Purchasing Principles and Management

Purchasing Principles and Management

EIGHTH EDITION

Peter Baily BSc (Econ), ACIS, FCIPS

David Farmer MSc, Ph.D, FCIPS, Dip. Man. Studies, Dip. Mktg.

David Jessop BA, FCIPS, FILog, ICSA, Cert. Ed.

David Jones PhD, MSc, BSc (Econ), MCInstM, MBIM, Cert. Ed.

FINANCIAL TIMES
Prentice Hall

An imprint of **Pearson Education**

Harlow, England · London · New York · Reading, Massachusetts · San Francisco · Toronto · Don Mills, Ontario · Sydney
Tokyo · Singapore · Hong Kong · Seoul · Taipei · Cape Town · Madrid · Mexico City · Amsterdam · Munich · Paris · Milan

Pearson Education Limited
Edinburgh Gate
Harlow
Essex CM20 2JE
England

and Associated Companies throughout the world

Visit us on the World Wide Web at:
http://www.pearsoneduc.com

First published in Great Britain in 1968
Eighth Edition 1998

© Institute of Purchasing and Supply, 1968, 1974
© Peter Baily and David Farmer, 1977, 1981, 1985, 1990
© Peter Baily, David Farmer, David Jessop, David Jones, 1994,1998

ISBN 0 273 62381 8

British Library Cataloguing in Publication Data
A CIP catalogue record for this book can be obtained from the British Library

10 9 8 7 6 5
05 04 03 02 01

Typeset by Tek-Art, Croydon, Surrey
Printed and bound in Great Britain by Redwood Books, Trowbridge, Wiltshire

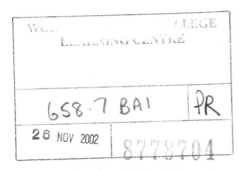

CONTENTS

PREFACE

We have reached the eighth edition of *Purchasing Principles and Management*. The original text was written almost thirty years ago by Peter Baily and David Farmer, and was in its day one of a very small (probably single figure) number of specialised texts relating to the field of purchasing and supply. Now, of course, there are many excellent books on the subject, and purchasing and supply chain management has become recognised as a crucial strategic activity by those concerned with organisational management; and as a recognised academic discipline with a growing number of university professors dedicated to the subject area. The visionary and pioneering work which Peter and David took part in, probably to some extent as a gesture of faith, is now fully justified. It is pleasing to see that the book continues to be seen as being of value, at the time of writing it still occupies first place in the Chartered Institute of Purchasing and Supply sales lists.

The book could not have survived for this length of time without continuous change, and of course the idea behind this new edition is to continue that process. It should be pointed out that the change process is evolutionary, and that we have taken care not to over emphasise the newer philosophies now widely adopted in our profession at the expense of well established thinking and practice. This book is not of the 'read this and it will change your life' genre, rather it is a reflection of current practice, accompanied by comment on the way things seem to be going, and by insights into developing ideas and practices.

The revisions for the eighth edition include the substantial rewriting of several chapters, and the inclusion of much new material reflecting changes in practice and thinking. We are very grateful for the contribution by Alexis Brooks of the Civil Service College of the revised Chapter 17 on the subject of buying for government and public services. This chapter contains detailed comment on the EC procurement directives, a theme not explored deeply in earlier editions.

The book is organised into four sections, the first, on the theme of objectives and organisation deals with the scope of purchasing activity, relevant strategic issues and considerations, the structure and organisation of purchasing, and with the development and evolution of the activity. The second section looks at the key purchasing variables of quality, quantity, time, price, source, negotiation. Part three concerns itself with important purchasing activities and applications, dealing with processes associated with buying in particular markets or economic sectors. The final section deals with systems, controls and personnel and includes an appreciation of the direction which research in purchasing is taking.

We persist with our hope that the book will continue to appeal to those in the practitioner and academic communities. We have attempted to strike a balance between the demands of a pure academic text and the sometimes simplistic treatment of ideas encountered in the literature aimed at managers.

We are grateful for the help and support of many colleagues and friends who have contributed in a great variety of ways to the book, and to the copyright holders of some of the included material. Specific acknowledgements are, of course, made at the appropriate points in the text.

Particular thanks are due to Maria Hanneman for her invaluable contribution to the organisation of the manuscript.

David Jessop
David Jones
January 1998

PART 1

Objectives and organisations

Chapter 1
PURCHASING SCOPE AND OBJECTIVES

Chapter 2
STRATEGIC ASPECTS OF PURCHASING

Chapter 3
PURCHASING STRUCTURE AND ORGANISATION

Chapter 4
PURCHASING EVOLUTION AND DEVELOPMENT

INTRODUCTION TO PART ONE

In the first section of the book we identify the scope and major objectives of purchasing and supply activities. Factors affecting the development of the function are discussed in both general and more specific terms.

In Chapter 1 we examine the main factors shaping the development of the purchasing and supply function. The contribution to organisational success is explained, along with the general movement away from reactive buying towards a proactive and strategic focus. References are made to how the purchasing activity is organised and functions in a number of influential organisations. The reader is directed away from considering price as the major area of concern in acquisition and towards total acquisition cost, comprising all the costs involved in securing a material or service. The buyer–seller relationship is considered.

In Chapter 2 the contribution of purchasing to organisational strategies is highlighted and some common strategic themes are identified. This leads in to Chapter 3, where we examine how the function might be organised in relation to different strategies. Alternative structures are identified and reviewed, and the question of centralisation versus decentralisation is discussed. Finally, we examine the place of purchasing and supply activities in the organisational structure.

Chapter 4 is concerned in the main with how the purchasing and supply function develops, and its stages of development. We discuss the factors, both internal and external, which are likely to affect the development of the activity. Various purchasing development models are examined, and measurement criteria suggested to enable a development audit of purchasing and supply.

CHAPTER 1

Purchasing scope and objectives

INTRODUCTION

All organisations need inputs of goods and services from external suppliers or providers. In this chapter we shall examine the developing role of the purchasing and supply function in managing these inputs, and comment upon the ways in which the activity can contribute to the efficiency of the organisation.

OBJECTIVES OF THIS CHAPTER

- To understand the development of purchasing from an independent function to an integrated activity
- To appreciate the influences which have effected the evolution of purchasing
- To consider the adoption of relationships based on mutual benefits as an alternative to the traditional transactional, adversarial approach
- To examine the 'total acquisition cost' as against price
- To consider purchasing in non manufacturing organisations
- To explain the 'supply chain concept' investigating events from primary supplier to the ultimate user.

DEVELOPMENT OF PURCHASING AND SUPPLY

Purchasing is seen by today's successful organisation as an activity of considerable strategic importance. However, not all businesses see purchasing as a function best undertaken by a specialised department, there are those who see the activity more appropriately performed close to the point of need of the goods or services being acquired. It is probably true to say, though, that a majority of larger organisations employ the services of a dedicated team of purchasing and supply specialists. This book is concerned with that specialised role.

The fact that the strategic role and contribution of purchasing and supply is well recognised in many leading commercial concerns, has meant that the *strategic* purchasing decisions may be taken at board level, rather than by a departmental manager.

The role and contribution of purchasing has increased quite steadily over the second half of the twentieth century, with a quite dramatic upsurge in interest in the activity taking place in the last few years. There are a number of reasons for this shift in importance and recognition, we summarise the main ones as follows:

Leading edge concepts

Organisations employing leading-edge approaches to the management of materials are putting into practice integrative ideas which are, at least in part, based on a strategic and integrated role for purchasing. The demonstrated success of these organisations is stimulating great interest, and as other organisations attempt to replicate their success, so purchasing is brought to the fore.

Approaches and concepts which might be considered under this heading are

- Best practice benchmarking
- Total quality management
- Just-in-time philosophies and lean production
- Supply chain concepts
- Tiering and empowerment of suppliers
- Relationship management
- Customer focus

The expression 'world class concepts' is sometimes employed to describe these and similar ideas, meaning something like 'world's best' or 'as used by the world's leading organisations'.

Advancing technology

Technology and associated complexity has meant that most businesses now specialise in a narrower range of activities and are compelled to buy a greater proportion of their requirements from those who have the specialist expertise, patents, intellectual property or design rights associated with complex or advanced technology.

Government and EC policies

There is today less freedom for purchasing policies and practices to be developed independently of external influences. As an example, the European Community Supplies and Services Directives impose obligations on public sector purchasers. It is recognised that a certain level of professional expertise is necessary to ensure that the organisation follows the rules.

The quest for greater efficiency in the public sector has led to a great deal of market testing, a process through which internal providers of services are assessed against the commercial providers in the marketplace. This has led in many cases to services being contracted out, and to an increasing purchasing or contract management responsibility for the core staff.

Finite resources

Some natural resources have, of course, always been finite. However, increasing recognition that their use and consumption needs to be planned has had a profound effect on the role of purchasing in contributing to the planned and responsible use of these resources, whether driven by simple economic forces or a growing sense of social responsibility.

Increasing proportion of revenue spent externally

For the reasons already mentioned it is generally the case that organisations are spending a greater proportion of their income externally, and less on internal costs such as wages and overheads. With the increased share of expenditure comes an increasing responsibility for purchasing.

Fewer but larger suppliers

Concentration in the supply market has had a profound effect in recent years. For example, the number of iron foundries in the UK has been decimated; the production of pharmaceutical products is almost entirely in the hands of a small number of large organisations; only a handful of large European chemical companies remain; and there is now no British car manufacturer of any significant size. This process of concentration through amalgamations, takeovers and the failure of the smaller and less viable business units continues. It poses obvious problems for purchasing and supply, and ensures a higher profile and more strategic role for the function.

Increasing environmental awareness

The recognition has dawned, perhaps belatedly, that it is good business sense to be 'green', and to be seen to be responsible in this respect. Recycling, the specification of renewable raw materials, a greater concern with the effects of waste and by-products, wider concern for the use of returnable packaging, and many other related concerns, all have implications for purchasing and are affecting perceptions of the function.

The increasing proportion of revenue spent externally

TOTAL ORGANISATIONAL EXPENDITURE	
Labour and overheads	**Externally provided resources**
Decreasing because of:	*Increasing because of:*
<ul><li>Automation</li><li>More efficient work</li><li>Competitiveness depends on access to 'best practice'</li></ul>	<ul><li>Greater specialisation on part of buying organisations</li><li>'Outsourcing' policies</li><li>Focus on core competencies</li><li>Development of specialised contractors</li><li>Easier access to world supply market</li><li>Complex technology restricts breadth of 'make' capabilities</li><li>Flexibility depends on external rather than dedicated 'owned' assets</li><li>Closer co-ordination with key suppliers</li></ul>

Fig. 1.1 Some reasons for the increased importance and recognition of purchasing

Many organisations are reporting that a greater proportion of their income is spent externally on goods and services than used to be the case. Figure 1.1 indicates some of the key reasons for this trend.

WIDER RECOGNITION OF THE CONTRIBUTION MADE BY PURCHASING AND SUPPLY

Clearly, supply of materials is not as important to some companies as it is to others. However, given that the average manufacturing company disposes of well over half its income on materials, supplies and services, and in some cases the figure approaches 90 per cent, it is significant in most concerns. To take an example, suppose that a company has total annual sales of £1m and that it makes a profit on that turnover of 10 per cent, equalling £100 000. The company spends 50 per cent of its turnover on materials and services and is able to effect a saving of 5 per cent on its material costs. The effect of efficiency (or inefficiency) with regard to the company's management of materials can then be shown in the following way:

£1m sales @ 10 per cent profit	£100 000
On £500 000 purchases, a 5 per cent saving in material costs =	£25 000
Giving a total profit of	£125 000

Now if the saving in material costs* were not achieved while the profit ratio was maintained at 10 per cent, it would be necessary to increase turnover by £250 000, or 25 per cent, to produce the same profit figure. Thus a 5 per cent saving in material costs in the average manufacturing company can equate with an increase in turnover of 25 per cent; which is not to say that we should not be concerned with increasing turnover.

The validity of this illustration depends upon several factors – e.g. at £1m turnover are the company's production facilities fully committed? – but it is a fact that every £1 saved is £1 extra profit. On the other hand, £1 additional turnover will only result in a proportion of that sum as profit and since the company in the illustration is average, a ratio of 1 : 5 in profit potential is not unusual.

The reader may be able to convert the illustration to figures relating to his or her own company. Those in chemical or car manufacturing will find that their purchases amount to approximately 70 per cent of turnover, with a proportional increase in potential. Most readers, however, will find that their 'spend' is similar as a proportion of sales to that in the illustration. Whatever that proportion, it should be noted that a 5 per cent increase in material costs which is not recouped in selling prices can have a similarly dramatic negative effect.

---

* It should be noted that the illustration relates to material costs, not price alone.

PROACTIVE PURCHASING

As the level of attention paid to purchasing and supply increases, the work tends to become more strategic in emphasis, concentrating more upon such activities as negotiating longer-term relationships, supplier development, and total cost reduction, rather than ordering and replenishing routines.

If we examine the responsibilities of buyers in organisations with a well-developed function – such as IBM, Nissan, Ford, Baxi, Hewlett Packard and others – we find that they spend only a small proportion of their time on administrative and clerical activities. Most of their activity concentrates on the establishment and development of appropriate relationships with suppliers. The emphasis in such organisations has evolved beyond simply reacting to the needs of users as and when they arise, to a forward-looking proactive approach that more fully reflects the contribution which the management of inputs can make. Figure 1.2 compares and contrasts reactive with proactive purchasing.

Reactive buying	Proactive buying
● Purchasing is a cost centre	● Purchasing can add value
● Purchasing receives specifications	● Purchasing (and suppliers) contribute to specification
● Purchasing rejects defective material	● Purchasing avoids defective supplies
● Purchasing reports to finance or production	● Purchasing is a main management function
● Buyers respond to market conditions	● Purchasing contributes to making markets
● Problems are supplier's responsibility	● Problems are a shared responsibility
● Price is key variable	● Total cost and value are key variables
● Emphasis on today	● Emphasis strategic
● Systems independent of suppliers	● Systems may be integrated with suppliers' systems
● Users or designers specify	● Buyers and suppliers contribute to specification
● Negotiations win/lose	● Negotiations win–win (or better)
● Plenty of suppliers = security	● Plenty of suppliers = lost opportunities
● Plenty of stock = security	● Plenty of stock = waste
● Information is power	● Information is valuable if shared

Fig. 1.2 Changing purchasing roles: reactive and proactive buying

The changing nature of relationships

A simplistic view of purchasing activity is that it is merely buying; that in essence it consists of finding a supplier who is willing to exchange the goods or services required for an agreed sum of money. This perception of purchasing has become known as the 'transactional' view, and is based on the idea that purchasing is concerned with simple exchanges, with buyer and seller interacting with each other on an arm's-length basis. The underlying interest of the buyer in this rather simple scenario is to acquire as much resource as possible for as little money as it is necessary to pay.

It is true to say that this transactional view is not obsolete; it is still an appropriate way of looking at the process whereby low-cost items, for which there are plenty of competing suppliers, might be purchased. However, it is no longer thought to be a suitable basis for most organisational purchasing expenditure.

Much more attention has been paid in recent years to the development of 'mutual' supplier–buyer relationships, where the benefits of doing business together arise from ideas of *sharing* as well as *exchanging*. In a mutual relationship the emphasis is on building a satisfactory outcome together, with, for example, such things as technology. Confidence and support are invested by both sides with the intention of adding value, a process not possible with a simple transaction. The organisations concerned seek to come closer together and to identify overlapping interests. These ideas will be referred to later in the text, but it is important at this stage to indicate the developing nature of purchasing and supply work, and the complexity which accompanies this development.

Figures 1.3 and 1.4 enable a comparison between the transactional and the mutual relationship. It should be noted that the list of shared benefits is by way of example only, and will vary between relationships.

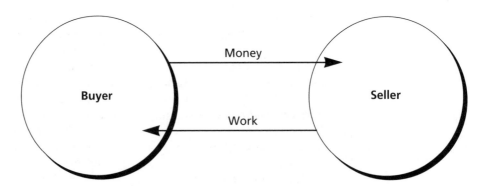

Fig. 1.3 The 'transactional' relationship

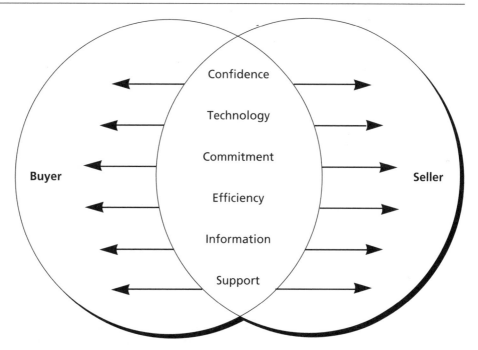

Fig. 1.4 The 'mutual' relationship

PROCUREMENT POSITIONING

Of course it is not the case that any organisation will wish to develop mutual or partnership relationships with all of its suppliers. Pareto's principle applies: it will generally be found that 80 per cent of expenditure will be with 20 per cent of suppliers; and it is likely to be the suppliers with whom large sums of money are spent who will be the ones with whom closer relationships are sought. A useful tool in assisting the determination of those suppliers with whom close relationships might best be sought is the 'Procurement Positioning' tool based on the work of Kraljic (1983) illustrated by Figure 1.5. The vertical axis, labelled 'Risk', is concerned with the degree of difficulty associated with sourcing a product or service, or the vulnerability of the client organisation to a failure of the supplier to provide the product or service on time, or to the failure 'in service' of a supply. The horizontal axis, 'Profit potential', is used to indicate the extent of the potential of the supply to contribute to the profitability (or efficiency) of the buying concern. This profit potential might be realised by achieving lower costs, either by paying a lower price for a good or service or by introducing more efficient buying methods.

It will readily be seen that there is no single best approach to relationships: a transactional approach might well be seen as appropriate for the routine purchases, whereas a strategic approach will be of obvious benefit to a mutual relationship in the critical sector. A buyer is likely to be uncomfortable with suppliers of services or goods in the leverage sector, and may well wish to

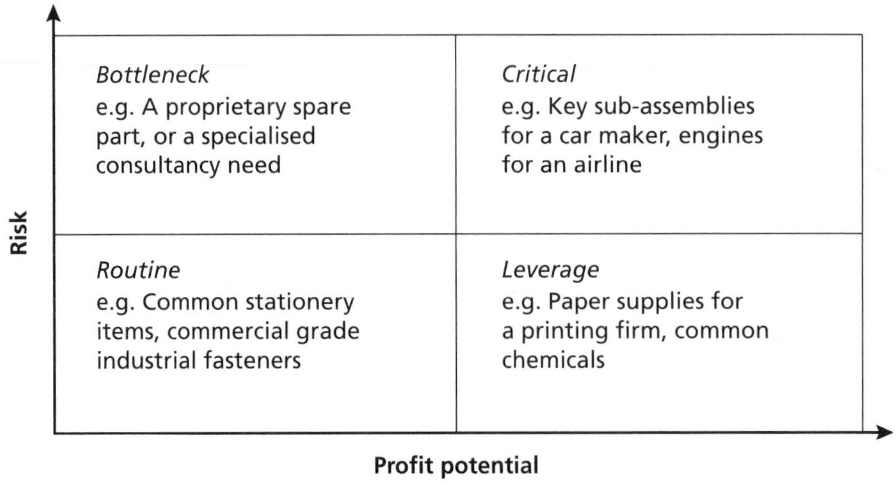

Fig. 1.5 The 'Procurement Positioning' tool

move the requirement to the routine sector – perhaps by developing additional suppliers – or to the critical sector, by attempting in some way to increase the seller's dependence. Where supplies and suppliers are in the leverage category, buyers are likely to feel quite comfortable, though of course we must expect that vendors will be keen to see their products or services repositioned as critical.

TOTAL ACQUISITION COST (AND TOTAL COST OF OWNERSHIP)

Buying price is probably the factor most often associated with procurement responsibilities. The function has an important role in judging the correct price for any purchase and this aspect of the task is seen at its most dramatic in the commodity markets. Since prices are affected by costs, at least in the long run, an important function of procurement is to work with colleagues and suppliers to eradicate unnecessary costs. These could result from over-specification; purchasing a non-standard item when an alternative standard is acceptable; unnecessary packaging and, where significant transport costs are involved, the design of the product in terms of transportation utility.

The total acquisition cost is more than simply price, and has a bearing on developing the wider role of purchasing into total cost management. It is the total you actually pay for goods and services, including such things as tooling, duty, inventory-carrying costs, inspection, remedy or rectification and so on. It is an obvious fact, yet a commonly ignored one, that a low price may lead to a high total acquisition cost. Of course, once materials or goods have been acquired, they may attract further costs while in use. With this in mind, some organisations prefer the expression 'Total Cost of Ownership' when referring to capital goods or materials which will be retained for some time.

Price is the most visible of the various costs which arise from making most acquisitions, and in many cases it will be the biggest component of cost too.

Fig. 1.6 The price/cost iceberg

The 'price/cost iceberg' helps us to remember the hidden costs, and to account for them in our business decision making.

The importance of purchasing and supply as a key function in the management of a business can be emphasised by considering the total acquisition cost of materials and services, and this is, of course influenced by the *specification* being purchased. In turn, this may involve marketing and a desire to have an attractive product to sell. It will involve production and the need to minimise disruptions in production and can involve resulting scrap or waste and even transportation costs. As many value analysis studies have shown, the cost-saving potential in this area is considerable and the procurement function has a vital part to play in the search for the optimum specification. One problem in corporate management is that there tend to be dominant functions in particular companies; in one it will be marketing, in another finance or production. This results in that function being given attention at the expense of the overall operation. We shall return to the theme of price and cost later in the book.

Specification

The procurement function has a part in working towards the optimum specification. This implies not only an attractive product for marketing to sell or for production to manufacture, but one which includes services, materials or components which are economic to purchase, and this in turn, presupposes that they are attractive for the supplier to produce or provide. All this necessitates some degree of compromise between the parties involved. A weak procurement function which simply purchases that which, for example, production asks of it is missing the opportunity of contributing in this way. Clearly, it is not for procurement to usurp the design function, or any other, but it should inform the various parties of the constraints and opportunities relating to the specifications and to delivery reliability.

Quantity and timing

Total material cost is also affected by *inventory levels*, and procurement has an important role with respect to stocks of raw materials and bought-in-parts, especially in times of rapid inflation. It is for procurement to judge supply-market conditions with a view to assuring the necessary levels of materials required to meet production and marketing needs. Price movements, availability, possible shortages or surpluses, physical and financial limitations all need to be considered.

Another important point affecting material costs is *timing*. One aspect of this relates to assurance that deliveries of necessary materials will be made to meet production schedules. Since inventory can be looked upon as insurance against supply failure, in theory perfect scheduling of deliveries would eliminate stocks. While this is rarely possible in practice, purchasing can certainly work with suppliers towards this end. This will involve better information flow on manufacturing schedules and fewer changes to those schedules; and, if such changes are inevitable, that they are announced as soon as possible. Procurement has an important role, too, in informing other functions of the costs related to such changes and working with them to reduce the number.

This includes making every effort to manage both internal and external environments in order to obviate unnecessary costs. For example, one company in the timber industry worked with its main suppliers to arrange shipments in ten one-monthly lots instead of all the material being delivered over a period of four to eight months which had been traditional. Coupled with packages of uniform length, this resulted in significant reductions in average inventory and handling costs.

Market considerations

Other procurement responsibilities include monitoring market prices, not only of the products or materials purchased, but of significant raw materials used in their manufacture; monitoring suppliers' prices, particularly where the item being purchased is 'special' to the buying company and a further important role is to provide information on pending price changes as early as possible to facilitate pertinent action by colleagues. Procurement should contribute to the strategic management of the business. It should participate in corporate planning and policy making on, for example, key make-or-buy decisions, long-term economic availability of raw materials, price changes, and the development of alternative strategies.

Supply continuity

Another aspect of total acquisition cost is the negative effect of supply failure on company sales. Material economics and assurance of supply are critical in a capital-intensive assembly industry dealing with oligopolistic suppliers as supply failure may adversely affect corporate objectives. Apart from the direct impact on costs, competitors may gain larger sales if supply failure affects production. This happened in the late 1960s and early 1970s in the UK car industry when foreign manufacturers increased their share of the UK market largely because component-supply difficulties adversely affected production in British plants. It is argued that the events of the late 1960s provided foreign manufacturers with a bridgehead which they have since expanded. It enabled Japanese manufacturers, for example, to establish an agency and distribution network in the UK without which they would not have been able to sustain their marketing effort. Since that time Nissan has established itself in the north-east of the UK and part of its strategy has been to develop UK suppliers to meet its exacting needs. What has been significant in this exercise is not the shortage of components from local markets but the adherence of existing suppliers to Nissan specification and delivery schedule demand.

Nissan produces over 3 million cars annually from manufacturing plants in 21 countries, and works with suppliers to continually improve their performance using 'Kaizen' techniques. Kaizen translates from Japanese as 'constant improvement' and is pursued through slow steady change. The Kaizen process encourages logical systematic thinking; it starts by recognising that things are never perfect and by identifying the areas where something can be done to improve matters.

It has been reported that the role of the buyer in Nissan UK has changed dramatically since 1986, from 'orderer' to 'consultant', spending time on strategic considerations.

Product Development

Clearly purchasing has an important role with regard to *product development*. Contemporary industry structure includes considerable specialisation and, with faster developing technology in many industry sectors, product life has shortened as the pace of change has increased. It follows that where product life is shorter the importance of getting the product right first time and on time increases. It is true, too, that there is a vital role for purchasing to play in keeping colleagues informed of supply market developments. With increasing specialisation it is reasonable to argue that more products are developed from innovations in the supply market than within the company itself. The earlier that intelligence is available, and the closer the relationship with the supplies, the more likely it is that the company can take advantage of the benefit. While the seller has an important part to play in informing the potential user of developments, the buyer too has a key role in searching for innovations. Indeed, as with many of the entrepreneurs in the cases quoted earlier, the buyer might even promote such developments, both in conventional markets and even more so in non-traditional markets.

In multinational companies another procurement task which can benefit the company as a whole is standardisation of components, materials or services between national units. For example, the car manufacturers, faced with national monopolies in respect of certain key components, developed alternative 'foreign' sources. Then interchangeability of components within

Europe affected vehicle design and thus marketing and manufacturing management. It appears that the emergence of the 'European car' may be as much the result of procurement considerations as of production and marketing strategy.

Figure 1.7 shows a hypothetical example of a component which might be bought by IBM in the United Kingdom. The Japanese supplier is the cheapest, but the total acquisition cost would be much lower if the item were purchased from the supplier in Scotland. IBM define total acquisition cost as: 'All costs, including the purchase price, related to the process of bringing a supplier's product and/or service to the point of consumption.'

NON-MANUFACTURING ORGANISATIONS

Discussion thus far has related largely to manufacturing businesses, but this is not to suggest that purchasing is unimportant in other types of organisations and it can be crucial in some. There are two headings under which other forms of purchasing may be classified, namely, purchasing for consumption and purchasing for resale. The latter grouping is dealt with elsewhere, although it is important here to recognise what a major part effective purchasing can play in the conduct of such businesses. Marks & Spencer, for example, is renowned as an example of a retailer which utilises its purchasing power effectively to give it advantage in the high street. It is interesting to note that the policies and strategies of the company from its beginning included purchasing as a

Commodity – Monitor Contract vol. 134K PROCUREMENT OVERVIEW Contract period – 52 weeks Description – Monochrome Monitor: Quote ref. – example Part No. – 1111111			
	Japan MATSUSUKI	Germany EUROMONITOR	Scotland VISIONTUBES
Ex-factory cost	10.000	11.000	11.500
Procurement m/power	0.070	0.154	0.057
Function manpower	0.050	0.165	0.034
Inventory finance	0.173	0.036	0.028
Capital tooling	0.037	0.060	0.022
Airfreight penalty	2.65	N/A	N/A
Freight – vendor	1.500	0.500	0.300
Freight – IBM estimate	0.300	0.120	0.100
Duty	0.490	N/A	N/A
IPO charge	0.066	N/A	N/A
Cancellation	1.400	0.440	0.230
Total uplift	5.236	0.974	0.472
Total cost	15.236	11.974	11.972
IBM contract spend	20,416,763	16,046,453	16,043,581

Fig. 1.7 Comparative total acquisition costs of the commodity to be purchased by IBM

Note: The figures are hypothetical and the suppliers fictitious

fundamental key. Those strategies have changed little over the years and stress quality, service and value and, given the current popularity of single sourcing, it should be noted that this has been a keystone of Marks & Spencer's from the outset.

Other successful retailers in the UK and Europe who have tended to dominate food retailing in recent years have also laid great store by purchasing. Clearly the food retailer who works with relatively tight margins has to maximise profit by moving the goods more quickly through the store. It is not uncommon for the more effective retailers to turn their stock over 52 times a year. Suppliers, in such circumstances find that what the economists call non-price variables are seen to be extremely important. Date/time scheduling is now common, for example, with the supplier being required to deliver on a stated day at a stated time.

The first heading or classification, namely, purchasing for consumption, covers a wide variety of activities; the UK Procurement Executive, the National Health Service supply organisation, and local authority supply organisations are three examples. These types of organisations are increasingly being required by government to work with less money, which has meant that strenuous efforts have been made to reduce costs through the more effective purchasing by such public organisations as the Prison Service, the Fire Service and the education sector. The task of the responsible executives in these services is to meet the demands that their service is in being to satisfy, within the constraints of lower budgets. Further discussion on these topics is contained in Chapter 17. In addition, purchasing specialists in organisations such as the railways, airlines, Telecom and electricity help to maintain the service their industry provides. Given the size of these industries, vast sums are spent on capital projects, maintenance and in some cases goods for resale. Clearly it is important to the viability of each of these industries that the procurement function be effectively performed as part of an efficient business system. By way of example, Figure 1.8 shows some of the goods and services necessary to operate a passenger aircraft.

THE OBJECTS OF PURCHASING

The foregoing discussion has touched on aspects of the objectives of the purchasing function, and these are now summarised briefly.

A well-known definition of procurement objectives is: to purchase the right quality of material, at the right time, in the right quantity, from the right source, at the right price. This rather hackneyed statement is criticised by some as being rather superficial and simplistic. This is probably valid comment, though the definition does provide a practical framework and has been useful to the authors in organising this textbook. A good objective should be measurable in some way, but who is to say, for example, what price is right? For present purposes, remembering the need to work as an effective function in the management team, the following broad statement of objectives is suggested:

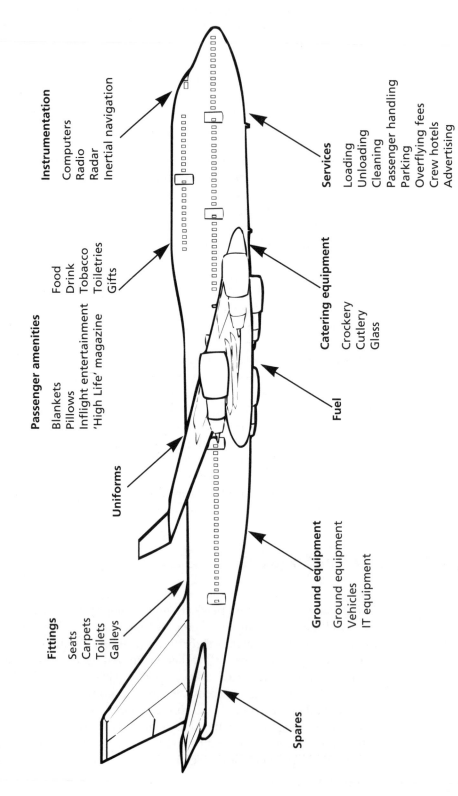

TYPICAL 747 DEPARTURE FROM LONDON

360 Passengers
20 Tons baggage, cargo and mail
35,000 Passenger support items

Fittings

Seats
Carpets
Toilets
Galleys

Passenger amenities

Blankets
Pillows
Inflight entertainment
'High Life' magazine

Food
Drink
Tobacco
Toiletries
Gifts

Instrumentation

Computers
Radio
Radar
Inertial navigation

Uniforms

Ground equipment

Ground equipment
Vehicles
IT equipment

Fuel

Catering equipment

Crockery
Cutlery
Glass

Services

Loading
Unloading
Cleaning
Passenger handling
Parking
Overflying fees
Crew hotels
Advertising

Spares

Fig. 1.8 Example of the scope of a procurement function: some of the goods and services necessary to operate a passenger aircraft
(*Source:* Courtesy British Airways)

- *To supply* the organisation with a steady flow of materials and services to meet its needs.
- *To ensure* continuity of supply by maintaining effective relationships with existing sources and by developing other sources of supply either as alternatives or to meet emerging or planned needs.
- *To buy* efficiently and wisely, obtaining by an ethical means the best value for every pound spent.
- *To manage* inventory so as to give the best possible service to users at lowest cost.
- *To maintain* sound co-operative relationships with other departments, providing information and advice as necessary to ensure the effective operation of the organisation as a whole.
- *To develop* staff, policies, procedures and organisation to ensure the achievement of the foregoing objectives.

In addition we might add some more specific objectives such as:

- *To select* the best suppliers in the market.
- *To help generate* the effective development of new products.
- *To protect* the company's cost structure.
- *To maintain* the correct quality/value balance.
- *To monitor* supply market trends.
- *To negotiate* effectively in order to work with suppliers who will seek mutual benefit through economically superior performance.

As we shall explain later, the orientation of the more highly developed purchasing role is now very clearly strategic, with the routine aspects of the activity either automated or undertaken by clerical staff.

THE SUPPLY CHAIN CONCEPT

The perception that purchasing is no longer a routine, administrative 'ordering' activity is now very widely, if not universally, held. The expression 'supply chain' has come into prominence, although there is competing terminology such as the expression 'value stream' preferred by the promoters of 'lean manufacturing'. 'Pipeline management' is another expression with a similar meaning.

What supply chain management is about is the linkage of the immediate seller/buyer relationship into a longer series of events. A company's suppliers have their own suppliers, and often our direct customers are not the ultimate consumers. Supply chain management sees the various buyers and sellers as being part of a continuum, and recognises the benefit to be derived from attempting to take a strategic and integrated view of the chain, rather than focusing on the individual links and thereby sub-optimising. In other words, the focus of managerial attention is not just the individual company or organisation, but the interactions between the series of organisations which constitute the chain. It might be helpful to visualise the firms in the chain, and the flows of goods or services and information passing between them as links. Figure 1.9 may help in this respect.

Consider Figure 1.10. It shows some of the major steps in the production of an automobile component in the form of a steel pressing. Iron ore is mined, converted into steel which is rolled into strip form, the component is pressed from the strip and then it is assembled, with others, to form the automobile. In

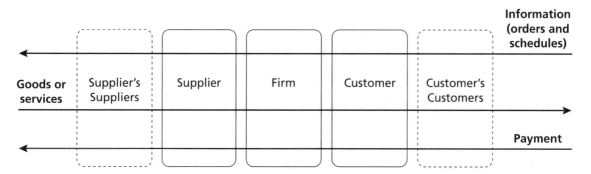

The supply chain responds to customer demand by supplying appropriate goods and services in the quantities and at the time required. The flow of cash is from ultimate consumer to original supplier.

Fig. 1.9 Supply chains and the principal 'flows'

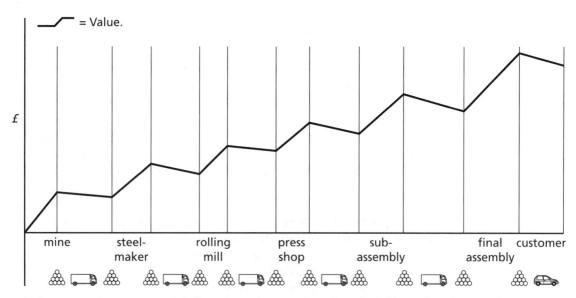

Value accumulates as materials flow through operations, but diminishes when non-productive costs of storage and handling are arising.

Also, the less waste there is *within* organisations the more steeply value rises.

Fig. 1.10 A simplified 'Value System'

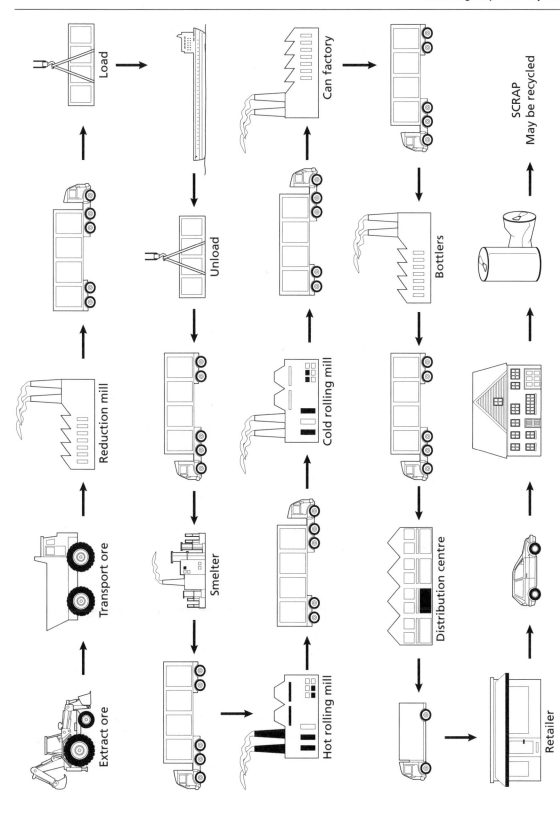

Fig. 1.11 The value stream of a soft drink can

practice there would almost certainly be many more steps, for example the steel component would be rather likely to become part of a sub-assembly prior to being incorporated into the car.

As work proceeds, value is added to the material (for the purpose of this illustration value is represented as the amount that the next 'customer' in the chain from iron mine to driver pays for the material, less any costs of process or conversion).

The various conversion or production operations begin with stocks of incoming material, and end with inventories of goods ready for the next operation. Transportation links the operations.

The diagram shows that cost is being added during storage and movement, but not value, and that if storage and movement can be minimised, value increases more steeply. In addition to the costs which are apparent *between* the main stages, there are also, of course, intra-organisational costs (costs *within* the main stages). For example if the steelmaker can become more efficient through the reduction of wastes associated with the steelmaking process, then the value adding slope will be a steeper one for that part of the chain. Value will be added more quickly.

Jones and Womack (1996) describe the value stream for a soft drink can, recognising that the most difficult component of a can of cola to produce is the can itself. They highlight the stark contrast between the actual value adding process time and the storage and movement time. They report that around eleven months elapses between the extraction of bauxite (aluminium ore) and the consumption of the contents of the can leading to disposal. Of this eleven months, only approximately 3 hours is spent on conversion of the product. In other words, for more than 99 per cent of the time, the value stream is not flowing; the muda (waste) of waiting and queueing is being funded.

Jones has referred to Purchasing and Supply professionals as 'the architects of the value stream'. There is a good deal of inefficiency in most supply chains; as purchasing develops its more strategic and holistic view of supply as constituting an extended process linking consumers with raw materials it is predicted that the benefits from increased efficiency will be great.

SUMMARY POINTS

- The chapter highlights the importance of a strategic purchasing function within organisations. It emphasises the necessity of purchasing being involved at all stages and levels of decision making.
- Purchasing has had to adapt to becoming more proactive. More emphasis is given to supplier relationships with both sides investing time and support to achieve mutually beneficial goals.
- Total acquisition cost is an all inclusive measure of the cost of ownership. It is influenced by certain factors which can be reduced with the involvement of an informed purchasing team.
- Purchasing for consumption and purchasing for resale are important considerations used in non manufacturing environments.

● Rather than focusing on individual relationships, the supply chain concept gives an overall view of the flow of goods and services from supplier to ultimate user and the flow in the opposite direction of payment and information. This concept taken further aims at optimisation of resources.

REFERENCES AND FURTHER READING

Burt D N and Pinkerton R L (1996) *A Purchasing Manager's Guide to Strategic Proactive Procurement*, American Management Association, New York.

Drucker P F (1968), *The Practice of Management*, Pan Books, London.

Erridge A (1995) *Managing Purchasing*, Butterworth Heinemann, Oxford.

Farmer D (ed.) (1985) *Purchasing Management Handbook*, Gower Press, Aldershot.

Gattorna J L and Walters D W (1996) *Managing the Supply Chain*, Macmillan Business, Basingstoke.

Heinritz, Farrell *et al.* (1991), *Purchasing Principles and Applications*, 8th edn, Prentice Hall International, London.

Kraljic P (1983), 'Purchasing must become supply management', *Harvard Business Review*, Sept–Oct.

Lamming R (1993) *Beyond Partnership, Strategies for Innovation and Lean Supply*, Prentice Hall International, Hemel Hempstead.

Reck R F and Long B (1988), 'Purchasing a competitive weapon', *Journal of Purchasing and Materials Management*, Fall.

Womack J P and Jones D T (1996), *Lean Thinking*, Simon & Schuster, New York.

CHAPTER 2

Strategic aspects of purchasing

INTRODUCTION

All organisations need to plan for the future, this involves development of frameworks to allow this process to take place. Once they have agreed strategic objectives, strategies can be formulated. It is essential that all business structures including purchasing, are involved in this process. Traditionally, purchasing has tended to be involved in day-to-day operational activities, and has not made the contribution to business that it is capable of. It must become involved in tactical and strategic decision making.

OBJECTIVES OF THIS CHAPTER

- To understand the levels of purchasing development and how they relate to potential strategic input
- To appreciate the importance of a well defined 'mission statement' which declares the organisation's intent and purpose
- To accept that strategies operate at different levels whilst all sharing the same focus
- To identify various forms of purchasing strategy aimed at gaining competitive advantage
- To examine influences on strategic choice.

A proactive strategic purchasing operation can give the organisation it represents a competitive advantage by reducing waste in the value chain. Purchasing strategies however cannot be developed in isolation, they need to be integrated with corporate strategy to succeed. Figure 2.1 shows the involvement of purchasing at a strategic, tactical and operational level.

Historically, the functions of marketing, finance or production have tended to dominate organisations. Some writers would argue that the particularly strong influence within organisations of manufacturing and the insistence on making products, rather than buying out, has led to major strategic problems in such companies. The inability of purchasing and supply, as a result of its lack of development, to effectively contribute to the make-or-buy decision has weakened the long-term survival prospects of many manufacturing organisations due to higher than necessary costs.

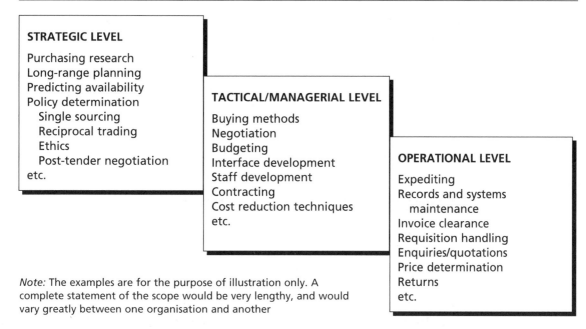

STRATEGIC LEVEL

Purchasing research
Long-range planning
Predicting availability
Policy determination
   Single sourcing
   Reciprocal trading
   Ethics
   Post-tender negotiation
etc.

TACTICAL/MANAGERIAL LEVEL

Buying methods
Negotiation
Budgeting
Interface development
Staff development
Contracting
Cost reduction techniques
  etc.

OPERATIONAL LEVEL

Expediting
Records and systems
  maintenance
Invoice clearance
Requisition handling
Enquiries/quotations
Price determination
Returns
etc.

Note: The examples are for the purpose of illustration only. A complete statement of the scope would be very lengthy, and would vary greatly between one organisation and another

Fig. 2.1 The scope of the purchase function

GROWTH IN THE STRATEGIC ROLE OF PURCHASING AND SUPPLY

The main reasons for the growth in purchasing involvement in strategic decision making are as follows:

- Purchasing is seen as an area for *adding value*, not simply reducing costs.
- Rapid product innovation requires a more integrated management team, involving all functions, and adopting a process rather than functional approach to management.
- There has been a move to holistic views concerning the integration of material and information flows, both internally and externally, for example:
  – MRP, MRP II and integrated information systems such as EDI
  – Supply chain concepts such as value streams and pipeline management.
- Active supplier involvement can reduce costs.
- A developing concern with strategic costs of supply rather than short-term price.
- The growth and development of the Chartered Institute of Purchasing and Supply in supporting the role of the activity.
- The influence of Japanese companies who, for a long time, have seen the activity as an important strategic entity.
- A greater awareness of the growth in bought out material expenditure and profit potential in purchasing.

One of the major problems faced by the purchasing and supply activity in many organisations has been the failure to take onboard a proactive strategic role. From the 1980s onwards organisations became more aware of the role the activity could take, particularly the strategic advantage it could give if properly developed. How effective the function is will depend to a large extent on the stage of development, i.e. is it clerical or strategic, reactive or proactive? Various frameworks have been developed to indicate the development or otherwise of the purchasing activity. It would not be possible for an undeveloped, reactive clerical function to make any real strategic contribution. It is therefore necessary to identify the stage of development reached by the activity and to engineer the appropriate development required.

PROBLEMS ASSOCIATED WITH ACTIVITIES AND VALUE

One of the major problems facing the traditional organisation has been the tendency to allocate and organise much of the work on a functional basis – purchasing, finance, production, etc. This type of approach has led to demarcation disputes and sub-optimisation, i.e. each function attempting to achieve its objectives regardless of the others. Newer ideas in management call for activities to be organised more on a process approach. This involves more of a team approach to problem-solving and concern with getting the job done. This in turn requires a more integrated management approach than a segmental one.

Figure 2.2 illustrates how the structure of organisations may be forced to change in an attempt to provide a more streamlined approach to the flow of goods into, through, and out of the organisation, in an attempt to maximise added value and minimise costs.

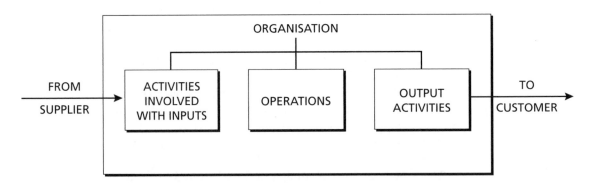

Fig. 2.2 Organisation structure and the flow of goods

Such **logistical structures** are more concerned with overall efficiency rather than functional efficiency, and give organisations a much better chance of integrating strategies successfully at all levels.

Organisations that fail to get purchasing involved in the strategies are likely to hinder or stop the development of such strategies.

THE CONCEPT OF STRATEGY AND THE MISSION/PHILOSOPHY STATEMENT

Before we can examine the role of purchasing strategy, we need to first explain what we mean by 'strategy'. In very simple terms, a strategy is a means of accomplishing long-term goals. The Harvard Business School defines strategy as 'The pattern of objectives, purposes and goals stated in such a way as to define what business the organisation is in, or is to be in, and the kind of organisation it is or is to be.'

Organisations will have single or multiple goals, which may, for example, relate to:

- profitability;
- market penetration;
- sales volumes;
- return on capital;
- customer satisfaction;
- environmentally friendly behaviour;
- social values; and/or
- maintenance of employment.

Many organisations indicate the strategies they are likely to follow in their mission statements. A mission or philosophy statement is a generalised objective or expression of an organisation's purpose – a master strategy. There follow some examples of mission statements, corporate missions and philosophies.

Developing a strategy

Process

In developing a strategy, the following need to be considered:

- What are target objectives?
- How are target objectives to be achieved?

Strategy is:

- moves and approaches which are on-going;
- new actions in the process of being mapped out;
- innovation, risk-taking;
- choosing among alternatives; and
- doing the right things at the right times.

It is vital, therefore, that the organisation, before it develops its strategies, is clear (in its mission statement) as to its intent. This involves defining the business profile and developing a mission statement.

DEFINING THE BUSINESS PROFILE AND DEVELOPING A MISSION STATEMENT

This involves management's vision of what the business is, or should be. Once established, this vision serves to:

- shape the future direction the organisation should follow;
- establish a strong organisational profile; and
- identify core business.

Major characteristics of the mission statement include answers to questions such as:

- Who are the customers, now and in the future?
- What are the principal products and/or services?
- Where are our major markets?
- What is the attitude towards economic goals (survival, growth, profitability etc.)?
- What are the fundamental beliefs, values and philosophical priorities?
- What are the broad strengths and competitive advantages?
- Does the mission statement motivate, stimulate and inspire?
- Do stakeholders agree with our mission?
- Does it give the flexibility we require?
- What is our attitude to quality?

EXAMPLES OF MISSION AND PRINCIPLES STATEMENTS

IBM principles

1 The marketplace is the driving force behind everything we do.
2 At our core we are a technology company with an overriding commitment to quality.
3 Our primary measures of success are customer satisfaction and shareholder value.
4 We operate as an entrepreneurial organisation with a minimum of bureaucracy and a never-ending focus on productivity.
5 We never lose sight of our strategic vision.
6 We think and act with a sense of urgency.
7 Outstanding, dedicated people make it all happen, particularly when they work together as a team.
8 We are sensitive to the needs of all employees and to the communities in which we operate.

(*Source:* Courtesy of IBM United Kingdom Ltd)

Chartered Institute of Purchasing and Supply mission statement

To be the centre of excellence for purchasing and supply chain management by:

- continuously improving the professional standards of practitioners
- raising awareness of their contribution to corporate, national and international prosperity
- representing the interests of individuals within the profession.

The Institute's objective is to promote the highest standards of professionalism in the Purchasing, Supply and Logistics function. CIPS acts as the central reference point on all matters affecting:

- the setting, testing and assessment of professional standards
- the arrangement of appropriate supporting educational and training facilities
- advice to individuals, businesses, Government, other national bodies, and to the European Commission
- maintenance of a strict ethical code to which all Members are required to adhere.

(*Source:* Courtesy of the Chartered Institute of Purchasing and Supply)

British Airways purchasing mission and goals

Mission: Improved profitability through the effective management of the airline's external resources.

Goals:
- To minimise the life-time cost of providing goods and services, meeting the company's needs for quality, timing and contractual protection.
- To make the most effective use of the international supplier base to enhance the competitive position of the airline.

Means:
- Recruit and develop a highly professional team, qualified and committed to deliver a consistently high level of performance.
- Exploit opportunities where our business skills add maximum value.
- Fully develop our relationship with suppliers to stimulate innovation and optimise performance for BA.
- Use global marketplace intelligence to maximum advantage.
- Further develop the working relationship with our client departments.
- Constantly monitor the performance of the purchasing team against measurable business targets in the areas of cost, quality and service.
- Maintain the highest ethical and professional standards.
- Constantly evaluate new developments in the purchasing field.

(*Source:* Courtesy of British Airways)

Nissan philosophy

> Our company's policy aims are to build profitably the highest-quality car sold in Europe. To achieve the maximum possible customer satisfaction and thus ensure the prosperity of the Company and its staff. To assist this, we aim for mutual trust and co-operation between all people within Nissan Motors (UK). We believe in teamworking wherein we encourage and value the contribution of all individuals who are working together towards a common objective and who continuously seek to improve every aspect of our business.
>
> We aim for flexibility in the sense of expanding the role of all staff to the maximum extent possible and we put quality consciousness as the key responsibility above all. We genuinely build in quality rather than inspect and rectify.
>
> (*Source:* Courtesy of Nissan)

Common objectives

There are a number of frequently encountered themes in mission or philosophy statements, for example:

- Total quality – continuous improvement.
- Satisfying or delighting the customer.
- Flexibility within the organisation.
- To be the best.
- World class.
- Total involvement of staff – teamwork.
- Prosperity.
- Expansion.
- Technologically advanced.

It is from these general mission statements that organisations determine strategies.

LEVELS OF STRATEGY

Strategies may be determined for various levels in the organisation, as illustrated in Figure 2.3. If an organisation has successfully determined strategies at various levels then those strategies should operate together harmoniously. This, of course, requires total involvement and commitment by all concerned.

Operational strategies are often reflected in vision statements, such as this example from IBM (UK) Manufacturing:

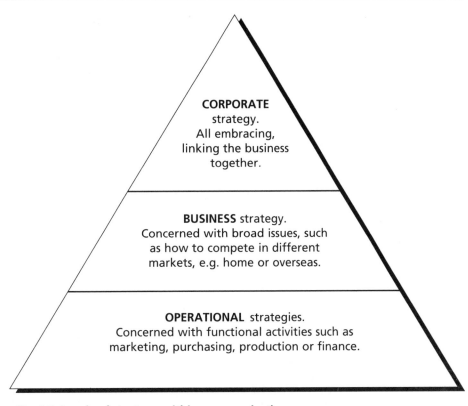

Fig. 2.3 Levels of strategy within an organisation

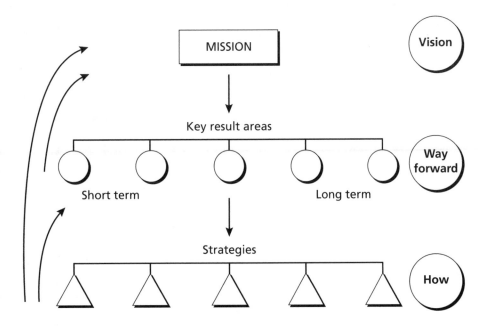

Fig. 2.4 Mission statements

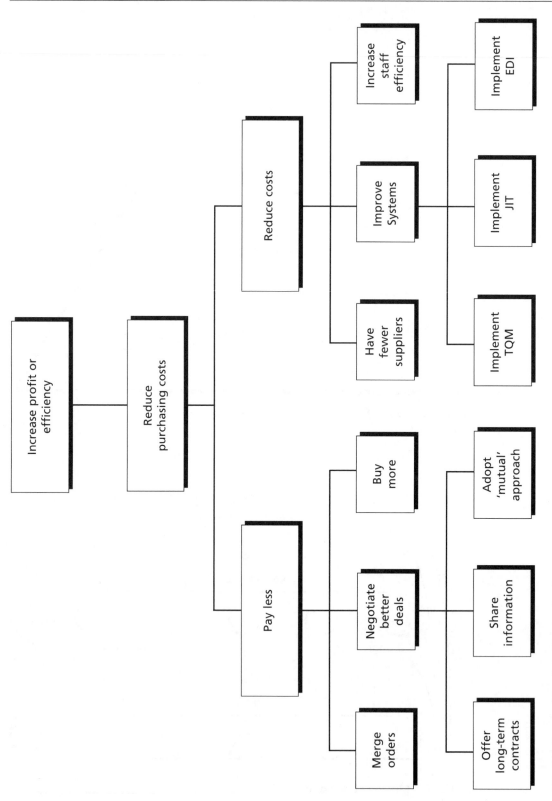

Fig. 2.5 Some objectives for purchasing

> PURCHASING VISION
> To be the best of breed procurement organisation benchmarked within and without IBM, and to support our customers with a World Class supplier base.

We can in Figure 2.4 show the interrelationship between mission statements, results required and strategies.

Good practice example

Many major purchasing organisations these days, are introducing strategic improvement plans for their suppliers. Such schemes identify several criteria that buying organisations would like to see considerable improvements to or zero problems. Such areas might include:

- zero defects;
- zero delivery times;
- zero administration errors;
- zero transaction costs.

Both buying and supplying oganisations would work together to achieve such objectives.

OBJECTIVES FOR PURCHASING

It might be useful at this stage to consider purchasing objectives in the form of a 'hierarchy'. Figure 2.5 suggests the way in which this might be done, though of course the chart will differ from one organisation to another. The illustration is given merely to illustrate the principle, and is not intended to encompass all possible ideas.

STRATEGIES AND THEIR SCOPE

In simple terms, a strategy may be thought of as a means by which longer-term ends are achieved. As any manager will realise, supply markets as well as sales markets offer opportunities to gain advantage and pose threats which may be detrimental to the business. It follows that whenever and wherever purchasing involvement in the development of business strategies is less than adequate, it is likely that exploitable opportunities will be lost while threats are neglected. In such circumstances it is probable that purchasing will be operating on an operational, fire-fighting, crisis-management basis.

It is a salutary lesson to recall that the once dominant UK motor and consumer electronic manufacturers operated in such a manner until they lost much market share to newcomers. The few who remain are now following currently popular supply strategies in an attempt to regain some of their lost business. One approach, which continues to gain favour, is for the purchasing organisation deliberately to set up 'solus' suppliers; to forgo the so-called benefits of market competition for what have come to be called co-makership arrangements.

This strategic approach, in keeping with others, does not guarantee success. For example, there may be supply failure through a strike or a fire. However, the strategists who have made these decisions did so having weighed the probability of failure against that of the benefits which they perceive.

Other purchasers deliberately avoid placing all their business with one source. Their strategy and tactics involve sustaining two or more sources in a market so as to stimulate competition while providing some insurance against the failure of one or other of the sources. This is a common strategy, whether recognised as such or not. Whether it is effective or not is another matter.

Another strategy, used successfully by at least one company in the copier market, involved designing a product to utilise standard, generic components instead of buying company-designed items. The benefits claimed for this approach included: lower unit cost (some people claim that a 'special' can cost up to three times as much as a 'standard'); better quality – since standard items are made in large quantities, they can provide the advantage of uniformly acceptable quality: and better availability. Among the issues related to this strategy is the necessity for buyers to work extremely closely with particular suppliers from the conceptual stage of product development. By this means the buying company incorporate, for example, the new components of the supplying company in its own product development.

IBM (UK) have identified a class of supplier as 'strategic', and seek in these suppliers technology leadership, highest product quality levels, design influence through early new product development, cost competitiveness, supply/market responsiveness, efficient administration and total customer orientation.

The make or buy decision is another which should be considered from a strategic viewpoint. One company which gained benefits from such thinking had had financial losses for three successive years before it undertook a complete rethink regarding its business. Up to the time in question they had bought raw material and components and had manufactured their end-product from design to despatch. Their business included such diverse activities as sheet-metal work, spray-painting, electrical and electronic manufacture, assembly-and-testing and calibration. The management argued that they could release 30 per cent of their workers by closing down what they thought of as basic activities. After negotiation with all parties concerned, they decided to retain only the design and final assembly-and-testing aspects of their work. Within eighteen months of taking this decision, the business was profitable and far more flexible. Purchasing had played a leading part in all the internal discussions. Among other things, they provided data on availability within the supply market of suitable sources, pricing and related product development. In addition, finding that no supplier existed in the vicinity of their plant for a particular activity, they set out to develop a supply source. As their own production wound down, this source was brought on stream along with the others. After one or two initial problems the new supplier merged effectively with the buying company's operation and was well satisfied with the business which resulted. Another strategic approach used effectively by far-sighted buyers during the recession of the early 1980s involved purchasing a proportion of a supplier's production output. Given the thin order books that were typical at the start of the period, many companies were delighted to get longer-term business. The terms that were acceptable in these circumstances were usually in the buyer's favour. However, because the contracts provided the supplier with a base-load, the latter also found them to be attractive. In the process of working closely together, communications between buyer and seller usually improved to the mutual benefit of both.

Some strategic options force the buying company to adopt a number of approaches so as to ensure success. For example, the much-discussed just-in-time approach presupposes that the buying company can rely absolutely on the incoming goods being to specification. Further, it usually means that it is necessary for the supplier's plant to be reasonably close to that of the buyer.

Where suppliers do not meet the buyers' requirements in one or more of these areas then a buyer might choose to upgrade its suppliers in order to achieve just-in-time performance. Rank Xerox in Holland followed this route with considerable success. Among the measures which they used in this work were:

- Statistical process control methods.
- A total quality control approach.
- JIT application to manufacturing (their own and that of the supplier).
- Continuous supplier involvement.
- Supplier interface improvement through computer-aided manufacturing (CAM).
- Where applicable, computer-aided design (CAD) and electronic data interface (EDI).

SELECTING A STRATEGY

Figure 2.6 illustrates some of the factors involved in selecting and developing a strategy. Clearly, tactical and operational behaviour must support the strategic approach selected. For example, if the aim of the strategy was to set up a range of dedicated suppliers – that is, suppliers who are the sole source for a particular item – it would be nonsense for buyers to seek quotations from other suppliers during the period of the agreement (at least with the implication that business might be placed). If the strategy involved developing a local source to avoid reliance upon a foreign supplier (involving currency management), it would be foolish not to support that supplier, even if, in the short term, it was more expensive.

As will be seen from Figure 2.6 many factors influence the choice of a strategy. Among them are:

- The position of the business in its supply chain. For example, is it a supplier of raw material, component or finished product? How many competitors does it have in its supply and end market?
- The number of effective sources in the company's supply market.
- The pace of technological development in the supply and end markets.

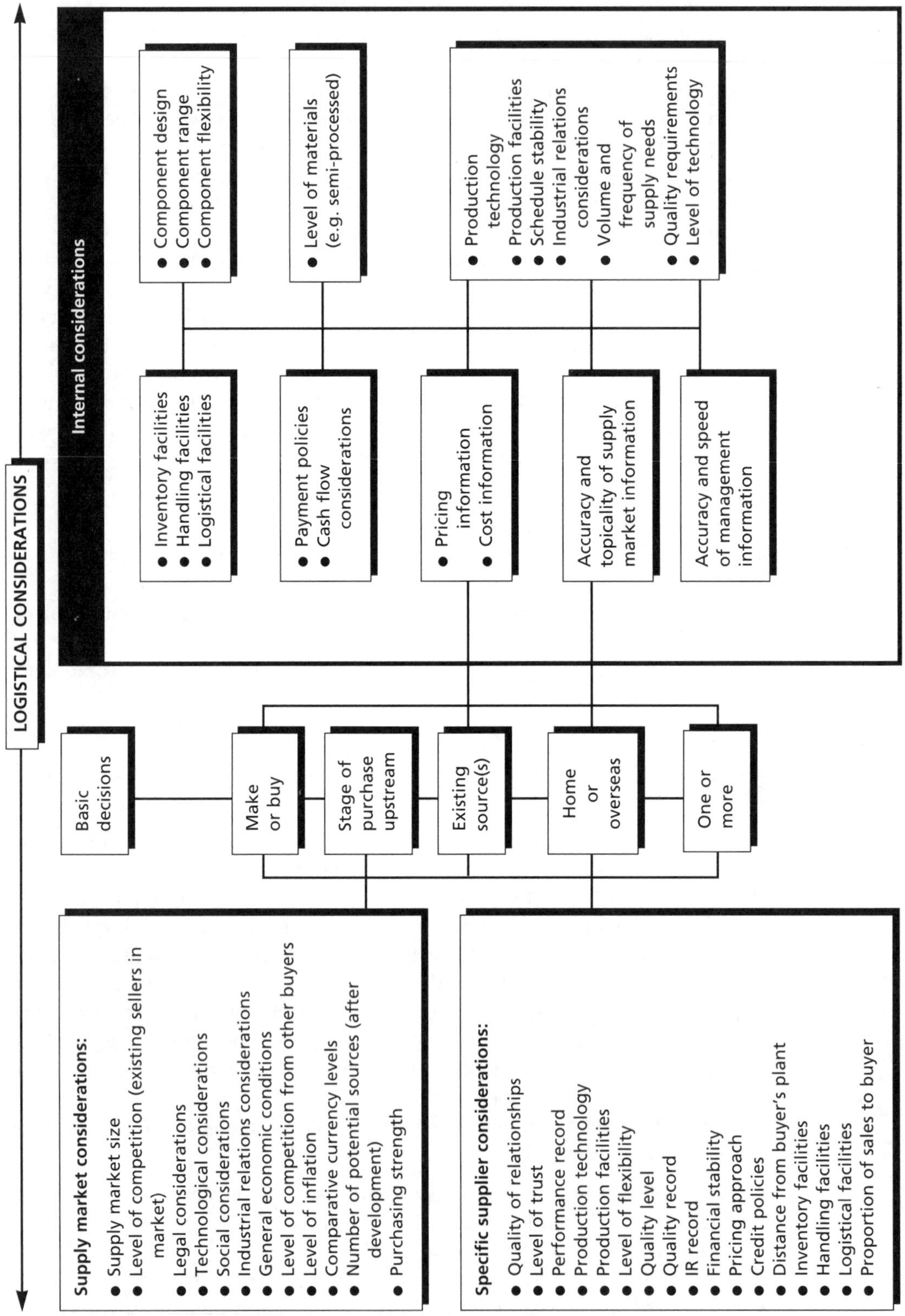
LOGISTICAL CONSIDERATIONS
Internal considerations
• Component design
• Component range
• Component flexibility
• Level of materials (e.g. semi-processed)
• Production technology
• Production facilities
• Schedule stability
• Industrial relations considerations
• Volume and frequency of supply needs
• Quality requirements
• Level of technology
• Inventory facilities
• Handling facilities
• Logistical facilities
• Payment policies
• Cash flow considerations
• Pricing information
• Cost information
Accuracy and topicality of supply market information
Accuracy and speed of management information
Basic decisions
Make or buy
Stage of purchase upstream
Existing source(s)
Home or overseas
One or more
Supply market considerations:
• Supply market size
• Level of competition (existing sellers in market)
• Legal considerations
• Technological considerations
• Social considerations
• Industrial relations considerations
• General economic conditions
• Level of competition from other buyers
• Level of inflation
• Comparative currency levels
• Number of potential sources (after development)
• Purchasing strength
Specific supplier considerations:
• Quality of relationships
• Level of trust
• Performance record
• Production technology
• Production facilities
• Level of flexibility
• Quality level
• Quality record
• IR record
• Financial stability
• Pricing approach
• Credit policies
• Distance from buyer's plant
• Inventory facilities
• Handling facilities
• Logistical facilities
• Proportion of sales to buyer

Fig. 2.6 A framework for strategy development

- The volatility of the supply and/or end markets.
- The degree of government involvement in the marketplace (e.g. the defence market).
- The ability of the buying company to manage a strategy (e.g. the quality and number of staff in the area and their ability to influence behaviour in the business).

The ability of the company to develop and apply effective supply strategies depends partly on the perceptions of managers at all levels. The manager charged with the development of a supply strategy should recognise that these perceptions are affected by the existing company structure, the quality of its internal communication system, the past experience of the company and its managers, and the resources available.

As has been suggested earlier, the development of a supply strategy involves company-wide considerations. These considerations differ by industry and by company. What should be common, however, is the need to develop advantages over the competition and use them effectively.

It has been argued that in developing an explicit business strategy it is necessary to outline a programme of future management actions, over the next 2 to 5 years. As far as the supply side of the business is concerned, there is much to be said for considering an immediate programme linked on a rolling basis to those longer-term actions. Then, since the ultimate purpose of the supply market is to satisfy the requirements of the company's sales market, that programme should be linked with other strategies. In so doing, it will be interesting to see if the philosophy of the business, attitudes to the roles of the various managers and the company's specific policies are challenged.

The task of the manager is to select those strategies which give his company novel, competitive advantage. There will be risk attached to the use of any strategy. Potential benefits need to be weighed against that risk as well as against the level of resources required by a particular strategy.

Even defensive strategies evolved to counter supply-market problems can be sources of competitive advantage. They might, for example, suggest a reappraisal of sales-market strategies related to positioning.

The key criteria in the development of effective purchasing strategies are the same as those that apply to marketing strategies. They should focus on the areas of greatest potential in terms of contribution; exploit the competitive advantage available to the buying company as a consequence of its particular mix of resources; emphasise creative management in use of those resources *vis-à-vis* competition (buyers or sellers); stress consistency and feasibility and specify who, what, when, why, which and how through an effective plan.

Although there may be advantages in copying the strategies of competitors, they need to be considered carefully in the light of the company's own strengths and weaknesses. There may be advantages, too, with the same caveat, of considering the strategies of companies; in other industries. Market growth rates, environmental aspects and legislative factors will be among other considerations.

Some questions to ask

The initial stages of strategy development necessitate analysis of the company's business activity. Some useful questions that may be asked at this point include:

- What is the current strategy? This question presupposes that a strategy exists. Even if there is no explicit strategy, in all probability an implicit one will exist.
- Does that strategy fit with those being applied in other key areas in the business, e.g. marketing and finance? How might that fit be improved?
- Have we identified the level of risk associated with the key components/ materials that we purchase? What threats are inherent in the marketplace? Risk can relate to, for example, supply security or to drastic price change.
- What strategies are being applied by our competitors, i.e. other buyers in the supply market?
- What opportunities are exploitable in our supply markets?
- Does the current company organisation structure (and its related communication system) allow purchasing to influence other aspects of the company's business strategy as well as being influenced by them?
- Is the departmental structure adequate with respect to item 6 above?
- Is purchasing influential with respect to product development decisions and to manufacturing strategy decisions (including make or buy)?
- What supply-chain issues suggest threat or opportunity?
- Is there advantage in collaborating with other buyers, e.g. in a group of companies; in a particular country?
- Could advantage be taken of under-utilised resources, e.g. plant, transportation, design?
- What changes are perceived in the supply marketplace?
- Do our key suppliers have balanced product portfolios? For example, are they bringing new products through at a rate fast enough to replace current products and to meet our own future development programme?
- Are there benefits to be gained from ownership/part ownership of one or more of the businesses in our key supply chain?
- What defensive strategies do we need to develop?
- What systems/information/staff development do we need to undertake to ensure that selected strategies are developed?
- What scope is there for the development of strategies concerned with import substitution?
- How might sustainable cost advantage be developed for our company with regard to key sources/materials/components?
- What strategies are suggested by shrinking supply markets?
- How can we improve the flexibility of our supply chain while improving its effectiveness? What strategies are suggested?
- What supply strategies currently being applied in other industries might be adaptable in our circumstances? (*See* Figure 2.7)

Note: * Strengths, Weaknesses, Opportunities, Threats

Fig. 2.7 Some influences on strategy decisions

EFFECTIVE SUPPLY-MARKET STRATEGIES

Effective supply-market strategies are based on analysis, weighing up probabilities, defining strategies and planning their implementation in detail. This involves:

1 Analysing the supply chains in order to find key points at which competitive advantage may be sought or threats exist.
2 Understanding the potential impact of particular strategic interventions upon the supply market; also to be able to conceive of the likely rearrangements that may occur and how competitors may react.
3 Having considered the alternative routes, selecting those which are likely to be most beneficial.
4 Predicting with reasonable accuracy the outcomes of such interventions.
5 Convincing colleagues within the business of the benefits of such interventions and of the need to balance them with end-market strategies so as to ensure that business-wide advantages are optimised.

Since there are no unchaining rules within any market, these tasks are demanding of the best executive. They illustrate the importance for the professional purchaser of allocating adequate resources – including a proportion of his or her own time – to strategic issues. After all, a company's perception of its strengths/weaknesses reflects its view of its power position relative to other parties in a marketplace. Recognition of opportunities and threats, and the ability to evolve effective strategies to adjust the balance in the company's favour, can be a powerful stimulant for business success.

Proactive purchasing activities need well trained and developed buyers who can work well in teams and access functional barriers. If they have been trained as order clerks they will have great difficulty taking on strategic rules.

THE PLANNING PROCESS

While top management must accept a large share of the blame for the lack of effective procurement activity, part of the fault also lies with purchasing people. Presumably, if the function is seen as being of sufficient importance to the long-term operation of a company, then relevant staff would be involved at the right level. If it is not, the management of the function has probably not presented its case well enough, or is seen not to have access to data or to be able to present that data in a suitable form for planning purposes. Involvement in planning necessitates a grasp of the operation of the business as a whole, as well as a clear understanding of the complex relationships within the company with regard to materials, and what information is required by whom.

Procurement needs to take a thoroughly professional view of its role in the business as a whole and that must include planning.

The following checklist indicates the kind of information which is required for effective integrated planning.

The external environment

- What technical developments are in train in both traditional and non-traditional market sectors which might affect our supply markets during the next five years?
- What effects will such developments produce, either to threaten manufacturing supplies or to suggest opportunities which can be exploited?
- What effect will forecasted changes in the supply market have on corporate management? For example:
  - What competition will there be for available supplies?
  - What non-traditional supply markets will need to be utilised because of component/material changes in our future product programme?
- Where a supply market is failing, will existing capacity be reduced by withdrawal of suppliers from the market? What effect will these changes have on the company?

PEST analysis (*See* Figure 2.8) is a technique which maybe employed in examining the external environment in a structured way.

Market research

- What arrangements exist for supply-market research?
- How could the link between this work, product research and sales market research be improved to overall advantage?

Supply strategy

- Is there a corporate supply strategy and policy? If they exist, are they clearly understood and are they being successfully implemented?
- Is our procurement organisation suitable to deal with the rapid changes taking place in many supply markets?
- Where there is increasing competition for available resources, what steps have been taken or should be taken to protect company interests?
- Where are we vulnerable (e.g. relying on a single source)? What if this source failed?
- What assumptions have we made about power supplies? Do these need to be reviewed?
- What are the anticipated supply-cost trends over the next five years?
- How do these projections affect our strategy (e.g. vertical integration, divestment)?

Product development and product life

- In which ways can purchasing work more effectively with R&D, e.g. through providing data on supply economics at an earlier stage?
- Are supply aspects considered in relation to product strategy at a sufficiently early stage? Are they given sufficient weight in that consideration?

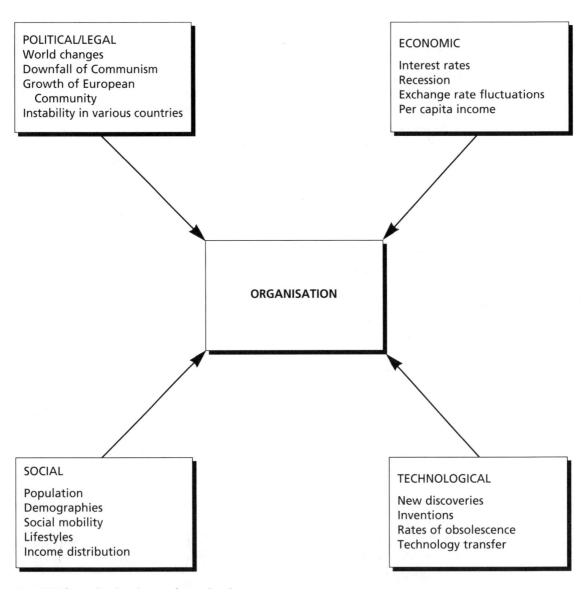

POLITICAL/LEGAL
World changes
Downfall of Communism
Growth of European
   Community
Instability in various countries

ECONOMIC

Interest rates
Recession
Exchange rate fluctuations
Per capita income

ORGANISATION

SOCIAL

Population
Demographies
Social mobility
Lifestyles
Income distribution

TECHNOLOGICAL

New discoveries
Inventions
Rates of obsolescence
Technology transfer

Note: PEST factors listed are by way of example only.

Fig. 2.8 A political, economic, social and technological (PEST) analysis

Source selection

- How long have we been dealing with our key suppliers? What proportion of our business do these companies hold? Do we envisage changing this mix? What advantages might accrue?
- When were checks last made on capacities and development plans of existing and potential suppliers?
- Is there a formal supplier selection procedure backed by relevant cost data? How could this be improved?
- What previous sourcing decisions need to be reviewed with respect to comparative currency changes? Could we develop local suppliers to obviate any problems which have arisen in this respect.

Planning

- How could supply input be improved for corporate planning? What difficulties could be avoided as a result of this improved input?
- In which ways might we organise more effectively to give key staff more time for consideration of longer-term matters?
- Is the current information-gathering system in the supply area flexible enough to react quickly to new data?
- Have the types of supply source and the approximate volumes which will be required of them been determined for the next five years?
- What historic make-or-buy decisions need to be reviewed in the light of current circumstances? How will changes affect us here? Which supply sources will need to be located? Which suppliers will need to be phased out? What raw-material/component-supply requirements would be added by a 'make' decision?

Staff

- What are the training needs of procurement staff? How can we best satisfy these needs?
- How can we best develop corporate supply attitudes and skills in keeping with wider and more challenging job specifications?
- What added skills are required in procurement staff in order to implement the broad corporate-supply programmes?

It is emphasised that these questions are only examples of those which might be asked of procurement. The broad implications of the task and its interrelationships with other functions demand that many more are asked. Figure 2.9 will suggest others, in particular with regard to the strategies to be developed by procurement managers in conjunction with their planning efforts. This diagram is a development of one originally conceived by Webster and Wind (1972), who were concerned with sellers being aware of what buyers may do. Clearly it is also important that buyers be aware of what sellers are likely to do.

Organising for planning

Herbert Simon's law that 'routine drives out planning and results in the urgent taking priority over the important' is very pertinent to many purchasing organisations. It brings to mind the organisation where two senior purchasing

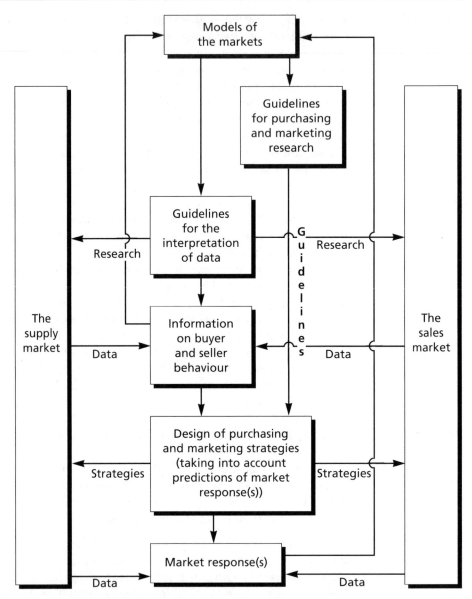

Fig. 2.9 Models and the design of purchasing and marketing strategies
(*Source*: Webster and Wind, 1972)

staff had suffered heart attacks within the previous six months. The urgent was taking priority over the important in that planning time was at a premium. As the manager concerned put it, 'We spent our lives fire-fighting.' A reorganisation of the workload and an earlier purchasing involvement in product development resulted in more time being available for planning. Senior purchasing staff now had the problem of how to use their new-found time. At first glance, this might be thought of as a non-problem. After all, which of us would not welcome more time? However, these were what we might term 'sharp-end' buyers. Their lives had been dominated by the telephone, the in-basket and by not stopping the line. They were not used to having 'thinking' time.

Given that the whole organisation was attuned to the previous type of activity, it was decided to capitalise on what was seen to be a first-class opportunity to promote the planning philosophy and develop closer links between the functions in the business. A short workshop was set up in which the requirements of the planning system were considered.

With respect to the purchasing function, the group concluded that they were expecting what they termed 'hard-nosed buyers' to act as researchers. In their marketing organisation they had salesmen (who could be compared to buyers). However, they also had a market research and planning department. It was this latter group, rather than the salesmen, which developed the planning systems and input. They reasoned that there was a similar need on the input side of their business.

As a result, in due course, a small section, of two people, started what was termed their purchasing research and planning section.

Among the early work performed by this section were: investigations into the supply/demand balance in key supply markets; a major buy-or-make study; and an analysis of the impact of pending legislation on one particular supply market. In particular, they sought to forge closer links with their product development colleagues. This proved to be one of the outstanding successes of the exercise, for virtually all major business decisions are influenced by the question, 'What products should we have in our range?' The product strategy which is evolved from the answer to that question probably becomes the core of the entire planning effort. Yet it is not always recognised that purchasing has an important role to play in developing that strategy.

No single formula

Chapter 3 points out the necessity to tailor an organisation structure to meet the particular need; this is also pertinent with respect to planning. From the foregoing discussion we can draw the general conclusion that a different set of characteristics will identify the planning/strategy development task from the buying role. However, it is important to remember that the organisation, systems and procedures which are developed will reflect, for example:

- The degree of internationalisation.
- The size of the company.
- The managerial style of the executives.
- The degree of centralisation.
- The authority extended to managers.
- The volatility of the supply market.
- The types of products and the pace of technological change which affects them.
- Managerial knowledge.
- The communication system.

Part of a system of plans

It is important to remember that purchasing input to planning must be considered as part of the whole. Clearly it does not stand on its own. The organisation exists to meet needs in its end-market and the role of purchasing is to ensure that the company is best placed to do this by maintaining efficient and effective management of the input – materials and information.

The following discussion places the purchasing involvement within this perspective. Strategic planning may be described as (Anthony, 1965):

> 'The process of deciding on the objectives of the organisation, on resources used to attain these objectives, and on the policies that are to govern the acquisition, use and disposition of those resources.'

From this definition we can consider any aspect of the business as a contributor to the process. In effect, planning involves a systematic process of making strategic decisions. The interrelationships of the key elements in the business impact upon these decisions. Thus, for example, if purchasing input is ignored, such problems as supply crises, materials price inflation, and technological development in the supply market may change the assumptions upon which marketing plans have been made. If such things occur, objectives based upon those assumptions may well prove untenable.

The planning system

Typically, plans have three phases:

1 an annual plan;
2 a medium-term plan (say 2–3 years); and
3 a longer-term plan (say from 3 to 15 years).

The time-scales of these plans differ from industry to industry and even by company within an industry.*

The three plans in the set are developed as a group, each interlinking with the others. The long-term plan is sometimes seen as a scenario document. This is designed to provide an annual control on what is termed a 'rolling' basis as to whether the business is proceeding in accordance with the selected strategy. Development features, in particular, are located in this plan.

The medium-term plan is also prepared annually on the same basis. However, this is usually far more comprehensive. Kingshott (1975) described his as being 'concerned with the impact of the trade cycle on the corporation's activities'. He listed the major purposes of this plan as including:

---

*One industry which is obliged to plan in double figures, in terms of time, is the extractive industry. The period of time from the conception of the need for the mine to the delivery of the first ores can frequently be as long as 10 years.

1 the development of corporate objectives;
2 forecasting cyclical fluctuations;
3 developing buying and selling plans;
4 identifying problems and opportunities;
5 identifying the need for policy decisions;
6 providing support for capital expenditure decisions; and
7 providing the basis for an annual plan.

With this type of approach the various elements of the plan are integrated one with the others, e.g. sales with production and material supply. Most writers argue that it is essential that the plan is developed on a multifunctional basis; as Kingshott put it, 'progresses through the chain of line management rather than emerges from a planning department'. A series of projections are derived from this plan relating to sales, purchases, manpower and financial performance indicators.

The annual plan is then a confirmation of the details of the levels of sales, production, purchasing and capital expenditure activities which were outlined in the medium-term plan. It also often includes key tasks agreed with functional staff. Usually the plan document and procedure will provide a basis for monitoring progress. It will seek to allow rapid analysis of variances sufficient to show what has changed, why it has changed and who is responsible.

As will be seen from the discussion in this chapter, the scope of the planning role for the purchasing function can be wide-ranging. However, the necessity for developing relevant skills, attitudes, systems, procedures and information will only become apparent when the impact of purchasing on the business systems is understood in the long, medium and short term. Much of this understanding will emerge from careful analysis of that system and of the complex environment in which it exists. The necessity for such analysis and action cannot be overestimated in our fast-changing world. Figure 2.10 outlines a model of a system within which this work may be undertaken.

To conclude, it is worth while repeating a statement made earlier in this chapter. Virtually all major business decisions are influenced by the question: 'What products should we have in our range?' The product strategy which is evolved from the answer to that question becomes the core of the entire planning effort. If strategic planning systems are to be effective and efficient, then it is likely that purchasing strategies will contribute to the success of the company's system; and that short-term opportunist buying behaviour will be superseded by a more professional approach. Strategic planning for a system that has input as well as output and which ignores the former can only be doomed to failure.

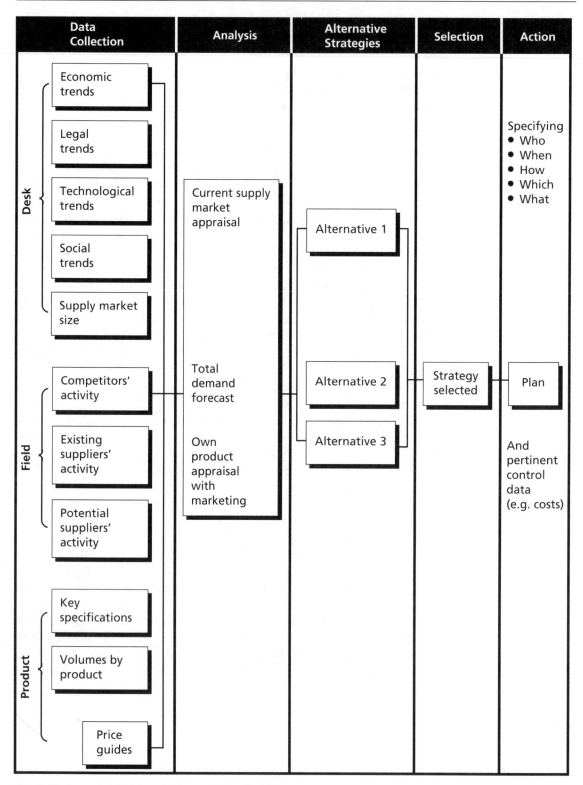

Fig. 2.10 A model for developing a strategic plan

SUMMARY POINTS

- Team approaches to problem solving are a feature of successful organisations. Overall efficiency is more valuable than individual departmental success.
- The chapter considers how an organisation's view of its business profile develops its Mission Statement which, in turn, determines its strategies.
- Viewing purchasing objectives as a hierarchy, world class concepts and co-makership principles are at the foundation level leading up to the ultimate objectives of increasing efficiency and profits.
- The external environment influences strategy selection. The perceptions of managers at all levels, the company culture and experience, will influence the effectiveness of those strategies adopted. The chapter stresses the need to adopt strategies which will develop and maintain competitive advantage.
- It is vital that purchasing be well informed on the external environment and its influences in order that it can provide effective input as part of the organisation's integrated planning activity.

REFERENCES AND FURTHER READING

Browning J M, Sabriskie N B and Huellmantel A B (1983), 'Strategic purchasing planning', *Journal of Purchasing and Materials Management*, Spring.

Cunningham M T (1982), 'Purchasing strategies in Europe', *International Journal of Physical Distribution Management*, 12 (2).

DTI (1991), 'Better value for money from purchasing', *Enterprise Initiative 1991*.

DTI (1991), 'Building a purchasing strategy', *Enterprise Initiative 1991*.

Farmer D H (1984), 'Competitive analysis – a must for effective purchasing management', *Long Range Planning*, June.

Kraljic P (1983), 'Purchasing must become supply management', *Harvard Business Review*, Sept.–Oct.

Nicholson A (1993), 'Strategic management for the professional', *Purchasing and Supply Management*, April.

Pearson J and Gritzmacher (1990), 'Integrated purchasing', *Long Range Planning*, 23 (3).

Soukup W R (1987), 'Supplier selection strategies', *Journal of Purchasing and Materials Management*, Summer.

Spinks T (1993), 'Gaining a strategic advantage', *European Purchasing and Materials Management 1993*.

Webster F and Wind Y (1972), *Organisational Buying Behavior*, Prentice Hall, New York.

CHAPTER 3

Purchasing structure and organisation

In this chapter we will examine how organisations structure their purchasing activities. The more developed the activity is, the more likely it is to be fully integrated with the rest of the organisation.

OBJECTIVES OF THIS CHAPTER

- To understand how purchasing relates to the company as a whole
- To realise the importance of a 'balanced' structure where all the functions work together towards the same objectives
- To examine how de-centralised buying *v* centralised, departmental organisation and support services affects the structure of the purchasing team
- To appreciate the importance of purchasing being highly placed within the organisational structure
- To look to the future role of purchasing in both upstream and downstream activities.

We will also examine new developments in supply chain management. Remember from the previous chapter that strategy determines structure in successful organisations.

Thinking of an organisation as a series of boxes on a chart is to misunderstand the scope of the topic. Organisational issues are many and varied and necessitate careful consideration when planning a new structure. There is little agreement as to what is the best approach in general terms, indeed it must be emphasised at the outset that a generally applicable organisation structure does not exist. Structures need to be developed to meet the specific requirements of an enterprise. These specific requirements include the objectives of the business, its strategies, resources, information system, the style of top management, their propensity and ability to delegate, the functions performed within the enterprise and the dominant cultures.

The manager who has the task of developing an organisation should always start with the basic question: 'What are we trying to do?' Since few people start to consider an organisation design with a clean sheet of paper, that question needs to be superimposed over whatever exists at the time.

Most organisations have been adapted over time to meet the requirements which those who have set them up have perceived as being important. Among the factors which will have influenced the design, as well as changes which have been made, will have been the comparative power of particular individuals or functions in the hierarchy which existed at the time. The more weakly placed functions, conversely, have little influence on the structure. 'Fashion' may have been another major influence, and, until recently, in most organisations purchasing lost out on all counts. Because this is the case, in considering the role of purchasing within the organisation, it is essential to ask the basic question suggested earlier as a fundamental prerequisite of organisational design. Not, of course, that purchasing will always emerge as of prime importance. However, wherever it is a primary function, it and the others involved, for example, in manufacturing development, production, sales and distribution, should be identified. Their several interrelationships should then be catered for in the design of the organisation.

STRUCTURE

We are concerned here with organisation as it relates to purchasing, but, clearly, the discussion needs to encompass the enterprise as a whole. Purchasing, after all, is a function which interacts with other functions in an enterprise. It does not function in isolation, for no organisation exists simply to buy other things. It follows that the liaison/co-ordinating aspects of any organisation should be to the forefront of our thinking in designing any organisation structure.

As to what is the most appropriate structure in a particular case, it is essential to keep in mind the point suggested earlier that a generally applicable organisation structure does not exist. In several respects, each enterprise is different from the next. Thus, a variety of factors will need to be taken into account in considering a particular case. For example, the size of the organisation, the type of market which it serves, the technology and processes involved, the type of people employed, the volatility of the markets in which the business operates, and its age.

Clearly, the organisation structure for a company which has six different product groups, several of which are sold in different markets, will need to be different from that which is appropriate for a single-product business and in addition so far as the purchasing function is concerned, its importance to the business system will influence its roles in the structure and, of course, how the structure and its related systems are designed.

Other influences which will affect the design of an organisation include geographic location; the type of market served (e.g. international, government); the length of the gestation period for the development of the product and usually the shorter this period, the more dynamic the enterprise needs to be; and the propensity of those who direct the enterprise to stimulate or depress both creativity and entrepreneurial drive.

Systems approaches

Systems approaches are often used to explain the development of organisation structures. The concept being that to be effective any system needs to be in balance. The argument put forward is that system-wide effectiveness is the goal rather than a sub-optimisation approach e.g. departmental efficiency (purchasing). Thus purchasing may achieve its objectives at the expense of the rest of the organisation. An example to illustrate this might occur when purchasing, in order to make savings, buys a year's supply saving say £10 000 but this decision cost others in the organisation money e.g. finance, stores, stock control etc. which may be a lot more than the £10 000 saved by purchasing. The more integrated systems are, the easier it is to see the cost implications of any decision leading organisations to move away from making decisions from a functional perspective to a total organisation viewpoint.

Systems theorists usually identify four system types. They are:

1 *Adaptive systems* which, as the name suggests, are concerned with adapting the organisation to its environment; with managing the sometimes rapid changes with which it is faced and with ensuring that the correct policies are adopted so as to ensure the continuance of an effective business.
2 *Operating systems* which are concerned with the day-to-day running of the business from the input through the processing to the output. Not only are such systems concerned with material and product flows, but also with money flows.
3 *Information systems* which are the antennae of the organisation, for none of the other system types can function without information.
4 *Maintenance systems* which exist to keep the organisation working effectively. They include control systems, so-called reward and punishment systems and the co-ordinating mechanisms which link the organisation with other systems.

If we relate these ideas to a manufacturing system, at the operating level that system may be represented as a box with input and output. It obtains materials/ components (input), processes them in some way and sells the resulting products (output). Clearly, the system can only operate viably if there is input to the process and if the output can be disposed of while achieving a financing surplus. Detrimental input factors, e.g. shortages, quality failure, will affect both the process and the output, just as similar negative factors in sales or

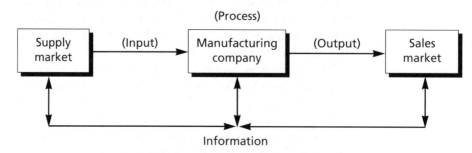

Information

Fig. 3.1 A simplified model of a manufacturing company

processing have an effect on input. Figure 3.1 is a simplified model of such a system, with the information system included.

The experience of the authors in considering many purchasing organisations is that the operating systems and the part of the information and maintenance systems relating to operations, are well recognised in designing most structures. However, the other system elements are given due consideration far less frequently. One result is that the business system of which purchasing is a part is less effective than it might be. For example, it is interesting to note that, even where the currently popular logistic-type systems have been adopted, frequently there is a tendency to focus upon day-to-day operating systems. It is our view that part of the reason for this is the lack of awareness among top managers of the scope of the purchasing function. Their diminished view results, e.g., in the employment of staff who are unsuitable for a broader role, which thus perpetuates the status quo. We will return to this later in the chapter.

The 'right' culture

Handy (1985) suggests that in considering the design of the culture of an organisation, one way to proceed is to examine the type of activity which characterises each part of it. He suggests that there are four principal activity types: steady state; innovation; crisis; and policy. It is interesting to note that while his view of marketing embraces innovation and policy (and not steady state), by implication at least, he sees purchasing as being only related to steady state. We would argue that while part of the purchasing function, e.g. supply aspects, may be categorised in this way, many of its activities should be embraced within innovation and policy. Nevertheless, given the foregoing caveat, it is useful to indicate here what Handy has in mind for each of these types.

Steady state   Steady state is the operational activity of a business. He argues that this often accounts for the work of 80 per cent of a company's personnel and that activities such as secretarial, accounting, production and sales come under this category. We would include supply 'call off' and progressing activities in the grouping.

Innovation   Innovation relates to any activity which is directed towards changing things that the organisation does or the way in which it does it. He includes research and development (R&D), parts of marketing, the development side of production and parts of finance in this. We would argue for the inclusion of parts of the purchasing function in this category (cf. for example, the developments in retailing in the UK and the considerable changes which have been made by, for example, Volvo and Rank Xerox in the industrial environment.

Crisis   Handy argues, not surprisingly, that no single part of an organisation will have a monopoly of crises or breakdowns. However, he recognises that the part of an organisation which interfaces with the environment is more likely to have to cope with the unexpected. Without doubt, supply 'call-off' is very much open to this. Indeed, we would go so far as to say that traditional buyers have tended, in a perverse way, to enjoy and be skilled at such fire-fighting. Effective purchasing management (e.g. improving the reliability of suppliers scheduling and quality), seen by Handy as a 'policy' type activity, will tend to minimise such crises.

Policy

Handy sees this activity as being concerned with setting the priorities against which an organisation operates. He includes within this the allocation of resources, and the initiation of action. He goes on to argue that while these and other activities form this as a category of their own, there is a degree of overlap with the other sets. A related statement which follows is indicative in our view of the problem with many organisations. He writes 'usually, each department will find the bulk of its activities in one or other set. That bulk will tend to determine the main focus and culture that is appropriate to it'.

Our point here is that the expectations of those who design organisations of the role of purchasing, and of those who undertake the tasks, will establish the 'culture' and the category in which purchasing has to operate. Handy suggests that: 'if the appropriate culture prevails where the set of activities prevails, then that part of the organisation will be more effective.'

Clearly, this has important implications for the effectiveness of the organisation and of the purchasing function. Where the 'culture' in purchasing is operational, reactive and seen simply as a service to production, in our view it will never be an effective element of its business system, nor, we would argue, will that system be effective.

We see the purchasing function as being a primary function, at least in most manufacturing organisations. After all, if you make things to sell you are obliged to obtain the components or materials with which to produce. Since the purchasing activity is undertaken in markets where others are involved in marketing and selling, it would be logical to assume that both buyer and seller will be attempting to manage their environment. To think otherwise is to give the lie to the established laws of economic activity.

If that is the case the appropriate culture with respect to purchasing should be one which assumes the involvement of the function in Handy's activity types in parallel with marketing. That means that there are 'innovative' and 'policy' aspects of the task plus 'steady state' and 'crisis'. The 'steady state' aspects have to be concerned with day-to-day system stability. In other words operational activity, the 'supply' side of purchasing, is different from the creative (innovative) or long-term (policy). This is an important factor which needs to be borne in mind when considering organisation for purchasing. Apart from anything else, the appropriate culture needs to be developed for each role both within purchasing and within the functions that interface with it.

An operational (steady-state) culture will hardly promote creativity, while a more creative one may not be conducive to meeting the day-to-day needs of a manufacturing system. It follows, too, and this is another factor to be noted, that people who can operate successfully in either of the environments may be inadequate in the other.

In the experience of the authors, most traditional purchasing organisations have tended to nurture people who are more comfortable in a steady state environment. Frequently, too, such staff seem to thrive on managing system failures (crisis) and enjoy the apparent power that doing this well provides. It might be said that while they are not able to influence policy (the origins of their problems in many cases), they obtain genuine job satisfaction from being able to deal with crises. Where and when the business system reinforces such a culture, then purchasing will continue to play a diminished role in the business.

It follows from all this that, in considering the development of an organisational structure for purchasing (or any other function), the scope of the task needs to be taken into account. Handy's activity types provide a useful model for consideration.

Centralisation/decentralisation

Given the growth of multi-national companies, conglomerates, holding companies and other groups, centralisation/decentralisation considerations have been much discussed in recent years. Cynics suggest that there are fashions which are followed in deciding between the two, and that the average executive will have passed through two reorganisations involving each during his or her working life; or that companies tend to copy the organisation structure followed by some more successful concern; or that leading management consultants promote their favourite organisation structure wherever they go. In some cases there may be justification for such cynicism, but effective management will endeavour to construct its organisation structure upon more objective foundations.

Most groups of companies or large organisations which operate several establishments adopt some compromise between buying everything centrally and buying everything locally, aiming to balance the advantages of strength with those of flexibility. Basically there are three alternatives:

1 complete decentralisation, allowing full autonomy in each of the units;
2 complete centralisation, which in practice means that apart from local purchases of small value, all purchases are made from a central office; or
3 a combination of the two.

The advantages usually cited for decentralisation are:

- The local buyer will have a better knowledge of the needs of his or her particular factory or unit, of local suppliers, and of transport and storage facilities.
- He or she will be able to respond more quickly to emergency requirements, partly because of shorter lines of communication and partly because he or she will have a greater awareness of local circumstances than someone sitting many miles away.
- The local buyer's direct responsibility to his or her immediate management will produce better liaison and tighter control by local top management

particularly where they operate as a profit centre. Since materials represent such a large proportion of works cost in manufacturing, a common argument revolves around authority and responsibility. That argument runs: if local management are not allowed, for example, to select and deal with their own suppliers, how can they be held responsible for output which relies so heavily on supplier efficiency?

Complete centralisation, on the other hand, has advantages which include:

- Economies obtained by consolidating like requirements of all units in the group, thereby improving purchasing strength in negotiating and facilitating supplier relationships.
- Avoidance of price anomalies between group units and of competition between them for materials in short supply.
- Better overall stock management and material utilisation.
- Economies of staffing and clerical effort together with uniformity in procedures, forms, standards and specifications.

Generally speaking, the advantages of one approach are the disadvantages of the other, thus a combination of both is often used to obtain the benefit from the best features of each, while avoiding the disadvantages of both approaches. A typical structure in such an organisation is illustrated in Figure 3.2 and in one of this nature the group or central office is often responsible for:

- Determining policy, standards and procedures and group specifications.
- The negotiation of contracts for common materials which are used by the group in any volume.
- Major plant and equipment and capital project contracts.
- Contracts for imported materials and for exports where relevant.
- Legal matters relating to supply.
- Co-ordination of group inventory.
- The education and development of supplies personnel within the group and the provision of advice on staffing and related recruitment.

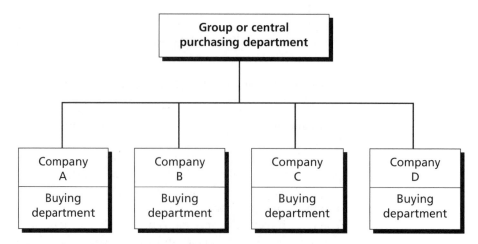

Fig. 3.2 A centralised/decentralised structure

Another approach sometimes used has a small group staff which has a relatively limited policy and co-ordinating role, and the largest user of a particular commodity or material in the group negotiates on behalf of all group users as 'lead' buyer. Thus, in the organisation illustrated in Figure 3.2, the buyer in company A might negotiate contracts for raw material X on behalf of companies B and C as well as their own. In the same way the buyer in, say, company D might do so on behalf of companies A and C.

In both systems, in matters outside the scope of the group office role, local buyers act autonomously. In some groups, the local managers are directly responsible to a member of their own board and have only an indirect or professional accountability to the senior supplies man in the group office.

Having established a particular approach within a group, it is still necessary to consider the problem of centralisation/decentralisation at plant or unit level. Over the last thirty years there has been a trend to centralise purchasing activity into one department. However, there is considerable difference between companies as regards the effective centralisation of these activities. In some instances it is still the case that the purchasing department merely comprises a rubber stamp which signs orders which have been negotiated by whichever line manager is concerned with the material or service in question: in others, full authority is vested in the purchasing manager as the only executive able to commit the company to expenditure. Even though as official signatories to purchase orders both have the same legal authority, their levels of decision-making authority are at different extremes of a continuum. Between those extremes exist a variety of authority levels, most of which in analysis relate to the degree of confidence which the remainder of the organisation has in the professionalism of the incumbent.

The advantages of centralising purchasing activity in an enterprise depend on the ability of the executive entrusted with this work to use the company's purchasing power most effectively. This will include consolidating requirements, developing sources, rationalising stocks, simplifying procedures, working with suppliers to eliminate unnecessary cost to mutual advantage, and working with colleagues to ensure an effective flow of information which will enable the objectives of the enterprise to be met.

Effective centralisation of authority to buy on behalf of the organisation, however, does not imply a dictatorial mandate. Several studies have shown that many people may be involved directly or indirectly in the decision to purchase. For example, in the case of a piece of capital equipment in a manufacturing concern, the following executives, in addition to the purchasing specialist, could bring influence to bear, depending on the seniority of the individual, and his or her level of authority, strength of personality, level of performance as a profit earner, and effectiveness of past decisions: the chief engineer, the production manager, the financial manager and the chief executive.

Effective centralisation does not imply that the supplies manager dictates which piece of equipment is to be purchased. Nor does it imply that his or her only role is to vet the commercial technicalities of the contract for the equipment, try to ensure that the price is competitive and that the equipment is delivered on time. For the best effect, he or she will be involved in the decision making from the initial stages where the need for equipment to perform the necessary function is identified; he or she should advise colleagues on sources and work closely with them on evaluating the alternatives. He or she should be seen by prospective suppliers as the decision-making authority, even if only to allow him or her commercial leverage in discussion with them. This does not imply that technical matters should be subordinated to commercial, but suggests that both are considered in parallel. Too often the converse is true and the buyer is given little scope to perform his or her function. If suppliers know that technical factors dominate and the order is theirs, the buyer has to negotiate with extremely limited power.

To take this example further, among the commercial factors which the buyer should take into consideration are: guarantees on the life of the machine, the position regarding spares, breakdown service, operative training, payment terms and conditions, delivery programme and check points, logistic and installation implications, price breakdown and relationship with the programme, level of after-service, etc. It is important to remember that effective comparison between alternatives at the quotation stage should include these and other considerations as well as the technical specification.

Departmental organisation

At departmental level the number of people employed, the volume and variety of goods and services purchased, the ability and authority of the departmental head, the capabilities of the people employed in the department, and the importance of the supply function to the operation of the enterprise concerned, are among the factors which will affect the organisation structure decision.

Nevertheless, there are basic organisation patterns around which variations occur. A simple form in a small department is often something like that shown in Figure 3.3. With the exclusion in some cases of the stock-control function from the buyer's responsibilities, this pattern is reasonably typical of a small departmental structure. Most departments, in the UK at least, are composed of less than four people. It should be noted, however, that an organisation chart is but one aspect of the matter. It tells us nothing of the scope of the job the buyer holds, etc., nor does it describe the informal aspects of the organisational activity (Strauss, 1962).

Figure 3.4, with similar caveats, illustrates one approach to organisation structure in a larger department.

The division of responsibilities in Figure 3.3 is generally quite straight-forward. The buyer assumes responsibility for the more important purchases, and their assistant deals with the more routine matters. In practice, the classic 80/20* relationship is evident in this division, for most of the money spent by the organisation will tend to be concentrated on a relatively small number of items.

---

* This is one application of the Pareto Principle that the significant items in a given group tend to be concentrated in a small area within that group. Eighty per cent of a company's purchases by value tend to be concentrated with 20 per cent of their suppliers: indeed in some cases the ratio can be as much as 90/10.

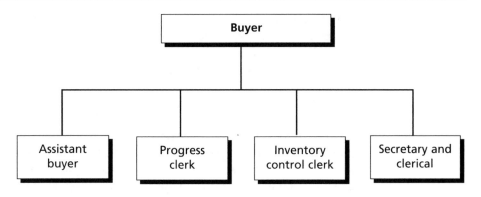

Fig. 3.3 A typical small department structure

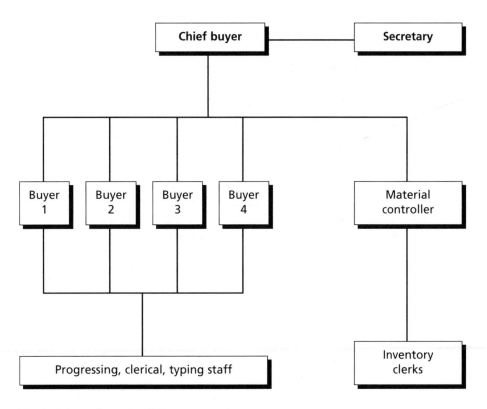

Fig. 3.4 A medium-sized departmental structure

In Figure 3.4, the allocation of responsibilities within the department is more complex. Generally speaking the chief buyer is responsible for the policy-making as well as the efficient management of the department as an element in the company organisation. He or she usually retains responsibility too for the most important contracts and purchasing decisions. In this type of structure a decision has to be taken as to how best to group the purchasing activities so as to be most effective. One common approach is to do this by commodity or material groups, where each buyer deals with a particular range of items; for example, one buyer may be responsible for raw materials, another for mechanical components and another for electrical/electronic materials. Apart from the advantage of specialisation in a particular range of goods, this helps to avoid duplication of research and negotiation effort at plant level. It should also facilitate data collection and communication inside the department and with other sections of the company as a whole. It can strengthen the buyer's negotiating position through consolidation of total requirements and can reduce time spent in negotiation. In addition, liaison with suppliers is often improved by this means.

However, if this approach to division of work is followed, it is important to bear in mind that provision should be made whereby a colleague can take over responsibility for a particular group of materials in the absence of the buyer normally responsible. One method which is commonly used to deal with this matter is to pair buyers. Not only can this help to overcome such temporary problems, but it can be a useful means of staff development. In the organisation shown in Figure 3.4, buyers 1 and 2 and buyers 3 and 4 might work together in this manner. In larger organisations (*see* Figure 3.5), each section will tend to become self-sufficient in this way. Development of staff in such cases, however, may involve moving people between sections.

Buyer specialisation by commodity or material group may often be the best way to subdivide the work of a supplies department, but it is not always the case. In the construction industry, for instance, individual buyers or buying sections are often responsible for all purchases for particular contracts. Often these contracts amount to huge sums and the construction site may be many miles from where the responsible buyer is located. In such circumstances, a single contract facilitates liaison, even though there may be advantages in concentrating purchases for negotiation. A combination approach is frequently favoured, where buyers assigned to particular contracts place orders against contracts negotiated on a commodity basis for the company as a whole. These contracts will, typically, be negotiated by members of staff who have been designated as major contract buyers. Usually this work is undertaken in addition to other functions.

Support services

One feature which should not be forgotten in considering the organisation of a purchasing department is the importance of support services to buyers. In larger organisations, more extensive support services are usually available: cost

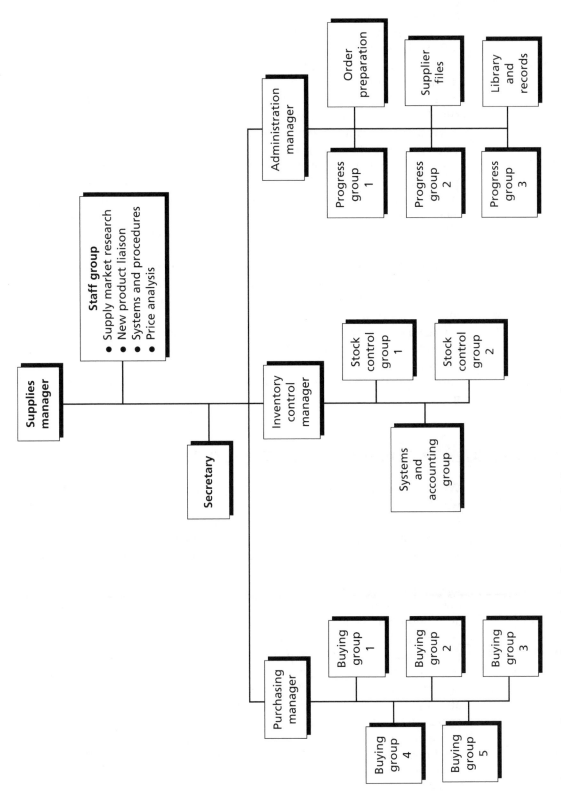

Fig. 3.5 A departmental organisation in a large single-factory enterprise

analysts, economists, legal advisers and other specialists are included among support staff in the interests of achieving organisational objectives. Computerised information systems also make a significant contribution.

In all cases the emphasis should be on teamwork: not only within the department but also between user and supplier. The buyer's role has been described as that of a 'catalyst' in promoting useful interaction between supplier and user. This is particularly important in technical matters where the buyer's co-ordinating role can be important in successful technical/commercial liaison between the buying and supplying organisations.

In departmental organisation it is important to make the most of the particular talents and strengths of the individuals in an organisation. Put people in jobs they can do best; use to the utmost the talents and skills available and constantly endeavour to develop individuals and the group as a whole. As Drucker (1968) emphasised, good organisation structure of itself will not ensure good performance; capable, well-motivated people are needed to make the organisation function. However, a poor organisation structure makes good performance impossible, no matter how good the individual managers may be. Improved organisation structure will therefore always improve performance.

Organisations require control, co-ordination and communication. These requirements need careful consideration in setting up any organisation whether it be at department, company or group level. It is important too, to ensure that the organisation and its related systems develop over time to match changing circumstances.

PURCHASING IN THE ORGANISATION STRUCTURE

Where should purchasing be in the organisation structure? This question, which the authors have been asked on many occasions, has no simple answer. In some cases the function may not be significant, and will be placed in a subordinate position in the hierarchy. The converse is true when the size of purchase expenditure relative to corporate turnover is such that a very senior executive is appointed to control the function, or when key supplies emanate from volatile markets, or when the proportion of the cost of a product which is bought in is significant. Between these extremes, on what might be thought of as a continuum, lie many variants.

There are organisations where the function is subordinated, most often to production. That position probably reflects traditional attitudes in the organisations as well as the quality of the supplies staff. 'If you pay peanuts you get monkeys!' A subordinate role and a commensurate salary, etc. will not attract staff with the ability to perform the function at a higher level. As a result, either the broader functions of purchasing are performed by other people, or it is assumed that they are. In such circumstances, competent purchasing staff may need to bring to the attention of traditional managements the potential of the function. Status is won; rarely is it given. Figure 3.6 is the outline organisation of a medium-sized manufacturing concern in which the purchasing function is

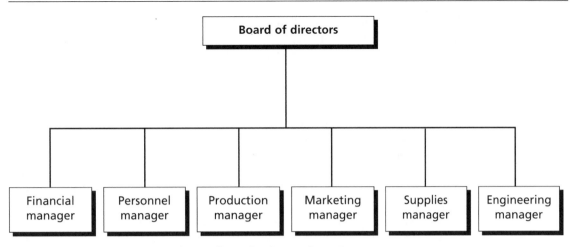

Fig. 3.6 Outline organisation of a medium-sized manufacturing company

recognised as a key element in company operations. Depending upon the perceived importance of purchasing, the function may, also, be represented at board level either in its own right or through a director with related interests.

When is purchasing important?

While each case will need to be examined on its merits, there is an argument for the provision of a more prescriptive guideline regarding the importance of purchasing. It was as a result of being asked to provide such a guideline that the following, so-called Farmer's Laws were developed. In the first case, the perceived importance of purchasing increased dramatically in a consumer electronics business as the time available to develop new products diminished. The management in the business concerned realised that there was an urgent need to involve suppliers and find ways to ensure that new products were right first time – faster. From this experience we can say that:

Purchasing increases in perceived importance in direct relationship with the reduction in the length of product life cycle time.

A second statement arose from the observation that the function appeared to be recognised as of significant importance when the business involved traded in commodity markets. This led to the statement that:

Purchasing is perceived to be important when the business concerned interfaces significantly with a volatile market or markets.

The third 'law' has a more general applicability. What should be noted here, however, is the absence of the word 'perceived' in the statement, for there are many organisations where, while the 'law' is valid, top management are myopic.

Purchasing is important whenever the organisation concerned spends a significant proportion of its income on purchasing goods and services to allow it to do business.

Where these 'laws' apply, what should the organisation expect of the head of purchasing? The person ought to be of a calibre consistent with other key managers. Like his or her colleagues he or she should be *au fait* with the objectives of the enterprise; indeed he or she should make a significant contribution to their development. In addition he or she should set objectives for his or her function, and the scope of his or her activity should exhibit accountability as well as authority.

The result of subordinating the supplies manager to some line manager may be reduced performance. Good buying requires objective consideration of many factors in the interest of the organisation as a whole, and line managers with a vested interest in certain aspects of organisational performance may not find this easy. Good buyers are also recognised as their company's experts on purchasing, people to whom colleagues at all levels turn for information and advice on supply matters. The calibre of the person in the subordinate position is rarely likely to be sufficient to meet this challenge.

Purchasing requires executives of a calibre commensurate with the potential of the function within the organisation concerned. Only by effectively centralising purchasing responsibilities and authority at the company level can this potential be realised. This is not because supply is more important than other functions; rather it is because the level of performance in the supplies area affects all those parts of the organisation where the work process results directly in profits or losses.

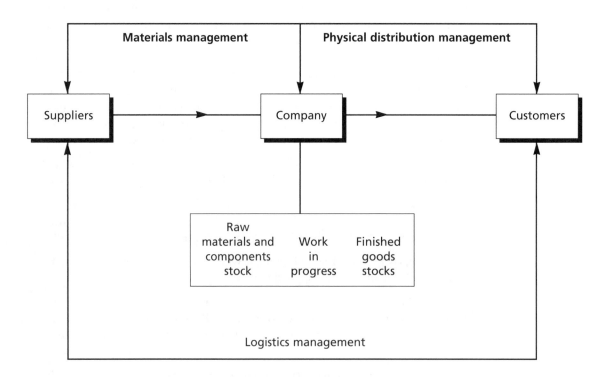

Fig. 3.7 A model of a manufacturing company showing one view of materials systems

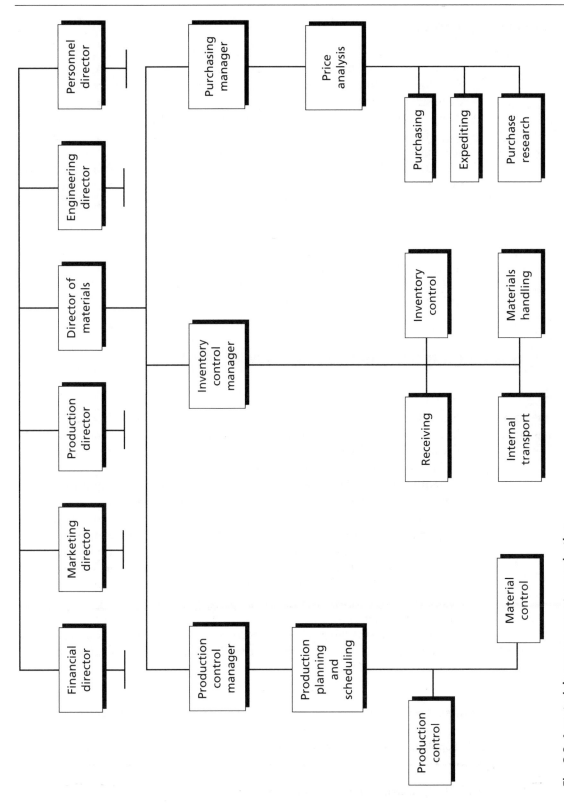

Fig. 3.8 A materials management organisation

The broader approaches

Several references have been made in this chapter to systems approaches. In broad terms these differ from conventional functional organisation systems in that they seek to avoid functional sub-optimisation whilst pursuing system-wide effectiveness. As implied earlier, this always involves trade-off decisions being made between departmental objectives. 'Materials management', 'logistics management', 'physical distribution management' and 'materials administration' are examples of such approaches.

Figure 3.7 illustrates what are generally regarded as the spheres of activity for each of these approaches. However, it is important to recognise that some advocates of, for example, 'materials management' and 'physical distribution management' define their scope of influence as being that of 'logistics management'.

Readers interested in these and other approaches will find relevant references at the end of this chapter. Other related organisational issues such as manufacturing resource planning (MRP), co-makership and just-in-time (JIT) are dealt with in other chapters.

NEW APPROACHES TO PURCHASING STRUCTURES

Strategic

Supply chain management

Purchasing and supply within organisations will vary in terms of its stage of development (*see* Chapter 4). The more advanced the activity, the more likely it will be involved with both upstream and downstream activities Figure 3.9. This in turn will affect organisation structures.

Traditionally the buyer was directly involved with relatively few internal functions and possibly the first tier of Suppliers. If, however, organisations are concerned with adopting World Class approaches, and concerned with driving out unnecessary costs from the supply chain they need to adopt flatter cross functional structures. Purchasing structures will need to be far more flexible if they are to deal with increased involvement both up and down stream.

In Figure 3.10, first tier suppliers are A, B and C. Traditionally, the buyer's involvement has tended to be limited to this first tier, similarly relationships within this organisation have also been limited. Time involvement in the supply chain means the buyer must become involved in the total supply chain, i.e. from TT to NS–NC, as shown in the diagram, if the unnecessary costs are to be driven out of this chain.

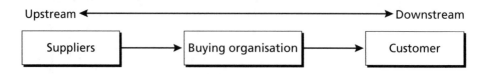

Fig. 3.9 Upstream and downstream activities

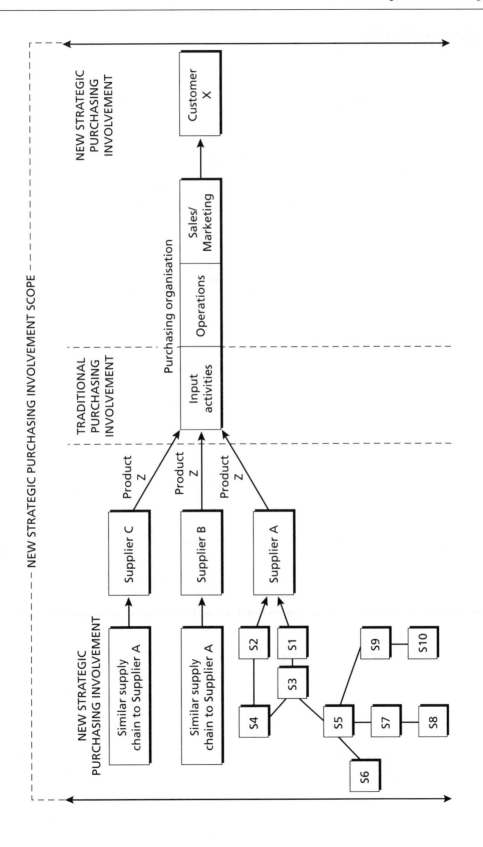

Fig. 3.10 Buyer involvement

PURCHASING DEVOLUTION

As purchasing takes on a more strategic role it will have to release much of the routine purchasing to budget holders, particularly in the areas where it can add little value. As purchasing evolves to become strategically proactive so it must devolve. It is therefore likely that in the future we will find new structures coming into place, with a small strategically tasked purchasing activity responsible for managing the supply chains, determining overall purchasing policy and involved with major negotiations while routine, lower value items are handled on a day-to-day basis by budget holders.

This new type of organisation structure is illustrated below in Figure 3.11.

Fig. 3.11 A new type of organisation structure

Within each profit centre, individual budget holders would be delegated to 'buy' within agreed parameters laid down by purchasing. A strategic purchasing activity would have to train staff and monitor such new developments.

Outsourcing of purchasing and 'virtual' organisations

Outsourcing   Outsourcing of activities that were traditionally provided by the buyer's organisation has grown considerably over the years. Today we even find that functions such as accounts, transport, computer services, marketing, even purchasing, can be outsourced. It is likely this would occur for the following reasons:

- Stage of purchasing development reached is not sufficient to give the organisation the competitive advantage required. Outsourcing the activity to a more advanced strategically proactive organisation will allow this advantage to be attained.
- The existing organisation structure cannot deal with rapid change.
- Existing structures and procedures make efficient/effective buying strategies impossible e.g. the public sector. In such cases outsourcing the purchasing activity to the private sector might give considerable gains.

'Virtual' organisations

Tom Peters and others talk about virtual organisations. Virtual organisation structures are minimal with the majority of work outsourced. The organisation communicates with its workers through the Internet or e-mail. Overhead costs are minimal with offices or meeting rooms hired when required. Most staff work from home or from their own offices. Structures in the normal sense do not exist.

The near virtual buyer working from home gets all the information he/she requires from integrated databases and responds accordingly. While such futuristic developments may seem far removed from what happens today, there are interesting developments in this area, particularly as the management of time becomes of key strategic interest.

CONCLUSION

To conclude this chapter it is worth emphasising a point made earlier: an organisation structure should be developed to meet specific needs. By the nature of things, those needs will differ from organisation to organisation. If materials management, or any other concept, has been successfully applied in company A, it does not follow that the same version will be suitable for company B. Thus the executive charged with developing an effective and efficient procurement organisation will need to take full account of the environment within which that organisation is to function, and the objectives and strategies which have been specified for it. This necessitates appreciation of its proper relationships with other functions in the business and the need to develop and support staff of the necessary calibre to achieve the objectives which have been set. In all organisational matters, it is important to have in mind the following precept:

It is better to have a less than perfect system which users and staff understand and want to make work than a highly sophisticated one without user and staff commitment.

SUMMARY POINTS

- There is no generally applicable organisational structure as each enterprise is unique. The size of the organisation, the type of market which it serves, the technology and processes involved and many other factors will all determine the structure.
- Systems approaches can be used to explain the development of organisation structure. The more integrated the system the better the chance of success.
- Handy suggests that an organisation's culture can be characterised by one of four types of activity; steady state, innovation, crisis and policy. The author disagrees with Handy's perception of purchasing lying in the steady state. While some aspects certainly do, proactive purchasing departments will have some involvement in innovation and policy making.
- Emphasis is given to the need of capable, well-motivated staff. (However, a poor organisation structure makes good performance impossible no matter how good the individual managers are).

- The adoption of world class concepts means purchasing has to extend its involvement down the levels of supply and up to the final customer, i.e. buyers must become familiar with the total supply chain in order to reduce costs and waste.
- Organisational structures should be tailored to meet specific needs taking into account the external environment and the objectives and strategies laid out.

REFERENCES AND FURTHER READING

Birchall D (1993), 'Managing the supply chain', *Logistics*, April.

Bowersox D, Gloss D, Helferich O (1986), *Logistical Management*, 3rd edn, Macmillan and Collier, London.

Bridges G and Mackenzie N (1990), 'Integrated supply and demand chains', *Purchasing and Supply Management*, April.

Dimanescu D (1992), *The Seamless Enterprise: Making Cross-Functional Management Work*, Harper Business Books, New York.

Farrington B and Waters D (1994), *Managing Purchasing: Organising, Planning and Control*, Chapman and Hall, London.

Freeman V and Cavatino J (1990), 'Fitting purchasing to the strategic firm: framework, processes and values', *International Journal of Purchasing and Materials Management*, 26 (1), Winter.

Fearon H (1973), 'Materials management: a synthesis and current review', *Journal of Purchasing*, February.

Handy C B (1985), *Understanding Organisations*, 3rd edn, Penguin, London.

Manion D (1993), 'Partnership selection at ICL', *Selected Readings in Purchasing and Supply* (eds. Jessop and Hines), CIPS, Ascot.

Morris N and Calantone R (1991), 'Redefining the purchasing function: an entrepreneurial perspective', *International Journal of Purchasing and Materials Management*, Fall.

Peters T (1992), *In Search of Excellence*, Harper & Row, New York.

Rajagopal S and Bernard K (1993), 'Strategic procurement and competitive advantage', *International Journal of Purchasing and Materials Management*, Fall.

Rich N, Hines P, Jones O, Francis M (1996), *Evidence of a Watershed in the Purchasing Function*, IPSERA Conference Papers, April.

CHAPTER 4

Purchasing evolution and development

Purchasing and supply activity is receiving more attention from senior management and from academics than was generally the case when the early editions of this book appeared. It is now widely, though not universally, recognised that a full contribution from supply activity can only be made if purchasing and supply is sufficiently developed. In this chapter we will examine in more detail what is meant by purchasing development and evolution. We will look at a purchasing development framework, and identify major factors likely to affect the process.

- **To appreciate that the supply activity has to be sufficiently developed in order to make a contribution**
- **To gain an insight into the external factors which influence the development of the purchasing function**
- **To assess the internal influences which can initiate change**
- **To examine the stages of purchasing development and the various methods used to indicate position**
- **To compare the benefits of outsourcing purchasing *v* investing in the development of an internal department.**

Organisations manage a range of input activities. By input activities we mean, principally: purchasing; stock control; stores management; and inbound transportation (*see* Figure 4.1). The ability of an organisation to meet its strategic objectives depends upon all parts of the organisation being appropriately developed for their responsibilities. There has, in recent years, been much greater attention paid to the input activities, and a good deal of concern for these activities is now generally demonstrated in the business world.

While all organisations have purchasing and supply activities, the contribution of these activities will be determined by the extent of their development. Here we discuss the evolution of purchasing and supply the extent and nature of its contribution at successive stages.

THE INCREASED INTEREST IN PURCHASING

Background factors

There are many reasons to account for the development of interest in purchasing and supply activity, some of these factors are suggested below, there are, of course, others.

- The increasing interest in appointing external providers by organisations keen to seek the most effective practices.
- Increasing specialisation has contributed to a great increase in external expenditure.
- There is an increasing emphasis on 'core business' activities by many concerns, this has led to a great increase in outsourcing, that is to say the appointment of contractors to undertake activities (usually of a service nature) formerly conducted 'in-house' employing the organisation's own staff and resources.
- Emergent ideas connected with quality, responsiveness and the elimination of waste have focused attention on the supply chain, and hence on supply.
- Leading organisations seem, at least partly, to be characterised by a strategic emphasis on supply. Others are seeking to emulate them.
- Organisations today need to be more responsive and flexible. They cannot be so unless their suppliers are too. Hence increasing attention to supply chains.
- Electronic Data Interchange (EDI) and systems integration between organisations has led to more attention being paid to the suppliers–customer interface.
- Powerful information technology has enabled a clearer view of the contribution that purchasing and supply makes.

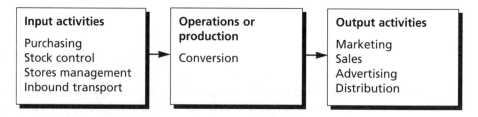

Fig. 4.1 Business activities

DEVELOPMENT FACTORS

During periods of high inflation, organisations with developed purchasing functions have done considerably better at controlling price increases than those where purchasing and supply was not so well developed. This has not gone unnoticed, and wider attention is today paid to those functions and departments involved with price negotiations. Top management has, in most cases, become far more aware of the need to develop a purchasing activity that could cope more effectively with inflation.

Historically, high levels of inflation were frequently accompanied by a booming economy associated with shortages. The handling of shortages can be coped with by paying the going price (or more) or ideally, by developing effective strategies to counter the problem. Those organisations with well-developed purchasing functions had often anticipated shortages and taken necessary action to deal with the problems by re-sourcing, using less of the product, liaising with designers in order to specify alternatives, or stockpiling when prices were low, where financially possible. While they were affected they were often able to cushion the effect and keep their organisations going.

Changing patterns of trade

With the growth of larger trading blocs such as the European Union, the opening up of Eastern Europe and improvements brought about by World Trade Organisation (formally known as GATT) markets have become international. The traditional administratively-orientated purchasing function had considerable difficulty in adapting to these changes. Most buyers would source for the most part within their domestic economy, whereas those more aware would be attempting to buy where the best value could be attained.

Government intervention

There are varying degrees of government and trading bloc involvement in the marketplace. This can take the form of price controls as in the 1970s, or control of monopolies and restrictive practices, health and safety and so on.

Of particular interest recently has been the privatisation of large parts of the former public sector and the movement of huge segments of the public sector back into private ownership. Audit reports had been particularly critical of procurement in the public sector, where purchasing had tended to be inefficient. With privatisation, purchasing functions quickly began to copy better practices found in the private sector.

In more recent years the public sector, comprising public health authorities, local authorities, defence procurement and what used to be nationalised industries, have spent considerable time and effort in attempts to improve their purchasing and supply activities. In some cases they still have some way to go to catch up with advanced purchasing organisations in the private sector, though of course not all 'best practice' comes with the private sector, and not all private sector purchasing is advanced.

Recent changes in local government have meant that now 'budget holders' are the major decision makers. They do not have to use centrally negotiated contracts, and in the pursuit of value for money, they can source with whom they like. In the past the centrally negotiated contracts did not necessarily offer what clients considered to be value for money. The net effect of these changes in the public sector has been that the central purchasing agencies have become more commercially orientated and have begun to 'market' their services to users.

The European Community directives have also put pressure on European purchasing to develop a more enlightened sourcing policy. Tenders over a given threshold (reviewed periodically) have to be advertised in the *European Journal*, thereby allowing greater opportunities for potential European suppliers.

Growth of the Chartered Institute of Purchasing and Supply (CIPS) and an increase in the general awareness of the purchasing activity

In the early 1990s the Institute of Purchasing and Supply was granted a Royal Charter. This was a landmark in the development of the purchasing and supply function, and it is now more widely regarded as a truly professional activity.

The institute has spent considerable time and effort at a national level demonstrating the importance and contribution of effective purchasing in both the public and private sectors. Its examination scheme and courses have done much to enhance the status of the purchasing function, and it is now represented on many government committees where purchasing issues are discussed.

This heightened awareness of the purchasing and supply function is certainly a factor in improving the general development of the activity across the UK. An example to illustrate this point has been the way the Department of Trade and Industry has published booklets on the benefits of a proactive purchasing function, and organised 'road shows' to increase awareness. It has also offered consultancy services to those smaller organisations who wish to improve their purchasing expertise.

'Leading edge'

Developing concepts and techniques, such as the following, have had an important impact on purchasing:

- EDI;
- Just-in-time;
- Lean manufacturing and supply;
- Integrated logistics;
- Total quality management; and
- Value stream concepts.

Figure 4.2 suggests that these ideas do contribute to improvement, but they are not the complete answer.

If purchasing is not sufficiently developed then the implementation of these ideas is impracticable. All the strategies require the development of more rationalised supply chains and suppliers who themselves are moving towards developed philosophies. Suppliers need to work closely with the purchasing organisation's staff in order to develop appropriate products and trading methods and to eliminate waste in all its forms.

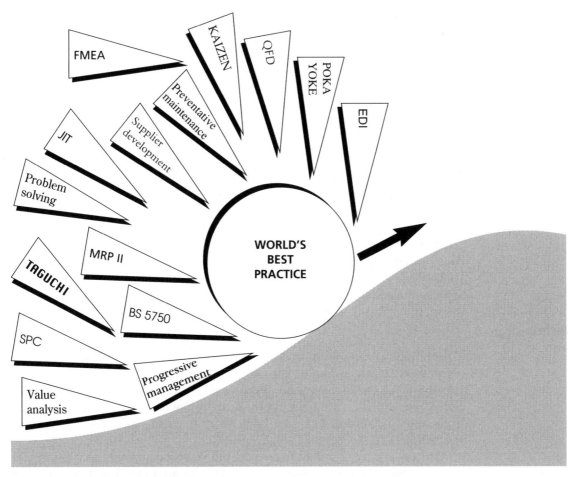

Fig. 4.2 A journey to 'world's best practice'
(*Source:* Welsh Development Agency)

Competitor activity

Pressure is often placed on organisations when attempting to develop new ideas to look at what competitors are achieving. The term 'benchmarking' is often given to this process, but we should mention at this stage that it is not simply copying good ideas. Demonstration of the real benefits that a developed supply function confers on the rest of an organisation has been a stimulant for other companies to improve that function, and this in turn has raised the profile of purchasing.

Customer demands

The customer is now seen as being all important. It is no longer acceptable to give a second-best service if you want to remain profitable and retain market share. Organisations are more 'customer driven', and these driving forces impact upon purchasing. Any inefficiencies in the supply chain must be reduced or removed. Major customers may in turn prevail on suppliers to improve the latter's own sources of supply as well as their operations. If, for example, a customer were to find that one of its main suppliers had an ineffective purchasing function, pressure would most likely be brought to bear on that supplier to make improvements quickly, otherwise the cost of supply would be unacceptably high.

Innovation

The pace of change has quickened over the years. Organisations must be able to develop new practices and products quickly and effectively. This in turn requires significant improvements in the internal interface between purchasing on the one hand and, on the other, production, marketing, finance and so on, as well as with external suppliers and customers. As product life cycles get shorter, reaction times are being compressed. Purchasing must be prepared to help initiate new ideas and developments. A good deal of attention is being paid today to 'time to market' initiatives. New products cannot be developed and marketed rapidly, without a proactive purchasing function.

Technology

Technological progression necessitates that organisations should have formulated plans to handle development. Purchasing needs to be actively involved. An example may be found in the development of electronic data interchange (EDI). It is imperative that purchasing has an appropriate supplier base and is involved with suppliers who can jointly develop and use this technology.

While we have examined some of the important factors that affect the development of the purchasing activity, there is no doubt that there are other external variables also at work, but these are more specific to particular organisations.

INTERNAL ORGANISATIONAL FACTORS

Although there is considerable pressure from outside to develop the purchasing function, it is often internal influences that initiate the changes. These internal influences include the following factors.

The level and percentages of bought-out material expenditure

Normally, as the external expenditure increases as a proportion of the total, greater attention is paid to the input activities. For example, in large automotive, electronic and retail organisations, percentages of bought-out material and services expenditure in relation to sales income run at between 60 and 75 per cent. Clearly, this expenditure is of crucial importance and needs close attention at policy level. It is interesting to note that this proportion has been increasing steadily for many years (*see* Figure 4.3).

Integrated systems

As a system becomes more integrated within an organisation and provides more and more information, so the likelihood of discovering inefficiencies within that system also increases. Input activities are therefore crucial to the development of integrated systems; their stage of development must match what is required to make the integrated systems work effectively.

The more advanced the computer systems, the greater the possibilities of reducing routine work carried out by input staff. Time can then be spent concentrating on more effective purchasing.

Integrated systems organise and disclose enormous amounts of information about the workings of the total system. Should senior management not be aware of the possibility of substantial savings and improvements in efficiency in the purchasing areas, they soon would be as integrated systems developed.

Structural changes

Moves towards materials management and logistic concepts have in their turn helped to develop the purchasing and supply function. In almost all cases the amount of attention paid to purchasing supply has risen.

Performance measurement

There has been more emphasis in recent years on measurement. Within organisations that measure the contribution of the purchasing and supply function, its status is usually affected in a positive way. Senior management become aware of its contribution to cost reduction and its strategic capabilities, and in consequence are far more likely to promote its development.

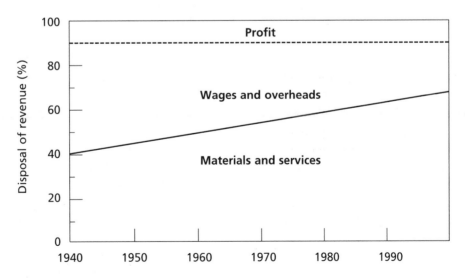

Fig. 4.3 The increasing importance of purchasing and supply in the manufacturing sector

MEASUREMENT OF PURCHASING DEVELOPMENT

Measuring the stage of development reached by a purchasing organisation can indicate whether development is appropriate for the needs of the concern. For example, it could be totally inappropriate to expect an essentially reactive organisation to take on board world class concepts. Failure would be inevitable.

It is useful, therefore, to identify the stage of development reached by a purchasing function so that further development can be planned.

Purchasing development framework

Perhaps the first attempt at developing such a framework was that undertaken by Jones (1983). Jones developed his model in order to establish whether or not organisations with well-developed purchasing functions were more effective negotiators than those where purchasing was not developed.

Criteria	Level 1	Level 2	Level 3
Sophistication levels	Simple informal buying process, price dominated, buyer acts as order clerk	More advanced buying process, price and other factors considered, buyer enjoys greater discretion	Advanced buying process, strategic aspects of buying considered, buyer full procurement executive
Buying stages			
Recognition and analysis of needs	Buyer receives requisitions from senior management, performs order clerk activity	Buyer participates in drawing up of specification/some discretion	Buyer participates fully in initiation of purchases/member of senior management team concerned with procurement
Search for supplier	Buyer passively receives catalogues from suppliers	Buyer initiates some supplier contact/ receives data	Buyer initiates two-way communications with suppliers
Evaluation and selection of supplier	Buyer buys what is specified to him at lowest price	Buyer concerned with non-price factors/ concerned with total cost to firm, not just price	Buyer concerned with strategic importance to firm of purchasing
Performance feedback	No involvement by buyer; assessment done by using departments	Some participation in feedback analysis	Buyer fully involved in wide-ranging assessment activity

Fig. 4.4 Buyer sophistication matrix
(*Source:* Barnes and McTavish, 1983)

STRATEGIC STAGES IN THE DEVELOPMENT OF A PURCHASING FUNCTION

Passive

Definition

The purchasing function has no strategic direction and primarily reacts to the requests of other functions.

Characteristics

- High proportion of purchaser's time is spent on quick-fix and routine operations.
- Purchasing function and individual performance are based on efficiency measures.
- Little interfunctional communication takes place because of purchasing's low visibility.
- Supplier selection is based on price and availability.

Independent

Definition

The purchasing function adopts the latest purchasing techniques and practices, but its strategic direction is independent of the firm's competitive strategy.

Characteristics

- Performance is primarily based on cost reduction and efficiency measures.
- Co-ordination links are established between purchasing and technical disciplines.
- Top management recognises the importance of professional development.
- Top management recognises the opportunities in purchasing for contributing to profitability.

Supportive

Definition

The purchasing function supports the firm's competitive strategy by adopting purchasing techniques and practices which strengthen the firm's competitive position.

Characteristics

- Purchasers are included in sales proposal teams.
- Suppliers are considered a resource which is carefully selected and motivated.
- People are considered a resource with emphasis on experience, motivation, and attitude.
- Markets, products, and suppliers are continuously monitored and analysed.

Integrative

Definition

Purchasing's strategy is fully integrated into the firm's competitive strategy and constitutes part of an integrated effort among functional peers to formulate and implement a strategic plan.

Characteristics

- Cross-functional training of purchasing professionals–executives is made available.
- Permanent lines of communication are established among other functional areas.
- Professional development focuses on strategic elements of the competitive strategy.
- Purchasing performance is measured in terms of contributions to the firm's success.

Fig. 4.5 A four-stage purchasing development model

(*Source:* Reck and Lang, 1988)

Jones suggests that there are 5 stages of development, calling stage 1 the least developed and stage 5 the most developed. Various criteria were measured and profiles produced. He indeed found that where the activity was well developed, the organisation negotiated not necessarily better prices but better deals, that is, deals based on strategic acquisition cost.

Buyer sophistication matrix

Barnes and McTavish (1983) produced a three-stage buyer sophistication matrix (*see* Figure 4.4) to help identify what stage of development an organisation's purchasing function had reached. The limitations of this matrix, however, is that it only measures six criteria and three levels. Nevertheless, it is useful in identifying, mainly to marketing staff, what type of purchasing function they are dealing with and how they should approach the buying organisations concerned.

Strategic stages in the development of a purchasing function

Reck and Long produced a more involved four-stage purchasing development model in 1988 when they began investigating the contributions purchasing could make to organisational strategic roles. These four stages of development and the characteristics of each stage are shown in Figure 4.5. This framework moves us forward, but its major defect is that only four stages are contemplated and the variables are not operational. It does, though, offer an opportunity in general terms to indicate stages of purchasing development.

Area of focus

Russell Sysons, writing in the September 1989 edition of *Purchasing and Supply Management*, saw purchasing divided into three principal areas of focus: transaction, commercial and proactive. The more developed the purchasing activity the greater its involvement in commercial and strategic activities. He illustrates the positioning of purchasing within the organisation in the two graphs shown in Figure 4.6. His illustrations show, that the more involved purchasing becomes in commercial and strategic areas, the greater its effectiveness to the organisation.

Purchasing profile analysis

The final framework for us to examine is that developed by Jones in 1997 as part of his PhD thesis concerning stages of purchasing development. The most important finding of the research is that purchasing has five stages of measurable development, these have been named:

1 Infant   2 Awakening   3 Developing   4 Mature   5 Advanced

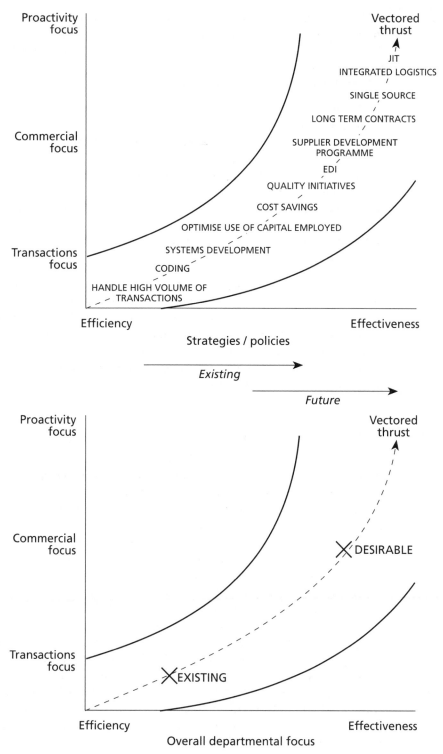

Fig. 4.6 The three principal areas of focus
(*Source:* Sysons, 1989)

Profiles can be produced for individual purchasing organisations identifying these stages of development, and indicating areas that may need further development. The framework is shown in Figure 4.7. Eighteen variables are assessed and profiles then produced.

From the research results it was possible:

- To identify the development of profiles that aided development of organisational strategies.
- To demonstrate that certain profiles, unless changed, could not support proposed organisational strategies.
- To provide a benchmark against which strategies could be developed to improve the status of the function.
- To show that 'best in class' organisations had very similar purchasing profiles.
- To establish that highly developed purchasing functions were more able to achieve optimisation of costs.

With the establishment of the purchasing development matrix it becomes possible for those managers responsible for the activity to identify where developments are required. The research has shown that developing some of the variables is more difficult than others. Attitudes are difficult to change, both within purchasing and in other parts of the organisation. It is important, therefore, that commitment to develop the purchasing functions comes from the very top of the organisation.

Outsourcing of the purchasing activity

There have been numerous articles recently suggesting that the purchasing activity might be outsourced, Benmeridja and Benmeridja (1996), or even eliminated, Evans (1996), and Stanwick and Jones (1996). Many of the arguments centre very much on the role of the activity and its contribution to the organisation. This idea is revisited later in the book.

Most writers and practitioners seem to agree that the old clerically reactive and transactional style of purchasing has only a limited role today. Such an approach cannot give the organisation it represents a strategic advantage by effectively contributing to the integrated supply chain. A purchasing activity – whether it be a purchasing department or a devolved activity shared by a number of people in the organisation – that is poorly developed is likely to slow development of the whole organisation. In such cases it might make economic and practical sense to allocate the purchasing activity to an outside organisation where there is appropriate expertise and influence.

All those purchasing activities below stage 3 of development are likely to be considered for outsourcing if the organisation needs a strategic proactive purchasing activity quickly and cannot wait or invest in the development of the purchasing activity that is required.

STAGE OF

MEASUREMENT AREA

		1 Infant	2 Awakening	3 Developing	4 Mature	5 Advanced
1. Activity breakdown analysis	A1					
2. Purchasing organisational structure	A2					
3. Purchasing services	A3					
4. Function position in the business	B1/2					
5. Extent of training/development of buyer	B3					
6. Relative remuneration levels	B4					
7. Measurement of purchasing performance	B5					
8. Standard of information systems	E1					
9. Computer technology	E2					
10. Standard of operating procedures	F1					
11. Interface development (buying centre)	H1					
12. Buying process involvement	H2					
13. Buyer characteristics/development	I1					
14. Degree of purchasing specialism	I2					
15. Supplier interface development	J1					
16. Policy on ethics	J2					
17. Hospitality	J3					
18. Quality of buyer–supplier relationship	J4					

Fig. 4.7 Purchasing profile analysis

Internal repositioning of certain elements of the purchasing activity, namely the handling of low value and transactional purchasing is likely to be devolved to users or requisitioners if purchasing is to evolve and spend more of its time on strategic purchases and all that this involves. Such internal repositioning of the activity to other functions is likely to occur at stages 3 and 4, otherwise purchasing could have difficulty in making the 'Quantum Leap', Sysons (1995) to fully developed status where most of purchasing's involvement is concentrating on strategic purchasing and supply chain management.

Figure 4.8 is an attempt to indicate likely contributions of the purchasing activity at different stages of development. If organisations measure, using profile analysis, the stage of development reached by the purchasing activity, they can begin to reflect on its likely capability. Unfortunately organisations often want the contribution offered by an advance on strategic purchasing activity but have not put the necessary corporate investment into the purchasing activity, which may still be at the awakening stage of development and not capable of making any real contribution to the organisation it represents.

Using the profiling technique, development shortcomings can be identified and appropriate development strategies produced.

Stage of development	Capabilities	Organisational contributions
Infant – Stage 1	Fragmented purchasing	None or low
Awakening – Stage 2	Realisation of savings potential	Clerical efficiency Small savings through consolidation 2–5%*
Developing – Stage 3	Control and development of purchase price/ negotiation capabilities	Cost reductions 5–10%*
Mature – Stage 4	80/20 recognised Specialist buyers Cost reductions Commencement of supplier base management	Cost reductions 10–20%* Acquisition cost 1–10%*
Advanced – Stage 5	Devolution of purchasing Strong central control Supply chain management	Cost reductions 25%* Cost of ownership Acquisition cost and supply chain management 30%+*
	Leverage buying Global sourcing Understanding and practice of acquisition cost and cost of ownership	

* = Estimates

Fig. 4.8 Purchasing development stages and performance capabilities

Purchasing overview

Rich *et al.* (1996) believe that purchasing has now reached a watershed, a process of 'gentrification' from academics, the CIPS and practitioners may have overstated the role of purchasing development overall, particularly in terms of its place in a fully integrated corporate structure. The development of world class concepts, lean supply, value chains etc. however require a strategic proactive function.

An article by Stanwick and Jones (1996) explores shifts in the conceptualisation of the purchasing function. It considers the effects of these changes, suggesting that they are so fundamental that they call for a redefinition of the profession. In turn they identify a four-stage purchasing evaluation structure based on:

- product-centred purchasing;
- process-centred purchasing;
- relation-purchasing; and
- performance centred purchasing.

This four-stage approach is also recorded by Stannack and Scheuing (1996), and similar purchasing development ideas are noted in this research.

These ideas, however, have one re-enforcing the view: that the purchasing function is very much affected by the stage of development it has reached within an organisation. The more developed the activity is the more likely it will be an integrated cross-functional strategic activity adding value and giving the organisation competitive advantage.

SUMMARY POINTS

- The chapter outlines reasons why there is increased pressure for purchasing and supply to become more developed. Ignoring this means that the adoption of leading edge concepts (such as total quality management) is not tenable.
- External factors influencing development include the effects of inflation and the opening up of new markets. Transactional approaches are unable to react to either of these situations. The privatisation of Public Sector industries has forced the improvement of purchasing within these organisations – often by emulating competitors.
- Internal influences such as the increasing level of bought out material expenditure and the implementation of integrated systems (reducing routine work) propels the purchasing function to higher levels. It is the internal influences which initiate change.
- The authors outline various models for measuring purchasing development. Making this assessment identifies areas that need attention. This research has shown that 'best in class' organisations have very similar profiles.

REFERENCES AND FURTHER READING

Barnes J G and McTavish R (1983), 'Segmenting industrial markets by buyer sophistication', *European Journal of Marketing*, 17(6).

Jones D M (1997), 'Purchasing evolution and development', unpublished PhD thesis, Strathclyde University.

Reck R F and Long B (1988), 'Purchasing a competitive weapon', *Journal of Purchasing and Materials Management*, Fall.

Stannack P and Jones M E (1996), 'The Death of Purchasing', *IPSERA*, April.

Rich N, Hines P, Jones T O, Francis M (1996), 'Evidence of a Watershed in the Purchasing Profession', *IPSERA Conference Papers*, April.

Benmeridja M and Benmeridja A (1996), 'Is it interesting for a Company to Outsource Purchasing and under what conditions?', *1996 IPSERA Conference Papers*, April.

PART 2

Key purchasing variables

Chapter 5
QUALITY

Chapter 6
THE RIGHT QUALITY

Chapter 7
TIME

Chapter 8
SOURCE DECISION MAKING

Chapter 9
PRICE

Chapter 10
PURCHASING NEGOTIATIONS

INTRODUCTION TO PART TWO

This part of the book is concerned with quality, quantity, time and price. Chapter 8, on source decision making, deals with selecting and dealing with suppliers, and the key topic of negotiation is also covered within this Part.

The purpose of this part is to bring together for the reader the important considerations that need to be taken into account when choosing a supplier, and to give an overview of the more commonly employed techniques in the consideration of the critical variables prior to supplier selection, and their management within an existing relationship.

Chapter 5 on quality is concerned with defining quality, and with the quality related themes of specification and standardisation. A note on ISO 9000 is included, and the themes of value analysis and value engineering are also addressed. Chapter 6 is concerned with quantity and looks at the traditional approaches by which demanded and supplied quantities are matched. In this chapter key provisioning approaches are dealt with and reference is made to the MRP system and JIT philosophies. Timing is discussed in Chapter 7, in particular 'lead time', expediting and planning. The issue of shortages is also covered here, as are some of the analytical techniques employed in time management in purchasing and supply.

It can, of course, be argued that finding the right supplier is the only really fundamental purchasing responsibility, and that if this is done properly then all of the other concerns fall into place as subsidiaries. Chapter 8 deals with source decision making, exploring such issues as the attributes of a good supplier, supplier selection processes and sourcing criteria. The important question of sourcing policy is also discussed here. There is a growing body of opinion which suggests that the right relationship is as crucial a consideration as the right supplier. This topic is briefly dealt with towards the end of the chapter.

Price is, of course, a matter of great concern to all of those who contract for supplies, and this is the theme of Chapter 9. Factors affecting pricing decisions, price, value, competition and market considerations are covered, and there is some new material on discounts. Contract price adjustment clauses and incentive contracts are also explained.

Chapter 10 is an important one, dealing with negotiation, a process of great importance to those concerned with purchasing and supply. There are definitions of negotiation, and an examination of the question 'what makes a skilled negotiator?' Negotiation is explained as a structured process, and the various elements of this structure are identified and expanded upon.

CHAPTER 5

Quality

INTRODUCTION

Product or service quality is increasingly seen as a 'qualifier' which must be demonstrably attainable before a supplier can merit consideration. Unless specifications can be understood and consistently met, a potential supplier is unlikely to win business from a buying organisation taking a professional view of the need to do business only with vendors who are tuned in to, and able to respond to the particular needs of customers. The shift in business and commercial practice from quality control to quality assurance is reflected in this chapter, as is the development of the extent to which attention is paid to the management systems employed by suppliers rather than the measurement or assessment of their products or services. In this chapter we consider the question 'What is quality?' We discuss approaches to specification and some of the relevant commercial practice. A note on value analysis and value engineering is included. Firms need to convince their customers that they can meet quality requirements *before* they can compete on price; and so ISO 9000, now firmly established as a key 'must know' for the purchasing professional is outlined in this chapter.

OBJECTIVES OF THIS CHAPTER

- To appreciate the move away from quality control (inspection techniques) towards quality assurance (prevention)
- To examine the different approaches to producing a specification and the role of value analysis
- To realise that total quality management requires the involvement of all suppliers and sub-contractors
- To assess the benefits of standardisation
- To introduce the BS EN ISO 9000 series of quality assurance
- To understand the economics of quality and examine the four broad cost groups.

WHAT IS QUALITY?

Quality is a word with several meanings and connotations. For example, it can mean excellence, as in 'this is a quality product', or it can be thought of as the extent to which a product or service achieves customer satisfaction. An idea gaining widespread support is that 'Quality is whatever the customer says it is'. The 'quality gurus' (Deming, Juran *et al.*) have become extremely influential, and have taught us that quality is an issue related to strategic advantage. Jones and Womack (1993) have advocated the pursuit of perfection, meaning the avoidance of all waste, though they state 'Perfection is like infinity. Trying to envision it (and to get there) is actually impossible, *but the effort to do so provides inspiration and direction essential to making progress along the path.'* So, quality can be defined in many ways. However, for the purposes of this chapter it might appropriately be defined or specified as the whole set of features and characteristics of a product or service that are relevant to meeting requirements. These can be few, or many (as shown in the coffee profile in Figure 5.1).

So, for the purposes of this chapter, 'quality' is simply 'fitness for purpose', or 'suitability'. There is a popular saying, 'there's no point in buying a Rolls-Royce to do the job of a Ford', and this sums up the concept adequately. Quality for a given application can be either too low or too high. The British

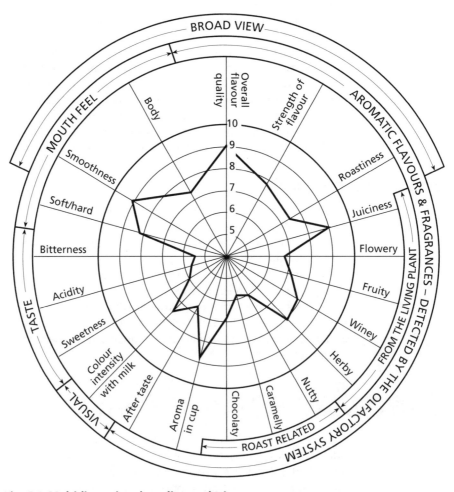

Fig. 5.1 Multidimensional quality analysis
(*Courtesy:* Nestlé)

Standards Institution as defined quality as 'The totality of features and characteristics of a product or service that bear on its ability to satisfy a given need'.

Performance quality and conformance quality

Supplies staff are concerned with quality from two points of view:

1 *Quality of design or specification* Have *we* specified the right material for the job, and have we communicated our requirement to the supplier in a clear and unambiguous way? This is *performance* quality.
2 *Conformance quality* Has *the supplier* provided material in accordance with the specification? We usually establish the answer to this question by inspection.

The words performance and conformance occur again later in the chapter, at the point at which we discuss specifications. Please take care not to confuse performance quality with a performance specification.

Attributes and variables

When inspecting goods we may be looking at *attributes* or *variables*. It is relatively easy to check for attributes, since they are either present or not. A domestic appliance is checked to see if the power lead accompanies it; a circuit board has 17 components attached; a gasket set has no missing items. These are all checks for attributes. Variables are much more difficult to inspect. A variable is something which needs to be assessed or measured, such as the dimensions of a mechanical part, the mass of a package of material, or the shade of colour of a printing paper. It is often economically sound policy to devise pass/fail tests of some kind that can enable variables to be assessed as attributes. Thus the inspection process becomes 'Does this item pass the test?'. The answer, which can only be 'yes' or 'no', is an attribute of the item.

Quality control and quality assurance

Inspection activities can be classified as quality *control* processes, along with the other activities which involve monitoring to ensure that defectives (or potential defectives) are spotted.

Quality *assurance* can be contrasted with control in that it (assurance) includes all the activities connected with the attainment of quality, including:

- Design, including proving and testing.
- Specification, which must be clear and unambiguous.
- Assessment of suppliers, to ensure that they can perform.
- Motivation of all concerned.
- Education and training of supplies staff.
- Inspection and testing.
- Feedback, to ensure that all measures are effective.

Total quality management

The 'total quality' philosophy takes this matter a stage further, and is based on the active involvement of all concerned. Attention is paid to systems procedures and processes rather than the focus being on the goods or service being supplied. Total quality in the supply chain would mean that suppliers, as well as customers and our own workforce, would be involved in determining quality. Inspection and supplier assessment are superseded by a shared approach to the elimination of defective work, with the emphasis on prevention rather than detection and cure. Suppliers must be seen as allies in this process, it is no longer appropriate that buyers should 'vet' suppliers, who should be bringing as much enthusiasm and commitment to quality management as their customers.

Key ideas associated with TQM as a policy are: 'teamwork', 'involvement' and 'process'.

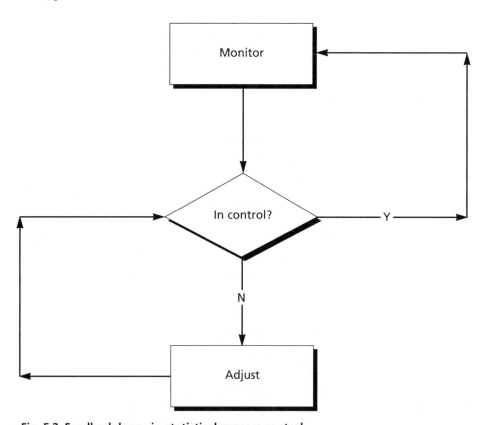

Fig. 5.2 Feedback loops in statistical process control

STATISTICAL PROCESS CONTROL

Statistical process control (SPC), an aspect of quality management, is often seen as a key part of a quality strategy. Basically, the idea is that statistical methods are employed to ensure that a quality capability is possessed by an organisation, and that quality is maintained by a monitoring, feedback and adjustment system. SPC is not, however, just a set of techniques. The idea is that a proactive approach is taken to the prevention of defective material or service, rather than the reactive 'correcting' approach of seeking to identify defective work already done.

SPC is not an approach confined in its application simply to the manufacturing context; the ideas may be applied in any situation where a process takes place. Every useful task or recognised activity may be viewed as a process. The inputs may be materials, information, skills, knowledge, tools and equipment, or any other factor which the task or process requires. Outputs may be products, services, information, documents or anything else that a customer requires.

A high concentration of effort on inspection or checking at the end of a process is indicative that attempts are being made to *inspect* quality in. This is contrary to the SPC goal of *building* quality in. If the inputs and process are co-ordinated properly, the outputs will meet the specification. This fact is of particular significance to the purchasing function. The goods and services acquired as inputs for the organisation are, of course, somebody else's outputs. If SPC is properly employed by the supplier, then we can have confidence that our inputs will be in accordance with the specification and requirements agreed.

SPC depends upon the operators of the process taking responsibility for quality. Inspection, in the traditional sense, is redundant. Attention must be paid to ensuring that the process is capable of meeting requirements; to ascertaining that the process is actually meeting requirements at all times; and to the empowerment of operators to make adjustment to the process so that outputs can be kept in control. Figure 5.3 shows in schematic form the process of monitoring and adjustment on which SPC is based.

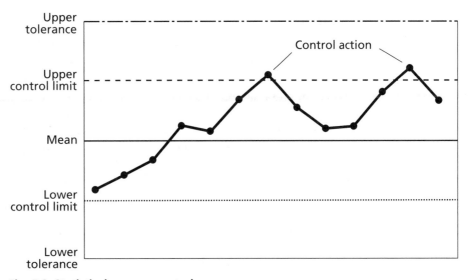

Fig. 5.3 Statistical process control

A commonly employed approach in SPC is the use of control charts which are designed to ensure that deviations outside a band of acceptability are detected in sufficient time to enable corrective action to be taken before defective items are produced. Figure 5.3 is an example of one type of chart; there are, of course, other types of control chart and, indeed, numerous other techniques employed in SPC.

Purchasing managers may derive benefit from working with suppliers on the implementation of SPC. There are potential benefits for both.

SPECIFICATIONS

There are basically two approaches to specification: *performance* and *conformance*.

Performance specifications

The idea of performance specification is that a clear indication of the purpose, function, application and performance expected of the supplied material or service is communicated, and the supplier is allowed or encouraged to provide an appropriate product. The detailed specification is in the hands of the supplier.

Where applicable, performance specifications are to be preferred in that they allow a wider competition, and enable suppliers to suggest new or improved ways of meeting the requirement. It is frequently the case that when services are being acquired or purchased it is not possible to prescribe a conformance specification due to the fact that the service provider alone knows how to do the work required and the buyer is able only to convey the intended outcome.

Conformance specifications

A slogan encountered in the purchasing function of British Airways states: 'Specifications restrict Innovation.' This is, of course, particularly true of conformance specifications – specifications where the buying organisation lays down clear and unambiguous requirements that *must* be met. The specification is of the *product*, not the *application*. This type of specification is necessary where, for example, items for incorporation in an assembly are to be bought, or where a certain chemical product is to be acquired for a production process.

Nevertheless, the production of effective conformance specifications is rather difficult to achieve on occasion. Even in situations where the greatest care has been taken, it is sometimes the case that a supplier will deliver material that meets the specification as they understand it, while the customer complains that the specification means something different and seeks to reject the supplies.

Conformance specifications take a variety of forms and can be drawn up by various departments.

PRODUCING A SPECIFICATION

In manufacturing, a design or engineering department usually has the responsibility for product design, which includes the specification of parts and materials. In service industries, user departments often prepare specifications. In distributive industries, which sell the merchandise they buy rather than products made by them, the selection of supplier-specified goods and the development of specifications for purchaser-specified goods is of central importance both in buying and in marketing, and reflects the organisation's policy on merchandising. In buying supplier-specified goods, retailers pick a brand or a make, or buy by sample, but in specification buying they draw up their own specifications, which are usually very detailed and thorough.

Specification is essentially a technical rather than a commercial activity. However, commercial staff have an important support role for their technical colleagues, in providing information about relative price trends and availability, keeping in touch with new developments, arranging contracts with potential suppliers and obtaining supplier help in formulating specifications.

Formal detailed specifications are not drawn up for the majority of relatively unimportant purchases. If the quality required is well within the range which is commercially available, it is usually left to the purchase department to pick the appropriate make or brand. If the article required is not a constituent of the product, or is purchased for internal use rather than for resale (such as factory seating or overalls), it will again often fall to the purchase department to specify what is to be purchased. The department is acting on behalf of the organisation as a whole in making such decisions, and care should be taken to seek the reaction and obtain the support of users before making a final choice between the alternatives available.

It can, of course, happen that purchasing staff are technical experts in what they purchase and carry primary responsibility for specification. The wool buyer for a textile manufacturer may well be responsible for specifying, as well as arranging for the supply of, the grades of wool which satisfy the particular needs of the manufacturer. Specialist buyers of print, packaging or furniture may also have this dual role, first, to collect and interpret the organisation's requirements to arrive at a specification and second, to review the market and negotiate a contract. The technical role of specification is in these cases not an extension of the commercial role of purchasing; it is a different role carried out by a single person because his or her qualifications make him or her the most suitable person for both roles.

An important stage in specification is to review alternative ways of satisfying a given need. Commercial as well as technical considerations affect the choice. For instance, copper is used for electrical conductors more widely than silver for commercial rather than technical reasons: silver has a higher conductivity but is more expensive. Aluminium has a lower conductivity than copper but is lighter, so that for overhead power cables where weight is important it can be a better buy than copper, depending on the relative prices of the two materials.

These price relativities change, and a specification which, at the time it was drawn up represented the best buy, may be capable of improvement in the conditions which apply in a later stage of manufacture. There is often little to choose between zinc alloy or aluminium alloy for pressure die castings, technically, but there may be a price difference. Natural rubber (latex) prices fluctuate and affect the commercial choice between rubber and such synthetics as neoprene.

The choice of production method is affected both by production volume and by technological development which makes new options available. For instance, a part might be purchased in small quantities as a mild steel fabrication for £50 apiece. In large quantities, a similar part might be purchased as a pressing for 50p apiece, once a press tool had been laid down for £2000 or so. Or technological innovation might provide some different way to produce an equivalent part at a lower cost.

Specifications usually state a tolerance: the permissible variation in important characteristics such as size and weight. Close tolerances simplify assembly and promote interchangeability, but increase the costs of production and inspection, and thus of purchase. In one case it was found that a dimensional tolerance of 0.0001 in. for grinding added 33 per cent to machining cost and 100 per cent to inspection cost compared with a tolerance of 0.001 in. It is widely accepted that some specifiers play safe by over-specifying, for instance by prescribing tolerances and limits which are too tight.

These are some of the reasons why value analysis examines such questions as:

● Would a cheaper material do as well?
● Is it made on the right tooling in view of volume?
● Are limits and tolerances too tight?

In some instances a technically equivalent end-product can be made to a variety of recipes using different ingredients. For instance, cattle feed cakes can be made from seventy different ingredients, from herrings to molasses, which can be combined in various ways to produce cakes having the same iron content, nutritional value, etc. Possible ingredients are mostly primary commodities and their prices vary rapidly and by large amounts. The choice of which ingredients to buy and, consequently, which recipe to use, at a particular time is a commercial rather than a technical decision. It is thus a decision taken by purchasing staff, usually after carrying out a linear programming calculation on the computer.

Specifications take a variety of forms, from a pile of drawings inches thick to a brand name. Every purchase order, large or small, critical or not, must communicate the requirement to the supplier, but the expense of preparing a detailed specification is justifiable only when the requirement is critical or unusual or volume is great and cost high.

One of the simplest forms of description is a brand name. If there is only one brand which meets requirements, this is the obvious way to specify. But if one brand has been tested and found satisfactory and other brands exist which may be just as satisfactory and have not been tested, it is preferable to specify in the form 'Brand X or equal'. Suppliers sometimes change the specification without changing the brand name, which can cause problems for the purchaser.

Where possible, national or international standards should be adopted in preference to specifications which are peculiar to the purchaser. If minor amendments would make a public standard appropriate to the need, it is good practice to state this specifically at the outset: 'generally to British Standard XYZ but with closer tolerance and harder temper', for instance.

STANDARDISATION

The systematic formulation and adoption of standards is referred to as standardisation. It is usually accompanied by variety reduction: a reduction in the range of items used, stocked, bought or made. This is not a process which happens naturally: engineers call for special parts which seem to them just a little better for the purpose than standard parts, users indulge individual preferences or even whims, and as a result the stores accumulate extensive ranges of different items to serve requirements which really differ little, if at all. A systematic standardisation and variety reduction programme can then be well worth launching. Benefits this can bring include:

1 fewer stock items and reduced stockholdings;
2 wider choice of supplier and increased scope for negotiation;
3 larger orders and the possibility of lower prices;
4 reduction to a simple routine of some parts of the work of design and purchase;
5 simplification of some orders, requisitions and other documents; and
6 less need for special explanations by letter, telephone, interview, etc.

It is not generally advisable to standardise on the cheapest since, when many versions of an article have been bought for substantially the same application, it may be expected that just as some versions were too good in the sense that they cost more than they were worth to the user, so other versions were not quite good enough. The objective in standardising is to select not the least expensive or the most expensive, but the right quality to meet the need.

No standardisation programme can succeed unless users are convinced that it is worthwhile. It needs to be marketed from the outset, and it is important to involve users in the variety reduction process; where possible, users themselves should decide which version will best suit their needs. Simply to issue a management edict that all standards must be rigidly adhered to does not work well. By ignoring legitimate differences in need it provokes people to develop their private differences in preference into apparent differences in real need. But just offering standards as available options does not seem to work well either, because of organisational inertia. In practice, standards are often mandatory for minor items where users' needs are unlikely to differ much, but for more complex items they become increasingly optional.

Most countries have national standardisation bodies. The British Standards

Institution (BSI) is linked with similar bodies in other countries through such supra-national organisations as CEN, the European Committee for Standardisation, and ISO, the International Standards Organisation.

EC national standards bodies have worked hard to harmonise their standards, although much remains to be done before the European Community is really operating on common standards throughout.

BS EN ISO 9000

The predecessor to this series of standards, British Standard 5750 was first published in 1979, and gained widespread recognition in the United Kingdom as an indication that companies which had gained registration were consistently able to supply their product or service to a stated level of quality. As such, BS 5750 certification became widely recognised by the purchasing and supply profession as a desirable characteristic in suppliers. This in turn led to competitive benefits being experienced by registered suppliers, and a rather rapid expansion of the numbers of registered organisations.

Following the introduction of BS 5750, many other countries saw the benefits associated with the scheme, and the idea was widely adopted abroad, usually with the support of the British Standards Institution. This wider interest in quality standards of this kind gave rise to the International Organisation for Standardisation (ISO) developing an international equivalent. This was published in 1987 as the ISO 9000 series of five standards. In turn, the British Standards Institution adopted, without amendment, ISO 9000 as the new (1987) edition of BS 5750. This adoption recognised the fact that ISO 9000 reflected several years of British experience with BS 5750, and was of international relevance.

The ISO 9000 series was also adopted as European standard EN 29000: 1987. Thus for many practical purposes BS 5750, ISO 9000 and EN 29000 are the same thing. The name adopted by the British Standards Institution for the standards has itself been standardised as BS EN ISO 9000.

The standards have a number of constituent parts, and contain three assessable quality assurance standards:

1 *BS EN ISO 9001* A model for quality assurance in design, development, production, installation and servicing.
2 *BS EN ISO 9002* A model for quality assurance in production, installation and servicing.
3 *BS EN ISO 9003* A model for quality assurance in final inspection and testing.

Firms need to apply only one of these parts. A company producing or supplying a simple standard product, with little or no design input may well work to BS EN ISO 9002, whereas if product design or development is undertaken by the firm then BS EN 9001 will be more appropriate. If final inspection is the most appropriate way of assuring quality, then BS EN ISO 9003 is likely to be adopted as the appropriate standard. An example of this type of activity might be contract cleaning services. It should be recognised that the standards are applicable to organisations producing services as well as goods, the requirements relate to the ways in which the firms operate and are managed, not to the products of the firms.

The BS EN ISO 9000 series of standards are of great interest to those responsible for identifying and selecting appropriate suppliers in that they provide evidence that a certified organisation is employing appropriate quality systems. They are not applicable to the *products* of the supplier, be they goods or services, but to the manner in which the supplier organises and conducts those aspects of the business with a bearing upon quality. The standard is employed by all major public sector purchasing organisations in the UK as a basis for determining a supplier's ability to produce satisfactory goods and services.

The following guidance notes are reproduced by permission of The Department of Trade and Industry and are adapted from tbeir booklet *Purchasers and BS EN ISO 9000*.

Claims of compliance with BS EN ISO 9000

A firm can implement a quality management system that follows the principles of BS EN ISO 9001/2/3 benefit from doing so and tell you about it. They are not legally obliged to have it independently assessed, but they cannot claim BS EN ISO 9000 registration until they have done so. If they are not registered, this does not lessen their achievement. But equally it does not give you the same assurance that an independent assessment does.

Claims of compliance with BS EN ISO 9000 may be based on:

Assessment by the supplier themselves

This is not very common, and such claims are of limited value, as they lack any input either from you the purchaser or any independent body. If you are buying from a self-assessed firm, you should:

- check that the process is supervised, preferably by people who have experience of or professional qualifications in quality assurance
- check they have proof of their ability to deliver to your requirements
- check that they can provide evidence that their system follows BS EN ISO 9000

Assessment by a second party

This may be by:

- acceptance on the tender list of an internationally recognised quality led company which assesses suppliers against its own quality system requirements, based on BS EN ISO 9000 (e.g. Ford, Rover, British Steel, Marks & Spencer)
- a few major organisations such as British Gas, British Rail Quality Assurance and the National Grid Company have schemes for assessing and certifying the quality systems of their suppliers

These schemes are assessed by UKAS on the same criteria as those used to assess accredited third party certification schemes, and they are recognised as Second Party Certification schemes.

Assessment by an independent third party

Explained in the note which follows.

Alternatively, suppliers may provide evidence from other customers that they have delivered reliable and consistent products or service, to specification, over a long period. While this does not prove compliance with BS EN ISO 9000 it is likely to provide an indication that the company manages its procedures to assure consistency of supply.

Independent assessment and registration

Independent assessment gives purchasers an impartial assessment of a supplier's system, if an assessment is successful the applicant company is awarded a certificate and included in the assessment body's own register of successful assessments. There are over 70 independent certification bodies, increasingly referred to as 'registrars', operating in the UK market. In January 1996, 51 of these were accredited by UKAS (*see* below), and three have been recognised as second party assessment bodies by UKAS. These 54 bodies are expected to provide assessment to the highest possible standards.

Accreditation is awarded to a third party independent certification body as recognition that the body has met internationally accepted criteria covering integrity and technical competence, and that its assessors have the capability to assess companies against the requirements of BS EN ISO 9000 in specific business areas to a consistent level. These bodies are assessed and accredited in the UK by the United Kingdom Accreditation Service (UKAS).

In recognition of their status, the UK government permits accredited bodies to use the National Accreditation Mark of Certification Bodies. Companies assessed by an accredited body may also use the Mark, subject to a registration within the certification body's accredited scope. The Mark is a clear and public demonstration that a company's quality system has been assessed by a competent and independent body. It is recognised internationally.

There are three levels of independent third party assessment. When considering the merits of using registered suppliers, you may wish to consider which level of assessment gives the amount of assurance you need. The highest of these levels results in a certificate of registration issued by an accredited certification body under its accredited scope. The next level is a certificate issued by an accredited body but outside its accredited scope. The third level is a certificate issued by a non-accredited body.

It is worthwhile remembering when considering the level of assurance you require that although accredited bodies are prohibited, for impartiality reasons, from providing consultancy services to the companies they assess, a number of non-accredited bodies both provide clients with their quality manuals and assess compliance to the manual against companies they assess. A number of non-accredited bodies both provide clients with their quality manuals and assess compliance to the manual against BS EN ISO 9000.

When specifying BS EN ISO 9000, Government purchasers wherever possible specify an accredited certificate. When this, or a second party certificate, is not available, then a non-accredited certificate from an accredited body is acceptable to most Government purchasers. A certificate issued by a non-accredited body is generally treated with great circumspection. You may wish to adopt a similar strategy when considering using BS EN ISO 9000 registered suppliers. Remember: the National Accreditation Mark is the mark to look for from companies claiming an accredited registration. However, when you use a supplier with an accredited registration it is important that you ensure their scope of registration is applicable to your needs.

An organisation wishing to achieve certification must, of course, first ensure that it has a quality system which meets the requirements of the standard. If advice and help is needed, then the regional offices of the Department of Trade and Industry are able to offer advice, and in the case of small companies, subsidised consultancy. Having developed and implemented a conforming quality system, then the company will be 'vetted' by an appropriate accredited certification body. The BSI does not itself offer certification. What happens is that the Secretary of State, following the assessment of a body by the National Accreditation Council for Certification Bodies, issues a statement that the body is competent to issue certificates within certain specified areas. This process is called 'accreditation' (*see* below).

UKAS was formed by the merger of the National Accreditation Council for Certification Bodies (NACCB) and the National Measurement Accreditation Service (NAMAS).

UKAS accredited certification bodies can use the National Accreditation Mark of Certification Bodies. So can firms registered under their accredited scope. This is an important indicator when considering what level of confidence can be given to a supplier's claim of independent certification.

Fig. 5.4 UKAS

It is important to remember that the BSI says that a company ought not to be rejected as a supplier solely because the supplier does not have a quality management system or ISO 9000 provided the company can provide other acceptable quality assurances. There has been some resistance to ISO 9000 by some small and medium-sized enterprises, who see the standard as imposing systems and procedures that are too rigid and bureaucratic, and which add cost without adding real value. Many larger concerns, while recognising the importance and value of ISO 9000 recognise that it is not appropriate for all their suppliers. For example, RS Components, a leading stockist and supplier of electronic and electronic components is a large and successful organisation which might be expected to require all suppliers to demonstrate that they are accredited under ISO 9000. They regard this as inappropriate and impractical, and instead insist that suppliers demonstrate that they have an appropriate quality regime in place that is working satisfactorily. Many companies in such industries as automotive and aerospace have their own quality systems and procedures which are rather more rigorous than ISO 9000. In the case of such concerns, accreditation would serve no useful purpose.

SUPPLIER ASSESSMENT

The next stage in the process of purchase quality assurance, after defining the specification, is to select one or more suppliers capable of working to the specification. Five methods used in assessing supplier capability in this connection are based on:

1 past performance;
2 reputation;
3 visit and appraisal;
4 third party certification; and
5 evaluation of sample products.

Vendor appraisal, supplier evaluation and vendor rating, are procedures used in this connection. Vendor appraisal is the term used when the performance of potential suppliers is assessed before an order is placed with them. Supplier evaluation refers to assessment after orders have been placed. Supplier rating (or vendor rating, as it is often called) refers to the calculation of an index of actual performance.

Past performance

The first method, basing the choice on past performance, can only be used for supplier selection when items are bought in large quantities from several suppliers. Records of quality performance need to be available to the purchase decision maker. Such records may also include quantitative data on delivery, performance, service, price and other matters considered relevant, which may be summarised and combined into a supplier rating. Buyers use this information, not only to give more business to better suppliers, and to phase out inadequate suppliers, but also to urge weak suppliers to improve their performance.

Reputation

The second method is widely used. A good reputation for quality can be a valuable trade asset, and in industrial markets it is mainly based on actual performance rather than advertising and other forms of publicity. Experienced buyers build up a lot of market knowledge, which they add to by talking to colleagues, sales representatives and buyers in other organisations. Potential suppliers can be asked to give references: the names of three customers who can be approached for a confidential report.

Visit and appraisal

The third method involves a visit to the supplier in order to make an assessment of quality capability. This takes time and can be expensive, but the expense may be a small price to pay for quality assurance. The visit may be made by quality control staff, purchasing staff or an interdepartmental team. The purchasing representative will make sure to meet any people who may need to be contacted if delivery or other problems occur. But since the purpose of the visit is to assess quality capability, most of the time will be taken up in examining production methods and facilities; inspection, test and measurement facilities both in production and in inspection departments; check and calibration routines for gauges and other test devices. Quality control procedures in use, including the use of control charts and other records and the way in which corrective action is taken will also be considered, and an attempt made to assess the standard of work in progress, policies and attitudes in relation to quality, and, so far as possible in a short visit, the quality of management.

More detail is given in Chapter 8, which also includes an example of a checklist such as most organisations use on these visits.

Third party certification

Third party certification is the term used for visits and appraisals made by some independent body – neither the first party, or buyer, nor the second party, or seller – the results of which are then published or made available to clients or subscribers in the form of a certificate of quality assessment.

Evaluation of products

The final stage in the process is the delivery of satisfactory goods by the supplier and their acceptance by the customer, thus completing the transaction once payment has been made.

This used to be considered the key to the whole of quality control: the inspection stage, when the purchaser checked deliveries and either accepted or rejected them. Now the view is that it is the supplier's responsibility to deliver goods which are acceptable, as conforming with specified requirements. Rather than inspect the goods, the purchaser inspects the supplier's arrangements for ensuring that the goods are acceptable. The earlier notes on BS EN ISO 9000 are relevant here.

Some goods still call for 100 per cent inspection, and there are also some goods which do not require technical inspection. Examples of the latter are works and office supplies, most branded goods, standard machine screws or cans of paint, and low-priced goods of minor importance.

Sampling inspection methods are now very widely used, especially when goods are delivered in large lots or batches. Checking every single one of a large batch of goods is tedious, time-consuming and expensive, and because of human errors it seems not to be as effective as checking a sample chosen on the basis of probability theory. Sampling procedures and tables for inspection by attributes are given in BS 6001, and BS 6000 explains clearly how to use these procedures.

A sample is taken from the batch, and the whole batch is rejected if more than a certain proportion is defective, or it is accepted if less than this proportion is defective. As quality expectations rise, the standard is becoming more severe. In the early 1980s, 5 per cent defective was often considered acceptable. Already 0.2 per cent or 200 parts per million is considered a normal target, with some companies looking for 50 to 100 parts per million and beyond. The pursuit of 'Zero defects' reflects a philosophy that perfection should be the goal.

Prompt notification to supplier, and if relevant to the transport firm which made the delivery, should be given if goods are rejected. Any delay could affect the legal position if a claim has been made.

Several alternatives are open when defective goods are received. Goods which are unacceptable are not all unacceptable for the same reason. The purchaser may:

1 refuse to accept the batch;
2 return the batch for replacement;
3 return the batch for credit;
4 arrange for supplier to make a 100 per cent inspection at purchaser's establishment to sort defective parts from good parts; or
5 make this 100 per cent inspection using purchaser's inspection staff.

Following the 100 per cent inspection, there are three further alternatives:

1 to return defective parts for credit or replacement;
2 to correct or rework defective parts; or
3 to use the defective parts, but with special care or for special applications.

A lower price would be negotiated for the last two alternatives.

Serious or persistent quality problems call for a thorough review of the situation and perhaps a visit to the supplier's establishment: to see the problem in the field and discuss it with production and quality control staff. Points to check include the following:

- Are specifications clear, explicit, unambiguous?
- Has supplier understood them?
- Do they specify the right quality or are they too demanding?
- Is there any assistance we can give, in quality control or production methods or in training staff?
- Should we change to a different supplier?

Vendor accreditation

Many major organisations have vendor accreditation schemes. These are mentioned in Chapter 8.

An important aspect of performance monitoring is the rating of quality, and statistics will normally be gathered on the quality of supplies received. From these statistics, supplier incentive schemes can be derived, such as supplier league tables, or 'vendor of the month' awards. Figure 5.5 illustrates the certification scheme used by Kodak in the UK, the idea being that suppliers will strive to qualify for a 'gold' certificate.

LEVEL 3   GOLD

- Processes under SPC
- Continuous improvement culture
- Proactive in design developments
- Audited quality system

LEVEL 2   SILVER

- Product control by supplier
- No inspection/test at Kodak
- Quality system established
- Quality team goals achieved

LEVEL 1   CERTIFICATE

- High conformance to specifications

Fig. 5.5 'Quality first' supplier programme: award recognition levels
(*Courtesy:* Kodak)

ECONOMICS OF QUALITY

It used to be the case that the level of quality control activity expressed as a cost worth incurring could be determined by looking at the cost of inspection, and at the cost associated with accepting defective supplies and detecting them later, perhaps at the time of use. No expenditure on inspection would result in all defective supplies finding their way into the system, and would result in high costs. A hundred per cent inspection would, for most supplies, be prohibitively expensive, so some optimum level of quality control was sought, seeking to minimise the total cost of quality. It was widely taught that the economic level of inspection would be attained where the cost of inspection was equal to the cost of failure. In this situation the important total cost would be minimised. What this concept failed to recognise was that the money spent on inspection and detection of defectives could be turned into an investment rather than a sunk cost if feedback could arise so as to prevent a repetition of the defective work. If such investments can be made and managed, the incidence of defective supply will become less, and the cost of quality will reduce over time. Current thinking on quality, inspired by charismatic individuals known as the 'quality gurus', suggests that we consider four costs of quality:

1 Prevention Costs – costs incurred in avoiding failure in the first place.
2 Appraisal Costs – costs incurred in checking and inspection.
3 Failure Costs – those arising from errors actually arising. Failure costs can be further divided into internal failure costs, arising from errors within the operation, and external failure costs which arise from an error being passed on to an external customer.

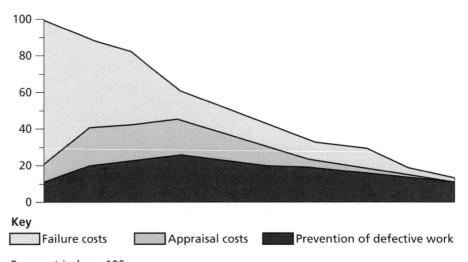

Key

☐ Failure costs   ▨ Appraisal costs   ■ Prevention of defective work

Base cost index = 100.
Shift is from no quality management to quality control to quality assurance.

Fig. 5.6 A schematic representation of change in quality cost over time

QUALITY CIRCLES

Quality circles have become a popular grassroots approach to the improvement, not only of product quality, but also of other aspects of company performance and the quality of working life. They go by various names: General Motors call them employee participation groups; Toyota refer to small group improvement activities.

They originated in Japan. Groups of up to 12 workers plus one or two supervisors or managers from the same department would meet once or twice a week on a voluntary basis to find better ways to do things: improving quality, increasing output, easier work, or getting along with each other better.

Quality circles have been adopted enthusiastically by British and American firms trying to improve quality and reliability, although there have been some difficulties. Management and workforce have to overcome traditional adversarial attitudes and learn how to collaborate for their common interests. This has often proved to be hard for both sides. Several attempts have sometimes been required before getting it right.

Quality circles seem to have made big contributions to the improvement of quality and reliability, as well as to other aspects of company performance, in those organisations which have managed to develop the right attitudes to make them work. The same can be said of a much earlier approach, which also relies on part-time group work: value analysis.

VALUE ANALYSIS/VALUE ENGINEERING

Value analysis (VA) and value engineering (VE) are terms which both refer to the same basic techniques. Sometimes the term 'value engineering' is used when new specifications are being refined before they are finalised, and 'value analysis' when the methods are used to reconsider existing specifications that have been in use for some time. Others prefer VE when the engineering design department takes the lead in implementing the technique, and VA when it is the purchase department which takes the lead. Often the two terms seem to be used interchangeably. The same technique is referred to, with the same aim of increasing value for money, whether by reducing the cost of providing a part, product or service to satisfy given needs, or by increasing the satisfaction resulting from a given part, product or service. Applied at the initial design stage, VA/VE assists in the launch of an attractive and competitive product: applied in the mature or declining phases of the product life cycle, it helps to prolong the profitable life and defend the market share of the product.

Successful VA/VE exercises have in thousands of instances produced savings very much greater than the cost of the exercise: savings not only in purchase cost or production cost, but also in the less quantifiable results of better co-operation between departments and more constructive relationships with suppliers.

The basic procedure is to ask: What is this? What is it for? What does it cost? What else would do the job? What would that cost? Usually a value analysis team is set up (a team, not a committee) with representatives at middle management level from such departments as purchasing, production, design, costing and, perhaps, marketing. The members are there not so much as departmental representatives, more because their departmental interests and their personal capability enable them to make contributions from different angles and with different kinds of expertise. The team operates part-time, and this is considered important because it means that members retain their main commitment to their departments. It is usually necessary to have one member who works full-time on value analysis projects; he or she is the designated value analyst and may act as chairman or secretary. The team should meet regularly, for instance once a week for three hours at the same time and place.

Having set up the organisation, the next steps are to select targets for analysis, preferably starting with profitable, high-volume items where reasonable prospects exist of making substantial savings, and to proceed systematically through the successive phases:

- information;
- speculation;

- investigation;
- recommendation; and
- implementation.

The information stage calls for the collection of facts and figures about the target item: its shape and size and cost of production or purchase, its weight, material analysis, processing and assembly operations, etc.

The speculation phase is seen as the heart of value analysis. It is a deliberate attempt to stimulate creative thought about the item. A common starting point is to attempt to define the function of an item in two words – a verb and a noun. Of course, an item may have more than one function; but the object of this exercise is to concentrate attention on what a thing is *for*, or what it *does*. Occasionally, it is found that what the item is for is lost in past history and what it does now is nothing, so that useful savings can be made by simply eliminating it. Defining the function in this way concentrates attention on the cost of performing the required function, rather than on the cost of whatever happens at present to be used for the purpose. What else could be used? Brainstorming, consulting suppliers, function/cost matrices and other techniques have been mentioned as sources of ideas. When new ideas are put forward, it is considered important to accentuate the positive and eliminate the negative; for instance, a poster may be displayed at team meetings which lists stock responses such as:

'We tried that in 1996.'

'Let somebody else try it first.'

'It's not the way we do things.'

'The customers will never agree.'

'Our business is different.'

'We've tried it before.'

'We've never tried it before.'

The investigation phase probes the merit of proposals and provides hard evidence for the next phase, the recommendation to management. The final phase, implementation, could be regarded as a routine matter once management approval has been received. Unfortunately, organisational inertia and individual resistance can frustrate the whole exercise unless as much effort is put into implementation as into earlier phases.

Footnote
NASA spent a great deal of money in encouraging the US pen manufacturer, Fisher, to develop and produce a pen for use in space. It had to be able to write upside down and function in zero gravity situations. The Soviets came up with a better value solution to the same problem: they used pencils.

SUMMARY POINTS

- Quality means different things to different people. It can be defined as 'fitness for purpose'. More strategically, it can be viewed as an issue related to competitive advantage.
- Statistical process control (SPC) is a mathematical system used to monitor an organisation's quality capability. It is a proactive approach to preventing defective work being produced. SPC devolves responsibility for quality down to the operator who is authorised to take corrective action should measurements stray outside of acceptable limits.
- Performance specifications encourage the supplier to be innovative providing an appropriate product/service to meet the need. Conformance specifications are clear and unambiguous, relating to the product/service rather than the application.
- Standardisation can be a difficult and lengthy process as it often requires individual preference be ignored. However, the benefits of variety reduction, lower stockholding costs, economies of scale on larger orders etc. can make the exercise well worthwhile.
- An organisation wishing to achieve ISO certification must ensure that it has a quality system which meets the requirements of the standard. While it is a useful award to hold, it may not be appropriate for all suppliers. For some the procedures may be too rigid, adding cost without adding value. (These companies should not be rejected if they can provide some other acceptable quality assurance system.) Other companies may employ far more rigorous quality procedures in which case accreditation would serve no purpose.

REFERENCES AND FURTHER READING

Atkinson P (1990), *Creating Culture Changes: The Key to Successful Total Quality Management*, IFS, Bedford.

Bicheno J (1991), *34 for Quality. A Guide to Gurus, Tools, Wastes and Techniques*, Moreton Press, Buckingham.

Call J (1993), *TQM for Purchasing Management*, McGraw-Hill, New York.

Department of Trade and Industry (1995), *Purchasers and BS EN 9000*.

Giunipero L and Brewer D (1993), 'Performance based evaluation systems under TQM', *International Journal of Purchasing and Materials Management*. 29 (1), Winter.

Jackson P and Ashton M (1993), *Implementing Quality through BS 5750 (ISO 9000)*, Kogan Page.

Juran and Gryna (1993), *Quality Planning and Analysis*, McGraw-Hill, New York.

Oakland J (1990), *Statistical Process Control: A Practical Guide*, Heinemann-Newnes, Oxford.

Oakland J (1993), *Total Quality Management: The Route to Improving Performance*, Butterworth-Heinemann.

Plank R and Kjjewski V (1991), 'The use of approved supplier lists', *International Journal of Purchasing and Materials Management*, 27 (2), Spring.

Womack J P and Jones D T (1996), *Lean Thinking*, Simon & Schuster, New York.

CHAPTER 6

The right quantity

INTRODUCTION

The right quantity to order is not always the quantity requested. This would be appropriate for a single isolated requirement, such as a replacement machine tool or a new factory, but most purchases are for regular requirements which recur. Several ordering policies are used for these repeat purchases. Different policies lead to different order quantities even though these must in the end add up to the same long-term requirement quantity.

OBJECTIVES OF THE CHAPTER

- To consider order quantities for stock control and for production control
- To examine the reasons for holding stock and approaches to reducing inventories
- To identify methods of stock control and their applications
- To appreciate the principles of Materials Requirements Planning (MRP)
- To introduce the Economic Order Quantity (EOQ) concept
- To understand the basics of the 'just in time' (JIT) philosophy.

Regular requirements are bought either for stock, or else for direct use in operations or production. Part of the function of stock planning and control, and of production planning and control, is to calculate what quantities are needed and when they are needed to meet requirements for stock or for production.

Stock planning and control could be defined as the policies and procedures which systematically determine and regulate which things are kept in stock and what quantities of them are stocked. For each item stocked, decisions are needed as to the size of the requirement, the time at which further supplies should be ordered, and the quantity which should be ordered.

Production planning and control could be defined as the policies and procedures which systematically determine and regulate manufacturing programmes and which establish requirements for parts and materials to support production. For each item required, decisions are needed as to the size of the requirement, the time at which it should be ordered, and the order quantity.

Requirement quantities can be aggregated or subdivided in various ways, and the quantity notified to the purchasing department as required is not necessarily the same as the quantity the purchasing department orders from suppliers.

Ordering policies used by purchasing include:

- blanket orders which group many small requirements together for contractual purposes;
- capacity booking orders, which reserve supplier capacity for the production of various parts, used in conjunction with make orders which specify later which parts are to be made;
- period contracts stating an estimated total quantity for the period and the agreed price, in conjunction with call-off orders which state delivery date and quantity;
- period contracts which specify a series of delivery dates and quantities (e.g. '1000 during the first week of each month');
- spot contracts and futures contracts in various combinations;
- 'open-to-buy' (OTB) and similar 'order-up-to' system sometimes used by stock controllers in the retailing sector;
- part-period balancing, lot-for-lot and other approaches favoured by production controllers in conjunction with materials requirement planning (MRP) or kanban systems; and
- the economic order quantity (EOQ).

We go on to consider order quantities in connection, first, with stock control, and, second, with production control.

ORDER QUANTITIES AND STOCK CONTROL

Every organisation holds some things in stock. Stock can be a nuisance, a necessity, or a convenience. Retailers and wholesalers see stock as the central feature of their businesses: what they sell is what they buy, and they aim to sell from stock rather than from future deliveries which have yet to arrive. Organisations such as manufacturers, health-care institutions and other service providers place stock in a subsidiary rather than a central position, but it is still an important element in operational effectiveness, and often appears on the balance sheet as the biggest of current assets, locking up a lot of money.

Why do we carry stock? The reasons include:

- the convenience of having things available as and when required without making special arrangements;
- cost reduction through purchase or production of optimum quantities; protection against the effects of forecast error, inaccurate records; or
- mistakes in planning; and
- provision for fluctuations in sales or production.

Carrying stock is expensive, and it is accepted that many organisations carry too much stock. A continuing drive to reduce stock without reducing service is needed to combat the natural tendency of stock to increase. Constructive approaches to stock reduction include:

- arranging for things to be delivered just in time instead of stockpiling just in case a need arises;

- devising ways to reduce ordering costs, set-up costs, and lead times so that optimum quantities are smaller;
- making forecasts more accurate, ensuring that records are right, better planning.

Order quantities directly affect the size of the stockpile. If twelve month's requirements arrive in one lot, average stock over the whole year (neglecting buffer stock) is equivalent to six months' requirements. But if only one month's requirements arrive, average stock over the whole year is equivalent to only half a month's supply. Frequent small orders for such regular requirements, instead of occasional large orders, can result in substantial reductions in the size of stocks. Unfortunately, this can also result in substantial increases in paperwork and administrative effort.

ECONOMIC ORDER QUANTITIES

Analysis of the costs involved led to formulae which enable an economic order quantity (EOQ) to be derived for any combination of the variables price, rate of usage or demand and internal costs. The EOQ is the quantity that results in the lowest total of variable costs. It should not be surprising to find that if the annual usage value is low in relation to the cost of ordering and processing deliveries, the formula indicates that orders should be placed infrequently, whereas if it costs appreciably more to hold a month's supply in stock then it does to order it, the formula indicates that frequent orders should be placed. For those of us who are not mathematicians, it may, however, be surprising to find that order quantity is proportional, not to the annual usage value but to its square root; so that if annual demand doubles, the order quantity should be increased by about 40 per cent.

Properly applied, the EOQ formula does in fact work well, resulting in lower stocks, fewer orders, and no reduction in service, thus justifying its name. It is *economic* in the sense that it is a thrifty, efficient order quantity which avoids needless cost. But it has often been applied inappropriately, and much of the criticism of EOQ approaches arose because many firms used them in situations to which they were unsuitable, with unfortunate results.

EOQ formulae

The basic EOQ formula is:

$$EOQ = \sqrt{\left(\frac{2 \times \text{annual usage quantity} \times \text{ordering cost}}{\text{unit cost} \times \text{stockholding cost}}\right)}$$

Writing u for annual demand or usage quantity;
p for the paperwork and administrative cost associated with an order;
c for unit cost or price each;
s for the cost of holding stock as a decimal fraction of average stock value, the formula becomes:

$$EOQ = \sqrt{2up/cs} \qquad (1)$$

Alternative versions can be derived from this, which show how many weeks' or months' supply to cover with an order, how many orders to place in a year, or which use weekly or monthly demand instead of annual demand. The derivation of the formula is straightforward. Demand is not affected by order quantity, and as a first approximation it may be assumed that buffer stock and price are not affected by order quantity. The total variable cost is then the sum of the remaining cost factors, the stockholding cost and the cost associated with ordering.

Since the average stock without taking account of buffer stock will be half the order quantity, q, the stockholding cost is given by

$$q/2 \times cs$$

and the cost associated with ordering is given by the cost per order, p, multiplied by the number of orders placed:

$$u/q \times p$$

Hence:

$$\text{Total variable cost (TVC)} = qcs/2 + up/q \qquad (2)$$

This is a minimum when

$$\frac{d(\text{TVC})}{dq} = 0$$

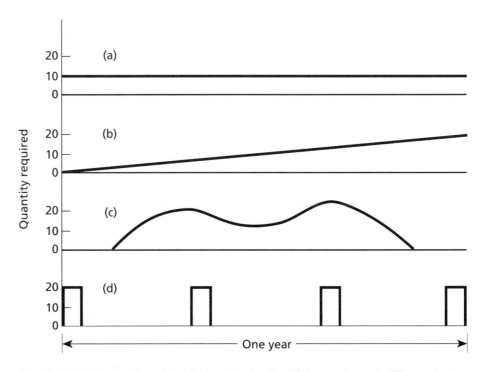

Fig. 6.1 Requirement profiles: (a) constant rate; (b) increasing rate; (c) seasonal rate; (d) periodic rate

Differentiating (2) with respect to q, rearranging and taking the square root, we arrive at the EOQ formula already given as (1).

The application of the formula is not difficult in practice. It can be solved on any pocket calculator which has a square root facility.

If, as is usual, stock records are computerised, suggested order quantities can be computed automatically, or a short table of representative values can be used.

EOQ formulae can be used with advantage if the stock range includes many minor stock items, used on a variety of products, for which detailed calculation of exact requirements and scheduling of as-required deliveries would not be feasible. For such items, both the size of the stockpile and the number of orders placed can be cut by using the EOQ.

EOQ formulae should not be used if price fluctuates, if the rate of use or demand is not approximately constant, or if the lead time is long and uncertain.

Of the various requirement profiles shown in Figure 6.1, the constant-rate requirement (a) is only one which is really suitable for use of the EOQ.

Stock turn rate and EOQ

Two common measures of stock control performance are service level, and stock turn rate. Service level measures success in meeting demand off the shelf. If every request can be met immediately, the service level is 100 per cent; if only eight out of ten, it is 80 per cent. The adoption of EOQ does not in principle affect the service level, although methods used to achieve the service level may not be the same for frequently ordered items as for infrequently ordered items.

Stock turn rate measures not the effectiveness of stock control in meeting demand but its efficiency in doing so economically. It relates the amount of money invested in stock to the use that is made of it. Achieving a high service level by ample stocks of everything that could conceivably be needed would result in a very low stock turn rate. At the other extreme, a high stock turn rate could be achieved by hardly stocking anything except the essential, very frequently used items – with, of course, a low service level as a result.

Stock turn rate is calculated by dividing average stock for a period of time into total usage for the same period. Thus if stock on the first day of June is £100 000 and stock on the last day of June £110 000, then average stock for the month is £105 000. And if the cash value of issues for the month (or sales) is £52 500, then stock turn rate is given by 52 500/105 000. The stock is 'turned over' 0.5 times a month; or once in two months; or six times a year.

In considering the effect of the adoption of EOQ on stock turn rate, it must be borne in mind that the latter is intended to evaluate the efficiency of the total stock investment rather than a single stock item. If the annual demand for a particular stock item is low in relation to the cost of procuring it, the EOQ formula will balance stockholding cost against procurement cost and indicate that a year's supply or more should be ordered. For that item, the stock turn rate will not improve, but fewer orders will be placed. Because a typical stock range includes a large number of items with a low annual usage value, the result is greatly to reduce the number of orders placed, compared with an ordering policy which treats all items alike, for instance ordering three months' supply whenever a stock item needs to be replenished.

Stock turn rate for a high usage value item will, on the other hand, improve when, instead of ordering three months' supply, the EOQ formula is used. Although high usage value items form quite a small proportion of the total stock range, they also tend to account for a large proportion of the sum shown in the accounts for stock. Usually, EOQ policies improve the overall stock turn rate by frequent ordering of high usage value items, as well as reducing the number of orders placed by less frequent ordering of low usage value items.

Price breaks and quantity discounts

Although EOQ methods are not used when price fluctuates up and down, they are used when lower prices are available if larger quantities are ordered for delivery in one lot. These lower prices may be expressed as percentage reductions to the nominal price, i.e. quantity discounts; or alternatively as progressive reductions in the net price as the quantity ordered increases, sometimes called price breaks. The foregoing analysis provides a systematic procedure to evaluate these.

The basis of the procedure is to compare the gross saving due to a price reduction with the extra cost due to increased stocks, in order to arrive at the net saving, if any. The gross saving is calculated by multiplying the annual requirement quantity by the difference between the normal price and the discounted price.

The extra cost is calculated from formula (2), first by using the normal price and order quantity, and second by using the discount price and order quantity. The net saving, if any, can then be calculated.

Sometimes the order quantity required to qualify for a lower price is excessive. In view of uncertainties about the future, it may not be safe to order more than a year's supply, and it is often not safe, to order more than two years' supply.

Example

The annual requirement for part X125 is 10 000 and the normal price £1 each. With the stockholding cost estimated at 20 per cent and the ordering cost at £10, the EOQ is 1000. Now the supplier offers a 10 per cent discount for deliveries of 5000 instead of 1000. Is it worth accepting?

The difference between normal price and discounted price is 10 per cent of £1, with an annual requirement of 10 000, the gross annual saving is £1000. The extra cost (from formula (2)) is £270. The net saving is thus £730 a year. Financially the offer is attractive.

If the discount offered is 2.5 per cent instead of 10 per cent, the gross annual saving is only £250. The extra cost is £307.50, so there is a net loss rather than a net saving. Accepting this offer would add to costs rather than reduce them.

Other methods in stock control

Reorder level methods of stock control are procedures in which, whenever the stock of an individual item is down to a quantity called reorder level (or order level, or order point), an order is initiated to obtain more stock. The order level is the average quantity required in the lead time plus buffer stock. Buffer stock is a reserve to take care of requirements running at above the average rate, or of delivery periods which exceed the normal lead time. The order quantity may be the EOQ, or may be determined in some other way.

Periodic review methods of stock control review large groups of stock items periodically. Stock on hand may be compared with a target stock figure for each item, and enough ordered to bring stock up to target. Target stock is typically enough to last until the next review, plus the quantity likely to be used in the lead time, plus buffer stock to cover variations. In many systems, orders need not be placed for every item which is below target level. Modifiers are incorporated, such as minimum orders (don't order until you need at least 12, for instance), order-with (if you're going to order A, order some B as well), etc.

ORDER QUANTITIES FOR PRODUCTION

Manufacturing industries were the basis of the British economy for two centuries. They are classified by product in the standard industrial classification used in official statistics, and the products cover an enormous range: transistors, electric motors, machine tools, cranes, small tools, lawn mowers, refrigerators, motor cars, double-glazed windows, garments, food products, garden gnomes, and furniture, for instance. Some make to customer's order, others make or stock in anticipation of orders.

Thousands of process technologies exist, but four fundamental approaches to their organisation are in use: project organisation, jobshop organisation, batch production and continuous production.

Project organisation is used for a single major product such as a bridge, a dam, a factory, or an oil rig. The project contract establishes the relationship between customer and contractor. Components, materials and services are ordered in the quantities specified in the contract for delivery at the time scheduled.

At the other extreme, continuous production is typified by an electrical power station or by any other plant which is designed to produce its output in a continuous stream.

Between these extremes, at least two-thirds of manufacturing industry exists. Jobshops go into production when they get a job from a customer. Batch producers make their products in small batches – six machine tools at a time – or large batches – 1000 agricultural machines at a time.

The standard system for calculating the quantities of components, sub-assemblies and material required to carry out a production programme for complex products is called Materials Requirements Planning (MRP). This can be carried out by manual methods but is now normally done by computer.

The MRP process starts with a production programme, or, as it is often called, a master production schedule, which schedules the end-products to be completed week by week during the planning period. It is based on customer orders, sales forecasts and manufacturing policy. There is quite an art to getting it right. Most software packages include facilities for making rough checks during planning to allow for capacity bottlenecks or scarce material constraints, as shown in Figure 6.2, so that a realistic production programme, which can be made to work, is scheduled.

The next stage is to explode the master schedule into detailed lists of all the parts required to make each product by means of parts lists, sometimes called bills of material (BOMs).

MRP procedure calculates gross requirements level by level, adjusting at each level for stock on hand and orders due in to get net requirements. These

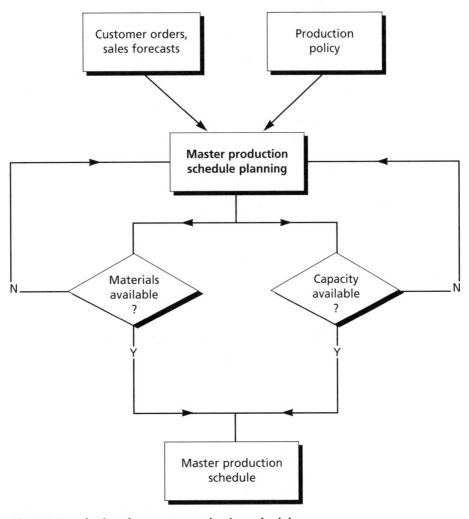

Fig. 6.2 Developing the master production schedule

are off-set by lead times to arrive at dates at which orders should be placed if net requirements are to be available in time. Planned purchase orders and planned works orders are calculated in the order generation part of the procedure, but remain in the system and are subject to amendment unless designated as firm orders. They become actual orders when released, and are then printed out or otherwise communicated to suppliers and to internal production.

Realistic, achievable production programmes and accurate information about stock on hand and orders due in are vital to success, and failure to provide them has led to many unsuccessful applications. Stock must be counted and stock records must be right (and this cannot be done by computer) before the order generation process (which can be done by computer) will work properly.

Nevertheless, MRP notched up many successes, when organisations which had used inappropriate stock-control methods for production planning reverted to common sense. Stock control is appropriate to a situation in which the demand for each stock item is independent of the demand for any other stock item, as in a retail shop where the demand for shirts in no way depends on the demand for shoes. In production planning, the demand for all the parts used to make a product is dependent on the demand for that product. Thus, if a car is supplied with five wheels, in planning the production of a batch of 6000 cars we know that we need 30 000 wheels. We do not need to apply stock control techniques of demand forecasting and provision of buffer stocks for forecast errors if the demand for wheels occurred independently of the demand for cars, except in allowing for orders for spares and replacements. MRP is the process, simple in principle, of calculating in detail the net demand for the components and material required to implement a given production programme, and allowing for lead times in order to plan production and purchase orders.

Several techniques are used in deciding on order quantities. The simplest is lot for lot, in which the order quantity is the same as the minimum quantity required for production.

Period	1	2	3	4	5	6	7	8	9
Net requirement	24				24				24
Planned order	24				24				24

The EOQ is quite unsuitable for use when the net requirement occurs in lumps at intervals of time, when another batch of the product is put into production as in the above example and as shown in Figure 6.1(d). If the EOQ worked out at less than 24, the order would not be enough to meet the net requirement. If it worked out at more than 24, the excess would just lie in stock until the next requirement date. The EOQ is based on the assumption that stock is consumed at an approximately constant rate, which is not valid for this sort of intermittent, lumpy demand.

If, however, there is some net requirement in most periods, unlike the above example, there is a case for applying the idea on which the EOQ is based of balancing set-up costs or ordering costs on the one hand and stockholding costs on the other, to arrive at a least cost solution. A version which has had some success calculates the cost of holding stock period by period, as in the following example.

In Figure 6.3, net requirements for nine periods are taken as 40, 20, 0, 80, 0, 20, 35, 40 and 45. Stockholding cost is taken as £0.50 per unit per period, and ordering costs as £25. The procedure is to calculate total ordering and stockholding costs for successive larger lots and to choose the order quantities which give the lowest cost per unit. The result is:

Period	1	2	3	4	5	6	7	8	9
Net requirement	40	20	0	80	0	20	35	40	45
Planned order	60			80		55		85	

This approach, which can easily be applied by computer, is called part-periods balancing because the stockholding cost and ordering cost are balanced period by period to give the lowest cost per part. It has the same basis as the EOQ in that it balances costs to arrive at a least cost solution, but does not require the assumption that stock is depleted at a uniform rate over the year.

A simpler way to calculate these order quantities on a similar basis is sometimes called the least cost algorithm. The cost of holding one part in stock for one period, taken above as £0.50, is divided into the ordering cost, taken above as £25, to obtain the part-period value, in this example 50. This part-period value means that it is economical to carry fifty part-periods, whether

Period	Net requirement	Order quantity	Periods stocked	Stock cost (£)	Stock + order cost (£)	Cost per unit (£)
1	40	40	0	0	25	0.625
2	20	60	1	10	35	0.583
3	0					
4	80	140	3	130	155	1.107
First order is 60 parts to cover periods 1 and 2						
4	80	80	0	0	25	0.312
5	0					
6	20	100	2	20	45	0.450
Second order is 80 parts to cover period 4						
6	20	20	0	0	25	1.250
7	35	55	1	17.5	42.5	0.773
8	40	95	2	57.5	82.5	0.868
Third order is 55 parts to cover periods 6 and 7						
8	40	40	0	0	25	0.625
9	45	85	1	22.5	47.5	0.559
Fourth order is 85 parts to cover periods 8 and 9						

Fig. 6.3 Part-periods balancing

this is fifty for one period or five for ten periods or one for fifty periods. In practice these figures are rounded up where appropriate.

So, applying it to the net requirement figures in the previous example: period 1 requires 40, periods 1 and 2 require 60, which is over the part-periods value; so the first order is for 60. Period 3 requires 0, period 4, 80; so the second order is for 80. If the calculation is continued, it will be found that the same order quantities are obtained as by the previous, more laborious method.

Software packages usually include lot sizing rules for determining quantity, such as predetermined order quantity or predetermined supply period, which can be useful. They also include modifiers, which can be extremely useful in the special circumstances for which they are intended; such as 'order with' to enable items that are related, for instance by coming from the same supplier or using the same tooling, to be ordered at the same time, or 'minimum' and 'maximum' to set upper and lower limits on the order quantity. Unthinking application of mathematical formulae can lead to ridiculous order quantities of 1.5 days' supply, or ten years' supply. These can be avoided by use of modifiers in the order quantity algorithms, as well as by making sure that the people responsible for order quantity decisions know what they are doing.

JUST-IN-TIME SYSTEMS

The just-in-time philosophy requiring the pursuit and elimination of waste in production and associated planning and purchasing were developed mainly by Japanese manufacturers, and were so conspicuously successful that everyone wanted to know how it was done and if they could do it too.

The basic idea is simple. If made-in parts are produced in just the quantity required for the next stage in the process, just in time for the next operation to be carried out, then work-in-progress stocks are almost eliminated. If bought-out parts are delivered direct to the production line without delays in stores or inspection, just in time for the needs of production and in just the quantity needed, then material stocks are largely eliminated too.

Stock turn rates of better than 30 have been achieved (although after years of

	Firm A	Firm B
Sales revenue	100	100
Cost of goods sold	60	60
Gross margin	40	40
General and administrative overhead	27	27
Cost of holding stock	5	1.25
Gross profit	8	11.75
		(46.9% more)

Fig. 6.4 Effect on profit of improving stock turn rate

effort and not overnight), compared with the rates of 5 to 8 which comparable businesses were getting with traditional methods. Stock turn rate is closely linked with profitability. If firm B achieves a stock turn rate four times as high as firm A, assuming that the two firms are in all other respects similar, then firm B will incur only a quarter of the stockholding costs incurred by firm A. Firm B could be much more profitable, as shown in Figure 6.4.

Perhaps the best known of the just-in-time systems is the kanban system developed by Toyota. Kanban is a Japanese word which means (among other things) the travelling requisition card on which the system depends. Two types are used: move cards and make cards. Both form part of a manual, visual control system, which is itself a sub-system of a more comprehensive process of planning resources and scheduling output, as shown in Figure 6.5.

Kanban is similar to the MRP planning system previously considered. The main difference is that, in order to make the kanban system work, it is necessary to smooth product mix, monthly and daily. So far as possible, batch production is made similar to continuous production.

Master schedules are smoothed so that ideally every product is made every day, and from day to day the same mix of end-products is produced, giving a smooth and continuous flow of parts through all work centres to the final assembly line. Changes in product mix are introduced gradually.

Dramatic examples of reduced set-up and changeover time have been reported. For instance, Toyota cut changeover time on a boltmaker from 8 hours to less than 1 minute, and set-up time for a wing and bonnet stamping operation from 6 hours to 12 minutes. Short changeover times increase flexibility and reduce lead times, thus greatly facilitating rescheduling to cope with such hazards of manufacturing as scrap, tool breakage, wrong forecasts, late deliveries by suppliers or revisions to the parts list.

A long process of small improvements leads eventually to a situation in which stock is much easier to manage because there is so much less of it, and it is out in the open where it can be seen, in production or in assembly.

Buffer stocks are not provided. Consequently, shortages (for whatever reason), bottlenecks and queues are highlighted rather than hidden. Vigorous attempts are at once made to find what causes the trouble and to devise a solution. Better quality control, training more people, and increasing available machine capacity (for instance by reducing set-up time) may provide a cure. What is sought is a solution to the problem, whereas buffer stocks are a way of living with the problem rather than solving it.

For bought-out parts, suppliers must be selected who can be relied on to deliver to the day and the hour stated on the order, straight to the production line without going through inspection and stores. Suppliers must have reliable quality control for this to be possible. Transport arrangements have to be reliable too, which has led to a strong preference for local sources using their own transport for delivery.

At a time when General Motors were dealing with nearly 4000 suppliers, Toyota had less than 300. Today the figure is much lower again, with a single figure supplier base per model envisaged. If production depends on suppliers delivering acceptable parts on time every time, many suppliers will have to be

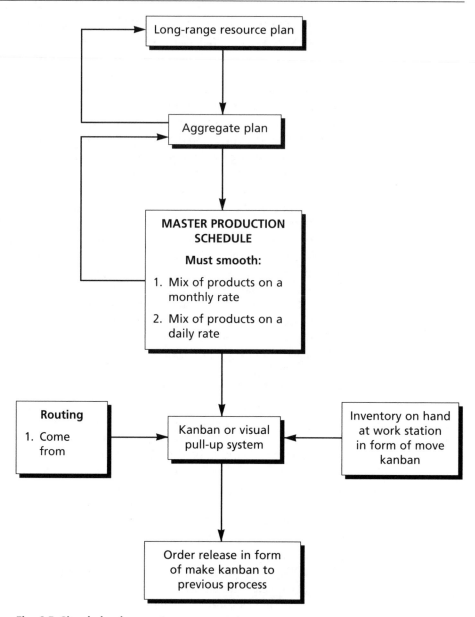

Fig. 6.5 Simple kanban system
(*Source:* Hahn, Pinto and Bragg, 1983)

dropped if they cannot meet requirements. Another reason for having fewer suppliers is the kind of relationship with suppliers which is required for JIT. The adversarial relationship, playing one supplier off against another, which has been traditional in Europe and America, seems unlikely to lead to long-term co-operation in reducing cost and increasing efficiency. Co-operative relationships with fewer suppliers are preferred. The concept of 'tiering' of suppliers dealt with in Chapter 8 is also relevant.

Order quantities are also affected. Traditional approaches such as EOQ, part-period balancing and the least cost algorithm tend to take the internal cost figures for buying and stockholding as constants and use them to calculate order quantities. Just-in-time systems treat nothing as constant. The cost figures can be driven down and Hahn *et al.* (1983) explained how. Ordering cost included six elements, it was argued: negotiation, paperwork, expediting, receiving count, receiving inspection, and transport. Transport and negotiation cannot be dispensed with, but when JIT is operating properly there is little need for paper work, expediting, receiving count and inspection. So buying costs are lower; and according to the formula, order quantities become smaller.

SUMMARY POINTS

- Ordering policies used include blanket orders; capacity booking orders; part period balancing and EOQ. The method used depends upon the industry, the usage, the production technique and the cost of ordering.
- Stock is expensive to hold therefore it is advantageous to reduce levels. The chapter explains the EOQ method of deriving an order quantity which results in the lowest total of variable costs. This technique is fine used on minor items used on a variety of products but makes limiting assumptions that price is stable and usage steady. It ignores lead time.
- MRP uses a master production schedule which it explodes into a bill of materials. Allowing for stock and orders due in, a net requirement of components required is produced. This initiates purchase and work orders taking account of lead times. The process can be computerised using specially designed software packages and is appropriate for dependant items for which there is 'lumpy demand'.
- Just in time assumes made-in parts are produced in just the quantity required for the next stage and bought out parts are delivered direct to the production line as they are needed. Thus Work in progress and stock are eliminated. This is a philosophy included in the list of World Class Concept. It requires reliable, co-operative suppliers and 100 per cent quality.

REFERENCES AND FURTHER READING

Ansari A and Modarres B (1990), *Just-in-Time Purchasing*, Free Press, New York.

Baily P (1972), *Successful Stock Control by Manual Systems*, Gower, Aldershot.

Baily P and Farmer D (1982), *Materials Management Handbook*, Gower, Aldershot.

Barekat M (1993), 'MRP II is dead – long live MRP II', *Selected Readings in Purchasing and Supply*, Vol 1, CIPS, Ascot.

Bauer *et al.* (1994), *Shop Floor Control Systems: From Design to Implementation*, Chapman and Hall, London.

Brown A (1993), 'Understanding technological change: the case for MRP II', *International Journal of Operations and Production Management*, 13 (12).

Cusumano M (1991), *The Japanese Automobile Industry: Technology and Management at Nissan and Toyota*, Harvard University Press, Cambridge, Mass.

Hahn C K, Pinto P A and Bragg D J (1983), 'Just-in-time production and purchasing', *Journal of Purchasing and Materials Management*, Autumn.

Harrison A (1992), *Just-in-Time Manufacturing in Perspective*, Prentice Hall, London.

Jessop D and Morrison A (1994), *Storage and Supply of Materials*, 6th edn, Pitman, London.

Monden and Yasuhiro (1983), *The Toyota Production System*, Institute of Industrial Engineers, Atlanta, Georgia.

Offodile and Arington (1992), 'Support of successful just-in-time implementation: the changing role of purchasing', *International Journal of Physical Distribution and Logistics Management*, 22 (5).

Vollman *et al.* (1988), *Manufacturing and Control Systems*, Dow-Jones/Irwin, III.

Womack *et al.* (1990), *The Machine that Changed the World*, Maxwell Macmillan International, Oxford.

CHAPTER 7

Time

This chapter is concerned with the importance of on-time supply, and includes a discussion of lead times and techniques employed in achieving appropriate timing.

OBJECTIVES OF THE CHAPTER

- To emphasise the importance of suppliers' responsiveness to customer needs
- To suggest the use of delivery performance records as part of supplier assessment
- To explain the need for expediting, how it is prioritised and organised and how it can be reduced
- To introduce network analysis and Gantt charts
- To consider the inclusion of liquidated damages, penalty and force majeure clauses in a contract
- To weigh up the courses of action to deal with sudden and endemic shortages.

TIME AND COMPETITIVE ADVANTAGE

Companies which can react promptly and accurately to the needs of their customers are, obviously, more likely to attract orders than those who cannot. Thus it can be seen that ideas such as responsiveness, time compression and time to market rightly earn their place in the developing management philosophies of the 1990s.

The recognition of 'time' as a key variable, and the need to minimise time as waste in the supply chain has led to an increased degree of concern with time and responsiveness in recent years. Attention is being paid to the benefits which might arise from increasing responsiveness at all stages.

Christopher (1992) states that in the past it was often the case that price was paramount as an influencer on the purchase decision. He goes on to suggest that, while price is still important, a major determinant of choice of supplier or brand is the cost of time. The cost of time is simply the additional costs that a customer must bear while waiting for delivery or seeking out alternatives.

If a company is seeking competitive advantage by becoming better able to respond to customer needs as they arise, then it follows that the company will require a greater degree of responsiveness from its own suppliers. While it might be argued that the possession of appropriate inventories might facilitate the same degree of 'responsiveness', it is unlikely that an organisation can carry the high levels of stock that such a policy would call for yet still remain price competitive. Even organisations who have promoted themselves as 'stockists' are beginning to question the value of substantial inventories, and are seeking to continue to provide high levels of customer service economically through working with suppliers who can themselves behave responsively.

Traditional 'batch and queue' manufacturing and supply is being challenged by approaches based on 'pull' and 'flow'. The production resources held by firms in supply chains are maintained in a state of readiness rather than employed on large batch production, and materials are made and supplied only when they are needed. The economies arising from the avoidance of waste when such approaches are adopted can more than outweigh the so-called economies of scale generated by the production of large quantities of stock.

ON-TIME DELIVERY

The achievement of delivery on time is a standard purchasing objective. If goods and material arrive late or work is not completed at the right time, sales may be lost, production halted, and damages clauses may be invoked by dissatisfied customers. In addition, most organisations regard cash as committed once an order has been placed, failure to achieve supply on time may slow down the cash-to-cash cycle, thus reducing the organisation's efficiency or profitability.

Purchasers are blamed, sometimes rightly, by user department colleagues if suppliers fail to deliver on time. To obtain on-time delivery, however, it is vital to ensure that user departments know what lead times apply, and any other necessary information. However, measures of this kind are not enough. Purchasing has a practical role in supply markets, convincing suppliers that they must deliver as and when agreed.

Most purchasers throughout industry and commerce, for most of their purchases, are happy with delivery times and regard late delivery as an exceptional event, which might require crisis action. Pharmaceutical wholesalers normally deliver two or three times a day, with a two- to three-hour delivery period for orders. Many building suppliers not only give same-day delivery but find it confusing to get more than 24 hours' notice of requirements. Mainly it has been with suppliers producing goods to customers' specifications, and whose work typically takes several weeks to complete, that problems have occurred in delivering on time.

Sometimes suppliers quote delivery dates which they cannot achieve. This may be an unscrupulous device to get the order, or the quote may be given in good faith but circumstances change and delivery dates are rescheduled. Sometimes the firms which fail to deliver on time may not be competent at production planning and control.

Frequently, of course, purchasers are themselves the source of the delivery problem, through issuing inaccurate delivery schedules, continually amended; or by allowing insufficient time for delivery.

The first step to obtain delivery on time is to decide firmly and precisely what is required and when it is required. Only in exceptional cases is this the responsibility of purchasing *per se*. Normally it is a materials-related department such as stock control or production planning and control which works out the timed requirement schedule, as explained in the last chapter. For occasional – as distinct from regular – requirements, it is often the user department which says that something is required. It is obviously not good practice for these requirement dates to be specified without regard to supplier lead times and market realities, since this is likely to lead to late deliveries. Purchasing should work on the problem of getting shorter lead times (and reliable suppliers) and should ensure that relevant departments know what they are. Care should be taken that a mutual understanding of the expression 'lead time' is achieved. Figure 7.1 shows that the expression has a variety of meanings. Having ensured that the requirement dates notified to the purchasing department are achievable, purchasing can properly be expected to go out and achieve them.

A vital step in achieving on-time delivery is to ensure that suppliers know and are fully aware that on-time delivery is an important element in their marketing mix. This means that they know that, when making a choice between alternative suppliers, the purchaser gives a lot of weight to their actual delivery performance. This in turn means that records need to be kept.

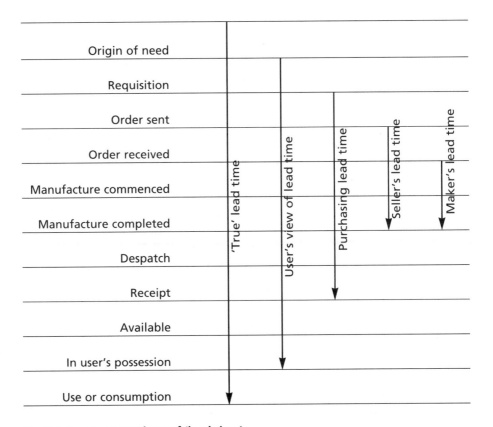

Fig. 7.1 Some perceptions of 'lead time'

If the due dates specified on orders or call-offs are correct, it is easy to measure and record supplier success or failure in delivering on time, and to tell suppliers how well they are doing. Delivery performance in many instances has improved significantly when recorded performance is used as a basis for talks with suppliers. In fact experience shows that when suppliers come to realise that requirement dates as stated on orders and call-off schedules are accurate and reminded that whenever they fail to deliver on time they will have to explain it, and that on-time delivery counts for a lot in the future allocation of business, then 94 per cent on-time delivery is often achieved.

In the case of suppliers making regular deliveries, a simple way to assess delivery performance is the percentage of deliveries in each review period which were behind schedule. This can be shown on a graph (*see* Figure 7.2).

Here it can be seen that supplier B's performance is getting better, whereas supplier A's is getting substantially worse, and calls for corrective action by the buyer.

A more complicated assessment would take account of the length of time by which a delivery was behind schedule as well as of the number of late deliveries. In one scheme this was applied as follows:

Days late	*Weighting*
Less than 11	1
11–20	2
21–25	3
More than 25	4

Mathematical or theoretical perfection is not what is sought; the aim of these schemes is to apply data available in goods received records to produce figures

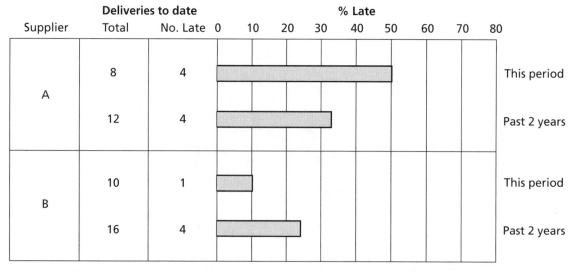

Fig. 7.2 Delivery performance

which can be used (i) to persuade suppliers to deliver on time, and (ii) to give preference in placing orders to suppliers who have demonstrated their ability to comply with delivery requirements.

If delivery problems exist, expediting is usually necessary. A simple phone call from the buyer or the user may suffice, or more extensive action may be called for, including the employment of full-time expeditors. There would perhaps in a perfect world be no place for expeditors, but we do not live in a perfect world.

EXPEDITING

In order to achieve the purchasing responsibility of delivery on time, expediting is frequently undertaken. A dictionary definition of 'expedite' is 'to assist the progress of something'. In the manufacturing industry, production operations may be subject to expediting, though all kinds of organisation are liable to engage in expediting in connection with bought-in supplies.

Expediting is best regarded as a planned, proactive, task. Expressions such as 'hastening', 'urging' and 'chasing' are sometimes used to describe the process of attempting to ensure that delayed materials do not cause too many or too severe problems. These terms imply that the work is often seen as reactive problem solving, rather than problem avoiding. Systems employed in the application of proactive contract management will be based on the application of effort where it is likely to be needed, and before the problem of late delivery arises.

It can be argued that expediting work does not add value to an organisation's activities or products in any way, and a principal objective of many concerns, achieved in some, is to reduce the need for expediting work to zero. In other words, to obviate it. The approach of continuous improvement is highly relevant here, and the 'partnership' philosophy or buyer–seller relationships can lead to significant improvements in this area.

Nevertheless, it would not be true to claim that expediting work is no longer a major aspect of purchasing – it is. In this chapter, therefore, it is appropriate that we take a look at an aspect of the work.

Prioritisation in expediting

If we accept that expediting work is to be undertaken, and that it ought to be proactive, then an obvious first question is: 'Where do we apply expediting effort?' Too often what passes for expediting is *ad hoc* 'fire-fighting' work. A fundamental requirement for any kind of planned activity is a systematic approach to prioritisation. We need to be able to concentrate on the important work, rather than simply the urgent.

It is possible to devise a points-based system which can be used to indicate in a reasonably objective way the contracts or orders where expediting work might be undertaken, and to suggest the degree of priority which might be given. The following factors exemplify the kinds of variable that might be taken into account when devising such a system.

Supplier
1 How good is their record?
2 What is their reputation?
3 How often do we use them?
4 How important is our order to them?
5 Have they a good record of co-operation?

Criticality
1 How serious are the consequences of late delivery likely to be?
2 Is the material of:
  (a) high priority (e.g. raw materials, key assemblies, fuel, production materials)
  (b) medium priority (e.g. standard components, parts for planned maintenance, furniture, packaging materials); or
  (c) standard priority (e.g. cleaning materials, internal stationery, paint (for buildings), office supplies)?

Alternatives
1 If the material is late do we have a substitute?
2 Is there an alternative supplier?
3 Are stocks held somewhere?
4 Do we know another user?

Organisation of expediting work

It is common practice for expediting work to be undertaken by the buyer, and it is a natural responsibility of the buyer to work with suppliers on the 'time' variable where a mutual 'partnership' type relationship has been established. However, it is commonly the case that a separate expediting section exists within the purchasing department, with expediting activities being either at the direction of the relevant buyers or at the discretion of the expediting staff themselves, sometimes liaising with user departments. The expediting group may be attached to the planning department, or to the function requiring the goods or services; the justification for this approach being that these people are better able to determine priorities. Another possible variation is that the expeditor is attached to a particular buyer, and performs expediting tasks (and possibly other duties too) as required by the buyer.

Reduction in expediting

The need for expediting may be reduced by ensuring that:

1 Lead times are known and accepted.
2 Mutual concern exists between buyer and seller.
3 Information is shared by buyer and seller.
4 Users do not frequently reschedule requirements.
5 Expeditors do not raise the alarm too often unnecessarily.
6 Capacity and capability of suppliers is checked pre-contract.
7 Specifications are clear, understood by seller and fall within seller's technical capability.

8 Specifications are not frequently altered.

9 Delivery required is specified properly (not, routinely, as 'ASAP', 'urgent' or 'ex-stock').

10 What the salesman says can be done reflects the actual situation.

This ten-point checklist is not intended to be exhaustive, but is indicative of the fact that the need for expediting is perhaps as likely to arise through buyer short-comings as seller failures.

NETWORK ANALYSIS

A group of techniques known as network analysis is often used to assist in the planning and control of certain types of project. Essentially, these are ways to organise and present certain information, such as what activities constitute the project, how these activities are related logically, their duration and cost, and the demand they make on resources. Critical path analysis is the network analysis technique which determines minimum project duration, and this is the one we shall consider.

This technique can be applied to any collection of related activities which has a definite beginning and a definite end. In the classroom, for purposes of explanation, it can be applied to such simple 'projects' as making a cup of tea or dressing in the morning. In the real world, it is applied only to complicated projects, for example:

- constructing and equipping a new factory;
- launching a new product;
- setting up a new department;
- building and civil engineering contracts, for example, a new motorway, a new department store, a new town; and
- major overhaul of a chemical plant or a blast furnace.

The word 'new' occurs frequently in these examples. Network analysis has notched up most of its successes on new projects rather than on the re-planning of operations which have been carried out for a considerable time. One of the first successful applications to be described was, in fact, a very large-scale procurement project which was in several ways unprecedented. This was the design, development, construction, equipping, staffing and getting into operation of the first fleet of nuclear submarines armed with Polaris missiles by the United States Navy. Much as the existence of these frightful weapons may be deplored, and still more their proliferation, a detached view can still be taken of the way this gigantic project was planned and controlled. It was actually completed ahead of time.

Network analysis calls for the production of a visual representation of the project in the form of a network of arrows which show the activities. Consecutive arrows stand for activities which must be carried out in sequence; parallel ones show activities which can be carried out simultaneously. Following this, the calculation of timing and, for certain applications, such other matters as cost, resource allocation, etc. is done. This part can be handled on a computer.

The following are the usual steps in the preparation of a critical path analysis of a project:

1 List the activities or jobs which have to be done to complete the project. Careful thought is needed as to what has to be done and how best to do it. A decision is also needed as to the level of detail to be shown. (Sometimes an outline network is prepared for top management, with detailed networks for operational use.)
2 Sketch a rough arrow diagram on rough paper or a blackboard. For each activity ask: Which activities must be completed before this starts? Which ones cannot start until this is complete? Arrows start and finish in junction points shown as circles or ellipses and known as nodes or events. Every activity shown by an arrow going into an event must be complete before any activity shown by an arrow coming out of that event can start. Consequently an event is defined as: 'A state in the progress of a project after the completion of all preceding activities but before the start of any succeeding activity'.
3 Find out how long each activity will take to complete and write its duration on the diagram.
4 Time the network, determining minimum project duration and critical path.
5 Re-draw the network, producing a neat version for circulation. Avoid crossed arrows and backward pointing arrows if possible. Earliest and latest dates can be shown in the event circles, which should also be numbered.
6 Re-plan if necessary to speed things up or to balance the use of scarce resources.

We illustrate this by the following example.

Project X: example of critical path analysis

An order has been received to make a batch of equipment. This involves preparation of detail drawings and works orders, buying out parts and materials, machining components, assembling, testing and shipping.

Activities involved and their durations in weeks are:

Detail drawings and works order	3
Purchase castings	5
Purchase forgings	6
Purchase assembly parts	2
Purchase crates and packing	4
Draw bar stock from stores	0.2
Machine castings	3
Machine forgings	3
Machine bar	1
Assemble	2
Test	1
Pack and ship	

Questions

1 Draw the network for the above.
2 If start time is week 0, what is the latest time at which castings could be issued for machining if the whole batch is to be completed on time?
3 In week 6 a serious fire at the crate manufacturer's works destroys work in progress and means purchase department have to find a new source for the crates. How much time have they got to get the crates in?
4 Draw a Gantt or other bar chart for the events and activities on the network.

Solution

Figure 7.3 shows the diagram as it exists on the completion of step 5. The initial activity, preparation of detail drawings and works order, is shown by the first arrow, referred to as 1–2 because it connects event number 1 to event number 2. On the completion of this activity, a number of others can be started: activities 2–3, 2–4, 2–5, 2–6 and 2–8. Event 9 is the completion of the whole project.

Conventionally, the start date is at first shown as time 0. Since the first activity, 1–2, has a duration of 3 weeks, the earliest date for event 2, that is to say the earliest date at which activities 2–3, 2–4, 2–5, 2–6 and 2–8 can start, is the end of week 3, and this is shown in the top right-hand quadrant of the circle known as event 2. Since activity 2–4 cannot start until week 3, and has a duration of 6 weeks, the earliest date for event 4 is 3 + 6, that is, the end of week 9, as shown in the top right-hand quadrant of the corresponding event circle. Proceeding in this fashion we reach event 9 and find the project minimum duration to be 16 weeks.

In most cases, the minimum duration is also the maximum duration since completion is required as soon as possible. We have found the earliest date for

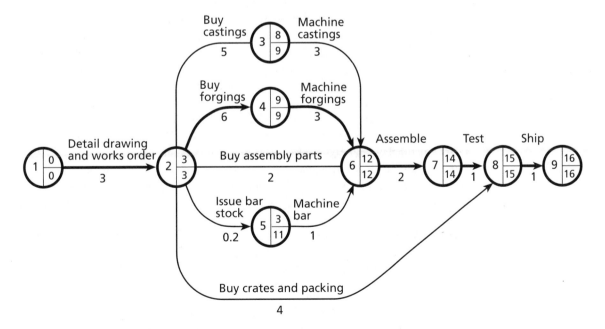

Fig. 7.3 Arrow diagram for project X

event 9 to be week 16; we now say that this is also the latest date for event 9. The latest date is written in the lower right-hand quadrant. Activity 8–9 has a duration of 1 week. Since the latest date for its completion is week 16, the latest start date for it is week 15, which therefore becomes the latest completion date for event 8.

The critical path is the sequence of activities which determines minimum project duration because its total duration is longer than that of any other sequence of activities in the network. Here it is activities 1–2, 2–4, 4–6, 6–7, 7–8 and 8–9. In all the events on this sequence, earliest date is the same as latest date, and the duration of each activity in the sequence is the same as the difference between dates for predecessor and successor events. The critical path is marked out by a heavy line.

Some activities however, are not on the critical path, for instance 2–3 and 3–6 which have a week of 'slack' or spare time between them. In answer to question 2, we can therefore say that the latest date at which castings could be issued for machining is week 9, as shown in the lower right-hand quadrant of event number 3. This is because the machining takes 3 weeks and must be complete by week 12, the latest date for event 6.

The answer to question 3 is also clear from the diagram. The crate purchase is shown as arrow 2–8, which has a latest completion date of week 15. The fire occurred in week 6, leaving 9 weeks to locate a new source and obtain the crates.

Two versions of the Gantt chart called for in question 4 are shown in Figure 7.4. Gantt and other bar charts are often drawn for ordinary time-only networks at the stage where the critical path network is converted into a detailed work plan. These charts show the expected duration of jobs by horizontal lines drawn against vertical divisions which represent time intervals; actual time taken is shown by differently coloured lines. Production controllers and buyers used charts of this type many years before arrow diagrams were invented. They are useful for controlling relatively simple projects, but they get less useful as the project gets more complex, because they cannot easily show the relationship between the various jobs in a work package or project.

Another network application is to combine time data with cost data. PERT/COST was developed not long after PERT/TIME and has been used for years on big US defence contracts, but has not been widely adopted, so far, outside this application. Costed networks can be used right through a large contract from tendering stage to final payment. Costs can be attached to individual jobs, but it is usual to attach them to groups of jobs or work packages. Builders now request progress payments based on completed sections of networks, and this is said to be easier for the client to check as well as enabling job progressing and collecting payments both to be done by the same method. Computer printouts for costed networks usually show:

- actual costs incurred to date;
- budget estimates for the rest of the project; and
- commitments for further expenditure, i.e. purchase orders outstanding.

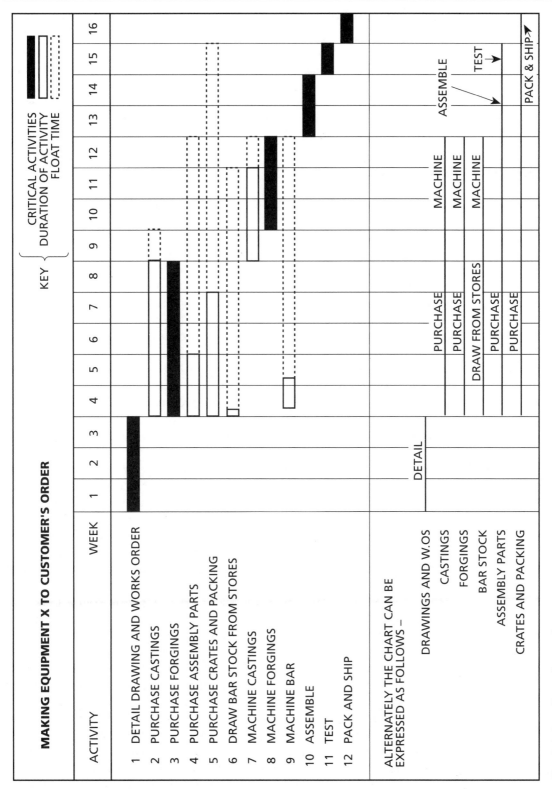

MAKING EQUIPMENT X TO CUSTOMER'S ORDER

KEY

CRITICAL ACTIVITIES
DURATION OF ACTIVITY
FLOAT TIME

ACTIVITY	WEEK	1	2	3	4	5	6	7	8	9	10	11	12	13	14	15	16
1 DETAIL DRAWING AND WORKS ORDER																	
2 PURCHASE CASTINGS																	
3 PURCHASE FORGINGS																	
4 PURCHASE ASSEMBLY PARTS																	
5 PURCHASE CRATES AND PACKING																	
6 DRAW BAR STOCK FROM STORES																	
7 MACHINE CASTINGS																	
8 MACHINE FORGINGS																	
9 MACHINE BAR																	
10 ASSEMBLE																	
11 TEST																	
12 PACK AND SHIP																	

DETAIL

ALTERNATELY THE CHART CAN BE
EXPRESSED AS FOLLOWS –

DRAWINGS AND W.OS	
CASTINGS	PURCHASE — MACHINE
FORGINGS	PURCHASE — MACHINE
BAR STOCK	DRAW FROM STORES — MACHINE
ASSEMBLY PARTS	PURCHASE
CRATES AND PACKING	PURCHASE

ASSEMBLE

TEST

PACK & SHIP

Fig. 7.4 Bar charts for project X

Critical path methods are more expensive than some older methods of planning and control because the planning is more detailed and the control more complete.

Reductions in operating costs ought, of course, to offset these increases in control costs. Plans should be better. When projects become urgent only critical jobs should need to be crashed – and obviously, selective overtime costs less than general overtime. One firm found that 'the costs of network analysis are so low that one can scarcely afford not to apply the technique'.

LIQUIDATED DAMAGES

In ordinary English law, a supplier who is in breach of contract by failing to deliver on time becomes liable to the purchaser to pay a sum decided by the courts, known as damages, to compensate the purchaser for any loss actually suffered, including loss of profits, as a result of this late delivery. Litigation is not part of normal purchasing procedure. Expense, delay and uncertainty associated with litigation make it a remedy of a last resort. There is a practical alternative based on this legal principle which is widely used in contracts for capital equipment and in major engineering and construction projects and this is to include in the contract a liquidated damages clause.

In this phrase the word 'liquidated' appears to mean 'decided in advance and expressed in monetary terms'. It is a quirk of the English legal system that the law courts reserve for themselves the right to impose penalties, but allow the parties to a contract to decide in advance between themselves the loss likely to be suffered by the purchaser as a result of late delivery, and to specify this loss in cash terms in the contract. Provided that the sum specified can be shown to be a genuine pre-estimate of loss rather than an arbitrary sum picked out of the air to frighten the supplier into compliance with the contract, the courts will enforce it in the unlikely event of litigation being required.

In some other legal systems it is open to the contracting parties to include in the contract a penalty clause, and this penalty may be payable in addition to any damages recovered by legal action. In the English legal system, the liquidated damages clause, which is often called a penalty clause in common parlance, is not seen as a penalty but as an agreement as to the amount payable by way of damages. Consequently some clauses emphasise this aspect by using wording as: 'seller shall pay to buyer x per cent of the contract price for each week of delay up to a maximum of y per cent of the contract price by way of liquidated damages and not as a penalty'.

The advantage to the buyer of such clauses is that they strongly motivate the supplier to deliver on time, and in case of difficulties with delivery they provide the expeditor with a powerful argument: 'It is going to cost you a lot of money if you don't deliver.'

However, they also have advantages to the seller. They limit his or her liability to a known amount. Marsh (1992) argues that 'no contractor can afford to be liable for a risk against which it is difficult to insure and which is out of all proportion to the value of the contract and to its anticipated profit' and that in such cases the supplier needs a liquidated damages clause as protection.

The supplier also needs the further protection of an additional clause exempting them from liability if the delay is due to the causes completely out of his or her control. Such clauses are often called *force majeure* clauses. Here is an example.

Force majeure

If either party is prevented from carrying out contract obligations by circumstances beyond its reasonable control including government intervention, strikes and lockouts but not including weather conditions, then the party affected shall not be liable for any delay resulting from such circumstances for as long as they last. If such delay extends for an unreasonable time the other party may cancel the contract without liability to either party, and buyer shall pay to seller an equitable sum for work done before cancellation.

SHORTAGES

Sudden shortages

Sudden shortages of key materials occur which call for fast action by purchasing staff. These shortages could result from various causes on the supply side, such as a strike, a fire or other disaster at the supplier plant, inability by the supplier to obtain key materials required for the order, defective production planning and control, or a change in supplier policy on product mix or customer targeting. They could result from a variety of obstructions which may appear between seller and buyer, ranging from currency difficulties and industrial action by transport workers to government action, revolution and war. They could also be caused by administrative error on the part of the purchaser, design modification, change in production plans, or action by the purchaser's own customers.

Emergency action to cope with a sudden shortage may take the following forms (in order of complexity):

1 Energetic attempts to get the delinquent supplier to produce the goods, to establish when they will supply, to persuade them to give priority to the particular buying organisation. Help may be offered with production difficulties or in locating materials which are holding the supplier up. Contact may be made at a higher level than usual, e.g. managing director or chairman level.

2 A crash search for another supplier to fill the gap. This may be a golden opportunity for some small local firm which has knocked vainly on the door for years. This search may extend widely – to Japan, Australia, developing countries. Emergency supplies may be purchased at premium prices from distributors.

3 Substitute materials investigation, working with quality control and design. (A food manufacturer, hit by revolution in Zanzibar, found clove oil an

acceptable substitute for cloves; an engineering manufacture, held up for a proprietary alloy, found that other producers could supply technically equivalent alloys under different brand names.)

4 Product specification could be reconsidered in the light of material availability.

5 Product mix could be reconsidered with a view to rescheduling the production programme, and manufacturing products which are not affected by shortages rather than those which are.

Endemic shortages

In addition to sudden shortages which call for emergency action, some purchasers face regular shortages which call for shortage planning and systematic development of 'tight supply' strategy.

Faced with frequent shortages, purchasers may plan material requirements further ahead so that purchasing can book capacity or even place firm orders for parts and materials to ensure supplies. Extra personnel may be drafted into expediting. Stocks of strategic supplies may be built up. Double sourcing may be adopted for items which would normally have a single source. For high-volume requirements requiring special tooling or development costs, this makes the purchase more expensive, and piece price may be further increased as a result of the lower volume per supplier when the business is split. Careful consideration is needed to see if the cost of having two sources would be even greater than the cost of losses from not having two sources. Furthermore, a second source should increase the security of supply, but will not guarantee it. A second source can normally increase output if the first source is blocked, but not by enough to make up the shortfall unless there is considerable idle capacity in men, machines and material which can be diverted quickly.

There are also fundamental reasons which lead many experts to think that shortages may become endemic. World population is increasing and natural resources are finite. Industrialisation is spreading with its greatly increased demands for energy and material resources. The fossil fuels in particular (oil, coal and natural gas) are being used up rapidly, and they are irreplaceable.

The pessimists think that for the West the era of cheap power and abundant supplies has come to an end: the sun that rises on Abu Dhabi has set on Birmingham. The optimists concede that some things have changed but think we will soon be back to normal. The realist, while hoping with the optimists, takes care to plan with the pessimists; he drinks to the boom but is not caught unprepared by a recession.

If management concludes that the organisation is at permanent risk, the whole supply market may be regarded as one of the areas which call for systematic forward planning. Detailed purchasing research on a world-wide basis can be undertaken to locate alternative sources; substitute evaluation can be undertaken systematically, with marketing, design, production and purchasing collaborating in an interfunctional material resources programme.

Purchasing will try to work out what shortages might occur, and how serious they would be, and what could be done to prevent their occurrence as well as what could be done if they did occur. Detailed contingency plans can be prepared for various possible threats showing alternative counter-moves.

Rationing and remarketing

How marketing departments allocate scarce products between customers is naturally of considerable interest to their customers. The simplest method of rationing is share and share alike; if the supplier can meet only 80 per cent of the demand, they could allocate to each customer 80 per cent of their smoothed historical off-take, or 80 per cent of what they bought last year for instance. This method is easy to apply and easy to defend. There exist, however, alternative methods of rationing, which the supplier may perceive as more likely to further his long-term interest.

For instance, customers can be grouped into several categories, with 100 per cent of requirements allocated to the most favoured category and 20 per cent of what was ordered last year going to the least favoured. Or the least favoured customers can be dropped altogether, either explicitly or by means of a letter, or implicitly raising prices and reducing service; this both simplifies the allocation problem and provides the company with some scope to exploit the shortage situation by accepting orders from desirable customers who resisted penetration in the past.

In classifying customers in this way – into most favoured and least favoured – initially, simple basic criteria can be used, such as volume and profitability of business, with subsequent adjustments for more complicated criteria such as last loyalty, future growth prospects, geographical location and likely buyer reaction; Philip Kotler and V. Balachandran (1975) have discussed this point. Some customers may be dropped because they are too much trouble – they haggle about prices, alter schedules and cancel orders too often; yet others may get a bigger share of available supplies simply because they are 'hard to please'. There is a difference between making unreasonable demands, and insisting that reasonable demands are met. It is well known that the buyers who get the best service are generally those who take the trouble to get to know senior officials in supplier firms and who demand good service. Suppliers may allocate a smaller share to buyers who are considered likely to be pleased with whatever they get, and larger shares to buyers who will not be satisfied unless they get most of what they require and who, if not satisfied, will switch sources as soon as the shortage is over.

Buyers are advised by Kotler and Balachandran to *market* their company's needs to their suppliers. They must convince suppliers that they absolutely need all of their requirements and that their loyalty and future business count for a great deal. When this does not work, they should increase their price offer for the scarce material and thus out-bid the competition. When this does not work, they might bring power to bear where they hold reciprocal resources needed by the supplier. In times of shortage, they add, the marketing problem shifts its location from the marketing function to the purchasing function.

SUMMARY POINTS

- Price used to be of paramount importance in choosing between suppliers – now the 'cost of time' is far more influential.
- Competitive advantage can be gained by being able to respond to customers needs as soon as they arise. This demands that not only is the supplier responsive but that his suppliers are too.
- Late delivery can mean lost sales, production downtime and invoke damage clauses. All of these have an effect on cash flow, reducing the company's efficiency and profits.
- Network analysis is a visual representation of the events of a project and the activities which have to be performed to achieve them. Timings to each activity give the critical path and the minimum duration of the total project. While costly to set up, the savings made in operating costs are normally far greater.
- Liquidated damages seek recompense for the buyer for the late delivery of an order. This is a sum agreed between the parties to represent a realistic pre-estimate of loss. Penalties may be in addition to damages, although the suppliers liability is limited.
- Sudden shortages call for immediate action. The buyer can: try to persuade the supplier to prioritise his customer's needs against other customers; find an alternative material/supplier; reconsider the specification. Endemic shortages can be dealt with by booking capacity; placing extra orders and double sourcing.

REFERENCES AND FURTHER READING

Christopher M (1969), 'Managing strategic lead times', *Logistics Information Management*.

Christopher M (1992) *Logistics and Supply Chain Management*, Pitman, London.

Jensen A (1992), 'Stockout costs in distribution systems for spare parts', *International Journal of Physical Distribution and Logistics Management*, 22 (1).

Karmarker U (1989), 'Getting control of just-in-time', *Harvard Business Review*, Sept–Oct.

Kotler P and Balachandran V (1975), 'Strategic remarketing: the preferred response to shortages and inflation', *Sloan Management Review*, Autumn.

Lester A and Benning L (1989), *Procurement in the Process Industry*, Butterworth, London.

Lockyer K and Gordon J (1991), *Critical Path Analysis and Other Project Network Techniques*, 5th edn, Pitman, London.

Marsh P D V (1992) *Contracting for Engineering and Construction Projects*, Gower, Aldershot.

Meitz A A and Castleman B B (1975), 'How to cope with supply shortages' *Harvard Business Review*, Jan–Feb.

CHAPTER 8

Source decision making

INTRODUCTION

It would be possible to argue that the most important purchasing decisions are concerned with selecting the right sources of supply; that is, if the correct source decision is made in a particular instance, then the buying company's needs should be met perfectly. In such circumstances it would receive the required goods or services at all times. However, the very simplicity of this statement belies the complexity of source decision making, for in arriving at the right decision many factors have to be considered. This chapter is concerned with many of the issues which are involved.

OBJECTIVES OF THIS CHAPTER

- To recognise the attributes of a good supplier
- To monitor the change in the traditional adversarial approach of sourcing to that of closer relationships with fewer, long term suppliers
- To identify the necessary capabilities and experience needed by a potential supplier
- To weigh up the advantages/disadvantages of single sourcing; reciprocity and intra company purchasing.

Effective source decisions will only be made when all relevant factors have been considered and weighted against the risks and opportunities which apply. Not all source decisions will justify the same level of attention, but major purchases will always repay careful decision making. For example, significant purchasers who dominate the demand side of a market need to devote a good deal of thought and time to the optimum supply market structure, and sometimes take direct action to develop new suppliers or support minor competitors. If one or two large companies dominate the supply side of a market, it may well be to the long-term advantage of purchasers to place orders in a way which keeps competition alive and prevents the market from degenerating into a monopoly. Conversely, in order to obtain the greatest benefits from longer-term relationships, the buying company might seek deliberately to develop a mutual relationship, sometimes called partnership sourcing or co-makership.

Sourcing thus involves much more than simply picking a supplier or contractor for each requirement in isolation. It involves continuing relationships, both with preferred sources which are actually supplying goods and services, and with potential sources which may have been passed over for the present but are still in the running. It involves decisions about how to allocate the available business, and what terms to do business on.

For its proper performance sourcing requires *supply market research*. This is a normal part of buying work, undertaken informally by buyers when they talk to representatives, visit exhibitions, read trade journals, and investigate the market before placing orders. Additionally it may be undertaken more formally as a support function to buyers by full-time purchasing research staff in a purchasing services section usually located at corporate headquarters. Supply market research identifies the set of actual and potential sources which constitute a supply market, investigates their capabilities, examines market trends and long-term supply prospects, and generally keeps an ear to the ground. It is part of purchasing research.

Another factor which needs to be kept in mind in making key resource decisions is, who else should be involved in the process? Three American writers, Robinson, Faris and Wind, back in 1967, identified what they called the 'decision-making unit'. They categorised the people involved as 'the user', 'the buyer', 'the decision maker', 'the gate keeper', and 'the influencer'. The writers were concerned with identifying source decision makers for marketing purposes. They wanted to know who actually made the decision, which person should they try to influence? Many marketing writers have built on that work since that time and readers who are interested will be able to learn more of these ideas from Chapter 21. For our purposes, it is interesting to note that one aspect of their findings showed then that different people played the major role in the decision when it concerned what they call a 'new buy', from those who were involved when it was a 'modified re-buy' or a 're-buy'. In general terms, at that time, the professional buyer's influence became greater as the decision moved from 'new-buy' to 're-buy'. In other words, the buyers, then, were largely concerned with the routine reorder, other people (e.g. designers, production personnel) were more influential when it was a new purchase. In the thirty years that have elapsed since this influential work was carried out, the impression is that, for some organisations, the same is still true, though there is today a much wider recognition that the role of purchasing transcends simply 'buying'.

ATTRIBUTES OF A GOOD SUPPLIER

While a definition of a good supplier which would be acceptable to everybody would be difficult to write, there are a number of attributes which might be regarded as desirable for a typical relationship. The following list is given by way of suggestion only:

- Delivers on time.
- Provides consistent quality.
- Gives a good price.
- Has a stable background.
- Provides a good service backup.

- Is responsive to our needs.
- Keeps promises.
- Provides technical support.
- Keeps the buyer informed on progress.

Most purchasing and supply staff find little difficulty in identifying the characteristics that they require in a supplier, for they see the identification and selection of appropriate sources as one of their primary roles. However, there is, generally speaking, a lower level of concern in connection with the attributes of a good customer, or buyer. The traditional view is that the buyer is spending money and suppliers should be encouraged to compete vigorously in order to gain acceptance.

However, this view is not so widely held these days, and there is an increasing belief that buyers and sellers are seeking a mutually beneficial long-term relationship through which advantages will arise for both participants in the trading process. Terms such as *synergy* or *symbiosis* are used to describe the buyer–seller relationship, indicating that an ideal arrangement leads to a '2+2=5' situation, where additional benefits arise out of an association between buyer and seller. None the less, if such a relationship is to come about, one of the first things a buyer needs to do is discover what suppliers are seeking in a customer, and attempt to meet these requirements.

DIFFERENT TYPES OF SOURCING

Before developing the present discussion it is worth recognising that the many implications of source decision making may vary by the type of purchase being made. For example, among the many different types of source decisions are:

- consumable supplies;
- production materials and components;
- capital purchases (e.g. machinery);
- intellectual property (e.g. software);
- subcontractors; and
- services.

Each type will involve different factors. For example, a mineral may only be available from a single country. However, it could be bought direct or through an agent or a distributor. Computer equipment may be bought outright or leased, and among the many factors involved in these decisions may be whether the proposed equipment is compatible with that which exists. On the question of production materials it will be necessary to consider the logistical implications, the proximity of the supplier and the frequency of delivery. Then decisions about subcontractors may involve consideration of the individuals who are to service the contract and the liabilities of the two parties. We will return to some of these issues later in the chapter, while subcontracting is dealt with in more detail in Chapter 11.

SOURCING DECISIONS

The traditional approach to source decision making involves the buying organisation in:

- establishing which suppliers make or supply the product or service (often by referring to a buyer's guide or industrial directory);
- selecting a short list from those available (say three);
- sending an enquiry to each of those three setting out the requirements;
- selecting the best supplier from those who quoted by comparing the offers; and
- placing the purchase order with them specifying such matters as volume, schedule, place of delivery, price and quality required.

Major buyers, of course, augment this procedure by a closer involvement with suppliers. Indeed, in recent years many major buyers have laid great emphasis on quality management at their supplier's plants. For example Rank Xerox in Holland had, at one time, 70 quality engineering staff working with suppliers to help them improve their performance. In addition, they ran training programmes for the staff of certain suppliers in order to hasten that improvement and took groups of suppliers to Japan to see what was being done there. Obviously, this kind of approach necessitates the use of far more resources than the traditional approach would require. However, Rank Xerox believed that it was necessary to take this action, did so and obtained some remarkable results. It is interesting to note that one factor which allowed them to pay so much attention to individual suppliers was their decision to reduce their direct supplier base.

Their strategy here involved reducing the number of production suppliers from 3000 to 500. Obviously, the fewer suppliers the greater time can be spent with each. It was also true that the company utilised a larger number of staff of better calibre. The results demonstrated that the effort paid off.

An influential research study by Professor New (1986) showed that UK firms tended to pay far less attention than should have been the case to source decision making and supplier management. The report found that 52 per cent of full factory cost was accounted for by purchases, and supported strongly the view that the unit cost performance of most manufacturing companies depended far more on the effectiveness of purchasing than on the control of labour performance. Purchasing effectiveness had a 'leverage factor' almost three times that of direct labour. Moreover, a specified percentage reduction in the purchase cost was probably far easier to achieve than the same percentage reduction in labour content. It is seen to be curious to contemplate the relative managerial effort put into direct labour control and purchasing effectiveness. Whole work study departments were maintained to control the direct labour content of unit cost, vast amounts of management time and effort were put into negotiations on work rating, yet in most plants the amount spent on purchased items was about three times that spent on direct labour, yet nothing like three times the management effort was directed towards purchasing efficiency.

It follows that when less than adequate attention is paid to purchasing decisions, supplier performance reflects that state of affairs. Since the source decision is so vital it is clear that, where proper attention is paid to such matters, the outcome will be of great benefit to the buying company. It is a fact that a greater awareness of this truth by successful manufacturing companies has been a major factor in their success in Europe and the United States.

Finding the right suppliers

As we indicated earlier, in order for buyers to be able to make the right source decisions they must know their markets. They need to know their main suppliers well, to visit them and talk to the people who process their orders and make decisions about them, to keep in touch with business plans, product developments, and what is going on inside key supply organisations. This could be described as part of demand marketing, which is not a new idea, even though in recent years marketing experts have concentrated almost exclusively on supply marketing, aimed at purchasers and potential purchasers rather than sellers. In addition, they should know where other potential suppliers are based and be aware of production costs, wages and distribution costs which apply in particular markets. Further, they should have clear criteria against which they will be able to judge the suitability of a particular supplier to meet the needs that they have.

Today, enlightened buyers are seeking suppliers with whom they can work to mutual benefit. This means that, in come cases, suppliers are selected prior to a design being prepared, on the basis that they are the kind of company with whom the buying firm wishes to do business. Such judgement, of course, must be based upon thorough assessment involving technical and commercial factors.

Major buyers expect key suppliers, selected after thorough appraisal, to set up production near their own plants. This, of course, implies what has been called quasi-vertical integration, where the buyer and seller, although owned by different shareholders, form an alliance. Philips, the Dutch-based multinational, called this 'co-makership' – a term which is now widely used – where the source of supply is selected with a long-term relationship in view. Obviously, where a supplier agrees to erect a factory near to that of the buying company, there must be a long-term arrangement in the minds of both parties. In such cases effective source selection becomes even more important.

Some criteria

In most cases where such decisions are made the selection process is comprehensive. Included among the criteria used by one company was the requirement that the supplier should have the 'necessary capabilities and experience'. This meant that a potential supplier:

● was viable in the longer term financially, technically, and in production terms;

- would be able to participate in the early phases of product design and development as a full partner in the process;
- would openly share information on the functional, assembly and in-services requirements of the parts, including cost and quality targets;
- would be orientated towards taking cost out of product and improving total system performance to mutual benefit;
- would be able to develop prototypes as well as manufacture volume production;
- would be prepared to agree cost structure targets;
- would work with the buying company so as to increase their flexibility in meeting changing demands and operate on a pull rather than a push basis, in the process, reducing their own wastes such as inventory holding, unnecessary inspection and excess work in progress as well as those of the buying company.

Another multinational, seeking partner suppliers of the same kind, formulated the following criteria. The supplier should have:

- Sound business sense and attitude.
- A good track record in supplying the market in which the buyer operates (or similar).
- A sound financial base.
- A suitable technical capability with modern facilities.
- A total quality orientation.
- Cost effective management.
- Effective purchasing – acquisition and control.
- Good morale among the workforce.
- Effective logistical arrangements.
- A customer service mentality.

THE SOURCING PROCESS

There are two ways to look at the sourcing process. So far in this chapter we have been looking at the big picture – at the major problem of matching total supply capability with total demand. In this section we look at the countless relatively minor problems which buyers deal with every day, of where and how to place orders for all the requirements notified to them: that is, how to match individual demand with supply availability.

The process usually starts with a requisition which informs purchasing that something needs to be bought. As shown in Figure 8.1 the buyer would check first if there is already some commitment by long-term contract, in which case an order could be placed immediately.

In the absence of such agreement, the buyer will ask if there is an existing source of supply whose performance is satisfactory; if so, the usual practice is to reorder from that source unless there is reason to review the position.

Reasons for reviewing the position include: price increase request; failure to meet specification; unsatisfactory performance as demonstrated by vendor

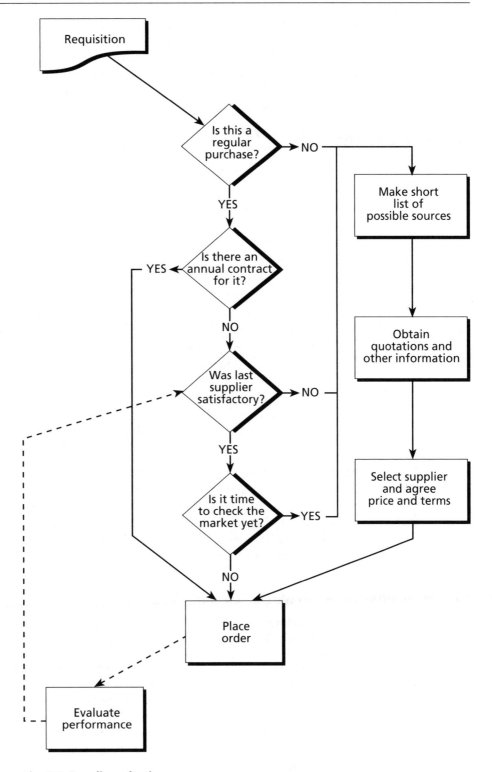

Fig. 8.1 Supplier selection
(*Source:* Baily, 1990)

ratings; internal pressure to save money; or simply that some time has elapsed since the position was last reviewed.

Research confirms that buyers are reluctant to change sources for regular purchases without good reason, and suggests indeed that they sometimes stay too long with a source which is not as satisfactory as others on the market.

SOURCE LOCATION

The location of potentially useful sources of supply is a major responsibility of the purchasing and supply executive. It is widely believed that there is normally a queue of suppliers who are willing to compete to meet the buyer's needs, but the reality is often very different, and the location of potential suppliers can be quite a challenge.

Three principal reasons why the location of suppliers might be difficult are:

1 *Technological advances* The buyer's needs are becoming more complex and difficult to meet, and fewer suppliers are willing or able to do so.
2 *Increasing 'concentration' in supply markets* The continuing process of mergers and takeovers is leading, in many industries, to a situation where there are very few, very large, suppliers who have less need to actively pursue business which will inevitably come their way.
3 *Increased specialisation* Specialisation amongst manufacturing concerns tends to lead to more 'buy' rather than 'make' decisions. This in turn means that a greater proportion of their needs are acquired from outside sources. These sources may not be aware of the developing needs, and will have to be actively sought by the buyer.

IKEA, the Scandinavian based international retailer of furniture and related products attributes a share of the reasons for its success to its suppliers. IKEA have followed a policy of developing relations with the most economical suppliers rather than necessarily dealing with traditional suppliers to the furnishing business. As an example of this, they chose to buy seat covers from a shirt manufacturer.

Sources of information on potential suppliers

When collecting and collating information on potential suppliers the following points ought to be considered:

- *Reputation* The reputation of a particular source may be ascertained through talking to professional contacts and colleagues.
- *Appraisal* A detailed investigation of potential suppliers may be carried out (see below).
- *Recorded performance.* The purchasing department may maintain records which may provide information on the past performance of suppliers who have been used in the past.
- *Approved lists* Individual organisations may maintain lists of companies who

have been assessed and approved. The approved lists of other organisations such as the MOD may be useful. Approval under ISO 9000 may be a qualification.

- *Catalogue library* Some companies keep a special library file containing the catalogues, price lists and other literature from potential suppliers. Some method of indexing these files by product is desirable.
- *Publications* The general or specialist trade press often contains information on the activities of companies who might be potential suppliers. These too can be filed and indexed.
- *Trade directories* There are plenty of directories published and available to buyers which provide information on sources of supply. The *Yellow Pages* directory is an example of this on a local general basis, but there are also national and international guides, usually specialised by industry.
- *Sourcing services* A number of agencies will provide information to buyers about potential sources of supply. Commonly, a computerised database is maintained to enable efficient matching of customer and source.
- *Representatives* Suppliers' representatives are useful sources of information on supply sources. They may disclose details of similar and competing products as well as their own.
- *Exhibitions* These events may provide the buyer with an opportunity to compare similar products from different sources.
- *Colleagues* Personnel in other departments within a company are often knowledgeable about sources of materials relating to their specialism.
- *Other buyers* Communications with fellow professionals in the purchasing field might be helpful in discovering new sources.
- *Agents* Stockists and distributors might provide comparative information on different manufacturers and their products.
- *Organisations promoting trade* Embassies and commercial attachés are usually keen to help buyers to find sources of supply in the territories they represent.

SUPPLIER EVALUATION

The evaluation of actual and potential sources is a continuing process in purchase departments. Actual sources with which one is dealing regularly can be evaluated largely on their track record: on the actual experience of working with them. This is often known as vendor rating, and a number of schemes have been devised for doing it systematically, as considered later. Potential sources can be evaluated only by judgement of their capabilities.

The extent of investigation into suppliers will be affected by the volume and value of possible expenditure. Most organisations spend 80 per cent of their annual budget with 20 per cent of their suppliers, and probably on 20 per cent of the range of items bought, and these big-spend articles justify thorough investigation. Unusual or first-time purchases, where the purchaser has little or no experience to call on, may justify extensive investigation, especially if the wrong choice of supplier could have expensive consequences. Parts made to purchaser's specification require more careful assessment of supplier capability than standard parts available off the shelf from several satisfactory sources. Task variables which determine the choice of supplier are traditionally stated as: quality, quantity, timing, service, and price.

Service includes before-sales service for some products, and after-sales service for others. Prompt and accurate quotations, reliable delivery times, ease of contact with persons in authority, technical advice and service, availability of test facilities, willingness to hold stocks; these are just some of the varied things that make up the package called service. Good service by the supplier reduces the buyer's workload, increases the usefulness or availability of the product, and diminishes the uncertainty associated with making the buying decision.

Financial stability is one of several supplier characteristics not mentioned as 'task variable', but which is nevertheless important. Buyers prefer suppliers to be reasonably profitable because they are interested in continuity and on-time delivery. A supplier with cash-flow problems will have difficulty paying their bills, and consequently in obtaining materials, their delivery times and possibly product quality will probably suffer. A supplier who becomes insolvent can be as big an embarrassment as a customer in similar difficulties.

Good management is also important. Well-managed suppliers improve methods, reduce costs, develop better products, deliver on time, have fewer defective products, and build high morale in their workforce.

On-the-spot surveys of facilities and personnel by technical and commercial representatives of the purchaser are often carried out to evaluate potential suppliers – although sometimes it may be possible to eliminate this on the basis of a supplier's reputation, as obtained from word-of-mouth and published information.

If the supplier's establishment is to be visited for evaluation purposes, most purchasers prepare in advance a checklist to remind investigators of what to look for and to record their findings. Many firms use multi page checklists, asking a great many questions such as 'What percentage of their tooling do they design themselves?' and 'What is the labour turnover?' Based on the answers, an analysis is completed, incorporating a marking scheme which might, for example, be divided into four areas: tooling (capability), machines, planning, and quality control. Finally, the supplier is evaluated for named products or processes as fully approved, approved, conditionally approved, or unapproved. Variations of the checklist approach are legion, and changes and improvements are incorporated as the needs of the organisation change.

Typical checklist questions are:

- Do they trade with our competitors
- Are confidential documents properly controlled?
- Does the buyer have technical support?
- How do they search the market and how often?
- How long have they been established
- What are their investment plans?

Overhead allocation, whether cost breakdowns are provided, the state of the order book, and the names of persons with authority to make decisions on delivery dates, are also looked into. The type of labour available in the areas is investigated, by observation, questions, and if necessary consulting the local Department of Employment office. Again, the checklist is used to fill out the form, with its marking scheme, and to arrive at a final judgement of the supplier as fully approved, approved, requiring minor improvement, or unapproved.

The contents of such checklists are devised to suit individual requirements. The last firm mentioned was, for instance, obviously concerned about keeping details of its bought-out component designs secret from its competitors. For checking the quality capability of a supplier it is, however, possible to standardise checklists to a greater extent, as considered in Chapter 5.

Another requirement of some purchasers necessitates the sellers being Electronic Data Interchange (EDI) connected. EDI is a method of sending information electronically between, for example, buyer and seller. By this means both parties eliminate paper work, reduce transmission errors and speed the information flows. Retailers and motor manufacturers have been early users of this process and, most frequently, it has been the buying company which has promoted the establishment of the facility. The advantages to the buying companies in helping minimise inventory while facilitating greater flexibility in response to demand are likely to result in fast adoption of the approach.

A further requirement in mass production industries in particular is for the supplier to be capable of delivering against a just-in-time (JIT) schedule. In this context JIT implies a supplier's manufacturing and delivery process capable of immediate response to a demand from the buying company, thus eliminating the need for the latter to hold anything other than a minimum inventory.

It is interesting to note the additional criteria which one company has developed to help ensure success in selecting this type of supplier. JIT arrangements are made with companies with whom the buyer wishes to make a long-term liaison. The approach necessitates absolute reliability in both quality and schedule terms. Thus potential suppliers have to satisfy the buying company on these counts. In most cases the company concerned has found that it has had to develop potential suppliers to the required level. They start by looking for suppliers who are near to the plant. Where that is not possible they have frequently persuaded effective suppliers to relocate.

Their initial focus is upon ensuring the quality of performance which they require, that is, specification and delivery schedule. In the process they work with the supplier in analysing the specification of the product so as to give the supplier every chance of producing the material or service as efficiently as possible. The specification includes statements like 'it must be possible for us to run our machinery at X units per minute'. The company makes every effort to develop mutual trust in the process. They aim to work with the supplier in partnership while 'eliminating 43 page contracts', and the joint aim of the partnership is continually to improve process quality control from an agreed level to a better one by a particular date. A team drawn from both companies works on a continuing basis with the brief 'How can we improve performance: e.g. quality, logistics, price?' One important factor from the buying company's viewpoint is that it agrees a target profit level with the suppliers and then works with them to take the cost out of the process.

Procurement Engineer's Vendor Evaluation Rating Form

Vendor name .... Date of evaluation ....

Address .... Commodity or process
under review

....

....

Evaluators: Commercial .... Technical ....

SUMMARY

As a result of this evaluation, the above vendor is

      Fully approved ....25 all areas ☐

      Approved ....20 all areas ☐

      ● Conditionally approved.............18 all areas ☐   *Tick appropriate box*

      ● Unapproved ....less than 18 any area ☐

For the following commodities

Product description

Range of recommended

Preferred quantity

Precision class

* Reason for vendor's conditionally approved/unapproved status

....

....

....

....

Evaluator's signature ....Procurement Engineering Dept

Fig. 8.2 Supplier evaluation

Procurement Engineer's Vendor Evaluation Rating Form

VENDOR RATING FORM

Rate factors   1 Fully approved
0.8 Meets minimum requirements
0 Unacceptable

	Rate	Wtg	Total
(a) Tooling capability			
1 Design		9	
2 Manufacture		6	
3 Maintenance		4	
4 Storage		3	
5 Tooling control		3	
Total		25 max	
(b) Machines			
1 Capacity		6	
2 Capability		6	
3 Operator skills		6	
4 Maintenance		4	
5 Environment safety – layout		3	
Total		25 max	
(c) Planning			
1 Detail method planning Operation sheets		8	
2 Detail estimating by operation		5	
3 Responsible to eng. change activity		2	
4 Work study practices		5	
5 Cost reduction consciousness		5	
Total		25 max	

Fig. 8.2 *(continued)*

Procurement Engineer's Vendor Evaluation Rating Form

(d) Quality control systems

	Receiving inspection			Control of manufacture			Final inspection		
	Rate	Wtg	Total	Rate	Wtg	Total	Rate	Wtg	Total
1 Quality assurance management		3			3			3	
2 Quality assurance planning		3			3			3	
3 Record systems		3			3			3	
4 Equipment and calibration		3			3			3	
5 Drawing and change control		2			2			2	
6 Corrective action procedures		4			4			4	
7 Non-conforming material		3			2			3	
8 Handling/Storage/ Shipping		1			1			1	
9 Environment/ General		1			1			1	
10 Personnel experience		2			3			2	
Total (25 max)									

RATING SUMMARY

Area of evaluation	Total rating	Status
Production tooling		
Production machines		
Production planning		
Receiving inspection		
Q.C. of manufacture		
Final inspection		

Status rating: 25 fully approved
20 approved
18 conditionally approved
Less than 18 unapproved

Fig. 8.2 *(continued)*

OTHER ASPECTS OF SOURCING

One or more suppliers?

Earlier we discussed cases where the buyer deliberately gives all their business of a particular type to one supplier. This is a single source approach and it is becoming increasingly popular. However, it is not always the right decision to make; in some circumstances it is better to have more than one source.

Many factors have to be taken into account before the right decision is made. In some instances there is no choice to make as only one supplier can be used because of patents, or technical or economic monopoly. In other instances, there is little real choice because the amount of business is too small to be worth dividing, or because one supplier is outstanding and without serious rivals. Where scope exists for a real choice, valid arguments can be found on both sides, and examples can be found where single sourcing has paid off handsomely as well as examples where advantages have been gained by dividing the business. There is no simple answer; each situation needs to be analysed. Some of the considerations which need to be evaluated are:

- Effect on price: aggregating orders with a single source may mean a lower unit price because of greater volume, will certainly reduce tooling costs if moulds, dies, or other costly equipment would have to be duplicated for dual sourcing, and may bring savings in transport costs. Splitting the business between several suppliers may, on the other hand, bring lower prices because of competition between them.

- Effect on security of supply: scheduling is simpler with single source, stockless buying or consignment stocking may be available, the supplier is motivated to give a good service because he has been entrusted with all the business. On the other hand, with a second source there is greater security if fire, flood, plant breakdown or strike interrupt supplies from the first source.

- Effect on supplier motivation, willingness to oblige, design innovation, and so on. Sometimes, single sourcing works well in this connection, but there are instances of complacent and indifferent suppliers who were stimulated to make radical improvements when their monopoly was broken. On occasion, purchasers have gone to considerable trouble and expense to build up a satisfactory second source. This suggests a fourth consideration.

- Effect on market structure: will single sourcing lead to a monopoly where there is no alternative supplier left in the market?

The captive supplier

A related problem is the captive supplier. Purchasing executives commonly consider it desirable to limit the proportion of a supplier's output which they take, and some figure from 20 per cent to a maximum of 50 per cent is often laid down in policy manuals and departmental guidelines. To take more than 50 per cent of a supplier's output makes a supply organisation dependent on the purchaser, limits the purchaser's freedom of manoeuvre and raises unwelcome moral and social issues if a design change or a change in the product mix on the part of the purchaser results for the supplier in a sudden loss of over half their output. Despite the general agreement that it is a risky marketing policy for the supplier to allow themselves to become a vassal of one purchaser, and questionable purchasing policy for a buyer to take the greater part of a supplier's output, nevertheless the situation can deteriorate gradually unless there are periodical reviews.

Merchant distributor

Goods are not necessarily bought direct from a manufacturer, and services may be provided by a franchisee or other intermediary. The distributor is assuming greater importance in some marketing channels for a number of products – mainly because, both to end-user and original maker, the distributor offers a solution to a number of problems. Increased costs of transport have led many manufacturers to re-examine their physical distribution systems and find in favour of greater use of distributors. Distributors in many cases offer additional services such as part finishing, which makes them more attractive. A further reason is the increased purchasing sophistication among end-users who are adopting efficient routine ordering systems for the 80 per cent of their purchases that account for only 20 per cent of their budget (blanket orders, for instance).

The distributor is a middleman who usually assembles, stocks and sells a large assortment of wares to users. Some are specialists, in software for instance. Non-specialists often handle clothing, tools and equipment, supplies such as screws and switches, and MRO items such as cleaning cloths and brooms.

Their main selling point is immediate availability; this point is stressed by the names 'stockholder' and 'stockist', which are often used. The availability may be achieved through a location close to the customer, or through a responsive system such as that operated by RS Components, who can usually supply an item from their catalogues to anywhere in the UK the morning following the day of order. 'Responsiveness' is a key competitive factor for most stockist/distributors.

Stockists are often used with advantage in maintaining stocks of stationery, small tools, spares and other articles in common use in perhaps a number of companies in their area. They guarantee to keep stocks to meet the various buyers' requirements and thus allow them to dispense with stocking these items themselves. The items may be called forward from the stockist as and when required, often under some monthly order arrangement which also saves paperwork. An extension of this idea used in some places is for the stockist to maintain an area in the buyer's own stores, which is kept replenished with an agreed range of materials or parts. The prices of these parts are agreed in advance and those used are paid for each month against an agreed stock check. This idea, sometimes called consignment stocking or a 'forward supply' arrangement is being used, too, by manufacturers as an extension of their service.

In the end, the decision to buy direct or from a stockist must be based on a comparison of the costs and benefits of the service offered with those of buying direct from the manufacturer.

Where?

Geographical location is another consideration: three-quarters of the buyers in one survey preferred local sources even if price was higher or quality inferior. The first reason for this is better communications generally: quicker deliveries, lower transport cost, personal knowledge of individuals on both sides, ease of contact when problems arise or something is needed urgently. The second reason is a wish to support the local community. It may be good business to support the local community and good politics too. However, the European Union directs through the EC directives that public sector organisations must publicise their intention to place orders of more than a certain 'threshold' value throughout the community. Local purchasing should not involve paying higher prices for worse products and inferior service, and it is not to be expected that good suppliers for everything can be found in the local area.

Companies pursuing with their supplier a just-in-time approach find mutual benefit through suppliers locating close to the customer organisation, and it has become a widespread practice for suppliers to set up subsidiary factories close to a customer's factory. Naturally, these factories tend to be dedicated units, geared to meet the needs of a particular customer, and with plant and equipment dedicated to the needs of the particular customer. A term which has evolved to describe this state of affairs is 'asset specificity'.

Reciprocity

Another thorny question, which many buyers, and particularly those in the manufacturing sector, have to face at some time in their careers, is reciprocity. This is a problem which is probably more in evidence in times of national economic recession. One effect of recession is to reduce the volume of business which is available to manufacturing companies. As a result, sales organisations, anxious to maintain as large a share as possible, are urged to greater efforts. One question, which is frequently asked at this time is: 'Which companies from which we make substantial purchases could utilise some of our products, but are currently buying elsewhere?' This is then followed by, 'Can we bring pressure to bear on these organisations to buy from us on the basis that we are customers of theirs?' Or the sales department may simply ask for the help of the purchase department in applying pressure to a possible customer who is a supplier.

The buyer is charged with making the best purchase possible for his or her company. When a selling organisation solicits his or her business on reciprocal grounds, he or she should consider why the approach has to be made on such a basis. Does it really amount to 'even though we aren't the best source, buy from us because we're good customers of yours?' The danger in deciding reciprocal trading questions on narrow departmental grounds is sub-optimising: that is, finding an optimum solution from the viewpoint of one department or section of the organisation which is not the optimum for the organisation as a whole. Gaining sales at the expense of costly and unsatisfactory purchases could be sub-optimising from the sales angle; making the best possible purchase at a high cost in lost sales could be sub-optimising from the purchasing angle. No matter how strongly sales or purchasing feel about such matters, the decision must be taken by general management in the interests of the whole company. The task of the buyer is to assist in taking the decision by advising on the costs and benefits involved, after carefully evaluating both short-term and long-term effects on the materials budget. Some of these long-term effects are difficult to evaluate. One reason why reciprocity is not popular in purchasing circles may be that effects which are difficult to evaluate tend to get left out of consideration when decisions are taken by general management, leaving the purchase department with a frustrated feeling that their side of the case has not been given a fair crack of the whip.

What happens, for instance, if one party wants to cut back on its purchases from the other? Has a reciprocal cutback to be negotiated? What does the buyer do if he or she succeeds in finding a new, greatly superior source? Normally, he or she would be free to switch source; but when the previous sourcing decision has been taken by higher management on reciprocal grounds, he or she will presumably have to raise the whole question once more with general management. Is a supplier who has won the business on reciprocal grounds going to keep up a high standard of service, or will complacency and a take-it-or-leave-it attitude develop? What does reciprocal trading do to purchase department morale; to its zeal in systematically comparing and evaluating sources and materials; to its opportunities to achieve cost reductions? The better the purchase department is at its job, the better placed it is to insist that full weight be given to such considerations in deciding reciprocity questions.

Supplier associations

Major Japanese manufacturers have for some time encouraged the formation of and participated in 'Kyoryoku Kai' or supplier associations. Early implementations of this idea were that suppliers were assisted in getting together by the customer, but the association would then operate without the active involvement of the customer. However, it is now generally the case that suppliers and their customers participate together. The idea of supplier organisations has, in recent years, been adopted by some American and European concerns, and seems to be paying dividends.

The basic thinking is that companies with a common interest in meeting the needs of a particular customer can, through the establishment of channels of communication and regular exchanges of ideas and information, better develop effective methods of meeting customer needs, with profit for all concerned. The participants are open and co-operative with each other, and usually work on a 'self-help' basis.

Figure 8.3 illustrates the principle of a supplier association, with the customer and the member suppliers freely exchanging appropriate information.

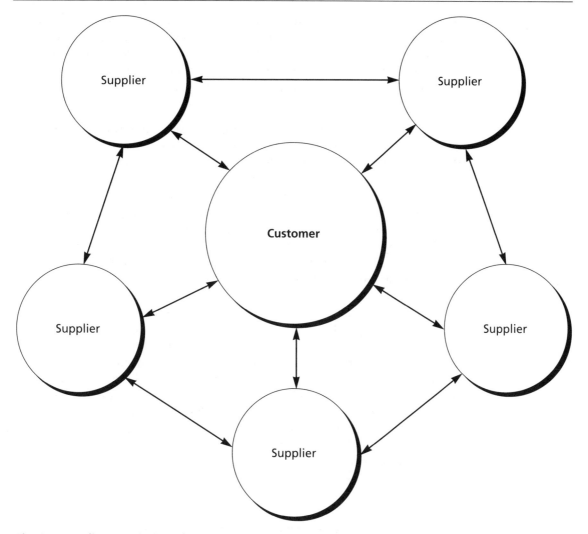

Fig. 8.3 Supplier associations: known in Japan as 'Kyoryoku Kai'

Intra-company purchases

Internal transactions within groups of companies can present problems similar in some respects to those raised by reciprocal trading. Different organisations lay down different policies on this, for instance:

- 'Group companies should be given the opportunity to quote against our requirements when they are able to satisfy our needs. It is understood by all concerned, however, that they cannot be allowed advantage simply because they are group members. In all cases they should be treated as any other suppliers.'

- 'Buyers are reminded that companies in the group provide the following materials and services... Please utilise these when and where possible.'
- 'The use of materials and services from other group companies is encouraged. Where a group company submits a quotation which is less advantageous than a competitor, it is to be given the opportunity to meet this competition on equal terms.'

These are from three different purchasing manuals, and it can be seen that the policies go from treating internal suppliers just like external suppliers, to using them when and where possible, to giving them preferential treatment. This is not necessarily a form of group philanthropy, since there may be sound policy reasons at top management level for giving temporary support to a weak group member. It does not seem efficient to compel other group companies to deal permanently with a member which cannot compete on level terms with outside suppliers. Unless there are special reasons, one would expect management either to upgrade the management of the supplier subsidiary to make it competitive on the open market, or else to divest themselves of the non-competitive operation.

An internal supplier can be a great help in times of shortages, and in principle could be the ideally responsive supplier. In practice, like any organisation with a captive market, it can tend to take internal orders for granted and give priority to external customers whose business has to be won, and may be more profitable. The purchasing manager should not permit this to happen. His or her organisational role gives him or her the right and the duty to insist on acceptable quality, competitive prices and a good service from the supplier subsidiary. If he or she fails to obtain this, in effect his or her own company is subsidising another group company and the latter is making profits at the expense of the former.

Market structure

Supplying organisations operate from within the context of what is often called the supply market (though some economists insist that there is no such thing, there are simply 'markets' which cannot be other than both supply and demand markets, since all markets involve buyers and sellers). The following types of market are common, and will have a bearing on the way in which both buyers and sellers operate.

- Monopsony, where there is a single dominant buyer, as is the case in the market for armaments in the UK where the Ministry of Defence is a monopsonistic buyer, or for certain categories of railway engineering, where Railtrack will be the sole UK customer.
- Monopoly, where there is a single powerful seller, for example water companies enjoy local monopolies in the UK, though this may well change in the future.
- Oligopoly is present where several sellers co-operate to dominate the market. The market for air passenger traffic within Europe demonstrates the characteristics of an oligopoly.

Price rings, cartels and restrictive practices

While collaboration between buyers through such vehicles as purchasing consortia is tolerated within the UK (though not necessarily elsewhere), collaboration between sellers comes under scrutiny through the Office of Fair Trading (OFT). That is not to say that any such co-operation is necessarily seen as a bad thing, but the OFT is concerned to see that any collaboration does not go against the public interest.

In 1994 the OFT published a booklet which gives some questions that buyers should ask in order to determine whether a cartel might exist. The questions are:

- Does the industry or the product have characteristics which make it easier to organise, police and sustain a cartel, e.g. few sellers, homogeneous products, similar costs of production?
- Are there factors which encourage suppliers to make a cartel agreement at a particular time, for example, the development of widespread excess capacity or a recession?
- Do prices change or behave in ways that would not be expected?
- Do price changes over time reveal so regular and systematic a leader/follower situation as to be inexplicable without some kind of contact between suppliers?
- Are similar phrases or explanations used in announcing price increases?
- Are 'give away' phrases sometimes used in correspondence or conversation, for example, 'The industry has decided that margins must be increased to a more reasonable level'?

SUPPLIER RELATIONSHIPS

The idea of working closely with suppliers is not new. Lord Nuffield in his pioneering days of motor car production in the United Kingdom worked very closely with his suppliers. He offered help in planning and organising production, and contributed to the development of components from the point of view of ease of assembly into the final product, as well as the final function. Marks & Spencer have for many years worked closely with suppliers, and other major concerns in the retailing business have established traditions in this respect.

The success in world markets of Japanese manufactured goods, and the increasing adoption by the Japanese companies of Britain as a manufacturing base has led to a great interest in and enthusiasm for Japanese management principles and ways of working. One of the many distinguishing characteristics of Japanese industry is the enthusiasm of working closely with their suppliers, attempting where possible to remove conflicts and tension. These ideas have been translated into English as 'partnership sourcing'.

In September 1990 the Confederation of British Industry launched the 'Partnership Sourcing' initiative. The project was led by Sir Derek Hornby, the former chairman of Rank Xerox, and reflected the view that traditional adversarial or confrontational attitudes towards suppliers were not conducive to the reduction of overall costs, quality improvement or innovation. With the involvement of the Department of Trade and Industry who fund the project, energetic efforts have been made to promote the partnership sourcing ideas throughout the UK, and considerable success has been achieved. Surveys have shown that a majority (nine out of ten) purchasing decision makers are aware of the concept, though a smaller proportion are actually employing the ideas.

The CBI and DTI define partnership sourcing as follows:

Partnership sourcing is a commitment by customers/suppliers, regardless of size, to a long-term relationship based on clear mutually agreed objectives to strive for world class capability and competitiveness.

The mission of the partnership sourcing initiative is summarised in the statement:

To bring about a fundamental change in companies' philosophy leading to the widespread knowledge, understanding and implementation of partnership sourcing within the UK.

A large number of influential business concerns in Britain have adopted the principles of partnership sourcing, and report considerable benefits. For example, Laing Homes, part of the Laing Construction Group have achieved great success. Instead of keeping information about programmers close to their chest, Laing Homes share information on where business is developing, allowing suppliers to plan production and in turn to help their own materials suppliers. Laing also report that at one time much of the timber used on construction sites arrived in random lengths of variable quality, with 20 per cent of shipments being rejected. As a result of an improvements project involving their supplier, Palgrave Brown, and the Timber Research and Development Association timber is now supplied to length, and of a consistent quality. Laing actually pay a higher price for timber, but the efficiency arising from the new scheme results in lower overall costs.

Another advocate of partnership sourcing is Texas Instruments (TI). At the UK headquarters and plant in Bedfordshire the US-owned company requests its customers work with TI as closely as possible when products (integrated circuits) are being developed. This helps to reduce costs while maintaining quality, and can reduce design-cycle times enabling customers to beat their competitors to the market with new products.

Details of the partnership sourcing initiative, and a range of relevant publications can be obtained from:

> The Confederation of British Industry
> Centre Point
> 103 New Oxford St
> London
> WC1A 1DU

Figure 8.4 summarises the principal characteristics of partnership sourcing.

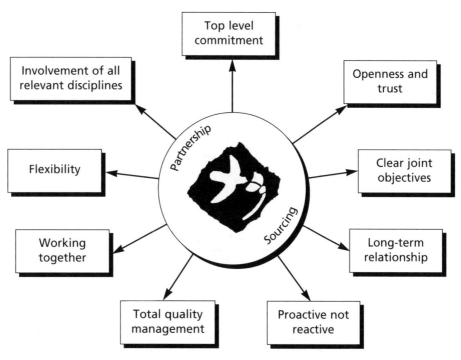

Fig. 8.4 The principal characteristics of partnership sourcing
(*Courtesy:* Partnership Sourcing)

TIERING OF SUPPLIERS

As is obvious from its name, this approach consists of organising supply through different 'layers' of supplier, with the immediate or direct suppliers being known as the first tier, and the second and subsequent tiers each being a stage further removed from the major manufacturer. Figure 8.5 illustrates the principle. The top tier is the final manufacturer, the first tier suppliers provide assemblies or systems, and the second tier suppliers typically provide components.

For many years now companies have sought to reduce the number of suppliers with whom they deal. 'Reducing the vendor base' was the jargon which accompanied this movement, and for many organisations this process consisted of simply identifying the better suppliers, trying to place more business with them, and discarding the rest. Most high volume manufacturing concerns can quote impressive statistics telling how they reduced their number of suppliers from thousands down to a couple of hundred or so during the 1980s.

Standardisation and variety reduction are linked to the idea of vendor base reduction, a narrower range of products bought is obviously likely to lead to dealings with fewer suppliers, as well as other economies. As an example of this policy in action, *Volkswagen* have targeted the avoidance of replications. Previously the group used 26 different cigarette lighters in their various vehicles lighters, now they use 5. Formerly 53 different exterior mirrors were specified, now there are 7.

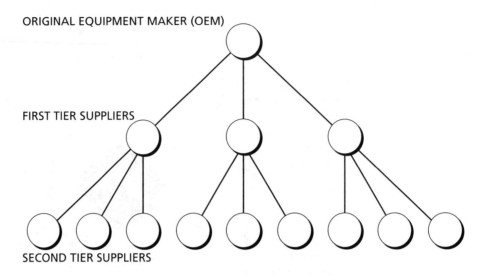

ORIGINAL EQUIPMENT MAKER (OEM)

FIRST TIER SUPPLIERS

SECOND TIER SUPPLIERS

Fig. 8.5 Tiering of suppliers

It is perhaps misleading to call the first tier companies merely suppliers. Supply is what they do of course, but as key vendors they work very closely indeed with the original equipment maker (OEM), collaborating in a great variety of ways, and becoming risk and benefit sharing partners in the OEM's business. Nor are they simply contractors (though this might be a more appropriate description than suppliers). There is a degree of mutual commitment and dependency which places them in the position of stakeholders in the OEM's business, with the investment being committed, development activity and, perhaps dedicated assets, rather than financial. The dependency is, of course, two-way, with the OEM heavily reliant upon the services of the first tier suppliers.

The tiering process is, however, a much more complex process than simply reducing the number of direct suppliers. In the auto industry, for example, it involves the identification of a supplier, or groups of suppliers, who can supply the OEM with systems, such as braking, electrical, trim, etc.; and empowering the key supplier to orchestrate the second tier suppliers to play their part in harmony. To some extent the second tier suppliers may be encouraged to do the same thing with their suppliers.

So, tiering is not just about reducing the vendor base. In fact it might be found that with the design and adoption of a structured, tiered supply framework, the number of suppliers to an actual OEM may increase, though of course the vast majority of suppliers will have no direct contact with the OEM. The direct vendor base can be reduced to very small numbers of contractors indeed. It has been recently suggested that a leading Japanese Automotive company is envisaging a situation where, for a particular model of car, there will be fewer than ten suppliers directly involved.

Figure 8.6 summarises the shift in the structure of supply in the automotive and similar industries.

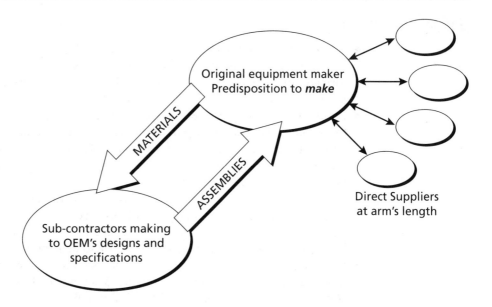

Fig. 8.6 Established pattern of supply in high volume manufacturing

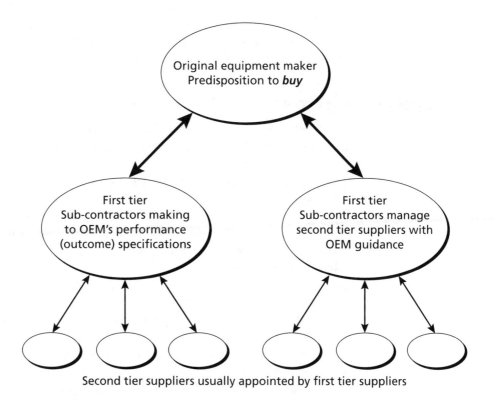

Fig. 8.7 Developing pattern of supply in high volume manufacturing

SUMMARY POINTS

- Those responsible for sourcing must have good knowledge of the market in which they are involved. Supply market research, undertaken either formally or informally, is essential. It also imparts awareness of substitute product markets.
- Professor New's Report 1986 showed that 52% of factory cost was accounted for by purchasing and that purchasing effectiveness had a leverage factor of almost three times that of direct labour. Thus a small improvement in purchasing performance would have far greater impact than the same percentage improvement in labour.
- Actual sources can be evaluated using vendor rating systems which are based on historical information. Potential sources have to be 'judged'. Questions regarding financial stability, management structure and order book commitments are amongst the criteria to be included on a site survey.
- Just in time manufacturer's rely on suppliers who can respond immediately to a demand from the buying company. They normally have to be located close to the manufacturer to enable prompt delivery.
- The chapter outlines the pros and cons of monopoly supply, also the sub optimisation problem common to both reciprocity and intra company purchase agreements.
- Tiering organises the precedent given to suppliers. Direct suppliers are first tier providing assemblies/systems. They are very closely linked, sharing the risk and benefits and are, in effect, shareholders in the Original equipment maker. First tier suppliers are empowered to direct the second tier suppliers, focusing them on the OEM's objectives.

REFERENCES AND FURTHER READING

Baily P (1991), *Purchasing Systems and Records,* 3rd edn, Gower, Aldershot.

Butterworth C (1995), 'Supply Tiers, The Purchasing Challenge', *Selected Readings in Supply Chain Management,* CIPS.

Farmer D and MacMillan K (1979), 'Re-defining the boundaries of the firm', *Journal of Industrial Economics,* xxvii, (3).

Griffiths F (1993), 'Alliance partnership sourcing – a major tool for strategic procurement', *Selected Readings in Purchasing and Supply,* vol 1, CIPS.

Hines P (1994), *Creating World Class Suppliers, Unlocking Mutual Competitive Advantage,* Pitman Publishing, London.

Kotabe M (1992), *Global Sourcing Strategy: R & D, Marketing and Marketing Interface,* Quorum, New York and London.

Lamming R (1993), *Beyond Partnerships: Strategies for Innovation and Lean Supply,* Prentice Hall, New York.

Merli G (1991), *Co-makership – The New Supply Strategy for Manufacturers,* Productivity Press, Cambridge, Mass.

New C C and Myers A (1986), *Managing Manufacturing Operations in the UK 1975–1985,* BIM, London.

Nishiguchi (1994), *Strategic Industrial Sourcing: The Japanese Advantage*, Oxford University Press, New York.

Office of Fair Trading (1994) *Cartels: Detection and Remedies, A Guide for Purchasers*, HMSO, London.

Robinson, Faris and Wind (1967), *Industrial Buying and Creative Marketing*, Allyn & Bacon.

Thompson K (1991), 'Scaling evaluative criteria and supplier performance estimates in weighted point purchase decision models', *International Journal of Purchasing and Materials Management*, 27 (1), Winter.

Womack J P, Jones D T and Roos D (1990) *The Machine That Changed The World*, Maxwell Macmillan, London.

CHAPTER 9

Price

INTRODUCTION

This chapter is concerned with examining how prices are determined both in the short term and long term. As you will appreciate from previous chapters any purchase decision is affected by many factors for example quality, delivery, responsiveness etc., not just price.

In this chapter we will look at various factors affecting the pricing decision. Techniques such as cost analysis, price adjustment clauses and learning curves will be evaluated. Finally we will look more carefully at moves to reduce costs in the supply chain and the concept of strategic acquisition costs.

OBJECTIVES OF THIS CHAPTER

- To look at the factors which enter into pricing decisions
- To define 'price analysis' as against 'cost analysis'
- To analyse the pricing methods of major contracts
- To suggest how escalation and price adjustment clauses might be employed in contracts where inflation is a problem
- To analyse the learning curve effect on the unit cost of production.

FACTORS AFFECTING PRICING DECISIONS

Three factors enter into most pricing decisions:

1 Competition and other market considerations – price mechanism.
2 Value as perceived by customers.
3 Cost of production.

These factors tend to pull in different directions, as shown in Figure 9.1, and any one may be the key factor in the price decision.

Supply and Demand

Pricing in nearly all types of business is affected by what economists call the price mechanism, that is the theory of supply and demand. There is the notion of an equilibrium price which means that at the equilibrium or market price, exactly OQ is both demanded and supplied (*see* Figure 9.2). In most free market economies the process of an equilibrium price helps to decide what is produced and what is not produced.

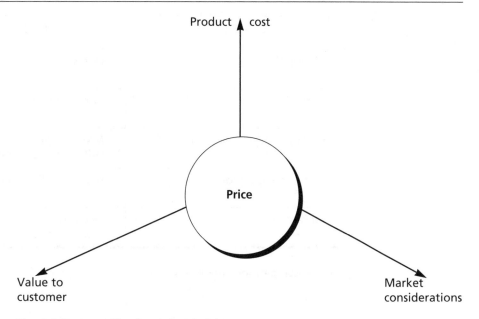

Fig. 9.1 Factors affecting price decisions

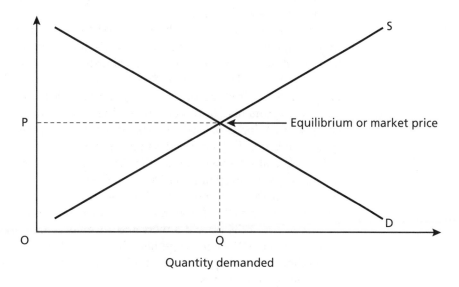

Fig. 9.2 Price mechanism

Competition and other market considerations

Organisations sell their products or services in a wide variety of market conditions ranging from perfect competition to monopoly. The characteristics of each type of market is shown below in Figure 9.3.

167

COMPETITION	CONDITIONS
Monopoly	One supplier
Duopoly	Two suppliers
Monopolistic competition	Many suppliers Differentiated product
Perfect competition	Many suppliers same product
Monopsony	One buyer Many suppliers

Fig. 9.3 Competition conditions

As you can see from Figure 9.3 above the extent of competition can range from one supplier in the case of monopoly to many suppliers in the case of perfect competition. In the case of monopoly, while there could be many suppliers of certain products or services, there may only be one buyer e.g. the National Health Service and drugs.

Conventional purchasing thinking held the belief that monopoly was bad and competition good. Government legislation adopted a similar line and attempted through various Acts of Parliament e.g. Monopolies and Restrictive Practices Act of 1948, 1956 and 1964, Fair Trading Act of 1973 and Competition Act of 1980, to reduce the power of monopolies and restrictive practices. Counter-arguments, however, maintained economies of scale more than compensated for problems associated with monopolies. More recently the European Union has increased its profile in this area.

It is generally believed today that the so-called economies of scale are not as big as was originally claimed and that responsiveness to changing demands of the customer make it difficult for larger organisations to be as efficient as they could. Today many buyers believe that unnecessary costs can be driven out of the price if buyers and suppliers can work closely together in a partnership. Working together they can drive out unnecessary costs throughout the supply chain, both upstream and downstream. This is achieved by such means as:

● reducing the number of suppliers in the supply chain;
● joint development of new products;
● having responsive suppliers;
● use of integrated databases; and
● assisting key suppliers.

Major Japanese buying organisations have been more concerned with selecting suppliers committed to policies of continuous improvement and

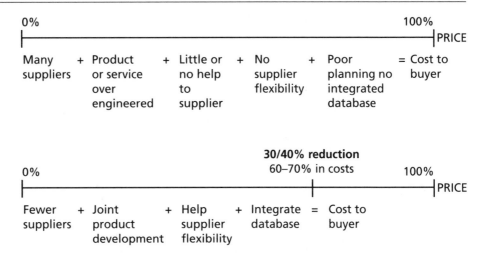

Fig. 9.4 Suppliers and buyers working together to drive out unnecessary costs

driving out unnecessary costs than the initial price of a product or service. They believe that with the right supplier partnership and by working closely together over a period of time prices can be reduced by eliminating unnecessary costs and inefficient practices. Thus while the price mechanism and market conditions may determine prices overall if both buyer and supplier work closely together they can drive out unnecessary costs and either reduce prices or increase profits.

Product life cycle and pricing

The product life cycle is shown in Figure 9.5. All products tend to go through a five-phase cycle of development: introduction, growth, development, saturation and eventual decline. Pricing policy can vary dramatically depending on where in the product life cycle a product has reached.

In the early stages of the life cycle differentiated prices can often be charged. Sales organisations may pursue policies of skimming, i.e. because their capacity is limited they can charge high prices for a limited time, but as their capacity increases and other suppliers offer similar products they move towards much lower penetration pricing to increase market share. Buyers will thus notice big differences in price over the life cycles of products.

Price and the cost of production

Cost-based pricing is widely used. Buyers may be able to insist that prices are justified by cost evidence when goods are produced specifically to their requirements.

Cost-plus contracts are sometimes used when the work is difficult to cost in advance, for instance when research and development work is involved. The final contract price payable under these contracts is the actual cost incurred

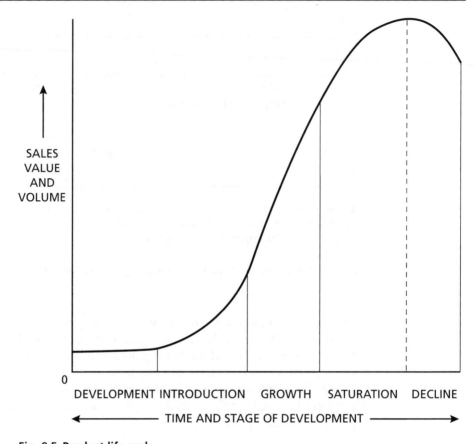

Fig. 9.5 Product life cycle

plus a fee, which may be an agreed percentage of cost, or an agreed amount, or a target fee with incentives as discussed later in this chapter.

Mark-up pricing, widely used in the retail trade, marks up the cost of purchase by adding a percentage to arrive at the selling price. The percentage mark-up varies, fast-moving goods such as greengrocery typically having a low margin and slow-moving goods such as jewellery or furniture having a high margin.

Target pricing is also used. If for instance a firm sets itself a target of earning 20 per cent on the £30m capital employed in the business, and if total annual costs are expected to amount to £60m, then the percentage added to cost of production to arrive at a selling price would be determined as follows:

$$\frac{\text{capital employed} \times \text{target rate of return}}{\text{annual costs}}$$

$$= \frac{30m \times 20\%}{60m}$$

$$= 10\%$$

This is not as simple as it looks, because cost of production varies with the quantity produced, which in turn depends on sales, which are affected by the price charged. An example of the costs associated with a manufactured item and its eventual price is given below in Figure 9.6.

Prime costs (direct materials, direct labour, direct expenses) +
factory overheads (fixed and variable expenses) = works costs

Works cost + administrative and sales overheads = total cost
Total cost + profit = SALES PRICE

Fig. 9.6 Costs associated with a manufactured item

Costing cannot be an exact science, as any buyer who negotiates cost-based prices, perhaps with a cost analyst sitting in with him or her, becomes aware. Apart from variable costs, which vary directly and proportionately with the quantity produced, the cost of production must include a contribution to overheads and profit. Sales revenue must, in the long term, cover the full cost of staying in business, including profit, if the seller is to survive, even though in the short term a firm which is short of work may accept prices which do not make a full contribution to overheads and profit in order to keep people and plant busy. There are other reasons why particular products may be sold at a loss, for instance to clear stocks, to price out competitors, to gain a toehold in a new market, but in general prices must cover overheads and profit.

Overheads are the fixed costs which a firm incurs to stay in business and which are fixed in the sense that they do not vary directly with output (e.g. rent, rates, the salaries of senior executives). (In the long run all costs are variable, just as in the very short run all costs are fixed.) One problem is how to allocate overheads when the quantity to be produced is not known accurately.

For instance, if a single-product factory expects to sell 100 000 products next year, with fixed costs of £200 000, the appropriate amount to include in product cost for overhead contribution is £2. But if sales are 20 per cent below target, fixed costs will be under-recovered by £40 000, and if sales are 20 per cent above target, there will be a windfall profit of £40 000. Such calculations may be charted on break-even diagrams similar to Figure 9.7. Within limits this may average out, but if a major customer takes most of the output at a price closely based on cost, it is right that the risk should be shared. At the end of the year the purchaser can check the seller's costs for labour, material and overheads and adjust the price in line with the actual level of sales. Thus, in the last example, if sales total 80 000 rather than the 100 0000 expected, overhead contribution needs to be £2.50 rather than £2, and if sales were as high as 120 000, the overhead per product would fall to £1.67.

Another problem occurs when fixed costs have to be allocated to products which have different cost structures. Product X and product Y, for instance,

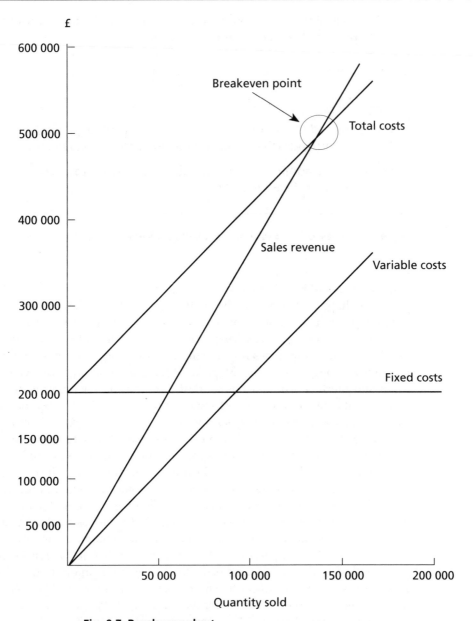

Fig. 9.7 Breakeven chart

both sell at a unit price of £100 each. But fixed costs account for 90 per cent of product cost for X and only 10 per cent for Y. Changes in selling price, and in quantity sold, will not affect profitability in the same way.

A 10 per cent price increase for product X would increase its contribution to overhead and profit by £10, an 11 per cent improvement, but a 10 per cent increase for product Y would double the contribution, from £10 to £20, a 100 per cent improvement. The profitability of product Y is thus much more sensitive to price changes than that of product X.

At the original price of £100, each product brings in a revenue of £10 000 a year if sales are 100 a year. A 10 per cent increase in sales volume would in each case improve revenue to £11 000 a year. In the case of product X the contribution to overhead and profit would increase from £9000 to £9900 and in the case of product Y the increase would be only one ninth of this, from £1000 to £1100. The profitability of product X is thus much more sensitive to volume changes than that of product Y.

Capital-intensive businesses, such as railways, hotels and chemical factories, can add appreciably to their profits by cut-price offers once sales at normal prices have reached the breakeven point. Any sale at a price which is above direct cost will make some contribution to profit once fixed costs have been covered. This is why railways offer special fares for off-peak travel, and hotel operators offer bargain breaks or cheap rates for weekend stays. Capital-intensive manufacturers such as chemical producers are able to dump abroad at prices which are not only below domestic prices but are actually below average cost of production, and still make a profit on such transactions if domestic sales have taken them above the breakeven point.

Price and perceived value

Another factor in pricing decisions is how customers value the offering. A supplier's market offering may include, in addition to the product itself, such things as reliability, durability, good service and prompt delivery. Perceived-value pricing is based on the customer's perception of relative value rather than on cost.

As mentioned in connection with the product life cycle, different customers have different orders of priority and some are willing to pay more than others for a given product. This fact is exploited in the use of skimming prices for new products. A high price is set initially to recover development costs and reap the greatest benefit before competition appears. After skimming the cream off the market, as it were, price is lowered in stages to reach wider and wider market sectors.

Quite a different pricing policy sets a low price from the outset to achieve maximum market penetration. This leads to low cost of production through economies of scale and establishes a dominant market position which competitors will find difficult to attack.

These are not the only alternatives in pricing a new product. Industrial suppliers often prefer to set a price which can be held for a considerable period and will yield the required profit over that period as a whole, partly because this is what most of their customers also prefer.

Another aspect of perceived value is the extent to which changes in price affect the quantity sold. Economists use the term price elasticity of demand for a ratio which measures this sensitivity to price change. Price elasticity can be defined as the ratio of percentage change in quantity sold to percentage change in price. An alternative formula is:

$$\text{Price elasticity} = \frac{\Delta Q}{\Delta P} \times \frac{P}{Q}$$

where ΔQ = change in quantity sold
   ΔP = change in price
   Q = quantity sold before price change
   P = price before the change.

Thus, if a certain item sells 1000 a month at the price of £100 each, and a 2 per cent increase to £102 results in a 5 per cent drop in sales to 950 a month, the price elasticity would be 5 per cent divided by 2 per cent, i.e. 2.5. Alternatively, using the second formula given above, we would obtain the same result:

$$\text{Price elasticity} = \frac{50}{2} \times \frac{100}{1000} = 2.5$$

In this example, the demand would be regarded as elastic. If a 2 per cent price change resulted in less than 2 per cent change in quantity sold, demand would be regarded as inelastic.

Sales of many consumer goods are sensitive to price changes, although there are some (e.g. salt, cigarettes and petrol) for which substantial increases in price do not greatly affect the quantity sold. Demand for industrial goods tends to be inelastic. The quantity sold is, within wide limits, not sensitive to the price charged, except where some close substitute exists to which customers can switch easily.

The main reason for this is because the demand for industrial goods is largely a *derived* demand. The demand for MRO items such as milling cutters and grinding wheels is derived from the demand for the finished products in the manufacture of which they are used. Quantities sold vary with the general level of activity in the manufacturing industries which use these items, and with sales of the particular products of individual manufacturers using them, but do not vary significantly with changes in the prices of the items. The demand for components and materials used in the manufacture of products is derived from the demand for those products. At least in the short term, the manufacturer cannot reduce the quantity purchased in response to a price increase, if they are to meet sales commitment or planned production.

HOW BUYERS OBTAIN PRICES

Four methods are widely used for communicating price:

- A price list is made available.
- Prices are quoted on request, based on an internal price list not available to customers.
- Individual quotations based on specially prepared estimates are made on request.
- Sealed bids or tenders are submitted.

Prices may also be determined by a process of negotiation. For non-standard goods, such as those made to the purchaser's specification or designed by the supplier for a special purpose stated by the purchaser, there can be no standard price list. Indeed final prices in the four methods mentioned above may be subject to a degree of negotiation.

Price lists are available for many standard articles such as small tools, lamps and nuts and bolts. They are commonly used for goods sold through wholesalers and through industrial distributors. List prices are often subject to discounts.

DISCOUNTS

The criteria for supplier discounts are many, any attempt to identify and describe all of them would be bound to fail. Nevertheless, it might be useful to point out the main categories of discount, and some of the types in each category. Figure 9.8 provides an 'at a glance' summary, and may well be self-explanatory for many readers. It indicates the following four categories.

Prompt payment

Many suppliers are prepared to offer a discount if the customer does not keep them waiting for their money. These discounts may be for cash or cheque with order, or for payment within a certain specified period of time.

It is the practice of some *customers* to insist on a discount for prompt payment, even where no discount has been offered by the supplier. In large-scale retailing concerns this approach is widespread. It is, of course, arguable that a supplier who expects to be pressured in this way will price products or services in such a way that they recover the sum they require *after discount*.

It is possibly unnecessary to point out that the buying organisation is only in a position to insist upon the supplier delivering on time and meeting the agreement to the letter when payment is made exactly as agreed. While not advocating delay in meeting obligations to the supplier, care should be taken that any discount for early payment is worth taking. In many cases the benefit

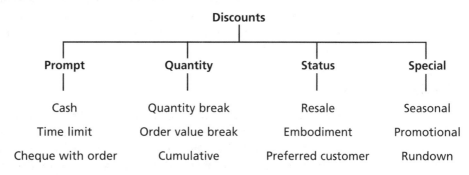

Fig. 9.8 Main categories of supplier discounts

is marginal, if it exists at all, and is obviously likely to be close to the cost of money in the marketplace, as evidenced by interest rates.

Quantity

Many suppliers use discounts as incentives to attract the customer to the purchase of more product. Discounts of this kind may be very attractive and should always be considered carefully, as they may reflect more than simple economies of scale. For example, it is possible that the supplier can make additional products at a 'marginal' cost, having recovered their overheads on the initial quantity.

Of course, taking more material than is needed in the short term is risky, and can result in waste. In addition there will be costs associated with the financing and storage of the temporary excess. As with all discounts, a balanced view is necessary.

Discounts are typically 'quantity break', where a lower price becomes available if more than a given amount of material is ordered. Order value may replace quantity as the threshold, and in some cases order values or quantities may be added together over a given time period to lead to a cumulative discount.

Status

Discounts may be offered according to the status of the buying organisation. For example, if the supplies are being acquired by an organisation acting as a stockist, agent or other intermediary, it is likely that the producer will adjust the price by means of a discount. This reflects the fact that the buyer is assisting the producer in the distribution of the product.

If the material is acquired for embodiment in the customer's product, then it may be seen as appropriate by the vendor to allow a discount, again recognising that the buyer is, in a sense, a distributor. A buyer of, say, ball bearings for incorporation in a machine tool as *manufacturer* is likely to receive a discount not available to another customer buying the parts for maintenance purposes.

Preferred customer status is another reason why discounts are sometimes offered. Entitlement to this status may arise from such factors as reciprocal arrangements, length of standing as a customer, membership of the same group of companies or a wish on the part of the supplier to expand sales in a particular market sector.

Special discounts

Many discounts fall within this category. It is frequently the case that seasonal discounts may be offered. Heating oil or lighting appliances may be available at a discount in the summer, the maintenance of air conditioning installations is more easily accommodated by the service provider in the winter, and discounts may be offered to attract this work.

Promotional discounts and special offers, familiar to all of us in the consumer goods market, are employed for much the same reasons where sales to organisations are concerned. A desire to increase brand or product awareness, or to increase market share may result in attractive short-term discounts becoming available.

As a final example, 'runout' discounts are widely offered. When the Ford motor company introduced the 'Mondeo' range, dealers, with the support of the manufacturer, cleared stocks of the replaced Sierra model by offering buyers very substantial discounts on the published list price. Obviously, this was very much a special discount, made available only by exceptional and temporary circumstances.

PRICE ANALYSIS AND COST ANALYSIS

In the consideration of quotations, some form of price analysis is always used; sometimes a more specialised technique, cost analysis, is brought into play, for instance to support negotiations about cost-based pricing.

Price analysis attempts, without delving into cost details, to determine if the price offered is appropriate. It may be compared with other price offers, with prices previously paid, with the going rate if applicable and with the prices charged for alternatives which could substitute for what is offered. Expert buyers deal with prices daily, and like their opposite numbers on the other side of the counter they acquire a ready knowledge of what is appropriate. When considering something like a building contract, which does not come up daily, they refer to prices recently quoted for comparable buildings.

When several quotations are received, some will usually be above the average and some below it. Any prices well below the norm should be examined with care.

If a supplier is short of work, a price may be quoted which covers direct labour and materials cost without making the normal contribution towards overheads and profit. Accepting such an offer can be beneficial both to supplier and purchaser; but it may be prudent to ask why the supplier is short of work. It can happen to anyone, of course; but in this instance have customers been voting with their feet because the supplier's work is not satisfactory?

Low prices may be the result of a totally different situation: a seller may have enough work on hand to cover overheads (i.e. expected sales revenue already exceeds breakeven point) and is consequently able to make a profit on any price which is above direct cost. Such offers are not necessarily repeatable; next time around, the price quoted may be higher to cover full costs.

Low prices may also be quoted as a special introductory offer to get new customers to give a fair trial to new suppliers. This may be regarded as compensation to the purchaser for the risk incurred in switching to an untried source.

Building long-term working relationships with proved suppliers matters more than a one-off cheap price, but this does not exclude all special offers.

Management may be pleased with an immediate cost reduction, but may also expect the buyer to do even better next year; this can be overcome if it is made clear that special offers cannot be made the basis for standard prices.

Low prices can also be quoted, because of mistake or incompetence. Suppliers should be allowed to correct their mistake or withdraw their offer if their bid is well outside the normal range of variation (e.g. 25 per cent below the average quoted price). Insistence on a contract at the quoted price can lead to bankrupt suppliers and unfinished contracts, and thus eventually to high costs.

High prices may be quoted as a polite alternative to refusing to make any offer by sellers with full order books. Buyers should not write off such suppliers as too expensive, since next time around they could well submit the lowest bid if conditions have changed. High prices may also be quoted because a better specification, more service, or more prompt delivery, etc. is offered. Obviously such offers should be considered with care. The best buy, not the cheapest price, is the buyer's objective.

Cost analysis examines prices in quite a different way from price analysis: it looks at one aspect only, how quoted price relates to cost of production. When large sums are involved and a considerable amount of cost analysis needs to be done, full-time estimating staff or cost analysts may be employed by the purchase department to do it. These people are well qualified to estimate price as their opposite numbers in suppliers' sales departments are to estimate a selling price; they have the same qualifications, engineering experience and costing knowledge, plus specialist knowledge of sheet metal processing, light fabrication, electronics or whatever is relevant.

Usually suppliers are asked to include with their price quotations detailed cost breakdowns. Some are reluctant to comply, but if one supplier does,

---

- Previous history of price increases.
- Competition prices – tenders/quotations – bid analysis.
- Product cost breakdown i.e.

  Labour %
  Materials %
  Overhead %   Check increases against
  Profit %   indices

- Breakeven analysis – the more business you take, the stronger your negotiating position.
- Learning curve – when labour costs are high.
- Value analysis – are costs necessary.
- Standardisation – reduce range.
- Buyer/Supplier business – what per cent of business do you give?
- Payment terms – could these be improved?
- Negotiations – used in conjunction with above.

Fig. 9.9 Price and cost investigation tools

others find it hard not to follow suit. Differences between a supplier's cost breakdown and the purchaser's cost analysis can then be examined one by one to arrive at a mutually agreed figure. Cost analysis is also used by purchasing management to set negotiating targets for their buyers.

Cost analysis is a useful technique for keeping prices realistic in the absence of effective competition. It concentrates attention on what costs ought to be incurred before the work is done, instead of looking at what costs were actually incurred after the work is completed. This seems more likely to keep costs down, as well as less expensive to operate, than the alternative of wading through a supplier's accounting records after contract completion, probably employing professional auditors to do it.

A summary of the price and cost investigation tools is given in Figure 9.9. It starts with the bid analysis where prices and other variables are compared. Further cost reduction exercise could then be concluded depending on the likely areas for cost reduction.

Strategic acquisition cost

Today increasing concern is being directed at long-term or strategic acquisition cost. This approach to costing is concerned with what the price of a product or service could be in the long term if the buyer and the supplier work closely together to drive out unnecessary costs in the supply chain.

When evaluating price the question may be asked have we captured all the costs? For example, have we allowed for lead time or capacity problems with the supplier, what about extra resources and support we may have to devote to suppliers if problems arise and so on. What could look like a good price from a supplier could suddenly escalate if problems occur.

Acquisition costs can be defined as all the costs involved in bringing a supplier's product to the buyer's organisation. It is made up not just of price and freight cost but any other costs in completing this activity properly, e.g. any quality or delivery problems need to be costed in. More buying organisations than ever are now attempting to measure these costs which are often considerably more than the price.

An example of a model for attempting to calculate true acquisition cost is given by IBM in Figure 9.10.

Quotes from various suppliers are systematically analysed, perhaps with an aid of a computer software package and estimates of other costs given. From this, a more accurate assessment of the price can be made.

Niels Schillewart presented a paper in 1996 to an International Purchasing and Supply Education and Research Association (IPSERA) conference on 'the total cost of acquisition (TCA) as an instrument for supplier evaluation'. He defines TCA as a supplier evaluation tool which takes all the costs associated with doing business with a certain supplier into account. Others go further and argue that to really reduce costs and prices one needs a much closer shared relationship with suppliers, though of course this may not be appropriate or practicable for all vendors. Lamming, Jones and Nicol (1996) call for more cost transparency. If *both* sides are more open about costings within a partnership

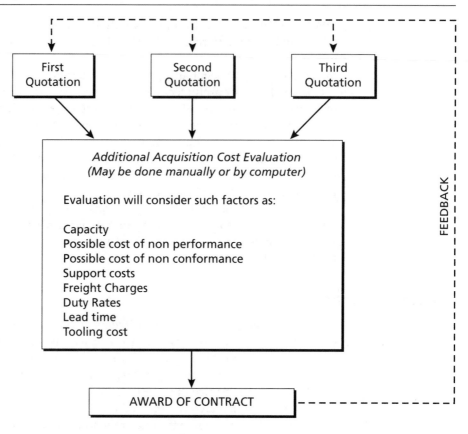

Fig. 9.10 Acquisition cost analysis

arrangement, unnecessary costs can be identified and driven out of the supply chain. As Lamming (1993) comments 'the objective of cost transparency is to reduce costs through joint development of good ideas, thereby improving the mutual competitive position of both organisations'.

PRICING MAJOR CONTRACTS

How to price major contracts is itself a subject on which many books have been written. Such contracts may involve any of the main engineering disciplines, civil, mechanical, electrical or chemical plant engineering – and some large contracts involve all three of them.

Often large sums of money are at stake and long periods of time are involved, so there is risk. Fixed price contracts are administratively convenient to the purchaser, but all the risk has to be taken by the seller. Cost reimbursement contracts are administratively convenient to the seller, but all the risk is taken by the purchaser. Between these two extremes there is a whole range of varied contract types, including fixed price with escalation, target price with incentive, cost plus fixed fee, cost plus incentive fee, etc. Apart from the risk of cost increases for labour and materials, and the effect of government intervention and of changes in taxation and in the financial cost of borrowing money, many contracts entail transactions between different countries, and changes in the rate of exchange between the currencies involved have to be taken into account.

With fixed price contracts the purchaser knows exactly what has to be paid and can provide for it in budgets. The seller, however, arrives at the fixed price by forecasting costs as best he or she can and then adding a contingency allowance to cover unprecedented cost increases. It would be prudent for the seller to make this contingency allowance as large as possible, which means that the purchaser pays a lot for the administrative convenience of a fixed price. If the seller is keen to win the contract and faces competition, the contingency allowance could be cut to a minimum. It may be cut too much, so that sellers have to appeal for *ex gratia* bailing out, or alternatively cut corners to avoid losing money on the contract. In times of severe inflation, fixed price contracts may not be to the advantage of the purchaser even if sellers are willing to sign them. When prices are stable and costs are reasonably predictable, purchasers will prefer fixed price contracts at least for contract periods not exceeding two years.

Fixed price contracts should not be confused with lump sum contracts. In lump sum contracts a single all-in price is payable for the whole of the contract. It may be a fixed price or it could be subject to escalation. A fixed price contract would not be a lump sum contract if it fixed the prices for various classes of labour and material without finalising the amounts to be costed out at these schedules of rates in the final invoice.

In cost-plus contracts, the seller is reimbursed for all costs legitimately incurred, plus either a fixed fee or a percentage fee for contribution to overhead expenses and profit. This type of contract is appropriate for research and development work, where total cost is usually impossible to predict. Close control is required.

When total cost can be estimated with enough accuracy to set a target cost, which is nevertheless capable of improvement and may also be subject to cost slippage, incentive contracts are often used. When the target cost is likely to be affected by changes in the cost of labour and materials, escalation clauses such as the British Electrical and Allied Manufacturers Association (BEAMA) contract price adjustment system are often used.

Incentive contracts

Incentive contracts are used when neither the supplier nor the customer can estimate the cost of the work covered by the contract with sufficient confidence to enable a fixed price to be agreed, but when a reasonable forecast can nevertheless be made of the actual costs of performing the work and a most likely (or target) cost can be agreed. A fee is also agreed for the profit which would be payable if the cost of the work comes out on target together with a ratio in which any under-runs or over-runs from target cost will be shared between the supplier and the customer. The supplier has a positive incentive to keep their costs down because by so doing they can increase profit or avoid contributing towards an over-run on costs. The incentive thus provided motivates the supplier to act in the customer's best interests.

An example is given below of a typical incentive contract, together with details of the outcome:

Example:

Target cost	£500 000	
Profit (at target)	£40 000	
Share ratio for over- and		
under-runs, 75% customer 25% supplier		
Outcome (i.e. actual cost =	£487 495	
Fee for profit payable: Target profit		£40 000.00
Supplier's share of under-run		
(500 000 – 487 495) × 25%		£3 126.25
	Total	£43 126.25

Thus:

	Expected Price (£)			Actual price (£)	
Target cost	500 000		Cost	487 495.00	
Target profit	40 000	= 8%	Fee	40 000.00	= 8.85%
			Share of u/run	3 126.25	
Total	540 000		Total	530 621.25	

Customer saved £9378.75   Supplier earned £3126.25 bonus

Escalation and price adjustment

Inflation is a general and persistent tendency of prices to rise, which, because it is general, is equivalent to a fall in the value (or purchasing power) of the currency affected. Britain suffered from severe inflation in the 1970s, and again in the late 1980s, and although not severe at the time of writing, inflation still remains a serious problem in many parts of the world. Buyers dealing on world markets, and multinational corporations, have to cope with inflation somewhere within their field of operations.

How are contracts to be priced when costs are rising by amounts which cannot be predicted with any accuracy? An option convenient for the seller is to charge the price ruling at date of despatch. Buyers reject this if they can; it gives them no contractual basis to challenge whatever price is eventually charged. Another option is to quote a fixed price which includes contingency allowances large enough to cover any cost increase which might conceivably occur. Fixed prices are convenient for the buyer, but this option cannot be to the purchaser's advantage despite its convenience. There are two better options.

**CONTRACT PRICE ADJUSTMENT CLAUSE
AND FORMULAE FOR USE WITH
HOME CONTRACTS**

**ELECTRICAL MACHINERY:
(for which there is no other specific Formula)**

If the cost to the Contractor of performing his obligations under the Contract shall be increased or reduced by reason of any rise or fall in labour costs or in the cost of material or transport above or below such rates and costs ruling at the date of tender, or by reason of the making or amendment after the date of tender of any law or of any order, regulation, or by-law having the force of law in the United Kingdom that shall affect the Contractor in the performance of his obligations under the Contract, the amount of such increase or reduction shall be added to or deducted from the Contract Price as the case may be provided that no account shall be taken of any amount by which any cost incurred by the Contractor has been increased by the default or negligence of the Contractor. For the purposes of this clause 'the cost of material' shall be construed as including any duty or tax by whomsoever payable which is payable under or by virtue of any Act of Parliament on the import, purchase, sale, appropriation, processing or use of such material.

The operation of this clause is without prejudice to the effect if any which the imposition of Value Added Tax or any tax of a like nature may have upon the supply of goods or services under the Contract.

Variations in the cost of materials and labour shall be calculated in accordance with the following formulae:

(a) Labour

The Contract Price shall be adjusted at the rate of 0.475 per cent of the Contract Price per 1.0 per cent difference between the BEAMA Labour Cost Index published for the month in which the tender date falls and the average of the Index figures published for the last two-thirds of the contract period, this difference being expressed as a percentage of the former Index figure.

(b) Materials

The Contract Price shall be adjusted at the rate of 0.475 per cent of the Contract Price per 1.0 per cent difference between the Price Index figure of Materials used in the Electrical Machinery Industry last published in the Trade and Industry Journal before the date of tender and the average of the Index Figures commencing with the Index last published before the two-fifths point of the Contract Period and ending with the Index last published before the four-fifths point of the Contract Period, this difference being expressed as a percentage of the former Index figure.

Fig. 9.11 Typical BEAMA clause for contract price adjustment

In both, the quoted price is based on the costs which apply at the date of tender, but the contract terms allow the price to be adjusted in line with cost increases which occur between date of tender and completion date.

In the first option, the seller is entitled to make the adjustment to the contract price which he or she considers to be justified by cost increases, and the buyer is entitled to request independent evidence that the adjustment is correct.

In the second, a formula is agreed for index-linking contract price: that is, for adjusting it in line with changes in published indexes of cost which are available both to buyer and seller. Contract clauses which define these arrangements are called contract price adjustment (CPA) clauses. They are also

---

BASIS OF CLAIM FOR CONTRACT PRICE ADJUSTMENT

Customer   John Smith   Customer's Order No   5002

A	Contract Price	£177 500
B	Tender or Cost Basis Date	20 Feb 1993
C	Date of order	12 March 1993
D	Date when ready for despatch/taking over	2 Jan 1994
E	Contract Period between C and D days	296 days
F	Data at one-third of Contract Period	19 June 1993
G	Date at two-fifths of Contract Period	8 July 1993
H	Date at four-fifths of Contract Period	4 Nov 1993
I	Labour Cost Index at tender or cost basis date	128.1
J	Average of Labour Cost Indices for period F to D	139.0
K	Department of Industry Index figures of Materials used in Electrical, Machinery or Mechanical Engineering Industries last published before tender or cost basis date	195.9
L	Average of Department of Industry Index figures commencing with index last published before date at G and ending with the Index last published before date at H	202.8

$$\text{M Labour Adjustment} \quad 47.5 \times \frac{J-I}{I} = \frac{10.9}{128.1} \times 47.5 = 4.0418\%$$

$$\text{N Materials Adjustment} \quad 47.5 \times \frac{L-K}{K} = \frac{6.9}{195.9} \times 47.5 = 1.6730\%$$

P *Total percentage Adjustment for Labour and Material = 5.7148%*

TOTAL PRICE ADJUSTMENT

$$= A \times \frac{P}{100} = £177\ 500 \times \frac{5.7148}{100} = £10\ 140$$

Fig. 9.12 Calculating the price adjustment

called escalation (or escalator) clauses. Some of them are very complicated. The Osborne formula for building works lists forty-eight basic work categories plus five special engineering installation categories, and cost variation in each of these is separately evaluated.

On the other hand, the BEAMA formula is about as simple as a CPA formula can be without becoming unrealistic, and consequently has been very widely used in all sorts of industries.

The British Electrical and Allied Manufacturers Association first agreed this formula many years ago on the basis that 40 per cent of a contract price could be attributed to labour costs, and 45 per cent to material costs, and these could be adjusted by reference to published indexes for labour and material costs. The remaining 15 per cent of contract price was regarded as invariable, because the intention was not to increase profits but to compensate the seller for cost increases. Subsequent alterations to these weightings have been made. A recent version is shown in Figure 9.11.

The BEAMA CPA Advisory Service sends monthly notifications of labour and material cost index figures used in the formula to subscribers. These are also available from government statistical offices. How these figures are used to make adjustments to the contract price may be seen in principle from the example in Figure 9.12.

LEARNING CURVES AND EXPERIENCE CURVES

We turn now to an empirical relationship between the cost of performing a task and the number of times it has been performed. In some instances cost decreases by a fixed percentage every time the total quantity made doubles.

Everyone knows that we can learn from experience. The first time a complicated product is built, fitters have to stop to consult drawings and work out how to do things. The second time, the work should go appreciably faster. By the time the twentieth product has been built, production time should be considerably reduced, and further reductions could well be achieved as the total quantity produced increases, although at a diminishing rate.

This can be shown on a graph, as in Figure 9.13b. It can also be drawn on a log–log graph as a straight line, as in Figure 9.13a, which is easier to work with. In this example, average labour hours to make the product reduce by 80 per cent every time the total accumulated quantity made doubles.

Learning curves can be very useful in working out the right price when complicated products, such as aircraft (one of the earliest applications) are made in relatively small quantities. The problem for the buyer is that average cost of production for the first order placed is not a good guide for the next order because of the learning effect. Obtaining quotes from other possible suppliers is not much help either; since they would have to start from scratch and thus would be in a similar position to the existing supplier at the beginning of the first order. There might also be problems with quality, tooling and delivery. Learning curves can be a big help in establishing the right price for a repeat order with the existing supplier.

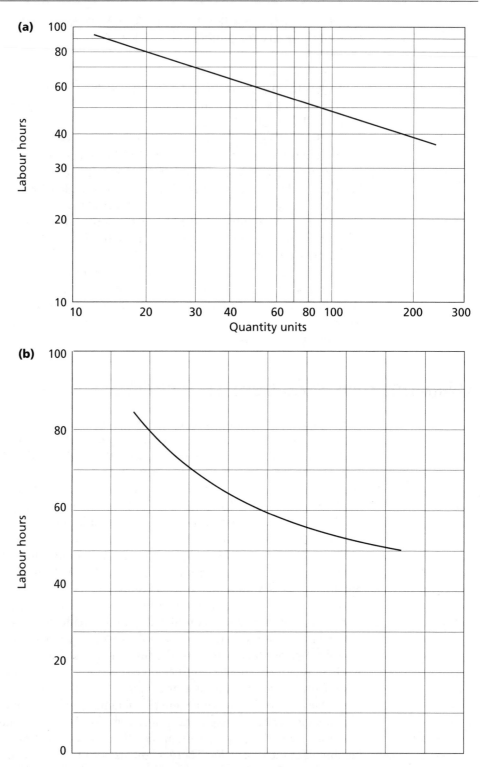

Fig. 9.13 Learning curve (80 per cent): (a) as usually drawn on log–log graph paper; (b) as drawn on ordinary graph paper

Learning curves refer to the reduction in labour cost because of reduction in the average time taken. Changes in rates of pay also affect labour cost, usually increasing it, so it is better to calculate the expected reduction in terms of time taken rather than in terms of cost.

The learning curve can be a most useful purchasing tool in situations of the kind to which it is relevant, and in such circumstances the buyer will find it worthwhile to spend some time acquiring a working knowledge of the tool and how to use it.

The term improvement curve is sometimes used to mean the same thing as learning curve, but it is also used to refer to the general improvement in production costs which many industries achieve. The learning effect in labour hours is one factor in this, but there are many other factors, such as increased scale, special-purpose machinery, changes in manufacturing process or product design. In recent years a 70 per cent experience curve effect has been observed in electronics. This is a most dramatic rate of cost reduction, but everyone has seen the prices of electronic watches, for instance, tumble. In power tools an 80 per cent experience curve has been seen. Knowledge of these experience effects can be useful to the buyer, but it is not a buying tool like the learning curve; its main use is in marketing and company policy, according to Hax and Majluf (1982).

CONCLUSION

Traditionally the buyer has had to concentrate his or her attention on price. Today by working closely with key suppliers and concentrating on driving out unnecessary costs throughout the supply chain, prices can be considerably reduced. Such a venture requires that cost transparency and strategic acquisition costs become part of the buyer's vocabulary.

SUMMARY POINTS

- The chapter explains how pricing is affected by market conditions, competition levels, the product's life cycle, cost of production and perceived value.
- The authors outline the various methods of costing and where they are most applicable – cost based pricing for specifically built goods; mark up pricing for retail goods, etc. All techniques aim to cover overheads and profit.
- Discounts may be offered for prompt payment, quantity or for seasonal/promotional reasons. Stockists/agents, in assisting the producer in distribution, will also attract a discount.
- Price analysis attempts to determine if the price offered is appropriate. The cost of alternatives and historical price may be used as a comparison. Lower prices may be offered as a way to enter a market, whilst a higher one may be a polite refusal or because the specification is greater than requested.
- Price increases may be agreed by mutual consent for the duration of the contract. More commonly, escalation formulae indexing linking contract price are used.

REFERENCES AND FURTHER READING

Ellram L (1993), 'Total cost of ownership: elements & implementation', *International Journal of Purchasing and Materials Management*, 29 (4).

Emmanuel C (1992), *Transfer Pricing*, London Chartered Institute of Management Accounting.

Hax A C and Majluf N S (1982), 'Competitive cost dynamics: the experience curve', *Interfaces*, 12 (5), October.

Hubbard R G and Weiner R J (1992), 'Long term contracting and multiple price systems', *Journal of Business*, 65 (2), April.

Imai M (1986), *Kaizen: The Key Japan's Competitive Success*, McGraw Hill, New York.

Sako M (1992), *Prices Quality and Trust: Inter-Firm Relations in Britain and Japan*, Cambridge University Press, Cambridge.

Lamming R, Jones D and Nicol D (1996), 'Cost Transparency: A Source of Supply Chain Competitive Advantage?', IPSERA Conference, April.

Lamming R (1993), *Beyond Partnership – Strategies for Innovation and Loan Supply*, Prentice Hall, New York.

Schillewaert N (1996), 'Total Cost of Acquisition as an Instrument for Supplier Evaluation', IPSERA Conference, April.

CHAPTER 10

Purchasing negotiations

INTRODUCTION

It is generally accepted that a key competence in a purchasing executive is an ability to negotiate. Negotiations may involve dealing with a single issue or many. They may be conducted on a one-to-one basis or between teams of negotiators representing different interests, and may be conducted over the telephone in a matter of minutes, or take many months to complete. It is also worth mentioning that negotiations are not necessarily confined to the buyer–seller relationship; many purchasing negotiations take place on an intra-organisational basis, involving the reconciliation of the views of supplies staff and colleagues. In this chapter we explore the nature of negotiation, and give some practical guidance.

OBJECTIVES OF THIS CHAPTER

- To understand negotiating as a 'mutuality of wants, resolved by exchange'
- To identify the activities carried out during the different stages of negotiation
- To analyse the characteristics of a skilled negotiator
- To recognise the key points of discussion stage behaviour and recognise negotiating ploys
- To introduce the concept of body language and how it can be interpreted
- To view how negotiating technique is influenced by long term interests.

NEGOTIATION

There have been many attempts to define negotiation for example 'to confer with others in order to reach a compromise or agreement' (Oxford Encyclopedic English Dictionary); or 'the process by which we search for terms to obtain what we want from somebody who wants something from us' (*Managing Negotiations*, Kennedy *et al.*, 1980). The latter definition points up a key factor: that negotiation implies some mutuality of wants, resolved by exchange.

It is perhaps worth mentioning at this stage that negotiation has two other meanings, not closely related to its 'bargaining' connotation. Negotiation may be employed by a mariner or navigator to mean something like 'finding a way', whereas a banker might employ the term to mean 'exchange for value' as, for example, a cheque or bill of exchange is negotiated. Purchasing and supply is certainly concerned with exchanging for value, and with finding new ways of doing business, but we shall confine our attention in this chapter to the more conventional usage of the term.

However defined, bargaining negotiation is seen as a process whereby agreement is sought. One should not forget that there are alternative ways of reaching agreement that do not involve negotiations and can be appropriate and effective in the right circumstances.

Alternatives to negotiation

Some alternatives to negotiation are:

1 *Persuade* Encourage the other side to accept the merits of a particular case with no concessions from yourself.
2 *Give in* Accept totally what the other side offers.
3 *Coerce* Insist that the other side meets your demands 'or else'.
4 *Problem solve* Remove the difference, so that there is no need to negotiate.

A vast amount of literature has emerged on the theory and practice of negotiation, and the topic continues to provide scope for a considerable amount of research and publication. The material available could generate several doctoral studies and much learned analysis and discussion at both a practical and academic level. Good theory, after all, mirrors and formalises descriptions of practice. Thus, helpful guidelines for the practising manager should have a close relationship with the theoretical findings of the academic.

We have drawn upon a considerable bank of knowledge in developing this chapter. A dilemma was to select a framework around which we might present a helpful section of the book for the diverse readership of this text. Our solution was to take our own framework, and relate other work to it as pertinent. In so doing, it is our intention that the practising manager or buyer might find the discussion helpful as it relates to his or her day-to-day negotiations, while the student who wished to consider the theories in greater depth would be provided with a starting point for his or her study. It should be emphasised that in using this framework we are not claiming its excellence over others. It is presented purely to provide a structure for discussion. However, it would be surprising if we did not believe it to be a sensible basis for such discussion, having used it as a structure in helping to develop negotiating skills in many thousands of managers around the world.

It should be noted, too, that in working with these managers we have learnt a great deal from them which has helped us hone the model and the ideas which are put forward in this chapter. Like salesmen, buyers need to be proficient in such skills as asking good questions, listening, interpreting trends in the negotiation, pre-planning a negotiation and ensuring that what is agreed is implemented. They need to be able, too, to analyse and interpret information and to be aware of the dangers of making unwarranted assumptions. Since negotiation is an interpersonal process, they need to understand something about human behaviour, needs and motivation: they need to develop interactive skills.

The three phases of negotiation

It is useful to consider negotiation conceptually as a three-phase process, as shown in Figure 10.1

The first of the three phases is the preparatory stage, when the information is analysed, the objectives are set and strategies developed. The meeting phase is concerned with the process of discussion, further information collection and analysis, and with the reaching of agreement between the parties. The final stage involves the implementation of the agreement within and between the organisations represented in the previous phase.

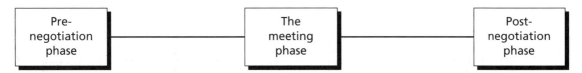

Fig. 10.1 The basic phases of negotiation

This is a simple model; apart from the elements of the meeting phase, which will be discussed later, the process of negotiation may involve several meetings. The preparation stage may then require consideration of phased objectives. For example, it may be that the first meeting between the parties will be concerned solely with exploratory discussions: both sides may need to clarify the issues of the negotiation and there will always be the need to obtain more information.

A subsequent meeting (or meetings) might be concerned with discussions leading towards the desired agreement. In some cases, agreement may be reached in one meeting, in others the situation might necessitate a further meeting(s) to conclude the agreement. Figure 10.2 extends the model by way of illustrating such a situation.

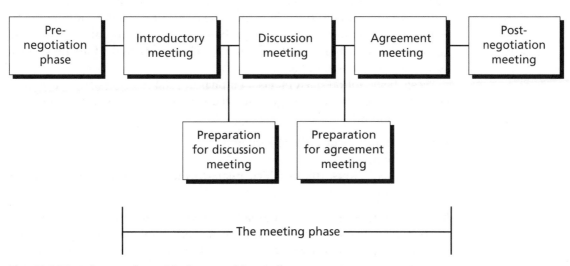

Fig. 10.2 The phases of negotiation – multi-meeting

This expanded model has applications even when the negotiation is concluded at a single meeting. Figure 10.3 illustrates the same model adapted for a single meeting.

In considering the elements of this model here, some of the key skills and concepts involved will be discussed. However, it is not the intention to attempt a comprehensive treatment, for this would be outside the scope of this chapter. None the less, as has been indicated, the reader, whether academic or practising manager, should be able to build from this base, perhaps in conjunction with the books and articles which are listed at the end of this chapter.

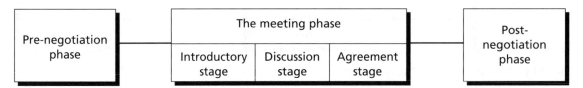

Fig. 10.3 The phases of negotiation – single meeting

What is a skilled negotiator?

Rackham and Carlisle (1978), who pioneered an analytical approach to negotiating skills development, argue that there are three criteria which relate to successful negotiators:

● They should be rated as effective by both sides.
● They should have a track record of significant success.
● They should have a low incidence of implementation failures.

They emphasise behavioural and interactive factors such as: 'image', integrity, status and self-actualisation. Then they stress one of the significant findings of our own research, which is that problems frequently occur in converting agreements into action. It is this feature which appears in the foregoing model as the 'post-negotiation phase'.

These behavioural factors also emphasise another important aspect of negotiation. This is that in negotiation there are two basic areas which need to be borne in mind:

● The corporate issues (those pertaining to the organisations involved in the negotiation).
● The human issues (those which relate to the individuals involved in the negotiation).

It is not that these issues are mutually exclusive; rather that concentration on one group to the exclusion of the other can result in invalid assumptions about the behaviour of the other party. A recognition of these, often interrelated but separate, aspects of a negotiation can be an extremely important feature of all phases of the model introduced earlier. In addition they have a considerable bearing on success.

Behavioural aspects of negotiation are probably those which have attracted the most academic attention in the literature. For example, Spector (1977) argues that:

'Persons, in the roles of negotiators are required to communicate positions, make demands and concessions, respond to changing signals and arrive at outcomes.'

He adds that the resolution of conflicting interests through negotiation is motivated by:

- The individual personality needs of negotiators.
- The personality compatibility among negotiators representing opposing parties.
- Negotiators' perceptions and expectations of the opponent – his or her strengths and weaknesses, intentions and goals, and commitments to positions.
- Persuasive mechanisms employed to modify the bargaining positions and values of the opponent to achieve a more favourable convergence of interests.

As will be seen, these features overlay and add to those described by Rackham and Carlisle. They emphasise the complexity of the negotiation process and demonstrate the problems of the behavioural scientist in grappling with studies involving so many variables.

It follows that the skilled negotiator needs to be aware of the many variables which may be present in a negotiation. Further, that if he or she is to be successful, he or she needs to be able to apply relevant skills at all phases of the negotiation process.

Preparation

A recurring finding of our own work is that the major source of difficulty for negotiators is inadequate management of the pre-negotiation phase. The implications of this finding include the fact that most managers believe they would have achieved better results had they prepared more effectively. Further, that those who are successful tend to have adequately managed the pre-negotiation phase.

Not every negotiation necessitates the same measure of preparation, and the amount of time spent will depend upon the complexity of the negotiation and its importance to the organisation concerned. The manager him/herself must decide, in each case, how long to spend on preparation. In cases involving long-term relationships (e.g. with key suppliers) it could be argued that preparation is continuous: certainly this is true of information gathering. However, the particular circumstances which apply in a given market at, say, May 1997 will probably be quite different from those which were experienced a year earlier. The economic climate, competition and the company's own situation are key variables which may have changed. A negotiation at the latter date will involve careful consideration of changes in the present situation, in addition to what has occurred in the past and what is likely to occur in the future.

Features of preparation

Kennedy identifies three key considerations in preparation for negotiation:

1 What do we want? This question may not be as easy to answer as we might at first imagine. Our wants may not become crystal clear until we enter discussion with the other side. They may, for example, include:
   (a) a lower price;
   (b) an improved relationship;
   (c) a bigger discount;
   (d) faster delivery; and/or
   (e) changes in quality.
   The range of negotiable variables in most buyer–seller relationships or transactions is very wide.

2 How valuable is each of our 'wants' to us? Perhaps, for example:
   (a) prompt delivery = high priority;
   (b) lower price = medium priority; and
   (c) quality changes = low priority.

3 What are my entry and exit points? Your entry point is really your 'opening bid'. Once disclosed, you are unlikely to better it, so the bid obviously requires careful thought. The exit point is your 'walk away' position. It is clearly desirable that this should be identified and understood at the preparatory phase, if only to obviate the possibility of striking a bargain which may be regretted later. If your exit point and your opposite number's exit points do not overlap then the probability of achieving a deal is severely reduced, though of course an apparent gap can be closed through negotiation, and an overlap achieved.

Figure 10.4 shows, first, a situation where the buyer's and seller's ranges of possibility do not overlap, and secondly, a situation where the gap is replaced by overlap, and a range of mutually satisfactory outcomes are possible. Note

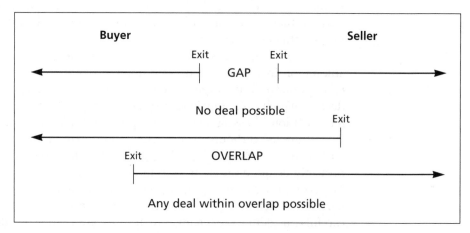

Fig. 10.4 Ranges of possibility

that the overlap does not suggest a single possible outcome; there is an infinite range of possibilities between the two exit points.

Rackham and Carlisle (1978) make a useful point regarding preparation when they suggest that 'it is not the amount of planning time which makes for success, but how it is used'. This apparently obvious conclusion is worth discussion for two reasons. The first is that their analysis indicates some aspects of the emphasis of the successful negotiator's pre-negotiation behaviour. The second is that those who are less successful may need, initially at least, to spend more time in preparation in order to cover the same ground. As with most areas of human activity, a major aspect of expertise is the ability to focus on the important issues and deal with them effectively in a given circumstance. Or as it has been put, doing the right things as well as doing things right.

Rackham and Carlisle suggest, for example, that the skilled negotiator considers a wider range of outcomes or options for action than his or her average counterpart. They show that the former typically considers twice as many outcomes/options per issue, both which they might introduce, and which might be raised by the other party. They emphasise that this wider-ranging analysis provides a major preparation for exploring every opportunity to obtain 'a better deal for both parties' (Karrass, 1972) during the actual negotiation.

Another of their findings relates to the time spent in preparation on areas of agreement as against those of potential conflict. They found that successful negotiators, while spending as much time on conflict areas, gave three times as much attention to common ground aspects as did average negotiators. They imply from this that concentration on 'common ground' areas may be the key to 'building a satisfactory climate'. Our own conclusion that the negotiator should build from a platform of known agreement supports this finding, though it will be clear that such an emphasis should not be confined to the preparation stage. Indeed, for best effect, it will extend through all the phases of negotiation suggested by Figure 10.3.

Our own observations suggest another important feature of preparation, that is, the necessity to differentiate between 'facts' and 'assumptions'. Many problems stem from the negotiator's inability to recognise whether the data with which he or she is working are factual or not. Clearly, if his or her objectives and strategies are based upon invalid assumptions, the negotiator will find him/herself in difficulty during the negotiation itself. A sound procedure which we have noted, used by successful negotiators, involves:

- specifying the key assumptions which are implied at the preparation stage;
- giving them some weight of probability, which helps signal the level of necessity to develop alternatives; and
- testing these assumptions, particularly in the introductory stage of the negotiation.

Among the advantages of this approach is the fact that negotiators may be forced to develop alternatives if the bases of their thinking are challenged. In other words, negotiators will be obliged to consider more options as a result of questioning. One consequence of this is that they will align themselves with the pattern of behaviour of the successful negotiators discussed earlier.

A further aspect of preparation which we have noted as resulting in negotiators being less effective in negotiations than they might have been is their perception of the strength of their position *vis-à-vis* the other party. Generally speaking, we have found that negotiators understate their own strengths, while overstating those of the other party. There is a tendency, too, to understate the weaknesses of the other party's position while over-emphasising their own. Not surprisingly, more successful negotiators are better at analysing both aspects.

It could be argued that the successful negotiator has learned:

- to increase the level of his or her perception of the strengths of his or her position; and
- to influence the views of the other party in line with his or her own.

Clearly, perceptions associated with relative strengths and weaknesses in negotiation have a great deal to do with assumptions. Thus this implies a further advantage for the negotiator in questioning the key assumptions which he or she is making. It also emphasises the need to consider such questions as: 'What do we believe to be the views of the other party on relative strengths and weaknesses?' 'What are our own?' 'Can we influence their views to our advantage?', and 'How might we do this?'

It is important in this analysis to recognise that 'strengths and weaknesses' do not simply refer to the negotiating positions of both parties. As will be seen from Table 10.1 a wide variety of variables may impinge upon a negotiation, including, for example: information, time and tenacity.

Table 10.1 Some 'personnel' factors in negotiation

Ability to:	Influence control; avoid conflict; deal with conflict creatively; interpret NV signs; analyse other party's position; form and use questions; listen; use verbal skills; maintain concentration and control discussion; persuade.
Traits:	Risk-taking propensity; level of commitment; level of loyalty; level of self-esteem.
Background:	Intelligence; fitness; age; race; sex; class; ethics.
Experience:	Of negotiation; of type of negotiation; of other party's company; of other party.
Approach:	Negotiating style; management style.
Status:	Personal conception of other party.

Collecting information

The information required in order to prepare for any negotiation will be unique to that situation. The manager concerned has to make a judgement as to the quality of the information which is collected. Quite apart from these two considerations, there will also be a time constraint on the collection of the data. In part, this will result from the resources allocated to the task and partly from the length of time available to the negotiation. Even the type of information which is collected in order to prepare will depend upon the circumstances surrounding the negotiation. None the less, the following questions are typical of those which the negotiator might ask of him/herself and his or her colleagues in a purchasing negotiation.

The current agreement (where one exists)

- What is the duration of the current agreement?
- What is the financial history regarding part transactions (e.g. pricing history)?
- What cost data are available?
- What has the supplier's delivery performance record been like?
- What has their quality record been like?
- What disputes have arisen over the period of the contract? Are they pertinent as far as the coming negotiation is concerned?
- By what date should agreement be reached?
- With whom will we be negotiating? (e.g. name the individuals; what is known about them)?

Some specification issues

- Has the supplier been given the opportunity to improve the value in the specification?
- What aspects of it are critical?
- Which can be varied to achieve the same function?
- How is conformity with specification to be measured?
- Who will do that measurement and where?
- If the item is a special item, is it possible to replace it with a standard?

Some delivery issues

- How frequently do we wish the supplier to deliver?
- In what quantities?
- How will the material/components be delivered?
- Who is responsible for packaging/pallets/containers?
- Which is the delivery address?
- Are there restrictions there (e.g. timing of delivery, size of lorry)?
- If the purchases are to be delivered in a container/rail truck, what is the position regarding demurrage?

Some financial issues

- In what currency is the transaction to be made?
- If a foreign currency, what rate of exchange is to be agreed?
- What dates are important in this respect?
- What credit terms apply?
- What are the general terms of payment (e.g. against letter of credit, free on board)?
- Does the supplier require stage payments?
- If so, are these terms negotiable?
- Is there a set discount for early payment?
- How could this be improved?

Some contractual issues

- Who is responsible for insurance?
- What is the level of cover? For what?

- Under which country's law is the contract made (in the case of a purchase from a foreign supplier)?
- Are customs requirements clearly stated?
- Has the method of transportation been agreed satisfactorily?
- Do the purchase terms clearly delineate responsibility for elements of purchase cost?
- Has the offer been accepted by the supplier in a manner which ensures a valid contract?
- Have your administrative requirements been clearly stated and understood?

Some personnel issues

- With whom are you going to negotiate? (individuals).
- What do you know about them?
- If a team is to be involved, what will it comprise?
- Do these people have the authority to come to an agreement?
- Which of these people will be responsible for ensuring that what is agreed is implemented?
- Which people at the supplier's factory/office are to be the key contacts?
- What should our team comprise?
- Who is to lead?

Some general issues

- What are our strengths and weaknesses?
- What are those of the other party?
- What is the duration of the agreement to be negotiated?
- What published data are available?
- What is the current contractual position?
- By what date should agreement be reached?
- What are the major issues?
- What key assumptions have been made?
- What information do we need to verify those assumptions?

Having assembled and analysed the relevant information it is then necessary to:

1 set objectives for the coming negotiation(s);
2 develop strategies/tactics in order to achieve those objectives;
3 prepare relevant data for easy reference;
4 if more than one person is to be involved in the negotiation, to develop a method of working which is understood and agreed by all concerned;
5 make the necessary arrangements for the meeting phase.

Objectives

Meaningful objectives are essential to successful negotiating, yet the authors' experience in working in negotiating training over many years is that rarely are they meaningful and clearly defined. This failure has proved to be particularly damaging in team negotiations where ambiguity has led to confusion, the disruption of team solidarity or the failure of a particular tactical approach. It can help to write down the agreed objective(s) for the coming negotiation. If they have been properly thought through, they will be the culmination of the manager's appraisal of the situation in hand; and writing them down will serve to ensure that those involved know:

- what is to be achieved; and
- upon what assumptions those objectives have been based.

It is important to recognise that the objectives which are set will be based upon an assessment of the situation given existing information. If some of the information proves to be faulty, then it may be necessary to change the stated objectives and probably the methods by which they are to be achieved. This is why the introductory stage of the meeting phase is important; the negotiators should seek to verify at least the data upon which they have based their tactics and objectives. Our own experience confirms that of Karrass (1972) as to the way skilled negotiators develop objectives. They tend to set upper and lower limits to a derived target, rather than simply stating a single point. In addition they tend to have higher aspirations.

The reasons for this behaviour stem from the problems associated with the validity of information at the preparation stage, which were discussed earlier.

Since negotiators deal with a mixture of fact and assumption, they cannot *know* that an objective is valid at the pre-negotiation stage. Thus they provide themselves with a range within which they work. Karrass argues that this often enhances the aspiration levels of the negotiators. It also allows them to calculate the various implications of maximum and minimum positions in their preparation. The effects of movement in either direction can then be monitored more easily during the negotiation proper.

Issues

To conclude this section of the chapter, the important aspect of issues should be noted. In every negotiation there is a series of issues which needs to be resolved. The weight of these issues in the eyes of either party will depend upon a mixture of their perceptions as well as real pressures which are being applied. Thus, an understanding of what is at issue as perceived by the negotiator, and his or her belief of what is accepted by the other party are vital elements in preparation.

Rackham and Carlisle, in illustrating how effective negotiators deal with issues which they perceive to be important, add a further element to this discussion. They note that skilled negotiators do not assume that they will be able to deal with issues in a sequential way according to their own plans. They note a propensity to plan around each issue in a manner which is independent of sequence. They argue that this approach provides the negotiator with greater flexibility. It also ensures that he or she does not make the assumption that the other party will be prepared to deal with issues in the negotiator's preferred sequence. Thus it increases the options which emerge for consideration.

THE INTRODUCTORY STAGE

Successful negotiators in the introductory stage (*see* Figure 10.3) tend to expend considerable effort in:

- Establishing an atmosphere conducive to agreement. This may include: social interchange; giving an impression of wishing to work to a mutually advantageous goal; the physical arrangements of the site; and re-stating the areas of agreement while avoiding irritators.
- Validating assumptions.
- Testing the other party's position, willingness to collaborate or propensity to oppose.
- Clarifying issues and the weight given to them by the other party.
- Trying to ascertain whether any new information will be introduced by the other party.

From our own experience, working with more than 7000 managers in small groups over the years, some prescriptive points may be made:

- *Be on time*. Being late necessitates an apology, signals a lack of organisation and results in the negotiator having to go into the negotiation hurriedly.
- *Emphasise the positive*. As suggested earlier, build from a base of known agreement, change 'but' to 'and' whenever qualifying a statement from the other party.
- *Make brief opening statements*. Listen, and be seen to be listening, to the other party.
- *Do not make quick decisions*.

In this, and indeed in all three stages of the meeting phase, the three skills used to the greatest effect by skilled negotiators are questioning, listening and observing.

DISCUSSION STAGE

Most of the actual negotiation time after preparation is spent on the debate stage. At this stage we are, amongst other things, endeavouring to first test our assumptions and find out what the other side wants.

In the course of the debate stage there will be discussion and argument. Ideally one should attempt to keep this as objective as possible.

There are a number of important points to remember here:

- Debate, while promoting the negotiation process, can also, if not handled correctly, hinder or deadlock deals.
- You cannot negotiate arguments. No matter how often you argue and disagree with the other side it does not help move forward the negotiation. We would advocate that you make proposals to overcome arguments. In other words, suggest a solution that could overcome the problem.

- Avoid destructive debate attacking/blaming the other side.
- Regular summarising during this stage helps to avoid later confusion.
- If the other side does not have an agenda, you could suggest one.
- Try to establish a rapport quickly with the other side – watch for the signals or body language that are indicative of how the other side feels and wishes to proceed.

Bargaining

During discussions we move on to the bargaining stage. This is the point when we convey the specific terms on which we would settle; for example: 'If you reduce your price by 3 per cent we will increase our order by 10 per cent.' Both the condition and offer are specific. Even at this stage, however, offers might not be accepted; there could be problems that take the two sides back into the preparation stage.

Ploys in negotiation

During discussions negotiators will from time to time be faced with one side using a ploy or tactic to try and gain advantage over the other.

Roy Webb of Negotiate plc, one of the better known negotiating trainers in the UK believes that such ploys are of limited value in long-term relationships. He comments as follows:

- All ploys have counters that a seasoned negotiator would be aware of.
- Reliance on ploys can often ruin a long-term relationship.
- Ploys, when recognised, can be disarmed.
- While a knowledge of ploys assists the negotiation, reliance on them exclusively should be avoided.

Examples of ploys

Nice guy/ hard guy
You are faced by two people, one difficult to deal with and aggressive, the other softer and conciliatory. The idea is that you become so afraid of the 'hard guy' that you make concessions to the softer negotiator.

Add ons
Basic deal only is negotiated. Everything else costs more money.

Deadlines
Telling the other side the deal has to be completed by a certain time otherwise it is off. The idea being to pressurise the other side into making a quick rather than the correct decision.

Russian front
Two choices are offered, of which one is so bad that you choose the second, less awful, option.

Empty larder
Attempting to convince the other side by lying that you have little to offer so that they will reduce their demands.

Approval from a higher authority

Telling the other side that anything you agree to over a certain amount will also have to be agreed back at base. The idea being to get the other side to agree to deals that do not require approval from a higher authority.

These are some of a large number of ploys that are used in negotiations and for which you should be prepared.

As one moves, however, towards building up long-term relationships with suppliers there is far less reliance and indeed positive avoidance of such tactics in an effort to enhance a strategic relationship between buyer and supplier.

Professor Gavin Kennedy argues that all ploys can be neutralised by the other side provided they have the necessary experience. The following are examples to illustrate (*see* Fig. 10.5a).

Negotiation ploys	Methods of dealing with ploys
Nice guy/hard guy	Either style match or adopt contrast style
Add ons	Carefully check what you are getting for your money before agreement
Deadlines	Avoid revealing what time you have to finish
	Agree to meet another time
Russian front	Do not accept poor deals. What is your best alternative to a negotiated agreement?
Empty larder	Ask for an explanation of any constraints in deal
	Offer what you can within those constraints

Fig. 10.5 Manipulative techniques and ploys

AGREEMENT STAGE

If a bargain is accepted we have agreement and the negotiations are concluded. Once there is agreement it is advisable to record full details of what has been agreed and to circulate these details to interested parties.

THE POST-NEGOTIATION STAGE

The final stage in our model follows the negotiation itself. Like Rackham and Carlisle, we have found that successful negotiators work to ensure that agreements are implemented. Less successful negotiators pay insufficient attention to this. It might be said that no negotiation is complete until what has been agreed is enacted.

Typically, skilled negotiators confirm with the other party what has been agreed. They also specify who is to do what, and by when, not only as between them and the other party, but also in their own organisation. Failure to perform will always have an adverse effect on relationships between the parties. It will, for example, result in a lack of trust or of belief in the other party's abilities or authority. Consequently, if there is another negotiation (and many purchasing transactions involve long-standing partners), this will have a bearing on the behaviour of both parties. The reader need only consider his or her own feelings at being let down on a delivery promise by a supplier. How does he or she approach the next negotiation with that party?

Our prescriptive guidelines for the post-negotiation phase include:

- Produce the first draft agreement. Despite the fact that you are reporting, honestly, what you believe to have been agreed, it will be your version, developed from your viewpoint. In addition, the other party will be freed from doing the initial draft – a fact which will be appreciated by most people. Clearly, the draft should be sent to the other party with the request for his or her comments and agreement. A sound piece of work can do much for ongoing relationships.
- Ensure the commitment of people in your organisation to making the agreement work.
- Prepare official contracts in line with the agreement.
- Remember no negotiation is successful until what has been negotiated is done.
- Find time to evaluate performance, first in negotiation, and second in enactment.

COMPETITION AND CO-OPERATION IN NEGOTIATION

When a negotiation takes place it is usually assumed that there is some conflict of interest between the parties involved. The logic stemming from this is that because of this conflict the parties involved will oppose each other in order to achieve their preferred ends. The word 'opponent' is then placed in a 'game' context where one side will 'win' over the other, and their gain will result from the other's loss. Yet the appeal of this thinking is bounded by a simplistic assumption that negotiation is a 'zero-sum' process. That is, that there is a 'cake' of x units which is to be shared between the parties. In a purchasing context, for example, A wishes to sell to B 10 000 components at £x each, whereas B wishes to pay £x – 10 per cent. An outcome in which B is obliged to pay £x for the items then places A as the 'winner'. However, the price of the components may be only one of the points at issue. For example, the rate of delivery, batch size and point of storage could all change the 'shape' of the cost package from the point of view of both parties. Thus by examining the many variables involved, the negotiators might be able to arrive at a more creative solution in which both parties gain.

It is, of course, a moot point whether one side will gain more than the other even then, and in a strictly quantitative sense have a larger share of the

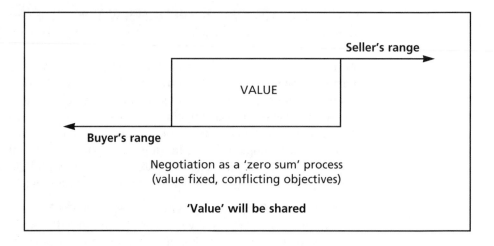

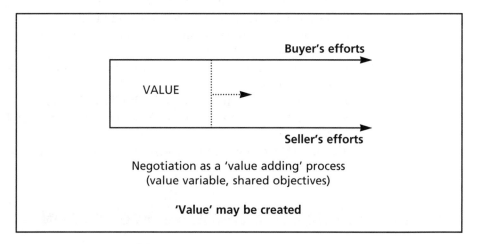

Fig. 10.6 Two views of the negotiation process

perceived 'cake', however, the psychological drive of a negotiator seeking (and being seen to be seeking) mutually advantageous solutions can be considerable. This does not imply that either side should be 'soft' with the other. Rather it suggests that they may each gain greater advantage by collaborating rather than competing. Figure 10.6 contrasts the 'zero sum' perspective with the collaborative approach.

It is reasonable to argue that in some circumstances it will be difficult, perhaps incorrect, to follow this approach. For example, the behaviour (past or present) of the other party, or environmental pressures, may suggest more aggressive/competitive behaviour. However, it is worthwhile making a further point which may influence the negotiator's behaviour in such circumstances. Most major buyer/seller negotiations tend to result in longer-term relationships being developed or extended. Thus a 'win' for either party when circumstances favour their position will tend to the converse when, for example, the market position changes. Consequently, immediate benefits need to be weighed against those pertaining to the longer term, and to the level of motivation of both parties to perform against agreed norms. There is, too, the important issue of trust.

BODY LANGUAGE

While over the centuries people have become more articulate, they have also developed an ability to hide how they really feel in situations. Thus as negotiators you may consider that the other side is being honest and open, but this may not be true. Although you may feel the other side is happy, this also may not be the case.

As a negotiator you must watch for the body language. No matter what people *say*, how they really *feel* can often be picked up from their body positions and gestures during the negotiations.

It is not our intention in this general text to go into any great detail in this area but below in Table 10.2 are a number of postures and what they might indicate.

Table 10.2 The interpretation of postures

Posture	Possible meaning
Leaning forward when making a point.	Interested; wants to emphasise a point.
Avoiding eye contact.	May be embarrassed; not telling the truth.
Arms folded. Body turned away from you.	Defensive; no compromise. Not interested.
Body turned towards you leaning forward.	Interested; warming towards your comments.
Looking away at watch or at a window.	Wants to leave or avoid any further discussion.
Hands supporting head and leaning back in chair.	Confidence.
Stroking nose regularly with a finger – avoiding eye contact.	May be lying.
Good eye contact. Fingers stroking face.	Interested in what you are saying.

One should, of course, be very careful in interpreting body language. You can get it wrong. Experienced negotiators, however, over a period of time get to understand the body language of the other side, which can contribute to increased effectiveness. A good negotiator must also be attuned to the way people answer and ask questions. From the other side's tone you can quickly pick up signals such as anger, impatience, annoyance and agreement.

NEGOTIATION STRATEGIES

How buyers negotiate with suppliers will be affected by their long-term interests. In the case of long-term strategic suppliers it is far more likely they will consider their negotiating approach in terms of:

- How it will affect future negotiations – e.g. a short-term manipulative or tactical strategy at the supplier's expense could jeopardise a long-term partnership agreement.
- Developing a supplier – a major buying organisation may well make considerable concessions to influence suppliers in order to encourage their development. However, with other suppliers a more aggressive negotiation stance may be taken.
- Reducing the supplier base – the preferred supplier may be given totally different treatment from others.

NEGOTIATION MIX

As you will now begin to appreciate, negotiations can take on different styles e.g. aggressive, assertive or submissive, or may be dominated by a manipulative as opposed to an assertive phased approach. During the negotiations body language will be studied. One cannot say definitely which is the best way to negotiate or which is the best style, much will depend on existing relationships and objectives. It is however argued by experienced negotiators that a purely short-term manipulative approach to negotiations based on *I win – you lose* leads to long-term problems. These days, particularly with a view to longer-term negotiation objectives, one finds a move towards more of a *win – win* approach based on trading wants and using the four-phased approach to reach a settlement.

CONCLUSION

Early in this chapter, three criteria to differentiate the successful negotiator were introduced. In conclusion, we put forward a more comprehensive list, which itself is far from definitive. Negotiation is a complex, fascinating subject which, since it involves people, contains many variables. This list and the related discussion are meant only to indicate the areas which we and other writers have noted as pertaining to successful negotiation. Those who negotiate successfully:

- Plan well.
- Can deal with pressure.
- Listen well.
- Understand people well.
- Observe well.

- Can handle confrontation.
- Have sound business judgement.
- Avoid excesses.
- Are creative thinkers.
- Are committed to their cause once established.
- Are skilled at dealing with risk.
- Are skilled at asking questions.
- Have higher aspirations.
- Can handle time effectively.

Finally, we complete this chapter with some practical hints derived from the experiences of major negotiators.

- *Negotiation is concerned with trading not conceding.*
- *Always trade something for something.*
- *Remember if you help me, then I'll help you.*
- *Attempt to educate the other side by putting a price on their demands.*
- *Listen to what they say.*
- *Avoid interrupting a proposal.*
- *Entry terms can influence the other side's expectations therefore open credibly, trade concession and do not fear deadlock.*
- *Good preparation is a must for successful negotiations.*
- *Don't tell lies, but there is no need to tell the other side about things that will give them an advantage.*
- *Avoid too many arguments, remember only proposals can be negotiated.*
- *Remember which phase you are in and act appropriately.*
- *Avoid sarcasm, blaming or point scoring.*
- *Agree an agenda.*
- *Avoid accepting the first offer.*
- *Test assumptions.*
- *Do not change the price, change the deal.*
- *Find out your best alternative to a negotiated agreement. It helps you to decide whether to agree or walk away.*
- *Value every 'tradable' in the other negotiator's terms.*
- *Identify your strategic objectives.*
- *Use ploys carefully and in a limited way. Remember if the other side feels on reflection after the negotiations they have got a bad deal it may ruin future deals.*
- *At the end of negotiations write down what has been agreed and show it to the other side for approval.*

SUMMARY POINTS

- Negotiation may not always be the appropriate way to reach an agreement – persuasion, complete acceptance, coercion or problem solving may prove a sound alternative.
- The author outlines three broad phases in the negotiation process: *preparatory* – analysing information, setting of objectives, and developing

strategies; *meeting* – introductions, clarification and the reaching of an agreement and *final* – implementation of the agreement.

- The chapter emphasises the importance of pre-negotiation preparation – evaluating the objectives, entry and exit points.
- A skilled negotiator considers a wide range of options; gives a great deal of attention to common ground aspects; is flexible dealing with issues as they arise. He/she confirms what has been agreed in a 'first draft' agreement which is then confirmed/commented upon by the other party.
- Negotiation style depends on the objective to be achieved – short term gain may use an aggressive, assertive style. This approach tends to lead to long term problems. A longer term 'win–win' approach based on trading wants is far more likely to reap reward – while one party may concede on price, it may be gaining on delivery or payment terms.

REFERENCES AND FURTHER READING

Beliaev E, Mullen T and Punnett E J (1985), 'Understanding the cultural environment: US–USSR trade negotiations', *California Management Review*, 27 (2), Winter.

Brynes J F (1981), 'Ten guidelines for effective negotiating', *Business Horizons*, 30 (3), May/June.

Coulson R (1983), 'Better results from bargaining', *Harvard Business Review*, Jan–Feb.

Fisher R and Ury W (1982), *Getting to Yes: Negotiating Agreement Without Giving In*, Penguin, New York.

Graham J (1985), 'The influence of culture on business negotiations', *Journal of International Business Studies*, 16, Spring.

Holmes G and Glasser S (1984), 'Guidelines for commercial negotiating', *Business Horizons*, 27 (1), Jan/Feb.

Karrass C L (1972), *The Negotiating Game*, World Books, New York.

Kennedy G (1985), *Negotiate Anywhere*, Hutchinson Business Books.

Kennedy G (1991), *Everything is Negotiable*, Arrow Books.

Kennedy G (1992), *The Perfect Negotiation*, Century Business Books.

Michelman J H (1983), 'Deception in commercial negotiation', *Journal of Business Ethics*, 2 (4), November.

Newman R G and Sowdo J (1988), 'Price analysis for negotiation', *Journal of Purchasing and Materials Management*, Spring.

Nielson R P (1990), 'Generic Win–Win negotiating solutions', *Long Range Planning*, 22 (5), pp. 137–143.

Pease A (1989), *Body Language*, Courier International.

Pease A (1993), *Body Language*, Sheldon Press.

Rackham N and Carlisle J (1978), 'The effective negotiator, parts I and II', *Journal of European Industrial Training*, 2 (6 and 7).

PART 3

Applications

Chapter 11
MAKE OR BUY DECISIONS
AND SUBCONTRACTING

Chapter 12
BUYING COMMODITIES

Chapter 13
BUYING INTERNATIONALLY

Chapter 14
CAPITAL GOODS

Chapter 15
PURCHASING FOR RESALE

Chapter 16
BUYING SERVICES

Chapter 17
BUYING FOR GOVERNMENT
AND PUBLIC SERVICES

INTRODUCTION TO PART THREE

Part 3 deals with specialist applications, covering areas of purchasing and supply activity that do not fall into the mainstream category. Chapter 11 is concerned with make-or-buy decisions and subcontracting, and deals with the major factors which influence such decision making, such as cost comparisons and strategic issues relating to make-or-buy. The do-or-buy question is also examined in relation to services. Subcontracting is a major theme of this chapter, and the problems of selecting and working with appropriate contractors are covered, with particular reference to the construction industry where subcontracting is, of course, a frequently adopted approach.

Commodities and their markets provide the theme for Chapter 12, which describes the major commodities and the way in which they are traded, and explains the reasons for fluctuating commodity prices. The way in which the terminal markets operate is explained, as is the role of the speculator. Futures, hedging, and some buying techniques for commodities are described in detail. This chapter includes a brief glossary of the terminology employed in commodity trading.

Chapter 13 deals with international trading, and includes a summary of the main problems encountered when sourcing internationally. The issues of payment, differing legal systems, communication, shipping and customs are all briefly visited. Countertrade is also covered in this chapter, and there is a brief introduction to the EC.

Capital goods are the theme of Chapter 14, an activity in which not all organisations employ their purchasing professionals. The nature of capital purchases is discussed and there is a note on the preparation of appropriate specifications. Investment appraisal and relevant criteria are topics which find a home in this chapter.

Purchasing for resale is, in many ways, similar to purchasing for consumption or embodiment, but there is a fundamental difference in that the goods are being acquired for onward sale to another party. For this reason a separate chapter (15) has been allocated to this topic. The buying procedures employed by retailers are explained, and there is an introduction to EPOS and other technology employed in this sector. Merchandising and brands are specialised themes covered by this chapter.

Chapter 16, on buying services, is concerned with differentiating goods from services, and discusses the EC services directive. The management of quality in service provision is also dealt with in this section. The final chapter of this section, Chapter 17 is concerned with buying *for* public services organisations, and provides an accompaniment to Chapter 16. EC Supplies Directives provide the main theme for this chapter.

CHAPTER 11

Make-or-buy decisions and subcontracting

INTRODUCTION

Make-or-buy decisions are decisions about the source of materials, goods, or services. The choice to be made is to produce the materials and goods and provide the service internally, or to purchase from a source external to the organisation (*see* Figure 11.1).

OBJECTIVES OF THIS CHAPTER

- To differentiate between make or buy decisions taken at lower levels (driven by operational needs), decisions taken at the highest levels (driven by strategic interests) and those in between taken for tactical reasons
- To identify what drives operational, tactical and strategic make or buy decisions
- To assess the advantages of subcontracting services
- To examine the case for out-sourcing the purchasing function
- To consider the responsibilities of the main contractor and subcontractors.

The significance of the choice to be made is measured by its effect on the organisation and the level at which the decision is taken. The most significant decisions fundamentally affect the nature of the business, the skills and numbers of employees, the style of management and the competitive position of the organisation. Less significant decisions can be routine choices to purchase from outside, these are easily reversible decisions taken at the operational level. This chapter deals with these decisions.

THE LEVEL AT WHICH MAKE-OR-BUY DECISIONS ARE TAKEN

The level at which these decisions are taken varies from the lowest level to which authority to make a purchase is delegated to the highest level, the directors or senior managers of an organisation – or somewhere in between. Decisions taken at the lower levels are driven by the operational needs of the organisation and those at the highest level by strategic interests.

We can think of these decisions as being located at three broad levels: operational, intermediate, and strategic. For example:

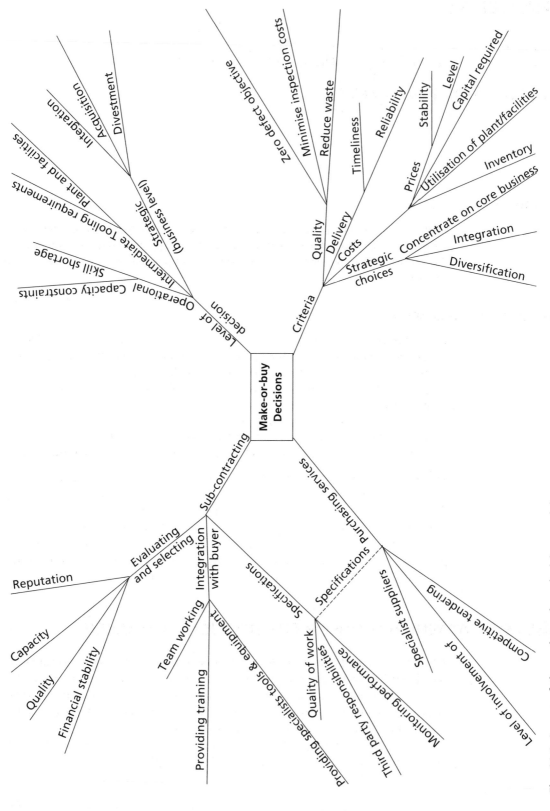

Fig. 11.1 A map of the make-or-buy decision model

- Decisions whether to source particular items internally, given the existing resources, are operational decisions which involve no changes in policy and are taken on a factual basis at departmental level. Internal sourcing (the 'make or buy' option) is excluded for any item which cannot be made on available plant using existing skills subject to capacity constraints. External sourcing (the 'buy' option) is excluded for items which can be made economically by the in-house manufacturing capacity.

- Tactical decisions might, for example, be concerned with considering the acquisition of additional equipment, personnel or other resources, without fundamental change in the asset basis, in order to manufacture internally what would otherwise have to be bought out; or, alternatively, the divestment of minor resources in order to source externally items which have previously been made internally.

- Strategic decisions on issues such as vertical integration and the acquisition of entire businesses in order to have an internal supplier of an important part or material are, in principle, senior management or director level decisions; as are decisions to close down or sell off major internal facilities in order to buy out instead of making internally. Questions such as 'What business are we in?', 'What business do we want to be in?' and 'What are the key strengths of our organisations and how are these best protected and developed?' are key, strategic issues.

TACTICAL DECISIONS

Tactical make-or-buy decisions will need to be reviewed as circumstances change. Some exigency is the usual reason for review; some common reasons for make-or-buy decisions at lower levels follow:

- Deterioration in an existing supplier's quality performance.
- Delivery failure or poor service by existing source.
- Large price increase.
- Volume changes: much larger or smaller quantity requirement for item concerned.
- Pressure to reduce costs.
- Desire to concentrate internal resources on areas of special competence.
- Need for design secrecy.
- Import substitution.

Emergencies cannot be prevented from happening, but too much 'fire fighting' implies a reactive management style; so, hurried, crisis decisions should be avoided as much as possible – a more proactive approach is called for. For instance, the whole range of materials, components and services purchased by the organisation should be reviewed to assess the likelihood of supply failure; and alternative sources, whether internal or external, could be considered on a 'What if?' basis: where could the goods be obtained if some problem occurred, such as those listed above? The supply market should be researched to discover changes which may have occurred in relation to such issues as copyright, patent protection and intellectual property to evaluate comparative costs and other factors relevant to the decisions.

OPERATIONAL DECISIONS

A general (but perhaps simplistic) rule is that prior to making a make-or-buy decision a comparison should be made between the cost of making (or, in the case of a service, 'doing') ourselves or buying in. If it is found to be cheaper to make ('do' if we are considering a service), then make it or buy it if that is cheaper. Why then is this simplistic – it seems straightforward enough? The reason is that a lot of decisions need to be made before a comparative evaluation can begin:

- What volume do we expect to require?
- What capital investment is required to make the goods?
- What will be our peak demand?
- How much risk is associated with the technology required?
- How much wastage (or cost of reworking) can we expect?
- What level of inventory will we (and our supplier) hold?
- For how long will the contract apply?
- What variations can be expected in materials costs?
- Can we make more by concentrating on our special competencies than we can save by carrying out the work internally?

Even when we have answered these questions there will be more; some more difficult, such as how much of our overhead should we attribute to the cost of making this item (carrying out this service)? So many assumptions taken together magnify the uncertainty associated with the decision. An omission of an important factor will distort the answer completely, giving a totally misleading picture.

Having said this, the argument is not that the analysis should not be conducted – it should! But great care should be taken to retain an objective view and be rigorously analytical. Qualified accountants will be able to fulfil the latter aim, but they will be reliant on the information provided to carry out the process. Professional bias may intrude, for example, the production department may wish to prove that it is cheaper to make because that is their business. This is human nature at work, so the purchasing manager should be alert to the possibility of bias, should examine any cost statements with care and should ask about things that seem relevant but do not appear in the statement. The purchasing manager should also challenge the realism of the assumptions upon which the cost statement is built – the decision-making process should, after all, be team effort.

Future prices and costs should also be considered in the light of the current and prospective economic conditions. Prices may be lower in times of recession and unrepresentative of what may be expected 2 to 3 years hence, when improvements in the economy lead to an increase in demand and rising prices. If substantial capital investment in specialist equipment is required to

If currently purchased from an outside source	If currently being manufactured within the company
• Does capacity exist within own company?	• Is there a matter of secrecy to be considered?
• If so, is such capacity likely to be available for the planning period involved?	• If the item is withdrawn from production, would redundancies result?
• Is the necessary raw material available now at economic rates?	• If 'yes', what action would need to be taken by management regarding those redundancies?
• Will that material continue to be available at economic rates for the planning period?	• If tooling is involved, what is its condition? Can it be used by the prospective source?
• If tooling is involved: (i) what is the cost? (ii) what is the expected life? (iii) what is the delivery?	• Will the machinery involved on current manufacture be fully utilised for alternative work if the part is withdrawn?
• Are we satisfied that the current supplier is the most economic source?	• Is there a possibility of development work being done on the part? If so, can this be done satisfactorily in conjunction with an outside supplier?
• Is there a patent and thus the possibility of royalties to be paid?	• Will the quantities involved interest an outside supplier?
• Is VAT chargeable (e.g. printing)?	• Do we know the true cost of alternative supply against manufacture (e.g. transport and handling costs) – present and forward?
• Is the current supplier doing development work towards an improved version of the item?	• Is the item part of an integrated production route involving several stages of manufacture? If so, can outside manufacture be satisfactorily co-ordinated with production schedules and machine loading in our shops?
• Has the current supplier had difficulty with either quality, quantity or time factors, and have his costs escalated as a result, thus affecting his selling price?	• What is the *forward* market position for the item concerned for the relevant planning period?
• If his quality has been affected: (a) has the supplier's quality system been vetted? (b) what has been the extent of quality failures? (c) is our production department confident that the specified quality can be economically maintained in internal production? (d) are we over-specifying?	• Are all drawings correct?
• If his other costs are escalating: (a) what are the reasons? (b) are we confident that we will not be affected in the same way?	• Is there any advantage in supplying raw materials/components if a decision is taken to buy?
• If the item is currently being imported, what is the cost breakdown? If duty is payable, what rate is applied? What duty, if any, will be payable on the relevant raw materials/ components if they are imported?	• Can we indicate to the potential supplier the remaining life of the product?
	• Can the potential supplier suggest ideas for taking cost out of the product?

Fig. 11.2 Make-or-buy checklist

produce goods internally, then the decision cannot be reversed within the economic life of the plant without losing money on the remaining capital value. It locks the purchaser into an internal source of supply.

Figure 11.2 provides a checklist which may help to ensure that relevant factors are not overlooked.

Other non-price considerations may also be relevant. One important consideration concerns the ability of the specialist supplier to innovate and find ways of improving the product or service. As discussed elsewhere in this book the success of the purchaser's organisation may be derived in part from improvements and increased value added in the goods and services being purchased.

STRATEGIC DECISIONS

C.K. Pralahad and G. Hamel wrote in the 1990 *Harvard Business Review* article that business development in the 1990s would depend on a corporation's ability to identify, to cultivate and to use its core competencies. These were prophetic words. Many organisations, large and small in both manufacturing and service operations have invested, and continue to invest, great amounts of effort in attempting to do just this. The fundamental questions of 'What business are we in?' and 'What business do we want to be in?' are, in essence, major make(do)-or-buy decisions and are at the root of corporate strategy. No commercial or public sector concern can undertake all the production of goods and services necessary to the business; and decisions of a strategic nature will need to be taken and adopted as a matter of policy for the concern in question. Decisions as to which classes of goods and services to outsource, and if partial outsourcing is to be pursued what the proportions should be, are core issues which, in many respects, actually define the business. Major issues of investment, location, planning and direction are, to a large extent, dependent on the make(do)-or-buy decision. These strategic decisions will be informed by many considerations, amongst them:

- Financial constraints: if we can't invest in everything connected with supplying the needs of our organisation, which factors do we invest in, and which do we outsource?
- Which of our capabilities provide competitive advantage? Should we outsource those which don't?
- Will integration (vertical or horizontal) bring benefits to our organisation? If so, how do we pursue this?
- What service, goods or commodities are difficult to acquire externally? Should we develop our own capability?
- If 'downsizing' seems to be an option for us, which bits of our operation do we shed, and which do we retain?
- Are we in the right business? Are we making things when selling them is what we're really good at, or are there opportunities to become producers of the goods or services that we sell?

Research undertaken by Ford and Farmer (1986) showed that make-or-buy decisions can have a considerable strategic impact on businesses. However, the researchers hypothesised at the outset that such decisions were made or confirmed by default or arising from subjective opinion, rather than arising from clear analysis. Sadly, while there were exceptions, the hypothesis was proven to be correct and one fundamental factor was the lack of involvement of the purchasing department in such discussions in most cases. In contrast to those, there were some dramatic examples of effective decision making with purchasing involvement.

Almost ten years later it was reported in the DTI publication *Make or Buy, Your Route to Improved Manufacturing Performance* that the Manufacturing Engineering Group at Cambridge conducted a survey with a view to discovering how managers in the manufacturing industry are making decisions in relation to make or buy. The main findings seem to be:

● Everybody recognises the need to treat make or buy as part of the business strategy.
● Only 50 per cent of companies have defined policies and procedures to support managers in their make-or-buy decision making.
● Only about a third of companies have committed resources to making sure expertise is available to carry out make-or-buy decisions.
● An overwhelming majority (85 per cent) would like to have a documented make-or-buy decision support framework.

It was reported that although the long-term impact of make-or-buy decisions is recognised, many firms adopt a short-term (one-year) view when considering the consequences, whereas it is suggested by the Manufacturing Engineering Group that three to five years would be more appropriate. It would seem that the make-or-buy decision is an area of strategic importance, yet one which is still not made in an appropriately rigorous way by all organisations.

A USEFUL TECHNIQUE

Lucas Engineering and Systems take the following considerations (amongst others) into account when making the make-or-buy decision in relation to a process.

● How important is the process to our business?
● How competitive are we in relation to others undertaking this process?
● How strongly does this process impact on our measures of business performance?
● To what extent does the process have an impact on other products/ processes?
● Is the process linked to any of the strategic issues confronting the business?

The information gathered in response to these questions is brought together on a chart similar to the one shown in Figure 11.1, which enables some comparisons to be made between the processes which might be candidates for a changed make-or-buy-status. Of course financial models and projections are used too.

BUYING OR 'DOING' – SUBCONTRACTING SERVICES

The benefits from buying services from specialist suppliers has been recognised for many years. More recently, however, the scope of services considered for contracting out has been extended considerably. In the 1980s and the 1990s, privatisation of activities in the public sector has been driven by the Government in order to improve the economics of the public sector service in question. For example, hospitals, schools and other public sector bodies were required to submit their cleaning and catering services to the rigours of competitive tendering, resulting in many being contracted to private companies. Although new to the public sector these decisions were little different from those made by, for example, Shell or IBM. The basic question asked would be: 'Could this service be more economically performed by a third party?' As discussed previously, this assessment is complex, but if following a careful evaluation the answer to the question is 'Yes', and all the quality and other non-price criteria are met, then the decision to subcontract would follow.

During the 1980s one resource which attracted the attention of many European manufacturers as a potential 'buy-or-do' decision was distribution. During the decade many manufacturers sublet to specialists either their transport or total distribution system. The following short section discusses some of the issues involved in such subcontracting, since they are fairly typical of those associated with most service-type decisions. Like other make-or-buy decisions, there are various stages which may apply with regard to transportation and storage. For example, a company may employ its own warehouses, lorries and related equipment and may employ its own staff to perform all the functions involved.

A variation on that arrangement would be that the vehicles involved in the distribution process were owned by a third party, though carrying the name and logo of the customer. The buying company, meanwhile, would own and operate its own warehousing. A third alternative would involve the third party in owning and operating all the elements of the distribution system on behalf of the buying company.

Each of these stages involves the buying company making buy-or-do decisions, and all the problems mentioned earlier in this chapter, in respect of comparing factual data, apply. Among the questions which need to be asked are those related to vehicle utilisation, life costing, cost of warehouse operations and effectiveness of the system, for example, in customer service terms. Another vital issue, where a total distribution decision is involved, is usually the level of stock held and the stock turn which applies. Order processing issues are also pertinent.

Among the data which need to be considered are the number of consignments involved in the process, the volume/weight ratios, the service level required and the number, frequency and location of the deliveries which have to be made. The comparison of such data may involve many unknowns, at least as far as some organisations are concerned. However, once the data are available, in conjunction with an experienced bona fide contractor, an effective comparison can be made.

It is interesting to note that the growth in the utilisation of comprehensive distribution services has reflected the ability of the contractors to make their case, and it would appear that many companies have, for the first time, become aware of the costs involved simply as a result of assessing the possibility of subletting their distribution. It is the same with many make-or-buy and make-or-do decisions.

PURCHASING – A CANDIDATE FOR OUTSOURCING?

A number of authorities have argued that if an organisation is to concentrate on its core competencies, then purchasing activity may well not be one of them, and the activity might itself be placed in the hands of an external agency. A number of contributors to the 1966 International Purchasing and Supply Education and Research Association conference held at the University of Eindhoven in the Netherlands presented papers suggesting or predicting the end of 'purchasing' in the traditional or established sense.

Benmaridja and Benmaridja (1996) suggested outsourcing the non-critical part of purchasing, and suggested a methodology for determining exactly what the non-critical parts are. Stannick and Jones (1996) argued convincingly that purchasing as defined by Burt (1984) as 'the systematic process of deciding what, when, and how much to purchase, the act of purchasing it and the process of ensuring that what is required is received in the quantity specified on time' was dying, to be replaced by 'the assessment, management and monitoring of supplier behaviour to optimise organisational inputs'. Compelling though the arguments put forward by Stannick and Jones are, the fact remains that at least some of the operations suggested by Burt's definition need to be undertaken by somebody somewhere. Perhaps the somebody might be a specialist services contractor, or a vendor rather than a buyer, and perhaps the somewhere will be remote from the customer's place of business.

Evans (1996) reports the case of an organisation which developed its interface with suppliers to such an extent that it had a small cadre of well regarded suppliers who worked strategically in alliance with the company. Supplier appraisal or sourcing work was no longer necessary, negotiations no longer took place, and the routine requisitioning, ordering acknowledgements and payments work took place electronically and automatically. Purchasing had improved to such an extent that there was no longer a need for the function. Quality issues were resolved by the quality department, manufacturing teams met regularly to discuss initiatives, and the accountants worked closely with their counterparts at the suppliers where prices were concerned. So, with no more need for a purchasing department the staff were redeployed and the department closed. Of course, this does not mean that the activities that many

219

regard as being part of the role of purchasing had all been rendered obsolete, but rather that they had been relocated in a more appropriate place in the organisation and its interface with suppliers. Direct supplier/customer linkages, at the appropriate level and between appropriate managers, had obviated the need for purchasing in an intermediary role. So, not 'outsourcing' of purchasing in this case, but some degree of internal re-sourcing.

SUBCONTRACTING

Organisations of all kinds subcontract aspects of their activity, and subcontracting is often viewed as a means of augmenting limited resources and skills while enabling the contractor to concentrate on their main area of expertise. A main contractor in project engineering normally assigns part of the contract work to subcontractors, who are legally responsible to the contractor rather than the client even when the client has stipulated which subcontractor is to be used. In other kinds of manufacturing, such as batch production, the term 'subcontracting' is used in a similar way, to denote work which could in principle have been performed internally but in practice is bought out because of a shortage of capacity or lack suitable facilities. What is bought, in subcontracting, is not standard merchandise or articles but the ability to do a job; capacity, expertise, time.

The short-term objective in the use of subcontracting in the sense of outside processing is often because of shortage of capacity to meet orders, often when the outside processors are also very busy. Moving on from this view, the need is to develop a policy which ensures an overall cost-effective use of manufacturing resources in the long term. Short-term capacity bottlenecks will still require tactical subcontracting but in the long term a well considered manufacturing strategy will be developed if Svenson's advice is to be followed. Svenson (1968) correctly foresaw an increase in the use of subcontracting. Reasons he gave for his conclusion, proved correct by events, were:

- Rapid technological innovation.
- Faster adoption of these changes in products and processes.
- Increasing specialisation by business enterprises worldwide.

The specialised subcontractor is better positioned to secure and maintain a grip at the leading edge of technological change and innovation (*see* Figure 11.3).

Selecting a subcontractor

All the issues discussed in Chapter 8 are pertinent in selecting a subcontractor. However, certain issues may need to be considered in a different light and additional issues may require attention. Key questions in major subcontractor selection include:

- What is the company's major specialisation? For example, are they jobbing machinists, or are they capable of working to close tolerances?

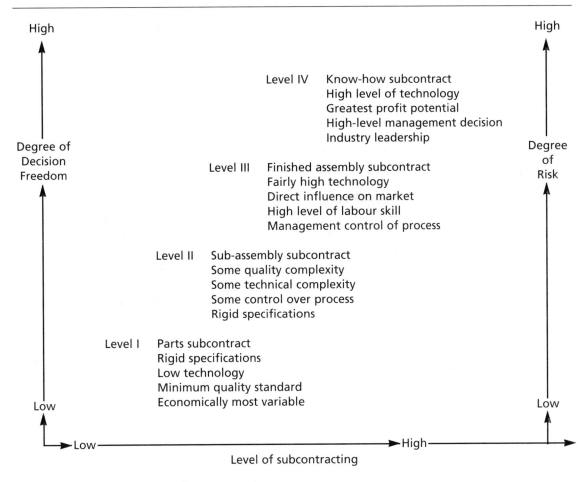

Fig. 11.3 Levels and content of subcontracting
(*Source:* Svenson, 1968)

- For whom have they worked? How long have they worked for these companies? Can we ask these customers about their service and quality performance record?
- What part of their capacity is on subcontract work? Can it be established whether the resources allocated to subcontracting will fluctuate in accordance with other sales?
- What is their capacity in terms of plant and output devoted to subcontract work?
- Have they a permanent and well trained labour force? What is their industrial relations record?
- In government work, are they approved by the relevant inspectorate?
- Are their quality-control procedures adequate?
- Are their engineering standards, procedures and controls adequate? How reliable is their forecast of availability of capacity?
- Are their production-control procedures adequate?
- Are they adequately financed?

- What is the state of their order book, current and projected?
- If tooling is required, can they make the tools themselves?
- Do they own their own transport? Is it reliable? If they use a carrier, which will be used? Are they reliable?
- In higher levels of subcontracting, does the company itself employ subcontractors?

Where possible, each of these questions should be transformed into a measurable quantity, then objective comparisons can be drawn between potential subcontractors or when reviewing existing subcontractors. The extent of such investigations depends upon the quality and importance of the work to be undertaken, but to do an effective buying job and build up data as a basis for comparisons, continuing appraisal is necessary. Companies change over time: new management, new policies and ageing machinery can change the direction and emphasis of a company's activities; external changes (e.g. in the state of the market) can affect performance. With new subcontractors, specification and standard of working should be agreed before they submit a quotation; the fact that a subcontractor is capable of meeting a given standard is no guarantee that it will be met. Samples made to the required standard, with drawings and written specification, can help in this connection.

In higher levels of subcontracting, close liaison between the contractor's and the subcontractor's staff is essential. The boundaries between the organisations should not become barriers to the team effort which is required to achieve success in completion of the work.

In manufacturing engineering, subcontracting refers to the award to some other concern of work which is normally undertaken by the buyer:

- is performed on material which is the property of the buyer and will be returned to them after processing;
- involves the manufacture of a component or assembly of a series of components designed by the buyer and over which the buyer retains some technical control;
- involves the provision of a complete manufacturing service for a company which does not have the local facilities (this might even extend into distribution); or
- is outside the normal scope of the buying company's activities (e.g. packaging; vehicle spares are often packed for the manufacturers by a specialist subcontractor).

Working with the subcontractor

Extending the team-working approach advocated above, it is good practice to make one individual responsible for all contacts with each subcontractor – that is, a team leader. The person handles all correspondence, drawings, bills of materials, telephone queries, etc.; he or she will also arrange visits to the subcontractor as and when necessary; all queries should be routed through this person, many of which he or she should be able to answer personally, or if not he or she will have access to the appropriate specialist who can.

In high-volume subcontracting, thought should be given to transportation and handling methods; box pallets used as transit containers and for handling and storage can cut handling costs, for instance.

Responsibilities for what work is required to be done by the subcontractor must be clearly defined, particularly where the contractor is to perform only part of a series of operations or processes. It must be made clear who supplies the material for the work, and when. Will it be supplied by the subcontractor or will it be supplied from the buyer? All operations to be performed should be specified in preliminary instructions and, if possible, requirements scheduled to fit in with the buyer's process. The subcontractor must also be informed of any special requirements or constraints for safety or other reasons.

Minor operations such as labelling or marking must be agreed at the initial negotiations, otherwise the buyer cannot assume that the subcontractor will carry them out. When work is in progress, the buyer is largely in the subcontractor's hands regarding changes for minor works not included in the initial negotiations. This can lead to a very competitive initial price becoming inflated to the point of being non-competitive, if not properly managed.

An understanding of the quality and workmanship required of the subcontractor must be reached at the outset. It must not be assumed that the subcontractor will be aware of the practices followed in the buyer's works. The buyer will usually be at a disadvantage if quality standards are raised when the contract is under way. Provision should be made for compensation by the subcontractor for spoilage or partially finished work, subject to accepted conditions of trade.

The design of a component made in the buyer's own workshop may have evolved from the original specification and the official drawings may be out of date. If a decision is taken to subcontract the work, then all drawings and process sheets must be brought up to the present practice including any further innovations required by the buyer: the subcontractor cannot be held to account for not following the latest practices unless informed of them.

It may be in the interests of the buyer to offer assistance to a subcontractor where the buyer possesses particular expertise. This may be in areas such as tooling, process engineering or purchasing. The subcontractor is an extension of the buyer's resources, therefore an improvement in the subcontractor's performance is in the interests of both parties. Training of staff in new processes and loan of specialised tools to accelerate the adoption of new technologies or innovations by the subcontractor are all helpful in assisting the development of the relationship with a view to long-term mutual benefit. The sooner the subcontractor can meet the specification at reduced cost, then any duplication is avoided and the buyer benefits through cost reductions and more effective use of their own resources.

It should be agreed:

- what tools and skills are required for the contract;
- what tools are available for loan to the subcontractor (these must be reserved for them);
- what training will be provided by the buyer;

- what tools will be provided by the subcontractor; and
- who is responsible for the upkeep of loaned equipment.

Inspection arrangements need to be clearly established. The buyer should ensure that materials or components sent to the subcontractor are as agreed in the negotiation, and that all previous operations have been properly completed. An objective of nil defects should be set for all work delivered by the subcontractor.

A buyer's representative may need to enter the subcontractor's premises during the contract period for progress or inspection. It should not be assumed that the seller will allow this unless the condition is agreed in the initial negotiation. If the right of access imposes limitations on the buyer's personnel while on the subcontractor's premises, these should be made known to anyone of the buyer's staff who visits the subcontractor.

Responsibility for transport in both directions should be defined at the outset, and care should be taken to schedule return loads so as to reduce costs; bad scheduling can result in additional transport costs. In some cases specialist transport requirements such as heavy or bulky loads may lead to the employment of a third party, which if it were arranged by the buyer would be an additional subcontract.

Procedures and documentation should also be clearly established at the outset and these should not conflict with existing supply procedures but should complement them. These procedures should cover likely happenings, such as the return of rejected materials, materials supplied to the subcontractor, the tools and equipment supplied to them. If more than one subcontractor is employed on a particular contract, each should mark their own work in some way to establish who has done work on a particular component in case there should be rejections.

The limits of the subcontractor's liability for damage to persons or property in respect of claims arising out of the contract need to be defined. The extent to which the buyer is indemnified in respect of such claims must also be stated.

Where tools, materials and equipment are loaned to a subcontractor, the buyer should see that they are insured. This may involve inspection and approval of the subcontractor's premises by the insurance company.

Subcontracting in the construction industry

Construction projects are often very complex in nature and the contractual arrangements usually reflect and amplify the complexity. A very complex construction project is often divided into phases which represent the major categories of work, for example, phase one would be ground preparation and foundations, and so on. The customer (more usually known as the client) may appoint one main contractor for the project or one for each phase. Sometimes the client nominates a particular subcontractor to complete one element of the project; in other cases the client issues a list of approved subcontractors. If the contractor seeks to appoint a subcontractor not included on the approved list, they will need to obtain the approval of the client.

The client will appoint a project manager to supervise the project to ensure timely completion to cost and specification. Large-scale construction projects are notoriously difficult to manage. In spite of careful preliminary investigation and planning, many exigencies often emerge as the work proceeds. The project manager's team incorporates specialists within the client organisation, but also includes members of the contractor's and subcontractor's organisations, all working within a common aim of completing the project.

Precise and detailed definition of the work which the contractor is to carry out and be responsible for is necessary. Particular regard should be given to the subcontractor's responsibility for making good other work, materials, equipment or access ways damaged in carrying out their services; omissions or ambiguity can be expensive. Responsibility for the provision of facilities, plant, storage and receiving, power and other services (often such common services are provided by the main contractor) should be stated. If assistance is given, this should be allowed for in the price, and steps taken to make such facilities available when required. Locations available to the subcontractor for storage or work should be clearly defined preferably before the subcontract is awarded. Subcontractors often cannot commence work until some previous stage has been completed, so it is important that schedules are realistic (part of the project manager's role). If building and civil engineering work needs to be inspected and approved in the course of construction, it should be laid down which organisation is responsible for informing the inspector that the work is ready to be inspected. It must be made clear who obtains the permission to carry out work which may interrupt traffic flow or the passage of pedestrians. Care taken in defining requirements will simplify supervision and inspection during the course of the project, to ensure that the subcontractor:

- works in accordance with the specification as regards materials and practice;
- does not use any material, equipment or facility without authority;
- observes safety regulations; and
- makes progress in accordance with the negotiated time and leaves the site or workplace cleared or ready for the next stage.

It is important to define the subcontractor's liability for damage to persons and property. The extent to which the main contractor is indemnified in respect of claims must be stated. Care must be taken that the main contractor's insurance policy provides adequate cover for the subcontract operation, particularly as regards third party liability.

Careful records should be kept by all parties in relation to activities on site covering relevant factors such as: interruption of works – duration and reasons – exceptional weather conditions, hazardous occurrences, variations to the contract etc. These records may prove valuable in respect of a dispute or claim for additional payment.

The increasing trend towards specialisation means more work is being subcontracted and this is a trend which is expected to continue. The choice of subcontractor and the management of the relationship is a key issue for organisations to which the purchasing function has a very important contribution to make.

CONCLUSION

Make(do)-or-buy and subcontracting decisions are being taken more frequently as organisations concentrate more on their own specialist abilities, leaving peripheral activities to other specialists in those fields. More work is being carried out by suppliers, making their choice and management increasingly important in the success of the buying organisation. Purchasing has an important specialist role to play in creating an analytical framework that will provide objective information to the decision-making process.

Subcontracting can be a contentious issue between production personnel, who see it as a temporary extension of their in-plant manufacturing capacity, and purchasing personnel, who see it as the purchase either of components or of facilities from outside and, consequently, their responsibility. Purchasing often argues that:

- those defining the need should not determine the source of supply; and
- technical personnel lack training in commercial transactions and rely too much on informal arrangements which are not recorded.

Other departments complain about internal communications as well as communication problems between the subcontractor and purchaser. It may be argued that purchasing personnel are not qualified to discuss technicalities, especially when state-of-the-art technology is involved. Sometimes companies employ engineers in purchasing departments to overcome such difficulties, or sometimes multifunctional teams are set up to consider the issues involved. Just as purchasing personnel may have technical weaknesses, technical personnel have commercial blindspots and it follows that firms are most likely to achieve their commercial and technical objectives when specialist staff from each area collaborate. Indeed, as the cases involved in the section on make(do)-or-buy strategy indicate, decisions which involve ceasing to perform certain tasks or continuing or strategic importance to the organisation. To use a word of Drucker's, they have great 'futurity'. What we decide today may have great impact on the future.

SUMMARY POINTS

- The decision to make or buy can fundamentally affect the nature of the business, the number of skilled/unskilled staff, management technique and the competitive advantage of the organisation.
- Operational decisions do not involve a change of policy. Tactical decisions consider the acquisition of additional resources or the divestment of minor resources, they do not affect the asset base. Strategic decisions include vertical integration, the acquisition of entire businesses in order to assure the internal supply of a component/service, the decision to close down or sell off a major internal facility.
- Make or buy decisions can intrinsically affect the long term success of a company. However, it is recognised that many firms only view the short

term consequences of 1 year hence when perhaps a 3–5 year view would be more appropriate.

- Subcontracting of services increased dramatically during the 1980 and 1990s when certain activities in the public sector were required to go to competitive tendering. Many large multi-nationals have also recognised that sticking to core business and divesting peripheral activities lead to a 'leaner' – more competitive organisation. Rapid technological innovation has also lead to increased subcontracting to enable changes to be adopted ahead of the competition.

- It is essential that a close relationship is developed between the buyer, contractor and subcontractors. Responsibilities and liabilities must be clearly defined for all. The contractor and subcontractors are an extension of the buyers resources thus continuing appraisal is necessary.

REFERENCES AND FURTHER READING

Baillie A S (1986), 'Subcontracting based on integrated standards', *Journal of Purchasing and Material Management*, Spring.

Burt D (1994) *Proactive Procurement*, Prentice-Hall, New York.

Benmeridja M and Benmeridja A (1996) *'Is it interesting for a company to outsource purchasing and under what conditions?'* Paper presented at IPSERA conference, Eindhoven University of Technology.

Cobbett R (1983), 'Subcontracting, the buyer's responsibility', *Purchasing and Supply Management*, September.

Evans E (1996) 'The disappearing department', *Supply Management*, July.

Hines P and Samuel D (1993) *The Economic importance and evaluation of subcontracting*, Paper presented at second international PSERG conference, Bath University.

Pralahad C K and Hamel G (1990) 'The core competence of the corporation', *Harvard Business Review*. May/June.

Stannack P and Jones M (1996) *'The death of purchasing?'* Paper presented at IPSERA conference, Eindhoven University of Technology.

Wild R (1989), *Production and Operations Management*, Cassell, London.

CHAPTER 12

Buying commodities

INTRODUCTION

The primary commodities are natural products rather than manufactured products. This affects the prices at which they are sold even though they normally enter into trade in processed or partly manufactured form rather than just as harvested or mined. Cocoa, coffee and tea, for instance, are dried and processed before they reach the market. Many primary commodities are bought and sold locally without entering into world trade. This chapter is concerned with those primary commodities which are in worldwide demand, and are traded worldwide, so that organised commodity markets have developed to facilitate that trade.

OBJECTIVES OF THIS CHAPTER

- To identify the different soft and hard commodities and their impact on the material costs of producers incorporating them
- To evaluate the different short term and long term price stabilisation techniques
- To consider the risks of speculation and measures undertaken to reduce them
- To appreciate the modern futures markets trade only in titles or rights to commodities rather than actual goods
- To evaluate various buying techniques
- To calculate the 'price of indifference'
- To insure against fluctuating prices by placing call and put options.

The main purchasing problem in buying commodities is the large fluctuations in price which occur, often in short time periods. Coping with this price variability presents a real challenge to any purchaser needing large quantities of commodities to support production in factories whose products are sold at prices which cannot be varied in the same way. It can also have serious effects on the material costs of producers using secondary products which incorporate price-variable primary commodities.

For instance, cable manufacturers buy copper; chocolate manufacturers buy cocoa; some carpet manufacturers buy wool; tyre manufacturers buy rubber; battery manufacturers buy lead; and some food-container manufacturers buy tin. All these materials – copper, cocoa, wool, rubber, lead and tin – are traded on organised commodity markets which offer facilities for hedging by means of futures contracts. Specialist commodity buyers are experts in these markets. Other buyers, however, who are not specialists and do not have the opportunity to become experts still have to make occasional purchases in these markets, or buy products at prices which are affected by the cost of the commodities used in their manufacture. They also need to understand why commodity prices fluctuate and to have some appreciation of the buying strategies which can be used in such conditions.

THE PRINCIPAL COMMODITIES

Aluminium This metal has been traded as a commodity since 1978 when the London Metal Exchange (LME) introduced aluminium contracts. The rather recent introduction of aluminium contracts is probably due to the fact that production is controlled by a few companies – Alcan, Kaiser, Reynolds and Alcoa. The tonnage of aluminium produced overtook the production of copper by the late 1970s.

Cocoa A very volatile commodity, with frosts, disease and other factors having a fairly unpredictable effect on the supply and hence prices. Main producing countries are Brazil, Ivory Coast and Ghana. The main cocoa markets are in New York and London, though Ivory Coast cocoa is traded in Paris.

Coffee Produced in many tropical countries, though Brazil is by far the biggest producer, with Colombia some way behind. As with cocoa, the two main markets are in New York and London.

Copper The London Metal Exchange is the most important copper market, and its prices adopted as the world reference price. Only a very small proportion of the world's copper is handled through LME trading, but producers and consumers often use the LME price as their basis for direct contracts. The Commodity Exchange (COMEX) in New York is the major pricing influence in the United States though in practice prices on all exchanges are closely related.

Cotton Provides half of the world's textile requirements, and is traded in Hong Kong, Liverpool, London and New York.

Gas oil A generic term covering a fraction of the products resulting from refining crude oil. In the United States it is often called heating oil, and in Europe 'diesel' is the usual name. Traded on the New York Mineral Exchange (NYMEX) and the International Petroleum Exchange (IPE) in London.

Gold Until the 1960s gold prices were fixed by governments on an international basis. This practice was abandoned in the 1960s and in 1982 the London gold futures market was established.

Grains Wheat, barley, corn (maize), rye and oats are the important cereals, and the trade in these commodities is dominated by North America. The main exchanges are in Kansas City, Minneapolis, Winnepeg and Chicago.

Lead Today the main application of lead is in the manufacture of batteries, and, to a lesser extent, it is used in the construction industry. Former important applications, such as plumbing, in pigments (as an oxide) and as a petrol additive, are all declining. Supplies are relatively plentiful, and much lead is recycled. Because of this, price movements tend to be limited.

Nickel   Introduced on the London Metal Exchange in 1979, nickel is mainly used in the production of stainless steel. Prices have changed dramatically in recent years.

Rubber   An interesting commodity, in that there is a synthetic substitute interchangeable with natural rubber for most applications. By far the greatest market is for the manufacture of tyres. Traded in several places, the most important market for rubber is the Malaysian Rubber Exchange in Kuala Lumpur.

Silver   The price of silver can be erratic because it is both an industrial metal and a medium for investment. Industrial materials tend to attract fewer buyers when the price is rising, but the opposite is true if the purchase is for investment. The London Metal Exchange is a market for silver, but the COMEX in New York occupies the key position.

Soyabeans   There has been a good deal of speculation in this commodity in the past, though by the early 1980s the market had become rather more stable. The main markets are as foodstuffs (soyabean oil for cooking and margarine manufacture) and as animal feeds (soyabean meal). Soyabean meal is 47 per cent protein, and hence a very high-value commodity.

WHY DO COMMODITY PRICES FLUCTUATE?

Anyone who buys food for a household or a restaurant is familiar with the way prices change for farm products. In England, the first new potatoes, Jersey Royals perhaps, appear in spring at very high prices. Potato prices fall as the months pass and the bulk supplies, first of earlies, and then of main crop potatoes reach the market; until by autumn old potatoes are selling for less than a tenth of the price of the first new potatoes in spring. The first asparagus reaches the market at astronomical prices; there is not a lot to sell, but at those prices there are not many who are willing to buy. Supply and demand are brought into equilibrium by means of these price changes. Price also changes from year to year; in some years potato prices stay high all year because the weather or some other reason has resulted in a major shortfall in supply.

These factors affect the prices at which 'soft' commodities trade on commodity exchanges, but there are additional considerations. As well as producers and consumers, participants in these markets include speculators, dealers and jobbers. Prices react continually to expectations of present and future supply, of present and future demand, of stock situations, etc.

Even though some commodity prices stay much the same for long periods of time, many commodity prices change by much larger amounts, and in much shorter periods of time, than the prices of manufactured goods. Also commodity prices move down as well as up, unlike most manufactured goods prices.

Soft commodities (agricultural raw materials) often fluctuate in price by 100 per cent, and sometimes by 500 per cent, in just one season. Price fluctuations of such amplitude are unwelcome both to consumers and to producers. A major cocoa consumer had to confess in the mid 1970s that purchasing staff had made 'transactions in the company's name on the cocoa terminal market which were not disclosed to the Board' – and which led to trading losses of £32.5m.

Hard commodities such as copper can also increase in price by 300 per cent in a year, only to be cut in half in a few months. Consumers and producers would both prefer more stable prices. This is generally agreed, although the actual level of price may not be so easy to agree. Price stability, however desirable, has not in practice proved easy to achieve.

Flood, drought, plant disease and crop failure can produce a shortfall of agricultural produce, while exceptionally good harvests can produce a glut on the market, and the natural results are high prices and low prices respectively. Wars, strikes, revolutions and changes in government policy have also had serious repercussions on the supply of commodities. Changes in economic activity in the industrialised countries, which are the main customers, have immediate effects on demand, and changes in taste or technology or the availability of substitutes have long-term effects on demand.

In the case of many commodities, the effect on price of any changes which occur in supply or demand is increased by the length of time it takes for any attempt to adjust supply to demand to take effect. Newly planted coffee, rubber and cocoa trees take years to come into full production. Small changes in metal output can be made with existing facilities, but a large increase in output might require a lengthy process of re-opening old mines, or digging new mines and providing housing, transport and shipping facilities to exploit them. A large reduction in output is equally difficult to achieve because of the serious effects on employment and export revenue which would result.

PRICE STABILISATION SCHEMES

It might at first appear easy for producer and consumer to agree on a stable price if this is what both parties want. There is considerable use by large manufacturers of direct contracts with the producer, the producer's agent or the shipper. Although the commodity markets provide a medium for hedging and speculation, a means for buying and selling commodities, and a consensus of trading views on market conditions, reflected in market price, the fact is that a large part of the world trade does not pass through these markets. If both buyer and seller prefer a stable price, surely they are free to negotiate a fixed-price contract.

In practice, however, if a price gets much out of line with world prices it becomes almost impossible to resist the pressure to renegotiate. Prices payable under direct contracts between producer and consumer are usually referred to the basis price set by the commodity markets for this reason. Prices for major individual contracts can be stabilised in general only if the world market price can also be stabilised.

A number of schemes have been successful in damping down short-term price fluctuations on commodity markets, although long-term changes are a different matter. Short-term fluctuations tend to occur about a mean, until a change in the supply/demand ratio triggers off an upwards or downwards trend.

A typical scheme would be administered by a governing body, such as a producer cartel, or possibly a council with representatives appointed by consumers as well as producers. This governing body would appoint and finance a buffer stock manager and fix the floor and ceiling prices between which he or she is to operate. The buffer stock manager buys for stock when price tends to fall, and sells from stock when price tends to rise; and if operating on sufficient scale the result is to stabilise market price. Such market operations have worked well for appreciable periods of time; but they break down once a definite upwards or downwards trend develops. They cease to work in the case of rising price when the warehouses are empty and the buffer stock manager has no more to sell, and in the case of falling price when the financial reserves are exhausted and he or she has no money to buy.

For long-term price stabilisation to be successful, the governing body needs also to monitor world demand and to make appropriate changes in output in order to keep the tonnage which reaches the market in line with market requirements. This is much more difficult to achieve than short-term buffer stock operations, because output is affected by unplanned events. Planned changes cannot in many cases be implemented quickly, and governments of some producer countries may feel that a change which is agreed to be in the general interest does not advance their own particular interest.

THE ROLE OF THE SPECULATOR

All futures markets offer opportunities for speculation, which is, of course, a very high-risk activity. Speculation will not normally be entered into by the producers or consumers of commodities, though there have been some spectacular windfall gains and unplanned losses made through the speculative activities of individual buying decision makers, sometimes without the knowledge or consent of top management. Most manufacturing and service organisations claim that speculation is at least discouraged, and is often forbidden, and it is common to find that procedures or policy manuals contain guidance to this effect.

However, professional investors or institutions may well have a proportion of their capital which they are prepared to put at risk in the hope of a very high return. The contribution of these speculators is *essential* for the smooth operation of the commodity markets. The speculators help to ensure the liquidity of the market, and ensure that the risks which the hedger is seeking to avoid are taken up.

HEDGING WITH FUTURES CONTRACTS

Both consumers and suppliers of commodities thus find themselves exposed to serious risk of loss (as well as of windfall profit) because of unpredictable changes in price. It is the sort of risk which might be insured against, in the same way as insurance is taken out against the risk of loss through fire, theft or flood, if this were feasible. Unfortunately, it is not feasible. Insurance is based on the fact that only a small statistically predictable minority of those at risk will actually suffer loss in a given period. Consequently, compensation can be paid to them from a fund which is provided by premiums collected from all those insured and calculated according to the degree of risk. Fire insurance is feasible because only a few of the buildings insured actually catch fire in a given period, but market changes affect all those trading in the market, not just a small minority.

Although normal insurance is not available, a different form of risk reduction technique is possible because, while price changes affect all traders, they affect some adversely and others favourably. Some stand to lose and others gain if the price rises, for instance; and those who stand to gain if it rises are also at risk of loss if price falls. In either case the risk can be reduced by hedging, which in this context means balancing a trading position by making compensating transactions in futures contracts.

Futures contracts should not be confused with, for instance, a construction contract to be completed in two years' time, or an order for castings to be delivered two months in the future. They are a special kind of commodity contract, which originated in the nineteenth century as world trade expanded and the markets developed arrangements whereby traders could agree on the sale or purchase of standard quantities of goods to standard descriptions for completion at a stated future date and at a fixed price. These contracts were made alongside the physical transactions in which actual goods were sold by sample and description for immediate delivery and constituted a facility whereby traders were able to reduce the risk of trading loss. Modern futures markets trade in titles or rights to commodities rather than actual goods (known as actuals, physicals, spot or cash). Futures contracts do not normally lead to actual deliveries of goods (although this is technically possible on some markets); they are closed out before completion by means of a reverse transaction.

How this works may best be seen by example. Suppose that, on 1 January, a copper cable manufacturer sells a quantity of cable containing 100 tons of copper and agrees that the price paid by the customer will be based upon the prevailing value of copper at the time of delivery of the cable to the customer. It will take three months to actually manufacture the cable, so on 1 January the manufacturer has to buy 100 tonnes of copper in order that they can start work. They pay £1700 per ton for this copper, the prevailing LME price on 1 January.

If the manufacturer does not take precautions, they are now at risk of the copper they hold losing value because of the changing market price. If the market price goes down they will not be able to recover what they paid

233

for the commodity. They could, of course, be lucky; the price could go up. However, they are in business to make cable, not to speculate, so they decide to hedge. On 1 January, as well as *buying* 100 tons of copper for production, they *sell* a commitment to deliver 100 tons on 1 April (a 3-month futures contract). They do not yet own this copper, and do not need to. It will be sufficient to get hold of the copper on 1 April in time to make delivery.

Figure 12.1 shows what happens if the price goes down to £1500 per ton. They will lose £20 000 on their physical copper. They paid £170 000 for it, and it is now worth only £150 000. Their hedged position saves them though. They can on 1 April buy 100 tons of copper for £150 000 to meet their obligations under the futures contract. Their receipts under that contract are £170 000, so they make a compensating gain here of £20 000.

The result would be the same if the price movement were £300 per ton, or any other figure. The gain on one contract would be compensated by a loss on the other. If the price went up instead of down, the profit on the physical copper would be balanced by a loss on the futures contract.

This is a simplified illustration, and as such is a perfect hedge. For technical reasons the spot price and the futures price may differ from each other, but they are seldom far apart. It is quite feasible to avoid most of the risk associated with owning a commodity by hedging in this way.

SOME BUYING TECHNIQUES

Time budgeting or averaging is a cautious policy which ensures that the cost of commodities consumed is the same as the market price. No expert knowledge is required and no risks are taken. The exact quantity required is purchased at the time of requirement and no stocks are held. If stocks have to be held, as is often the case, this simple policy cannot be used.

An ingenious formula approach, known as £-cost averaging or budget-buying, does even better by ensuring that the cost of commodities consumed is less than market price, provided that average market price can be predicted successfully and that actual prices fluctuate in random fashion about this average. The idea is to spend a standard sum based on the average price at regular intervals of time. This 'budget' amount buys a larger amount when actual price is below average and a smaller amount when price is above average. Let us suppose that 1 ton a week is required of a commodity of which the average market price is £100 a ton, and that in three successive weeks, actual market price is £150, £50 and £100. With the back-to-back or averaging policy, 1 ton would have been bought each week; but with the budget-buying policy £100 would be spent each week, the budget amount to obtain 1 ton at the average market price. In the first week, £100 would buy two-thirds of a ton at £150 a ton. In the second week, it would buy 2 tons at £50. In the third week, it would buy 1 ton. Over the three-week period, budgeted buying would have resulted in 3.66 tons being bought for £300, at an average cost below the average market price. The averaging policy would have resulted in 3 tons being bought for £300, at cost equal to the average market price.

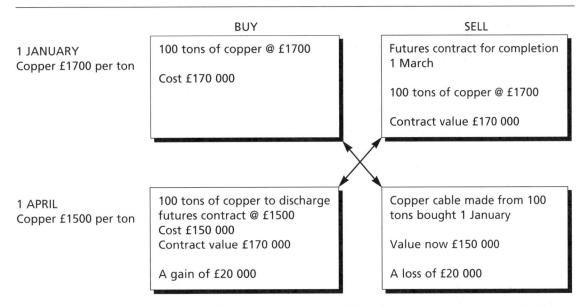

	BUY	SELL
1 JANUARY Copper £1700 per ton	100 tons of copper @ £1700 Cost £170 000	Futures contract for completion 1 March 100 tons of copper @ £1700 Contract value £170 000
1 APRIL Copper £1500 per ton	100 tons of copper to discharge futures contract @ £1500 Cost £150 000 Contract value £170 000 A gain of £20 000	Copper cable made from 100 tons bought 1 January Value now £150 000 A loss of £20 000

Fig. 12.1 A simple 'buyer's hedge': the two transactions made on 1 January compensate each other

A more sophisticated approach developed by operations research workers is known as dynamic programming. To illustrate this technique, let us suppose that 100 tons a week are required of a commodity the price of which fluctuates randomly between £200 and £300 a ton, and that the buyer is authorised to purchase up to ten weeks' supply (1000 tons). We will also assume that futures contracts are not available. Having found a method of determining each week how much to buy, we will then reconsider these simplifying assumptions.

In order to establish a yardstick, by which we can measure how well the dynamic programming technique works, let us first see how well we could buy if we knew in advance what the market price would be each week. Over a fifty-week period, let us assume that prices each week are going to be as shown below:

Actual market prices

Weeks	Weekly prices in £/ton				
1–5	277	265	220	209	280
6–10	234	246	202	205	204
11–15	215	240	206	287	288
16–20	217	218	277	266	214
21–25	268	227	285	211	217
26–30	226	295	268	297	273
31–35	275	264	227	245	201
36–40	287	220	202	219	236
41–45	245	242	296	272	298
46–50	278	281	252	231	288

Assuming we start with no stock, we must buy 100 tons in the first week to meet the first week's requirements, but as price is falling we buy only one week's supply. The same applies in weeks 2 and 3, but in week 4 the price of £209 is the lowest until week 8, so we buy 400 tons to last until week 8. In week 8 the price of £202 is the lowest which is going to apply for a considerable time, so we buy 10 weeks' supply, the maximum authorised. Each week we look ten weeks ahead and buy as little as necessary to meet requirements until we can stock up at a low price. With the advantage of advance knowledge of price we would be able to supply the fifty-week requirement at an average price of just below £210 a ton, as follows:

Week number	Opening stock	Price paid	Amount bought	Total expense
1	NIL	277	100	27 700
2	NIL	265	100	26 500
3	NIL	220	100	22 000
4	NIL	209	400	83 600
8	NIL	202	1000	202 000
10	800	204	200	40 800
13	700	206	300	61 800
20	300	214	100	21 400
24	NIL	211	1000	211 000
25	900	217	100	21 700
35	NIL	201	1000	201 000
38	700	202	300	60 600
39	900	219	100	21 900
49	NIL	231	200	46 200
	Totals		5000 tons	£1 048 200

Average price paid = £209.64/ton

If, on the other hand, we took no chances and had no advance knowledge, and simply bought 100 tons a week at the going price, the average cost would be £248 a ton.

INDIFFERENCE PRICES

In order to decide a buying rule for the practical situation in which advance knowledge of market prices is not available, the procedure is to determine a *price of indifference* at which it does not matter if an order is placed or not. If market price is above the price of indifference, no order will be placed, and if it is below the price of indifference, we make a further calculation to decide how much to buy. Clearly the price of indifference is affected by the amount of stock in hand; with nil stock we cannot afford to be indifferent but must buy whatever the price. We will denote the prices of indifference by $P_0, P_1, P_2 \ldots P_{10}$, where the suffix denotes the number of weeks' stock in hand. These prices can easily be calculated on the simple assumptions we have made; that:

1 demand is 100 tons a week;
2 orders are for multiples of 100 tons;
3 maximum stock is 1000 tons; and
4 price varies randomly and evenly from £200 to £300 a ton.

With nil stock we must buy whatever the price; but as price will not exceed £300, P_0 is £300.

With one week's stock, the price of indifference is determined by the fact that we must buy next week if we do not buy this week. Next week's price we do not know, but on the average will tend to be halfway between £200 and £300, so we should buy this week if the actual price is below £250; and this gives the value of P_1 as £250.

With two weeks' stock, the situation is more complicated. If we do not buy this week, next week we will be down to one week's stock and P_1 = £250. The chances are even that next week's price will be below £250, and if it is on the average it will be £225. Consequently,

P_2 = (probability of price being below P_1) × (expected price if it is)
    + (probability of price being above P_1) × P_1
  = 0.5 × 225 + 0.5 × 250
  = £237.5

With three weeks' stock, a similar calculation can be made:

P_3 = (probability of price being below P_2) × (expected price)
    + (probability of price being above P_2) × P_2

Since prices are assumed to be evenly distributed, if the price is below P_2 it will on the average be halfway between £237.5 and £200, so:

P_3 = 0.375 × 218.75 + 0.625 × 237.5
   = £230.5

Proceeding in this way we obtain the following prices of indifference:

P_0 = £300
P_1 = £250
P_2 = £237.5
P_3 = £230.5
P_4 = £225.8
P_5 = £222.5
P_6 = £220.0
P_7 = £218.0
P_8 = £216.4
P_9 = £215.0
P_{10} = £214.0

These are shown in graphical form in Figure 12.2.

Now we can work through the 50 weeks' prices previously given once more. In week 1, with nil stocks, P_1 applies and we must buy. The quantity to buy is also derived from the above list; if market price was £218, equivalent to P_7, we should buy enough to supply 7 weeks' requirements. But in week 1, market

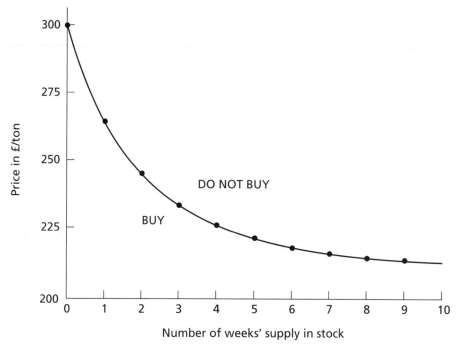

Fig. 12.2 Indifference prices

price is £277.5, higher than P_2, so we buy just one week's supply. In week 2 we again buy just 100 tons. But in week 3, price is £220, corresponding to P_6, so we buy six weeks' supply, in addition to our requirement for the current week. Proceeding in this way, by the end of the year our buying record is shown below.

Week number	Opening stock	Price paid	Amount bought	Total expense
1	NIL	277	100	27 700
2	NIL	265	100	26 500
3	NIL	220	700	154 000
4	600	209	400	83 600
8	600	202	400	80 800
9	900	205	100	20 500
10	900	204	100	20 400
13	700	206	300	61 800
16	700	217	100	21 700
20	400	214	500	107 000
24	500	211	500	105 500
33	100	227	300	68 100
35	200	201	800	160 800
38	700	202	300	60 600
48	NIL	252	100	25 200
49	NIL	231	200	46 200
	Total		5000 tons	£1 070 400

It can be seen that the 5000-ton requirement would have been bought for an average price of £214 a ton. This is much better than the average market price of £248, which is the best that could have been achieved by the risk-reducing policy of averaging, or in this case buying 100 tons a week. Although it is not quite as good as the average price of £210, which is the best obtainable with complete advance knowledge, it really is quite close to it.

It may be objected that anyone can set up a simplified illustration and devise a winning strategy; how applicable is this to the real world? Well, the simplifying assumptions that demand was a fixed 100 tons a week, and that prices varied once a week, and that buy decisions were made in multiples of 100 tons, are made only for ease of explanation and can be relaxed without affecting practice. The assumption that a maximum of ten weeks' supply could be bought reflects the fact that in reality some limit must always be set to the buyer's discretion and that he or she must seek authority from higher management if in his or her judgement commitments can with advantage be made beyond that limit. Finally, it was assumed that price distribution was rectangular, or flat between the two limits stated. In practice a price forecast with its likely error distribution could be used instead. Kingsman (1975) has given a fuller account of this technique, which he says can also allow for futures contracts as a less expensive alternative to holding stock.

TRADED OPTIONS

One way in which a buying organisation may protect itself against fluctuating commodity prices is by means of traded options. These are, in essence, insurance policies. The party requiring insurance cover pays a premium to another party who is willing to provide the cover. In this process the buyer of an option acquires a right (but not an obligation) to buy or sell a commodity under certain conditions in exchange for a premium. It follows that the holder of the option may or may not exercise the right, though the seller of the option *must* meet his or her obligations if called upon to do so by the buyer.

An option conferring the right to buy is known as a 'call' option; a 'put' option is one which confers the right to sell. It is sometimes erroneously said that 'put' and 'call' options are opposite sides of the same transaction. This is not the case – the markets for the two kinds of option are entirely separate from each other. A 'put' option provides protection against declining prices, a 'call' option protects against rising prices.

The use of options may provide protection for a manufacturer whose raw materials are commodities, and who has to quote prices for their manufactured goods, but knows neither whether they will be awarded a contract, nor the price they will have to pay for the raw materials should their bid be accepted. Hedging will not be appropriate in these circumstances, as it requires the manufacturer to take delivery of the physical commodity, though they are, as yet, unaware as to whether their bid will be accepted. The problem can be overcome by using a traded option. The company should purchase call options, which confer the right to buy. If the company's offer is accepted by the customer, the company can take up the option and enter into a standard futures hedge, but if the offer is declined or rejected, the company either will simply not take up the option, or may trade against it and possibly make a profit from doing that. In short, options allow those employing them to delay making a commitment to the actual acquisition of a commodity until it is appropriate to so do.

We conclude with a brief glossary of commodity market terminology.

SUMMARY POINTS

- Soft commodity prices can fluctuate by 100–500% in one season due to weather conditions. Commodity price is also affected by speculators; dealers and jobbers; expectations of present and future supply and demand.
- Supply is affected by drought, flood, strike, war, revolution whilst demand can change with economic activity, changes in taste and the advances of technology bringing alternative materials to the market.
- Suppliers and buyers may agree to a direct contract in order to stabilise price avoiding the commodity market. This will work if the price is in line with the market price. In the short term, producer cartels can control price administering a 'buffer stock'. This works until there is a definite upward or downward price trend, in which case the stock or the money to service it, is exhausted. Long term price stabilisation requires the monitoring of world demand and the alignment of output to meet it.
- The chapter illustrates various buying techniques – time budgeting (no risk and no stock); cost averaging/budget buying (undercutting market price) and dynamic programming (complex operational research approach).
- Traded options incur a premium to insure against fluctuating prices. A 'put' option protects the supplier against declining prices and a 'call' option protects the buyer against rising prices. Manufacturers bidding for work use this technique of conferring the right to buy should their bid win the tender. (Hedging would not be an appropriate strategy at the bid stage.)

GLOSSARY

Arbitrage Buying in one market, e.g. London, and selling in another, e.g. New York, in order to profit from price anomalies. This in fact smooths out the anomalies.

Backwardation Exists when the futures price is *lower* than the spot price.

Basis Difference between cash price and futures price.

Bear One who speculates for a fall in price.

Bear market A market in which the price is falling.

Broker One who buys or sells for others in return for a commission.

Bull One who speculates for a rise in price.

Bull market One in which price is rising.

Call option An option which confers the right to purchase a particular futures contract at a specific price.

Commission Charge made by a broker for buying or selling contracts; rates of commission are fixed by market authorities, and brokers are not allowed to depart from them.

Contango When the spot price is lower than the futures price.

Forwardation Same as *contango*.

Long Owning physical commodities or futures contracts which are not fully hedged.

Put option An option which confers the right to sell a particular futures contract at a specific price.

Premium The 'price' of the option; the amount of money transferred between buyer and seller for the benefits and rights conferred by the option. The premium represents the maximum amount that the option buyer can lose.

Prompt date The day on which delivery against a declared option contract must be made.

Short Selling physical commodities or futures in excess of what is owned.

REFERENCES AND FURTHER READING

Buckley J (1986), *A Guide to World Commodity Markets: Physical, Futures and Options Trading*, 5th edn, Kogan Page, London.

Gibson-Jarvig R (1989), *The London Metal Exchange: A Commodity Market*, Woodhead Faulkner, Cambridge.

Kingsman B G (1975), in Farmer DH and Taylor B (eds), *Corporate Planning and Procurement*, Heinemann, London.

Kingsman B G (1985), *Raw Materials Purchasing: An Operational Research Approach*, Pergamon Press, Oxford.

Seidel A D and Ginsberg P M (1983), *Commodities Trading: Foundation, Analysis and Operations*, Prentice Hall, New Jersey.

Buying internationally

The continuous internationalisation of trade has meant that foreign sourcing can no longer be regarded as exceptional activity in commercial purchasing. It would be difficult to find any organisation today that did not acquire at least a proportion of its requirements from foreign sources. For many organisations, and not just the multinational corporations, foreign sourcing is mainstream sourcing. For this reason, careful consideration was given in preparing this edition to the question of whether a separate chapter on this subject was necessary, the argument being that since importing can be regarded as mainstream work, the themes might be dealt with under 'purchasing systems and procedures'. The final decision was to retain the chapter, but we should like to suggest that purchasing from a foreign source is not different in any *fundamental* way from purchasing from a domestic source. The same value for money objectives are pursued, and much the same range of methods and systems are employed in this pursuit. Exactly the same problems need to be thought about and overcome, though, of course, *additional* problems need to be dealt with, and these form the main theme of this chapter.

OBJECTIVES OF THIS CHAPTER

- To appreciate why it may be necessary/preferable to source materials/goods from abroad
- To consider the problems associated with foreign sourcing
- To introduce 'incoterms'
- To define countertrade as a form of barter
- To outline the role of the European Union in relation to international purchasing.

WHY BUY FROM ABROAD?

Most purchasers would prefer to buy from suppliers located nearby, who speak the same language, belong to a similar culture, do business in the same legal system, work to the same standards and have no currency exchange problems. Shorter lines of communication and quicker delivery periods which are less subject to delays are further arguments in favour of local sourcing. So why is international trade increasing?

Reasons for sourcing abroad include the following:

1 The buyer may be compelled to go abroad to get what is required. Many raw materials are not produced at all in the UK; for instance cocoa, coffee, cobalt. The UK traditionally imported raw materials and exported manufactured goods. Some countries on the other hand export raw materials and import manufactured products which are not produced by their domestic industries.

2 The buyer may prefer to buy from a foreign source which offers features not available on domestically produced goods of a similar type. Technological innovation occurs all round the world. This is very noticeable in consumer goods, and is one reason why the UK currently imports more finished and semi-finished goods than it exports.

3 Although goods of the type required are produced domestically, domestic capacity may not be enough to meet demand, so the gap has to be filled from abroad.

4 There may be strategic reasons for foreign purchases, for instance to improve supply security by having a second source in another country.

5 It may be possible to buy equivalent goods more cheaply abroad, because of larger quantities, lower wages, better productivity, better plant, or the rate of exchange.

6 Countertrade may compel your firm to buy abroad. Sometimes it is not possible to win an export order without agreeing to a reciprocal import order.

PROBLEMS IN BUYING ABROAD

The main problems associated with foreign sourcing are as follows.

Communication problems

These arise not just because of language difficulties, which in any case are minimal for a UK buyer as English is, arguably, the standard language of international trade, but also because of time differences between countries, and differing meanings attaching to trading terminology and technical vocabulary.

Consensus ad idem, agreement on the same thing, is fundamental to a valid contract. It is, therefore, important to ensure that understanding is mutual. Even though both parties may be employing English or some other shared language in conducting their business, it is possible that if one party is less familiar with the language than the other, differing meanings may be attached to words or contract terms. Difficulties arise in connection with interpretation when contracts are entirely domestic; the probability of problems of this kind arising is much increased in international contracts.

Currency differences

The conversion of one currency into another does not, of itself, pose any great difficulty if the currencies are 'convertible', but the extent to which exchange rates fluctuate does cause considerable problems. The risk and uncertainty associated with the change in relative values between the exporters' and the importers' currencies has to be taken into account and managed. This is not an easy task.

The rate at which one currency exchanges for another tends to change continuously because of changes in the demand for and supply of each currency. These exchange rate fluctuations can and do affect international transactions in the same way as price changes.

For instance, suppose a British firm buys an American machine tool on three months delivery for $10 000. The rate of exchange is $1.70 = £1 when the purchase is made, so the customer sees the price as about £5882. During the three-month delivery period, the exchange rate alters to $1.90 = £1; and so the amount payable becomes £5263. This looks like a price reduction to the purchaser, although the seller still gets the price in dollars as quoted. If the rate altered the other way, the buyer would suffer the equivalent of a price increase, although the seller would not benefit from it.

It may be possible for the buyer to eliminate this uncertainty as to the amount payable by stating the contract price in the buyer's currency. This puts all the uncertainty on the seller. The buyer knows exactly what will have to be paid, but the seller does not know how much will be received.

Sometimes contracts are negotiated in which the risk is shared equally, for instance a clause might be included such as this:

> The amount payable will be calculated by converting the agreed dollar price to sterling according to the formula:
>
> £1 = ($x = $y)/2
>
> where $x is the dollar value of £1 at the date of the contract, and $y is the dollar value of £1 at the date payment is due.

Prices can also be stated in a third currency, or a notional currency such as the ECU. The ECU (European Currency Unit) has not replaced the individual European currencies, but functions alongside them, with an exchange value calculated daily according to a complex formula from the weighted average of individual exchange rates. The EU maintains its accounts in ECU, as do some companies. The ECU is widely traded, and can be used as the denominated currency in international contracts.

Many European countries subscribe to the ERM, or exchange rate mechanism, which is an agreement by members to allow their exchange rates to vary only to a very limited extent, with any departure from fairly narrow limits only to be made by mutual consent. Countries control their exchange rates by altering exchange rates, changing economic policies, and buying or selling their own or other currencies. At the time of writing the UK government has suspended its membership of the ERM, but has declared its intention of rejoining. It has also declared misgivings about the common EU currency, advocated by many, which would replace pounds, marks, francs and the other currencies of member states.

The standard way purchasers cope with currency risks is to make a forward purchase of the amount of foreign currency required to settle the bill. The banks provide a marketplace in which these purchases can be made.

On a large scale, currency futures are traded in the same way as commodity futures (discussed elsewhere in this text). They are even sometimes traded in the same markets, such as the Chicago Board of Trade, perhaps the biggest marketplace in the world for transactions of this kind.

Forward rates are quoted in the newspapers. Whether forward rates are at a premium or at a discount against spot rates, once the purchaser has made the forward currency purchase, the amount payable is certain.

A multinational business which buys components in France and Italy, to manufacture goods in the UK, for sale in Germany, and is controlled financially from the US, is exposed to a combination of exchange risks which might best be handled by a small central group of foreign exchange experts. Buyers without access to such internal expertise can get advice from banks or external consultants.

Payment

The international transfer of funds poses its own difficulties, and a third party, usually a bank, will probably need to be involved to facilitate this process. Of course, this service will cost money, a cost not applicable in domestic sourcing. Most transactions in the domestic market are on open account (credit terms). Typically the customer is allowed a month from the invoice date, or the date of delivery, whichever is the later, to settle the account. More precisely, *net monthly account* terms mean that the account must be settled by the end of the month following the month of delivery or invoicing, whereas *net cash 30 days* means that the account needs to be settled within 30 days of delivery or invoicing.

Trade within the EC is frequently conducted on open account, although sometimes the delay and expense associated with international cheque payments make it preferable to use telegraphic transfers, mail transfers, banker's draft or international money orders to settle the account. Telegraphic transfer is an instruction by telegraph from the buyer's bank to the seller's bank to transfer to the seller's account a stated sum of money. Mail transfer is a similar instruction sent by post. Banker's drafts are issued in any currency by banks, and the seller can usually pay them into an account at a local bank. International money orders are useful for small amounts.

Major international transactions outside the quasi-domestic market of the EC are frequently settled by bill of exchange or letter of credit. There is a basic conflict of interest between seller and buyer which assumes greater significance when the relationship is an international one. Basically the problem is that the seller will not wish to release his or her goods to the buyer until payment has been made, or he or she is certain that payment will be made. The buyer, of course, is in a similar position. It is unlikely that the buyer will release funds until he or she has possession of the goods, or at least a guarantee of their delivery. Because of these conflicting interests the contracting parties will usually employ the services of an intermediary, usually a bank, which will make payment only when evidence of performance is produced, but can be relied on to actually make the payment under such circumstances. The essential difference between a bill of exchange and a letter of credit is that in the case of a bill of exchange the bank is looking after the interests of the exporter, whereas in the case of a letter of credit the importer has the greater protection from the bank.

A bill of exchange is 'an unconditional order in writing addressed by one person to another signed by the person giving it requiring the person to whom it is addressed to pay on demand, or at a fixed and determinable future time a sum certain in money to, or to the order of, a specified person or to bearer'. There are two principal types of bills of exchange:

1 *Documents against acceptance (DA),* meaning that the importer accepts the documents giving title to the goods and signs a bill of exchange drawn on him or her which is to be met at a given future date. With this form of bill of exchange a certain amount of deferment can be attached to payment, while making as certain as possible the fact that the importer will pay.
2 *Documents against payment (DP),* which means that the importer is obliged to pay *before* the documents are released to him or her.

A documentary letter of credit is a promise in writing by a bank to an exporter that the goods will be paid for, providing that the exporter complies exactly with the terms and conditions laid down. The promise is, of course, made on behalf of the importer. The bank will naturally need to be sure that the importer has the necessary funds. There are three types of letter of credit, namely:

1 A *revocable* letter of credit, which means that the importer may instruct his or her bank to revoke it at any time prior to payment becoming due. Such letters are rarely used these days, as the degree of trust necessary between the two parties would mean that a direct payment might be made.
2 An *irrevocable* letter. Once one of these has been raised, it cannot be withdrawn under any circumstances. If the exporter performs his or her obligations he or she is virtually certain of payment.
3 A *confirmed irrevocable* credit provides dual protection. A bank in the exporter's country agrees to pay if the importer's bank fails to do so.

Of course, computer technology has made possible significant advances in the efficient transfer of funds through electronic data interchange (EDI). For example, the Eurogiro system is based on a network of computer systems which allow each member to exchange transactions with the other members directly.

Differing legal systems

When purchasing internationally it is important to establish whether the courts of the exporter's country, those of the importer's or the courts of a third country have jurisdiction in the event of a dispute. In the case of a contract made in England or Wales, and in the absence of an express term to the contrary in the contract, then the English courts will normally assume jurisdiction.

There remains, however, the question as to which law is the proper law of the contract. If the law of another country is relevant, then the applicable rules will have to be established by an expert witness. It is quite possible to have a situation where matters relating to the *form* of the contract may be liable to be decided by the legal system of one country, and matters to do with *performance* fall to be decided by the legal system of another.

The proper law of the contract is the law which the parties stipulate. Under English law the parties are free to stipulate in their contract the legal system which is to be applied. Sometimes the legal system of a country not connected with either contracting party is specified, for example because the goods are likely to pass through several owners in the course of trade, and a particular legal system is the generally accepted one in that particular trade.

It is sometimes the case that parties neglect to stipulate their intention as to which law shall be applied. When this is the case then the courts will infer the proper law from the contract and the circumstances surrounding it.

Consider the not unlikely scenario of a consignment of goods of Japanese design, manufactured in Malaysia and shipped from Singapore. The goods are sold by a British agent to a customer in France, and are to be shipped in a Norwegian-owned ship, registered in Liberia. The goods are to be paid for in US dollars. Obviously, the questions of jurisdiction and the prevailing law can be quite complex.

Of course, most buyers from overseas will buy through agents, and even where direct purchases are made the buyer is likely to employ an appropriate specialist to advise on, or, more likely, organise such matters as shipment, insurance, handling, clearance, payment and other related matters.

Incoterms

When buying from overseas it is important to establish and be aware of the obligations of both parties in respect of 'terms of delivery'. Both buyer and seller will have obligations concerning the transportation, insurance and shipment of the goods under their contract for the sale and supply of the goods. Misunderstandings can easily arise, and it is desirable to take appropriate steps to prevent problems of this kind from occurring.

The International Chamber of Commerce (ICC) based in Paris first published a set of shipping terms, with their standard interpretations almost 60 years ago. These 'Incoterms' as they are known, remain in service today, though the ICC has, of course, continuously revised and updated them to take account of contemporary practice.

The current edition of Incoterms was published in 1990, though there have been very minor revisions since that date. There are two major groups of Incoterms; those relating to the carriage of goods by sea and those relating to all forms of transport including multimodal. The responsibilities of buyer and seller are clearly prescribed in the Incoterms guide, available from the ICC. There are 13 Incoterms in all, as follows:

- EXW   Ex Works
- FCA   Free Carrier
- FAS   Free Alongside

- FOB   Free On Board
- CFR   Cost and Freight
- CIF   Cost, Insurance and Freight
- CPT   Carriage Paid To
- CIP   Carriage and Insurance Paid to
- DAF   Delivered At Frontier
- DES   Delivered Ex Ship
- DEQ   Delivered Ex Quay
- DDU   Delivered Duty Unpaid
- DDP   Delivered Duty Paid

Litigation between buyer and seller is generally a complicated and expensive business, and is to be avoided if at all possible. This is particularly true in the case of international transactions. Fortunately, there is an alternative in the form of *arbitration*. This is relatively inexpensive and much quicker, and involves a panel of independent arbitrators examining the case with a view to finding a solution which reflects the rights and interests of both parties. The International Chamber of Commerce in Paris is the leading body for the provision of arbitration services in connection with international trade, and has a set of rules for conciliation and arbitration. Arbitrators can be appointed for any country by the court of arbitration in Paris. The London Court of Arbitration of the London Chamber of Commerce and Industry also offers arbitration services, as do some other chambers of commerce. Panels of expert arbitrators are maintained and advice is available on arbitration clauses suitable for use in international contracts.

Transport

All five basic modes of freight transport – road, rail, air, water and pipeline – are used in international transactions. More than one mode may be used in delivering goods: a consignment may make part of the journey by road and the next part by air. The Channel Tunnel now provides more choice and competition in road and rail haulage to and from Britain.

Severe delays occur in the transport arrangements for some international transactions. Strikes and congestion at ports in the Middle East and in Africa have led to ships queuing for months to be unloaded. One way to counteract these delays is to hold stocks in the country of import. This can be expensive. A big selling point of air freight is that buffer stocks can be low because of the 'lead time economics' of air travel: fast delivery, in effect.

Customs

Import and export procedures between countries which are members of the EC are being considerably simplified, with the single market and the abolition of import taxes. For purchases from countries outside the EC, however, careful administration is needed to avoid unnecessary expense.

It is important to reduce the length of time goods are in Customs. Every day's delay can add to costs. Inaccurate, incomplete or incorrect information on documents such as invoices, waybills, import licences and letters of credit causes delay. Whether information is given to consignments from different sources for one destination. Consolidation is the term used for air freight, groupage for overland transport.

A major air forwarder may have as many as a hundred consolidation routes to airports around the world, with agents meeting consignments on arrival and breaking them down into packages for delivery to individual addresses. Consolidation enables customers to benefit from bulk rates, with up to 50 per cent reduction in cost. Airlines also benefit from these arrangements, and over 80 per cent of UK air freight is handled by forwarders.

Groupage is used in overland transport to enable several consignors to share the journey cost. Consignments from several sources which are going to the same destination are collected together to make a unit load. This can delay things while the load is being accumulated, although it does reduce transport costs.

Substantial differences occur between the prices quoted, so buyers would be well advised to obtain several quotations. In one instance five quotations were obtained for transport, insurance and documentation of a consignment of 2500 lb ball valves door-to-door from Perth to Hamburg. The highest quote was 64 per cent above the average while the lowest was 51 per cent below the average. Of course, price is not the only thing to consider, and when price differentials are as large as this, non-price differences must be considered with care.

COUNTERTRADE

Countertrade is a form of barter. It takes place whenever goods are traded internationally, not in exchange for cash or currency, but for other goods. Countertrade is widely practised in international business, and facilitates transactions with countries which are unable or unwilling to export in a more conventional manner, perhaps for one or more of the following reasons:

- One or both trading partners have no (or limited) foreign exchange.
- A country wishes to promote exports, and is prepared to accept goods rather than hard currency in payment to facilitate this.
- There may be political pressure to balance trade between two countries.

The most straightforward form of countertrade is the full compensation arrangement, where a single contract is established between two parties, and goods are exchanged for other goods. Of course, it is unlikely that a coincidence of wants will be experienced in practice, and one party to the transaction is likely to need to sell the goods received under the contract. When British Aerospace supply military aircraft to Saudi Arabia in exchange for oil from that country, or a European car maker sends vehicles to a South American country in exchange for sheepskins, it does not mean that the supplying company is likely to have a use for the materials exchanged.

What happens under a full compensation arrangement is that the goods are valued in money, and the party who wishes to liquidate the materials received will do so by arranging for the sale of goods, usually with the assistance of an experienced third party.

Counterpurchase arrangements are also widely employed, where two separate contracts are formed simultaneously. A company in country A agrees with a company in country B to ship goods from country A to country B in exchange for money. At the same time agreement is made that country B will ship goods to country A, also in exchange for money. Although the two contracts balance each other, so that the net effect is simply that an exchange of goods has taken place, it is easier to manage two conventional contracts, to assign rights and responsibilities, to arrange insurance and so on.

There are, in practice, many kinds of arrangement under which countertrade exchanges may be made, some of them extremely complex. The arrangements have in common the fact that the outcome results in one of the parties discharging some or all of their obligations by supplying goods or services rather than by paying money.

THE EUROPEAN UNION (EU)

The EU is a single market. That is to say that it is one area for the purposes of customs duty. Once goods from any source outside the EU have been imported into any EU country and the appropriate duty, if any, paid, then the goods are in 'free circulation'. No further customs duty is payable on transfer of the goods to any other EU member state. It should be noted that, in contrast to customs duty, VAT and excise duty are imposed by each member state independently. There are some anti-dumping duties specific to the UK and these may be levied, even though the goods are imported from another state within the EU and as such are in free circulation. As a general rule the regulations and reliefs from duty on importation into the EU are common throughout the member states, though there may be differences in detail on the way in which they are supplied. The membership of the EU at the time of writing is Belgium, Denmark, France, Germany, Greece, Eire, Italy, Netherlands, Portugal, Spain, Luxembourg, Austria, Finland, Sweden and the UK though this membership is likely to increase through the admission of a number of other European countries.

The EU has issued many directives to ensure that the market within the membership is a free and open one; two of particular interest and concern to purchasing and supply executives are the Supplies Directive and the Services Directive. A familiarity with the detailed requirements of these directives is essential for all organisations in the 'non-excluded' part of the public sector, and for those organisations providing public utilities and services. The directives require that an opportunity to tender for supply or service contracts in excess of a given value should be extended equally to organisations in all EU states, and that the procedures by which contractors and suppliers are selected and notified shall conform to regulations designed to ensure openness.

The European Economic Area agreement was signed on 2 May 1992, and extends most of the EU's single market measures to Austria, Finland, Iceland, Lichtenstein, Norway and Sweden. These countries, plus Switzerland, which is not a party to the European Economic Area Agreement, comprise the

European Free Trade Area (EFTA). The European Economic Area is the world's biggest single market, covering a land area with both a Mediterranean and an Arctic coastline, and accounting for over 40 per cent of world trade. Under the EEA Agreement, EFTA will adopt most of the EU's existing single market legislation.

SUMMARY POINTS

- Communication problems (language, time difference, interpretation) complicate foreign trade. Exchange rate fluctuations can be dealt with by making a forward purchase of the amount needed in the same way as a commodity.
- Within the European Community, payment will involve the transfer of funds by telegraphic means, mail, bankers draft or international money orders. Outside of the EC, Bills of Exchange or Letters of Credit which require an intermediary are used.
- There are two types of Bills of Exchange – documents against acceptance (allowing deferment of payment) and documents against payment (importer is obliged to pay before the release of the documentation). The three types of letters of credit are revocable, irrevocable and confirmed irrevocable.
- In the event of a dispute, it is important to establish which court has jurisdiction. Matters relating to the form of the contract and matters relating to performance may be decided by separate courts (sometimes the court is of a country not connected with either contracting party).
- Countertrade may be a straightforward single contract between two parties 'swopping' goods or it may be performed using two separate contracts simultaneously, each assigning rights and responsibilities.

REFERENCES AND FURTHER READING

Branch A E (1990), *Elements of Import Practice*, Chapman and Hall, London.

Bugg R and Whitehead G (1990), *Elements of Transportation Documentation*, Woodhead Faulkner, Cambridge.

Butler J (1988), *The Importer's Handbook 1988*, Woodhead Faulkner, Cambridge.

Coombs P (1978), *Handbook of International Purchasing*, Cahners Books, Boston.

Hickman T K and Hickman W M (1978), *Global Purchasing*, Ore Irwin (USA).

Whiting D P (1986), *Finance of Foreign Trade*, M & E Handbooks, Pitman Publishing, London.

CHAPTER 14

Capital goods

INTRODUCTION

Many organisations appear to believe that in the acquisition of capital equipment they need not involve their purchasing professionals. In such cases engineers, and production and financial staff tend to be closely involved. Purchasing staff are drawn in simply to sign the contract or get a discount. Yet the commercial implications of capital purchases are as important as the commercial implications of production materials or components. The main emphasis of this chapter is on explaining purchasing's role.

OBJECTIVES OF THIS CHAPTER

- To identify purchasing's contribution to the acquisition of capital equipment
- To outline the differences between the purchase of capital and non-capital goods
- To appreciate the importance of 'performance' specifications and how dealing with them can be simplified by tabulation
- To involve purchasing from the earliest stage of identifying a need through the process of supplier selection, commercial input into contract clauses and appraisal of after sales service
- To assess the various methods of investment appraisal.

THE ACQUISITION OF CAPITAL EQUIPMENT

It is evident that operators, and production and finance staff need to be involved in making purchasing decisions concerned with capital equipment. Depending upon the type of capital purchase, each may have a significant part to play in, for example, identifying the type of equipment required, examining the alternative sources which may be able to provide that equipment, and in specifying the performance specification and budget factors that are involved. However, in our experience, decisions made by such a group without purchasing/commercial input frequently lead to contractual difficulties; for example, the equipment does not function to the level which the supplier's specification promised. In many such cases the buying company is obliged to seek compensation from the supplier, with little commercial leverage other than, say, 10 per cent of purchase price retention. In our view, proper participation of the buying professional would help to ensure that such circumstances were avoided. Even where the outcome is the same, effective pre-contract negotiation can ensure that the buyer is protected, at least to some degree.

We are sometimes asked for advice from purchasing personnel who feel that it is necessary to convince users that the purchasing function can contribute to the making of appropriate decisions in relation to the acquisition of capital equipment. In this respect, Figure 14.1 is based on an overhead projection transparency used to stimulate discussion on the role and contribution of purchasing.

This chapter comments on the role that the buying professional has to play in purchasing capital equipment or in making other types of capital purchase. It should be noted, however, that the buyers we have come across who play a full part in the capital purchase decision have always earned the respect of their fellow professionals. They tend to have reputations which imply that they have expertise to offer. Where that is the case they are welcomed as and even sought out to be part of the capital purchase team.

Procurement executives who aim to make a useful and constructive contribution to the capital expenditure decision, and one which will be recognised as such by other members of the decision-making unit, need diplomacy as well as top management backing. Alternative assets differ in their features, and technical assessment of these features is required. This technical assessment, followed by a financial assessment – Will it pay? Can we afford it now? – is usually the main part of the investigation, but examination of commercial aspects can also be very rewarding, and here astute procurement people can make a real contribution.

Because the equipment will have a working life of several years, it is important to consider such matters as product support, availability of spares, after-sales service, the financial soundness and management stability of the supplier. Cost of use after service is important, and is affected by reliability and the possibility of down-time.

The acquisition of capital equipment. Purchasing's contribution
• Location of sources
• Vetting of suppliers
• Negotiating (active role/consultancy)
• Cost/benefit analyses
• Life cycle costing
• Advice on residual values
• Organisation of product trials
• Establishment of total supply cost
• Lease/hire/buy comparison
• Contact drafting
• Contract management
• Provisioning of support materials
• Co-ordination of procurement team

Fig. 14.1 The role and contribution of purchasing

Contract price is negotiable as are payment terms. In addition it does not necessarily follow that a request by the supplier for stage payments needs to be accepted. It may well be the normal terms of trade of a particular manufacturer that he receives X per cent with order, Y per cent when ready for despatch, Z per cent upon delivery with the balance being paid a stated number of months after commissioning. However, depending upon, for example, the state of the supplier's order book, he may well be prepared to forgo any payment prior to commissioning. Indeed we have been involved with one company in the printing industry where a Swiss supplier agreed to give the buyer eighteen months' credit against a 10 per cent deposit. This is not to say that such arrangements can always be negotiated. Rather it is to emphasise that such negotiations should be undertaken in a manner which seeks the best commercial and technical outcome from the buyer's viewpoint. Frequently this involves challenging the apparent 'givens' of a tender for capital equipment.

The buyer should always seek some level of retention; for example, 10 per cent of the purchase price may be retained by the buyer until, say, one month after the equipment has been demonstrated on a production run as meeting its specified performance level. Contract terms of this kind can be negotiated by purchasing in the more straightforward cases. In more complicated cases (e.g. involving trade-offs between technical alternatives as well as commercial and financial alternatives) negotiating teams are set up with representatives of the various specialist functions.

WHAT ARE CAPITAL PURCHASES?

Buying capital goods, such as buildings, plant and machinery, and computers, differs in several ways from the purchase of non-capital goods. Unlike merchandise, production materials or office supplies, capital goods are not bought for current needs, to be used up in a short time, but are bought for long-term requirements, to be used for the production of goods or services. Capital goods have, as a rule of thumb, working lives greater than one year.

Capital expenditure is treated differently, for taxation purposes, and in accounting. Special tax allowances or cash grants may be available for investment in new equipment or for factories in certain areas of the country. Consequently, tax considerations, usually ignored in non-capital purchases, can be significant in capital purchase decisions; they can affect timing, they can make a big difference to the expected return, and they can be crucial in deciding whether to go ahead with the purchase.

Often the initial price is high, so that commitment to one capital project means that rival proposals have to be rejected. Even if initial price is not high compared with current expenditure, capital goods tend to be highly specific so that the cost of a wrong decision could be much higher than for current expenditure items. Alternative uses of a high-bay automatic warehouse, a crankshaft transfer line or a special-purpose machine tool may be negligible. If stocks are built up to meet increasing sales which fail to occur, stocks can be run down by selling back to suppliers or by deferring further purchases; but if specialised plant is procured to cope with the sales increase, it will not be so easy to dispose of it.

Most capital expenditure is postponable. Individual consumers would not last long if they stopped their intake of food and drink, and manufacturing organisations which stopped acquiring parts and material for production would soon be out of business. Individual consumers can postpone, however, the replacement of consumer durables such as a car or refrigerator with no great loss of amenity so long as the existing equipment works, and manufacturers in the same way can defer the replacement of old plant until prospects look brighter or the financial situation improves. This has unfortunate consequences for capital equipment suppliers; their order books alternate between feast and famine. When their customers experience a minor recession, they suffer a major recession; the business cycle hits them in amplified form, with some time lag.

CAPITAL REQUISITIONS

Because of these special features, special procedures are commonly used for capital purchases. In small or medium-sized organisations all capital expenditure has to be authorised by the board. In larger organisations, authority to approve capital expenditure up to a specified cash limit is delegated to local directors, division or area managers, profit centre managers, or others below main board level; but above this limit, the projects which make large demands on organisation finance, or affect capacity and method of working for a long time, are still referred to the main board even in large organisations.

Most capital decisions will be influenced by a range of interests. Figure 14.2 suggests some of the interests which may contribute to the acquisition of a fork lift truck.

Delay in obtaining authorisation for capital expenditure resulting from such procedures can lead to excessive haste to get on with the work once authorisation is forthcoming. The requisitioner may have been waiting months for approval, and as soon as he or she has it he or she may phone the chosen supplier with the good news, chivvy purchasing to get the order off before contractual details are finalised, and generally ignore commercial aspects in his or her natural zeal to get the equipment installed.

In such circumstances the buyer is forced to negotiate from a disadvantageous position. The seller, having been told that the order is his or hers and that delivery is required as a matter of urgency, is in an extremely strong position from which to negotiate. The professional buyer should seek to ensure that company procedures are in place which obviate such difficulty. It is our view that their involvement should begin at the earliest stage when a need is defined, and that, in conjunction with their technical and financial colleagues, they should undertake the market search for qualified suppliers and suitable equipment. After all, commercial as well as technical negotiations

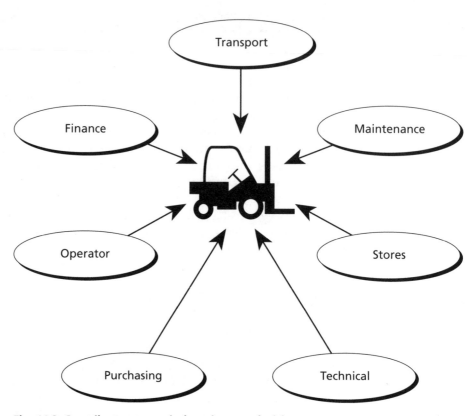

Fig. 14.2 Contributors to capital equipment decisions

commence in those early stages and while engineering colleagues would be primarily focused upon technical issues the buyer would be concerned with the many commercial issues as they unfold.

The purchase department needs to insist that enough time be allowed to negotiate contract details. Where possible it is better for purchasing to participate at an earlier stage so that commercial as well as technical aspects are agreed and are included in the proposal put up for approval.

As an example of difficulties which can be encountered if these things are neglected, a case occurred in which a company ordered a new design of production equipment costing over a million pounds. Engineers in the buying company had been assured that the equipment would be fully installed and operational in six weeks and would reach target output by week 8. Nine months after delivery, actual output was less than half of target output, which caused embarrassment with customers whose orders were held up. The company had inserted a 5 per cent retention clause in the contract, but apart from that was unable to obtain compensation from the equipment supplier. When negotiating a contract for production equipment which is wanted because of its indicated performance, it is necessary to include performance criteria in the contract and to relate payment, at least in part, to achievement of the agreed output norms.

SPECIFICATION OF CAPITAL EQUIPMENT

In an article in *Purchasing and Supply Management* in July 1993, Nigel Moore, writing on the theme of specification of capital items said:

> Sometimes specifications are improved by being split into a general requirements section that is changed infrequently and a particular requirements section that is customised to each individual order or contract. [The particular requirements section forms the basis of the tabular format specification shown in part in Figure 14.3 comprises three main sub-sections]:
>
> 1. A section on the **required equipment, services or works.**
>   The entries are kept short and must be read in conjunction with the information in the vertical columns, Table A, Table B and Inspection.
>
> *Table A*   This is completed by the specifier to show what is required.
>
> *Table B*   This is completed by the vendor to show what is being offered.
>
> *Inspection*   This is completed at the time an inspection of the works or equipment is carried out.
>
> 2. A **site details** section (not shown). Relevant details and factors about the location that could affect the design and performance of the plant, equipment, services or works.
>
> 3. A section on **additional information** that is required from the vendor (not shown).
>
> The general or 'wordy' specification can remain to support this particular requirements specification. It could be updated to provide further clarification of terms and to ensure that they cannot be misinterpreted. The tabular format can have wide application as the contractual and specified requirements are not changing. The only departure from the traditional is the way the information is presented. It can be used for supply of equipment or services and scope of works on site. Usually the information is presented in a logical order of importance. Often this is based on the cost and difficulty for the vendor to comply with as part of fulfilling the subsequent contract. Typically this could include:
>
> - Scope of supply including any extra items (for example, tests).
> - Overall performance requirements.
> - Any specific design requirements.
>
> The detail can be made as comprehensive as desired or kept to the minimum. Consequently the specification can comply with EN 29000 by stating functional or performance requirements.
>
> Table A is pre-printed to show the standard practice. The specifier needs only to complete the remainder and he or she is prompted on what information to provide. This can entail, for example, filling in a blank line or crossing out the options that do not apply. Consequently his or her job is made easier. Often all the vendor has to do is enter a 'Yes' to confirm compliance, although data can be written in where appropriate.
>
> When the completed documents are returned from potential vendors, it is a simple task to compare their offers with the specification. The bid tabulation merely requires lining up the Table Bs. It takes little extra time to compare offers even if there is a

large number of tenderers or alternatives. Possible copying errors or difficulties extracting information from the vendors' offers are removed.

At the tender evaluation stage, differences are highlighted and can be resolved before the order is placed. Even meetings with vendors are made easier as the specification forms a convenient agenda and when photocopied on to a larger sheet can be used to record the minutes. The process of issuing enquiries, evaluating tenders and placing orders is consequently speeded up.

The vendor also benefits. There is much less paperwork to look through and try to understand. The major part of the vendor's price and costs can be worked out by just examining a few sheets, instead of reading many pages. This is especially useful as tendering departments are often overworked and tender submissions are against tight time limits. Alternative offers can be submitted with greater confidence that they will be seriously evaluated.

Perhaps the greatest advantage to both specifier and vendor is that when the order is placed, there are markedly fewer opportunities for extra costs through copying errors, mistakes, misunderstandings and omissions. They also have a simple document to refer to during the contract and the last column can be used at any time by the specifier or the vendor to check that what has been agreed is actually being provided. Typical uses are for drawing checks and final inspection before despatch or handover

THE PROJECT APPROACH

Whatever the size of the company, any purchasing professional worth his or her salt ought to be seeking to make an effective contribution to the control and management of capital purchases as suggested earlier. The person concerned should be the one who searches the market to locate suitable sources for the equipment. This presupposes that the requisitioner has developed a preliminary specification. Too often this is not written in sufficient detail to allow proper research to be done. The specification should indicate desirable performance criteria and delivery date as well as any special requirements such as safety and other legal requirements in the country where the equipment is to be used. The buyer could then:

1 Draw up a list of potential sources – worldwide if appropriate.
2 Obtain relevant data about sources.
3 Get names of current users of the suppliers' products for possible use as referees.
4 Obtain prices for alternative equipment, including ex-works price, transport and installation cost.
5 Find out lead-time details – ex-works, delivered, installed, operational, and up-to-target output.
6 Establish expected equipment life, recommended spares and maintenance schedules.
7 Obtain statements of operating costs and performance criteria.
8 Find out what after-sales service suppliers are prepared to provide.

Next, the team can consider available alternatives and where feasible draw up a shortlist of companies able to meet technical and commercial requirements.

BATTERY AND CHARGER REQUIREMENTS			
1.0 EXTENT OF CONTRACT	Table A	Table B	Inspection
1.1 Supply, Design, Testing, Delivery site/~~FOB~~	Yes	*Yes*	....
At site installation, commission	Yes/~~No~~	*Yes*	....
(a) Delivery: date req'd/length of time in months	*10 weeks*	*15 wks*	....
(b) Quantity:	*Two*	*2*	....
1.2 Testing to EN/IEC (incl. tolerances)			
1.2.1. All equipment previously type tested	Yes	*No*	....
1.2.2. Witness tests at work by purchaser	Yes	*Yes*	....
2.0 OVERALL PERFORMANCE REQUIREMENTS			
2.1 Supply standing load and recharge battery	Yes	*Yes*	....
(a) Time to recharge battery ....hours	*10*	*8*	....
2.2 Battery only supply standing load curve	Yes	*Yes*	....
(a) At rated min./max. ambient temp. degrees C	20/30	*20/30*	....
(b) Min. Battery terminal volts V	*45*	*45*	....
2.3 Equipment suitable for specified location	Yes	*Yes*	....
(a) IP Number external during normal operation	32 min.	*45*	....
2.4 Design life min...years	25	*Yes*	....
(a) Battery expected service life min.............years	3/~~10~~	*5*	....
2.5 Packed for transport to site	Yes	*Yes*	....
(a) Suitable 6 months min. indoor/outdoor storage	Yes/~~VTA~~	*Yes*	....
3.0 GENERAL REQUIREMENTS			
3.1 Spares + consumables required for ....years	2	*Yes*	....
(a) List of spares + future availability + prices	RWT	*Yes*	....
3.2 Finish (colour/RAL/vendor's std)	*Grey*	*Yes*	....
4.0 DOCUMENTATION			
4.1 Quality Assurance, Quality Plan to BS 5750-1	RWT/~~No~~	*Yes*	....
4.2 Manual copies: ....*5*.............Loose leaf, A4 size	Yes	*2*	....

Note: Table A lists specified requirements. The information provided in Table B forms the basis of the vendor's technical offer. Comments in brackets provide clarifications of information required.

Abbreviations: RWT = Return with Tender; VTA = Vendor to Advise; incl = including the following; m = minute; min = minimum value; max = maximum value.

Fig. 14.3 Format of a particular requirements section of a specification

Each company will be appraised individually, as well as being made aware of the terms and conditions applicable. Detailed discussions with shortlisted sources may be necessary to ensure that they understand what is required, when and how it will be done, and what criteria will be used to assess performance. Suppliers and referee customers may be visited in this stage.

Finally, one supplier is selected and the contract is negotiated. It should state the responsibilities of both parties and the procedures to follow in commissioning the equipment. It may well be the whole team which negotiates, but the purchasing professional, whether or not designated as team leader, should play the key role in commercial and contractual matters, and in communication between customer and supplier about the contract.

In these negotiations many issues need to be covered. Among the commercial issues the most obvious is price. What does the price include, what is excluded? Is it a delivered price or an installed one? If there are to be extras what is the means by which their value will be calculated? In what currency is the purchase to be made? If a stage payment agreement has been made it is necessary to specify under what circumstances the price may be varied. If there is a long lead time and the supplier wishes to protect themself in an inflationary period, it may be necessary to negotiate the application of a formula, for example, BEAMA.

As far as specification is concerned, leading companies are moving towards a functional rather than product specification; for example, that a particular machine should be capable of producing N widgets every minute over a period of Y hours continuous running. Where that is the case, many buyers are seeking to agree contracts where the buyer retains a substantial percentage of the purchase price until the equipment performs as specified. Others agree payment against a performance bond where money is held, as it were, in trust until the equipment meets the specified output figures.

Other important areas for consideration include warranty terms and a clear understanding as to when title passes. Also, given the assumption that title does not pass until satisfactory commissioning, who is responsible for insurance relating to associated risks and liabilities until that time.

Time, of course, is always an element and in some major capital negotiations decides to refurbish one of its stores, each day which passes without trading results in lost sales. Consequently time becomes a major focus given the extent of the opportunity costs associated with the store not trading.

Spares provision, training of operators, a clear understanding of what facilities (e.g. electricity, water, cranage) are to be provided by the buyer, safety and arbitration arrangements, and a clear agreement as to when title passes, are further considerations.

INVESTMENT APPRAISAL

In a sense, almost any expenditure can be seen as an investment: the immediate expenditure procures a return which is not entirely immediate but extends some way into the future. A comparison can be made between what is likely to happen if the expenditure is made; and what is likely to happen if it is not made: if, for instance, the money is spent on something else. Such 'appraisals' are more important when the amount to be spent is larger because, in committing a larger proportion of available resources, the expenditure cuts down the options which remain open. The individual consumer is likely to give more thought to the purchase of a house or a motor car than to the purchase of a shirt or a drink for this very reason.

Capital expenditure of the sort we are considering is concerned with the acquisition of permanent physical assets used in the production of goods or services, and thus very definitely represents an investment. To appraise properly the costs and benefits associated with a particular proposal requires the life-cycle cost approach referred to above. The standard procedure is to prepare a detailed statement of the net cash flow per period throughout the life cycle (which may be the end of the project or asset life, or else up to a planning horizon). Net cash flow is the difference between cash received and cash paid. Positive cash flows, which increase available cash, may include payments from customers, savings in operating costs, reductions in the tax bill and tax refunds. Negative cash flows, which reduce available cash, may include payments to suppliers and employees' wages and salaries, interest on loans and repayment of loans, and tax on profits attributable to the project. The sequence of net cash flows for the life cycle is the earnings profile – a term used particularly when there are substantial differences between earnings (or profits, or savings) in different parts of the life cycle.

Complete accuracy is unattainable even for the simplest proposal, such as the replacement of worn out machinery. For more complicated projects such as launching new products or opening up world markets, great uncertainties exist in estimating the future streams of costs and benefits which constitute the earnings profile. Nevertheless, the attempt must be made, since without some figures to work on most investment decisions would just be leaps in the dark.

Once the cost–benefit analysis or earnings profile has been prepared, a decision has to be taken as to whether to go ahead with the project. Even if it looks likely to be profitable, most organisations have many calls on available resources. A number of other paying proposals may be put forward, some of which have to be turned down because resources (financial, human, management) are limited. The process of calculating or estimating earnings profiles for investment proposals and applying various criteria to assess their profitability is known as investment appraisal.

The criteria applied to assess investment projects include payback period, average rate of return and discounted cash flow methods, of which the two most widely used are net present value and DCF yield or internal rate of return. Since the procurement executive who is involved in the capital expenditure decision may encounter any of these, we will explain them all with the aid of examples which may point to the shortcomings of some of them. In most of the examples there is no specific reference to tax because this is the province of the accountant – not because it is unimportant. Taxation incentives in a development area could treble the expected yield of an investment in plant and machinery; taxation is also an important factor in deciding whether to buy or lease a facility.

INVESTMENT APPRAISAL CRITERIA

The payback criterion, popular because of its simplicity, consists of calculating how long the investment will take to pay for itself: the time taken for savings or profits (net positive cash flow) to accumulate to an amount equal to the initial outlay (negative cash flow). Its disadvantage can be seen from an example. Suppose the choice is between Project A and Project B, both requiring an initial outlay of £3000. Project A earns £1000 a year for three years, £600 in the fourth year and nil after that. Project B earns £750 a year for eight years. The payback criterion would prefer A, which pays for itself in three years, to B, which takes four years to pay for itself, even though B continues to earn money for twice as long as A.

The crude 'rate of return', criterion is applied in several ways. Typically, the average annual earnings are calculated and then expressed as a percentage of the capital invested. For instance, Project A has total earnings of £3600 over four years; therefore the average annual return is £900; as a percentage of the capital invested, £3000, this is a 30 per cent rate of return. Project B earns £750 a year, a 25 per cent rate of return.This criterion would also prefer A because B gives a lower rate of return. The fact that it earns it for a longer period is left out of account.

Table 14.1 Discount factors for DCF calculations.
(This table shows the present value of 1 discounted for various numbers of years at various rates of discount.)

Rate of discount	5%	6%	7%	8%	9%	10%	11%	12%	13%	14%	15%	16%	17%	18%	19%	20%
Year																
0	1.000	1.000	1.000	1.000	1.000	1.000	1.000	1.000	1.000	1.000	1.000	1.000	1.000	1.000	1.000	1.000
1	0.952	0.943	0.935	0.926	0.917	0.909	0.901	0.893	0.885	0.877	0.870	0.862	0.855	0.847	0.840	0.833
2	0.907	0.890	0.873	0.857	0.842	0.826	0.812	0.797	0.783	0.769	0.756	0.743	0.731	0.718	0.706	0.694
3	0.864	0.840	0.816	0.794	0.772	0.751	0.731	0.712	0.693	0.675	0.658	0.641	0.624	0.609	0.593	0.579
4	0.823	0.792	0.763	0.735	0.708	0.683	0.659	0.636	0.613	0.592	0.572	0.552	0.534	0.516	0.499	0.482
5	0.784	0.747	0.713	0.681	0.650	0.621	0.593	0.567	0.543	0.519	0.497	0.476	0.456	0.437	0.419	0.402
6	0.746	0.705	0.666	0.630	0.596	0.564	0.535	0.507	0.480	0.456	0.432	0.410	0.390	0.370	0.352	0.335
7	0.711	0.665	0.623	0.583	0.547	0.513	0.482	0.452	0.425	0.400	0.376	0.354	0.333	0.314	0.296	0.279
8	0.677	0.627	0.582	0.540	0.502	0.467	0.434	0.404	0.376	0.351	0.327	0.305	0.285	0.266	0.249	0.233
9	0.645	0.592	0.544	0.500	0.460	0.424	0.391	0.361	0.333	0.308	0.284	0.263	0.243	0.225	0.209	0.194
10	0.614	0.558	0.508	0.463	0.422	0.386	0.352	0.322	0.295	0.270	0.247	0.227	0.208	0.191	0.176	0.162
11	0.585	0.527	0.475	0.429	0.388	0.350	0.317	0.287	0.261	0.237	0.215	0.195	0.178	0.162	0.148	0.135
12	0.557	0.497	0.444	0.397	0.356	0.319	0.286	0.257	0.231	0.208	0.187	0.168	0.152	0.137	0.124	0.112
13	0.530	0.469	0.415	0.368	0.326	0.290	0.258	0.229	0.204	0.182	0.163	0.145	0.130	0.116	0.104	0.093
14	0.505	0.442	0.388	0.340	0.299	0.263	0.232	0.205	0.181	0.160	0.141	0.125	0.111	0.099	0.088	0.078
15	0.481	0.417	0.362	0.315	0.275	0.239	0.209	0.183	0.160	0.140	0.123	0.108	0.095	0.084	0.074	0.065
16	0.458	0.394	0.339	0.292	0.252	0.218	0.188	0.163	0.141	0.123	0107	0.093	0.081	0.071	0.062	0.054
17	0.436	0.371	0.317	0.270	0.231	0.198	0.170	0.146	0.125	0.108	0.093	0.080	0.069	0.060	0.052	0.045
18	0.416	0.350	0.296	0.250	0.212	0.180	0.153	0.130	0.111	0.095	0081	0.069	0.059	0.051	0.044	0.038
19	0.396	0.331	0.277	0.232	0.194	0.164	0.138	0.116	0.098	0.083	0.070	0.060	0.051	0.043	0.037	0.031
20	0.377	0.312	0.258	0.215	0.178	0.149	0.124	0.104	0.087	0.073	0.061	0.051	0.043	0.037	0.031	0.026
21	0.359	0.294	0.242	0.199	0.164	0.135	0.112	0.093	0.077	0.064	0.053	0.044	0.037	0.031	0.026	0.022
22	0.342	0.278	0.226	0.184	0.150	0.123	0.101	0.083	0.068	0.056	0.046	0.038	0.032	0.026	0.022	0.018
23	0.326	0.262	0.211	0.170	0.138	0.112	0.091	0.074	0.060	0.049	0040	0.033	0.027	0.022	0.018	0.015
24	0.310	0.247	0.197	0.158	0.126	0.102	0.082	0.066	0.053	0.043	0.035	0.028	0.023	0.019	0.015	0.013
25	0.295	0.233	0.184	0.146	0.116	0.092	0.074	0.059	0.047	0.038	0.030	0.024	0.020	0.016	0.013	0.010

More accurate appraisal techniques take account of the fact that a pound received today is worth more than a pound which will not be received for two years. The present value of money receivable in the future can be calculated quite simply. The procedure is the inverse of the compound-interest calculation by which the future value of money invested today can be worked out.

For instance, if £100 is invested for three years at say 10 per cent interest, it will amount to £100 + 10 per cent at the end of the first year, i.e. £110. At the end of the second year it will amount to £110 + 10 per cent, i.e. £121. By the end of the third year it will be worth £121 + 10 per cent, i.e. £133.1. Now if we can say that £100 invested today at 10 per cent interest will be worth £133.1 at the end of three years, we can also say that if £133.1 is due three years from now, it must be worth £100 today, using a discount rate of 10 per cent.

Published tables show interest factors: we could have looked up 10 per cent for three years and found the factor of 1.331. Multiplying £100 by this factor would immediately have given the future value of £133.1 which we worked out longhand. Similar tables are published for discount factors: 1/1.331 = 0.751, the discount factor for three years at 10 per cent. If the future value of £133.1 is multiplied by this factor of 0.751, we have the present value of £100. Table 14.1 gives such factors.

Some problems on present value (ignoring inflation)

Example 1

Would you rather be given £100 now or £200 in five years' time, given that the current interest on a safe investment is 10 per cent?

The present value of £200 in five years' time is 0.62 × 200 = £124.
The present value of £200 in five years' time is greater than £100, and if present value were the only consideration I would rather have £200 in five years' time.

Example 2

Capex Ltd is trying to decide whether to replace an old machine. The purchase price of a new one is £10 000 and it is estimated that it will result in a saving of £3000 per year for five years in operating costs. Should Capex Ltd go ahead with the purchase? Use a discount factor of 10 per cent.

Year	Cash flow (£)	Present value (£) (discounted at 10%)
0	−10 000	
1	+3 000	+2 727
2	+3 000	+2 478
3	+3 000	+2 253
4	+3 000	+2 049
5	+3 000	+1 863
		+ 11 370

In present value terms, the new machine will save £11 370 in operating costs over the next five years. Purchase of a new machine at a price of £10 000 is justified.

Example 3

To pass its annual inspection, Mr Jones' old car will need repairs costing an estimated £200. He has been offered a ten-year-old Mini (with a new MOT) for £500. He estimates that the 'new' car will save him £80 a year for five years in fuel and repair costs. He could sell his old vehicle for £80. Should he buy the 'new' car if he can borrow the money he will need this year at an interest rate of 12 per cent?

	£	
Purchase price of new car	−500	
Selling price of old car	+ 80	
Cost of repairs for MOT	+ 200	*(saved by purchase of new car)*
Net cost of purchase	−220	

Year	Net cash flow (£)	Present value (£) (discounted at 12%)
0		
1	+80	+72
2	+80	+64
3	+80	+56
4	+80	+50
5	+80	+46
		+288

By purchasing the new car, Mr Jones would save £68 on present value terms.

Example 4

Project A can now be compared with Project B on a more rigorous basis. Using a 10 per cent discount rate we obtain the following figures:

	Project A		Project B	
Year	Cash flow (£)	Present value (£)	Cash flow (£)	Present value (£)
0	− 3000		− 3000	
1	+1000	909	+750	682
2	+1000	826	+750	619
3	+1000	751	+750	563
4	+ 600	410	+750	516
5			+750	466
6			+750	423
7			+750	385
8			+750	350
	− 3000	− 2896	− 3000	− 4004

Project B is obviously much more profitable than Project A. This was not shown by the payback and crude rate return criteria applied earlier, which indeed suggested the opposite.

Example 5

In fact, in the last example, Project A is not profitable, since the present value of the earnings, £2896, is less than the initial outlay to obtain the earnings, £3000. One factor in determining the present value of the earnings is the discount rate: if a lower discount rate were applied, the present value would be higher. What discount rate would show Project A as breaking even?

As we have only four figures to consider, the effect of various discount factors can easily be calculated. The one which comes nearest to breaking even is 8 per cent:

Year	Cash flow (£)	Present value at 8% (£)
1	+ 1000	926
2	+ 1000	857
3	+ 1000	794
4	+ 600	441
		3018

Would Project B still be the more profitable at this lower discount rate?

Example 6

Project C and Project D each require an initial investment of £2600 and each have a three-year life. While C produces earnings of £2000 by the end of the first year, £1000 by the end of the second year, and £200 by the end of the third year, D has quite a different earnings profile: £200 in the first year, £1000 in the second, and £2000 in the third. After the third year there are no cash earnings either for Project C or for Project D.

On the payback criterion, C is preferable since it pays for itself sooner. On the crude rate of return criterion, there is nothing to choose between them since they both produce average earnings of £1066 a year, or 41 per cent. If present value is created at a discount rate of 10 per cent, we see that D actually loses money:

Year	Discount factor	Project C earnings (£)	PV (£)	Product D earnings (£)	PV (£)
1	0.909	2000	1818	200	182
2	0.826	1000	826	1000	826
3	0.751	200	150	2000	1502
			2794		2510

The net present value, when the initial investment of £2600 has been deducted from the PV of the earnings, is minus £90 for Project D, and plus £194 for C.

The discount rate

The present value of future payments depends on how much they will amount to, on how far away in time they are located, and on the discount rate which is used. The amount and the timing of the payments are estimates of facts, but the discount rate is not factual in this sense; it is a matter for decision.

Financial experts see it as a technical decision, at least as complicated as such technical questions as the life of electronic components or the strength of embankments. It may sometimes be the cost of capital finance, although this is multivalued; firms raise finance from several sources at various costs. Risky projects may be thought of as calling for risk capital while virtually risk-free projects can be funded at safe rates.

The two most popular DCF criteria for investment appraisal are: net present value (NPV), and internal rate of return (IRR) or DCF yield. In example 2 above, the gross present value of the savings of £3000 a year is £11 595, a positive cash flow; the negative cash flow required to buy the machine is £10 000. Consequently, the net PV, the difference between the two, is £1595. Similarly, in example 3, the NPV of the car purchase is £34.

The IRR criterion is to find what discount rate would make the NPV equal to zero. In example 5, we saw that a discount rate of just over 8 per cent would make the present value of the earnings equal to the initial outlay, giving a zero NPV. This is the rate of return which the investment will actually earn. It can thus be seen as a more rigorous version of the crude 'rate of return' criterion used by some firms. It can also be regarded as showing the actual cost of capital finance at which the project would break even; for instance, if Project A in example 5 could be financed by a loan at 7 per cent, it would show a small profit. The method of finding this discount rate, which will determine the DCF yield by making the NPV zero, is basically trial and error, but short-cut methods have been developed which reduce it to a quick and simple routine.

A common reaction to DCF methods is that they are too complicated; they lend a spurious appearance of precision to estimates which are basically far from precise. As the economist J. M. Keynes wrote in the 1920s, 'the outstanding fact is the extreme precariousness of the basis of knowledge on which our estimates of prospective yield have to be made'. The contemporary economist Paul Samuelson writes: 'The world as it is today was predicted by nobody' – so how can we expect to succeed in our life-cycle costing exercises? What is the point of taking our earnings profiles, riddled as they must be with assumptions, pious hopes and power ploys, and putting them through the DCF calculation process?

The point is very simple. It is that DCF methods, which are theoretically sound, do not increase whatever error is in the data. Unsound criteria such as payback (if used uncritically) make the data even more misleading. Admittedly, it will hardly be economic to apply procedures to small routine replacement investments such as typewriters, and it may not be practical to apply them to major non-routine decisions such as diversification, or to investments which must be undertaken because of legislation or other compelling cause; but between these two extremes extends a great range of 'middle management' investment proposals for which DCF criteria are now considered normal.

This elementary introduction to investment appraisal has referred only in passing to such matters as sensitivity analysis, taxation, and the comparison of proposals which have different life cycles or differently shaped earnings profiles. Readers wishing to find out more about these matters should study some of the excellent books available.

CONCLUSION

Contracting for a North Sea oil rig, a new hotel, a major computer installation or a replacement machine tool would in each case have its own special set of problems. In buying capital goods each case is likely to be different, but in each case the purchasing department has an important part to play.

Market and source information can be obtained for the project team. Help can be provided in evaluating available alternatives. Good communications should be established with preferred suppliers. Time-scales should be made known to all parties. Performance criteria, and who is responsible for what, need to be spelled out.

Perhaps the most important of the purchasing department's duties is to ensure that all important aspects of the contract are considered and agreed, and what is agreed is written into the contract and that the supplier performs against the terms of the contract.

SUMMARY POINTS

- The chapter outlines the differences between the purchase of capital goods and non capital goods. Capital goods are bought to meet long term needs; are normally highly specific and highly priced (thus the cost of a wrong decision could be critical). Most capital expenditure is postponable.
- Performance specifications are widely used in the acquisition of capital goods. Once this is complete, the buyer can then short list potential sources, obtaining the relevant data including lead times, expected equipment life, recommended spares and maintenance schedules.
- With high levels of investment, decisions are normally referred to the main board who may take some time to reach an agreement. It is imperative that no hasty actions are taken by the requisitioner once approval has been given – full regard must be given to the commercial implications. By being involved from the earliest opportunity, purchasing will be able to input sound commercial and contractual knowledge throughout the project.
- Investment appraisal serves to assess the costs and benefits associated with a proposal. The Life Cycle approach profiles the net cash flow. The chapter also outlines the methodology behind the following approaches: payback period, average rate of return and discounted cash flow.

REFERENCES AND FURTHER READING

Berliner C and Brimson J (1988), *Cost Management for Today's Advanced Manufacturing*, Harvard Business School Press, Boston.

Brealey R A and Myers S C (1988), *Principles of Corporate Finance*, McGraw-Hill International.

Freeman M and Freeman K (1993), 'Consider the time value of money in break-even analysis', *Management Accounting*, 17 (1), January.

Morgan M (1993), 'How the Japanese account for long-term risk: some lessons for western companies', *Multinational Business* (MTN), Issue 4, Winter.

Partridge G E (1985), 'Purchasing capital equipment', in *Purchasing Management Handbook*, ed. D H Farmer, Gower, Aldershot, Ch. 19.

Perry J H (1987), 'A conceptual framework for evaluating capital equipment purchases', *Journal of Purchasing and Materials Management*, 23 (4), Winter.

CHAPTER 15

Purchasing for resale

INTRODUCTION

Purchasing for merchandise for resale while having much in common with other types of buying also has some major differences. Buyers in other sectors of the economy can learn much from studying some of the good practices found in the retail sector. Buyers in major retail organisations such as Marks & Spencer, Tesco's etc. are likely to be far more involved with their supply chains and customers than in other sectors of the community.

OBJECTIVES OF THIS CHAPTER

- To analyse the role of the retail buyer and their involvement with the supply chain
- To differentiate between selector, buyer and merchandiser
- To understand retailing research and the different methods of collecting data
- To define all the aspects involved in merchandising
- To appreciate the value of brand names and how they compete with 'own brand' labels and generics.

Decisions have to be made in terms of what to buy, quantities, prices, delivery terms, and mode and timing of payment. In addition, there may be negotiations covering training of retailer's staff by the seller, sale or return, sales promotion deals, and so on.

There are, however, differences. What retailers, wholesalers or other members of the distributive sector buy, they also sell. The 'what to buy' decision must be taken with a strong feeling for what will sell. There is a much greater overlap between the marketing/selling activities and buying than any other sector. Almost certainly a trained buyer in Marks & Spencer or Tesco would have spent a considerable time on the sales side prior to becoming a buyer.

This chapter concentrates on the distinguishing characteristics of purchasing for resale.

The retail sector in the UK accounts for some £140 billion (1995/96) out of a gross domestic product of some £600 billion. If this sector is run inefficiently it adds unnecessary costs to finished goods as they are produced in the secondary sector i.e. manufacturing.

RETAILING

It is interesting to note that a small proportion of retailers account for most of retail sales. Chain stores – for example, Tesco, Sainsbury's, Asda, Marks & Spencer, the Co-op – account for about 70 per cent of the total food and drink retailing in the UK. The rest is made up of smaller independents and multiple independents (e.g. Spar).

The majority of the buying for the larger organisations is centralised. Sainsbury's and Tesco each employ hundreds of buyers backed by teams of agronomists, technologists, quality controllers, and researchers. 'Buying is the glamour job in retailing,' according to one expert, 'Store sizes are going up, and they need to find more lines to fill them. So they're constantly searching.' The pressure is on the buyers to come up with more innovative and up-market 'niche' products. Certainly, the range and quality of food products on offer in the supermarkets has greatly improved in recent years. This should be good for consumers and it should be the key to success for those retailers who manage to stock what consumers want, at prices they can afford, which is also the key to success for small specialist outlets.

Marks & Spencer employ a range of specialists involved in the buying activity who, while they all work together, each have specific roles.

To take clothing as an example, the selectors are responsible for identifying suitable lines for sale in Marks & Spencer's stores. They visit fashion shows and other influential events. This may involve travelling widely, identifying appropriate merchandise. Buyers determine the budgets/estimates and, working closely with selectors, decide whether or not lines will sell. Buyers have the final say in any decision, and also have some involvement in identifying appropriate merchandise. Once a line has been selected buyers require the supplier to produce samples for examination, trials and testing by various technologists. Finally, the merchandiser will decide on levels of stock to hold in the stores and which stores will carry various lines. These three activities – selector, buyer and merchandiser – which do overlap from time to time, are co-ordinated by HQ in Baker Street.

Most large retailers are organised in broadly the same way. In smaller organisations and department stores, the buyer may be responsible for selecting, buying and certain merchandising functions as well.

RETAILING RESEARCH

In deciding what to buy, the buyer's intuition and feel for the market are considered especially important in connection with fashion goods, the demand for which is very hard to predict. There is always some scope for intuition and feel for the market, but marketing research is intended to provide a factual basis for rational decisions, especially for such relatively standard lines as food and drink. Marketing research has been defined as: 'the systematic gathering, recording and analysing of data about problems in marketing goods and services'.

An early version of retailing research was the retail audit which Nielsen invented in the United States. A representative group of shops is selected – representative of chemists, groceries, off-licences, or whatever is the research subject – and checks are made at regular intervals, usually twice a month, of what stock is on the shelves and in the storeroom. Sales for each item audited are calculated from the figures for this and the previous stock check and from quantities invoiced in the period between the two. Increasingly, electronic data capture at checkouts makes this sort of information immediately available to retailers for their own merchandise sales and this is leading to new forms of retail audit.

ELECTRONIC POINT OF SALE (EPOS)

With the introduction of bar coding or article numbering, we now have a situation where every stock line can be uniquely identified. 'Bar codes' – the familiar panels containing numbers printed as a series of narrow and wide lines and spaces – are used to identify merchandise. These codes can be read quickly and accurately by sensors at the checkout or till, and numbers matched with a computer file, enabling the description, current price (not encoded, but 'looked up' by computer), and other details of the product specification to be accessed. Compared with checking by hand, scanning is three or four times faster. We can update information on sales as changes occur, in terms of dates and times, amounts bought, prices paid and so on. This system greatly facilitates data collection compared with traditional methods.

'Real time' information is available on patterns of stores traffic, sales, and profitability on every line carried. This information can be passed on to the suppliers of the merchandise concerned. EPOS is an example of electronic data interchange (EDI): that is, the transfer of structured data by agreed message standards from computer to computer by electronic means. As goods are sold, information is transferred directly to major suppliers via the buying organisation, in this case the retailer. There is no need for huge amounts of paper documentation, and savings are considerable. Figure 15.1 is a schematic representation of an EDI system.

Probably the most developed EDI systems are those used by retailers in connection with EPOS. Indeed, this usage has been seen by many manufacturing organisations as a benchmark against which to judge their own development in this field.

Much of the information generated from retailers' EPOS systems can provide valuable real time information to suppliers selling merchandise to the retailer. Such information is:

- how well a product is selling;
- the effects of promotional activity from the supplier;
- shelf space allocations;

EDI
ELECTRONIC DATA INTERCHANGE

- Transfer of structured data, by agreed message standards from computer to computer by electronic means

Examples
- EPOS   Electronic point of sale – retailers' bar code
- Dish   Shipping
- Tradanet Wide cover – DIY Electronics

Advantages
- Quicker transfer of information
- Lower costs of production

Requires
- Few suppliers/customers
- Strategic view of relationships
- 'New thinking'

Fig. 15.1 Schematic representation of an EDI system

- the effects of other merchandise changes; and
- the effects of price increase or decrease.

It can quickly be fed back to suppliers for decision-making purposes. This type of information is often only made available to suppliers as part of a negotiated 'deal' i.e. they pay for it.

When Selfridges introduced a new EPOS system from Siemanns NIXDORF into their store during 1993/4 they developed far more accurate information. This new system helped to avoid the problem of buyers overbuying on stock. The system also improved merchandise planning.

MERCHANDISE PLANNING

All retailers need to plan what goods to sell. At the top level, merchandise planning is about the nature and purpose of the business: 'what we sell is what we are'. Merchandise planning at this level is part of corporate planning. At a lower level, merchandise planning is about what to order next month.

Marks & Spencer, for 50 years one of Britain's most successful businesses, built its success on providing high-quality goods at low prices to meet mass market needs (previously unidentified), by establishing close and long-term relationships with carefully selected suppliers. Marks & Spencer took 5 per cent of the food market and 15 per cent of clothing sales in the later 1980s, but their success story had been built on identifying and targeting a mass market which was already splitting into segments. They came up with radically new lines, many of them not traditional retail goods, such as charge cards, personal loans, unit trusts and insurance policies, together with an overseas expansion designed to make Marks & Spencer the first genuinely international retailer since Woolworth in the 1920s.

Merchandising is a term used differently by different organisations. For instance in Firm A, merchandising means collecting the information which buying needs to do its job. In Firm B, merchandising means deciding what merchandise will be sold, deciding on a supplier or suppliers, negotiating buying prices and setting selling prices for the first buys, the buying department as such dealing only with repeat orders. In Firm C the terms merchandising and buying are used interchangeably. These three examples are taken from three actual firms.

Merchandising in its broadest sense would comprise:

- *Merchandise planning* Preparing sales forecasts, setting merchandise budgets, developing model stock plans.
- *Buying* Evaluating potential suppliers, selecting suppliers, negotiation, ordering.
- *Distribution* External transport arrangements, receiving goods, marking, internal transport.
- *Control* Stock turn rate, financial control, unit control, and other measures.

Corporate objectives normally include targets in all of these areas, and strategies will be devised in most areas.

A retailer develops a product mix: that is to say, a particular combination of products to meet the needs of one or more target markets. This is not a once-for-all process. The right mix for today might not be the right mix next year. New products appear on the market, old products sometimes lose their appeal, consumers' preferences alter. The target market is itself subject to change.

The product mix includes ranges of merchandise. A product line or range of merchandise is a group of related products. Products can be related in several ways to form a range of merchandise, for instance, various kinds of canned soup, or children's clothing, or wallpaper. In developing a range of merchandise, retailers consider such questions as:

- Is this product suitable for our store image?
- Is it appropriate for our target markets?
- What is the likely demand?
- Who are the suppliers?
- How readily is it available?
- On what terms could we buy it?

Model stock plans

A model stock plan specifies the stock of the articles which the retailer intends to be available off the shelf. In planning the stock, retailers consider assortment, variety, width and depth.

Assortment

Every retailer has to decide what combination of goods and services to offer for sale. The assortment may be exclusive, like a camera shop that sells only Kodak cameras; wide, like a shop that sells cameras alongside many other lines related in some way, for instance as leisure activities; deep, like a camera shop which stocks many different makes of camera, film, enlarger, and accessories; or scrambled, stocking many unrelated lines. The assortment a retailer chooses is related to the target customers at which the retailer is aiming.

Variety

Variety is the number of lines carried by a shop. A fish and chip shop does not offer the variety offered by a Chinese take-away, for instance. Variety has two aspects; width and depth:

1 *Width* refers to the level of specialisation; it measures the number of different product groups or lines offered.
2 *Depth* refers to the level of choice; it measures the number of items in each product group or line, size, colour, style, price.

A narrow and deep assortment would be appropriate for a product specialist, for instance a shoeshop. A wide and shallow assortment might suit a variety store.

Logistics and retailing

Huge amounts of money have been spent by the larger retailing concerns to find more efficient methods of moving merchandise from suppliers to their various stores up and down the country. Considerable savings have been achieved by using third party carriers. Larger retailers like Tesco, Sainsbury's and Marks & Spencer have led the way in establishing a more efficient approach to the total logistics problem of getting the merchandise to the customer at the lowest cost, through employing specialist logistics concerns to contribute to efficiency.

STOCK ANALYSIS AND SALES ANALYSIS

Stock can be analysed in many ways – for instance into fast movers and slow movers. For a retailer this is a form of sales analysis: which lines sell best? As one retailer said: 'There are some types of merchandise in which we do very well, for example newspapers and magazines where the turn round is measurable in hours rather than weeks. On the other hand, some of our slower selling lines such as the less familiar book titles are held for much longer periods, but this is essential for maintaining a service to our customers.'

Pareto or ABC analysis is a very useful method of stock analysis. This groups stock items into high demand value items, which tend to be few in number, medium demand value items, and low demand value items, of which there are many. According to one retail chain store: 'We organise our stock control on ABC lines; that is, the A lines are the top 1 per cent accounting for 30 per cent of the volume, the C lines are 85 per cent lines accounting for 20 per cent of the volume, and the B lines are somewhere in between. The figures are not precise. Our A lines, the top 1 per cent, are partly controlled by a top sellers system. Branches report the stock level of each of these lines at weekly intervals and from this we calculate rates of sale. The system has been highly successful in keeping stock levels down to very acceptable figures while maintaining service levels to the branches in the region of 94 per cent. Our books are mainly C items in stock control terms, that is they are 85 per cent of the lines which account for 20 per cent of the volume. For example, we hold 31 000 lines at our main warehouse of which 25 000 are books.'

Unit stock control is the term used in the retail trade for procedures intended to ensure that the quantity available in the shop, of each article on sale, is not too little or too much, to meet sales targets profitably. What is controlled is the physical quantity, or number of units, available as stock-in-trade. Financial stock control on the other hand aims to control the amount of money committed to stock-in-trade. Since these two kinds of stock control have different aims, it makes sense to use both of them.

The traditional basis of unit stock control is counting the stock. The simplest version, sometimes called 'eyeballing', is the periodic visual check, unsupported by records. This can work well in a small shop if the shopkeeper knows the stock well enough to keep a suitable assortment without records, and can predict demand without records, especially if the merchandise is not costly and can be obtained quickly. Millions of shops around the world use systems of this kind. 'Two-bin' systems are sometimes used. For example, two cases of an item are bought. One is put on the sales floor and the other in storage. When the case on the sales floor is empty, the other case is brought out of storage and one more is ordered.

Periodic actual count gives tighter control. Different classes of merchandise could be counted at different intervals of time: daily, weekly, or monthly, for instance. Count records plus order records enable demand for each item in stock to be calculated, providing a basis for forecasting future demand for it.

Perpetual inventory shows what is in stock at any time of any item. Electronic data capture at checkouts and the use of computers have finally made this feasible. Point-of-sale devices have become much more than cash registers; they can carry a complete stock record, analyse sales, work out order levels and reorder automatically. Reporting increased sales and higher retail profits in 1989, W H Smith attributed much of the increase to their computerised tills, which enabled them to respond much more quickly to demand.

Just-in-time also affects retailing probably more often than the average manufacturing organisation. At one time, most retailing organisations allocated huge areas to hold stock not actually on the shop floor. Today, very few retail organisations can afford to lose selling space by holding reserve stock. What you see on the shelves and counters is frequently what the store holds as stocks. It is therefore imperative that suppliers resupply stock exactly when it is required. Failure to supply on time means lost sales and profit. Flexibility is essential, EPOS provides the way ahead, linking customer demand with deliveries.

BRANDS

Brand names can be valuable property, as Rank Hovis McDougall demonstrated when its portfolio of brand names (Mothers Pride, Hovis, Bisto, etc.) was valued in the 1988 balance sheet at £678 million.

For a small shop, the national advertising and reputation which attract customers to well-known brands on sale can be very useful. A larger retailer wishing to establish its own distinctive image may prefer to sell exclusive brands which are not available from any other retailer. For instance a distributor such as Curry may negotiate with a producer such as Hotpoint for a special version of their latest model to be sold only through Curry, who thus benefit from Hotpoint's well-advertised brand name while still being able to offer a unique product.

For a major chain, there are advantages in selling goods under its own brand name. Marks & Spencer probably invented own brands in 1928, when Simon Marks registered St Michael as the Marks & Spencer brand name. He picked this name partly because St Margaret was the brand name used by Corah, who had just been persuaded to sell direct to M & S instead of through wholesalers, partly because Michael was his father's first name, and partly because the archangel Michael was the guardian angel of the Jews.

In a typical Sainsbury's supermarket, 5000 out of 6500 lines may be own brands. Many BHS goods are own brands, Peter Dominic have their own brand of lager, and there are plenty of other examples.

There are two versions of 'own branding'. In one, the manufacturer supplies standard production line goods, but with the retailer's brand label rather than the manufacturer's. In the other, the retailer draws up a specification and finds a manufacturer to make goods to it.

The advantage to the manufacturer of the first version is getting a large order for goods which are being produced anyway, without incurring any expense in advertising or sales promotion. The advantage to the retailer is the lower price this makes possible, enabling their own brand to be stocked next to the manufacturer's brand on the shelves, identical goods at lower prices.

The second version of own branding is specification buying. Major retailers like this because as well as improving margins it helps to establish the retailer's image. Specifications can be very detailed, covering everything from what pesticides a farmer can use to how often packers must wash their hands. Not only the dimensions of the product, but the raw materials, the production processes and the quality control methods are specified. Specifications may even list the suppliers' suppliers from which raw materials can be obtained.

Generic brands

This is where one uses the basic product – for example, Corn Flakes can be sold for considerably less than Kelloggs Corn Flakes, which are branded. Similarly with pharmaceuticals – for example, aspirin may cost a fraction of the price compared with a brand name drug, although both may offer the same benefits. There is a considerable movement to provide more generic products as well as the brand equivalents. This enables retailers to tap the lower spectrum of the market.

SUPPLIER SELECTION

Standard criteria for supplier selection are quality, price, terms, delivery and service, together with actual performance on previous orders. These are discussed elsewhere in this text, since they apply to most purchase decisions taken by an organisation. Additional criteria which may be taken into account by retailers include merchandise criteria and promotion criteria.

Merchandise criteria include the suitability of the merchandise for the store's requirements, how well it fits the store's image and the needs of its target customers; its availability – whether it can be delivered in the quantities, to the locations, at the times required; and perhaps adaptability, whether the supplier is willing to meet any special needs, such as supplying exclusive brands or own brands.

Promotion criteria include the type and amount of promotional support which a supplier provides. Apart from the support given by the supplier's national or local advertising, there may be an advertising allowance or joint advertising by producer and retailer. In-store demonstrations, display materials and other consumer inducements may also be provided.

Other problems in supplier selection include how many suppliers to use; whether to concentrate orders for a particular line with a single supplier, or divide them among several suppliers. A related question is how much of a supplier's output to take. It is sometimes argued that it is undesirable for one customer to take more than a third of a supplier's production, but Marks & Spencer have taken 90 per cent of Dewhurst's output, 95 per cent of Gent's, 80 per cent of Sussman's and 75 per cent of Corah's, although on average they take about 30 per cent of a supplier's output. We find a similar pattern of increasing mutual dependence in manufacturing industry, due to JIT and the trend to closer relationships with fewer suppliers.

In specification buying, the role of the buyer (or 'selector', as Marks & Spencer call them) is rather different from the traditional retail buyer's role of selecting from lines offered by competing suppliers. It is much closer to the industrial buyer's role. Indeed Marks & Spencer has been called a 'manufacturer without factories'. As one supplier said: 'they don't buy products from us, they buy production capacity'. A typical buying office at Marks & Spencer includes the selector and assistant selector (buyers); the merchandise manager and merchandiser; the technical manager, technologist and quality controller; plus secretary, admin assistant and clerk. This is the buying team, all next to each other in the same office, not in separate departments.

NEW DEVELOPMENTS IN THE RETAIL SECTOR

The following is a brief summary of some of the issues facing the retail buyer and likely consequences.

Greater concentration of retail outlets

The trend towards bigger out-of-town retail establishments is growing. Often the effect of this is that an even greater range of products and services will have to be offered to the customer. The buyers traditional breadth and depth of merchandise is likely to increase as a result requiring more back-up services to assist the buyer.

Moves towards own brands

All Marks & Spencer merchandise is own label. Their profits are also much higher than the average retail organisation. The growth of own label brands puts even greater pressure on the retail buyer to expand in this area. Along with this is an associated problem referred to as passing off. This occurs when a retailer produces a branded product with similar labelling and package design to an existing product so as to cause confusion in the customers' mind, the effect being to increase sales of the new branded copy product at the expense of the genuine article.

- More routine purchasing decisions being taken by the computer and EPOS system in terms of routine buying. This should give the retail buyer more time to spend on supplier development, negotiations and customer care.
- Direct ordering by the customer from their own computer systems. This would enable the retail buyer more time to carry out market research on new merchandise.

CONCLUSION

Buying in the retail sector has many of the characteristics found in most buying jobs. The major difference is likely to be found in the scope of the buyers role. Retail buyers are far more involved in the running of the retail organisation, the customer and the supplier base than the average buyer in other non-retailing organisations. Some of the best purchasing practices can be found in large retail organisations in terms of EPOS, supplier development, supply chain management and the customer buyer interface.

SUMMARY POINTS

- The 'what to buy' decision is directly related to what will sell. This decision may be taken by a team comprising of selectors, buyers and merchandisers (in large organisations) or by an individual buyer who is responsible for all three aspects.
- Barcoding means that every stock line can be uniquely identified. Electronic point of sale systems scan product codes and collect real time data relating to product turnover, stock levels, profitability. This greatly aids the retailer and the supplier by providing information on the effect of promotional activities etc.
- Merchandising comprises of four aspects; planning; buying; distribution and control. Targets set in each of these areas form the basis of corporate objectives.
- *Unit stock control* looks at the physical quantity available as stock in trade and uses various methods from 'eyeballing' to electronic data capture. *Financial stock control* aims to control the amount of money committed to stock in trade. Most retail organisations hold all stock on the shelves – hence the importance of timely and accurate restocking.
- When undertaking a supplier appraisal, merchandise and promotion criteria are also assessed. Is the supplier adaptable? What type of promotional support will they offer?

REFERENCES AND FURTHER READING

Baily P J H (1991), *Purchasing and Supply Management*, 6th edn, Chapman & Hall, London.

Foster A and Thomas B (1990), *The Retail Handbook*, McGraw-Hill.

James R (1996), 'Winning promotions', *Supply Management*, August 1996.

Kotler P (1992), 'Silent satisfaction', *Marketing Business*, issue 6.

Mazur L (1993), 'Tools of the trade', *Marketing Business*, March.

McRae C (1991), *World Class Brands*, Addison-Wesley.

Sinfield, Gassenheimer, Kelley (1992), 'Co-operation in supplier-dealer relations', *Journal of Retailing*, New York University, 68 (2).

Swindley D (1992), 'The rise of the buyer in UK multiple retailing', *International Journal of Retail and Distribution Management*, 20 (2), March/April.

Williams G (1996), 'Store Wars', *Supply Management*, May.

CHAPTER 16

Buying services

The acquisition of services is an important part of purchasing and supply work, so much so that many organisations spend a greater amount with service providers than with suppliers of goods. Service supply is further gaining in importance as more and more organisations 'contract out' aspects of their work. This contracting out may arise from a wish to concentrate more closely on the core business, and hence focus on the specialist skills which give rise to competitive advantage. Alternatively, and particularly in public sector concerns, the pressure to contract out services arises from the need not only to be efficient, but to demonstrate that open and competitive buying methods are employed. The widespread public sector practice of 'market testing' to ensure that work performed by organisations is undertaken at least as efficiently as would be the case if contractors or other providers were employed has given rise to a considerable increase in the external sourcing of services. Compulsory competitive tendering by local authorities in the UK has resulted in a greater emphasis on the acquisition of services from external providers; services formerly supplied by 'in-house' supply. This chapter is concerned with the acquisition of services in as much as such acquisition processes differ from those employed in the acquisition of goods.

OBJECTIVES OF THIS CHAPTER

- To assess the differences in purchasing services as opposed to tangible goods
- To compare the relative merits of conformance and performance specifications
- To consider outsourcing as the external provision of functional activities
- To outline the various approaches to service provision
- To highlight the main features of the European Community Public Contracts Directive
- To summarise the main provisions relating to the supply of services of the 1982 Goods and Services Act.

What is meant by 'services'?

Any kind of supply where the main component is a task of some kind, rather than the provision of some tangible good or material. A service is a performance of some act of value which, unlike the situation where goods are sold, does not result in the customer's ownership of anything. Almost any kind of service might be required, the list which follows is only a representative sample of some of the more commonly bought services, a complete list would be impossibly long:

Accountancy	Computing	Importation	Research
Advertising	Consultancy	Insurance	Security
Arbitration	Decorating	Legal advice	Training
Banking	Designg	Logistics	Transportation
Catering	Freight forwarding	Maintenance	
Cleaning	Grounds maintenance	Medical	

SPECIAL FACTORS

There are a number of factors which differentiate services from tangibles, and which give rise to particular difficulties associated with their acquisition.

Impracticability of storage

By their nature, services cannot be stored. This means that they must be provided at a time which exactly coincides with the need. It is neither possible for a supplier to stockpile them in anticipation of a need arising, nor for a user to carry inventories to protect against uncertain supply or demand. Of course, not all services are time critical. It will probably not matter too much whether the windows are cleaned on Monday morning or Tuesday afternoon. Other services, while not 'storable', are provided continuously (e.g. insurance services, power and other utilities) and pose no significant scheduling problems for the user.

None the less, the majority of services are likely to be the subject of careful planning and programming to ensure that they are provided at the right time and to the right location, with any failure giving rise to significant consequences. As an example, consider the design of a timetable in a school or college. The matching of tutors, appropriate groups of students from a range of courses, in suitable accommodation at mutually available times, is a puzzle that taxes hundreds of academic minds at the start of each academic year, and which has, as yet, defied attempts to formalise and render it completely susceptible to a software-based solution.

If the requirement for a service is not steady, or is difficult to predict, the challenges associated with its provision are enormous, and normally require a very great investment in standby resources. The armed forces provide an excellent example of this type of situation.

Inspectability

Tangible materials can be measured, weighed, tested and inspected in any number of ways in order to ensure that they conform to the agreed specification. This is not so with services, which are generally rather more difficult to test for quality. Quality may be specified in 'conformance' terms, by saying things like 'the consultant shall be on the client's premises until 3 p.m. on Friday', or 'the work shall be completed and recommendations made by such and such a date'. More appropriately though, at least in most cases, 'performance' specifications are employed. Examples might be 'at the end of the training programme participants shall be competent to operate a one ton counterbalance forklift truck', or 'vehicles maintained under this contract shall be capable of travelling safely at 90 k.p.h. and returning 5 km per litre.

A most important characteristic of services is that the results can not be seen prior to purchase, so preliminary assessment will tend to focus more strongly on the service provider, rather than his or her product.

Do or buy?

This question is related to the make-or-buy decision which may be made when tangibles are being acquired. However, though the question occurs occasionally with tangibles, usually there is no real alternative to buying the material. In the case of services the do-or-buy question is more commonly posed, and may frequently be reduced to a consideration of the pros and cons of employing persons with the necessary competencies to undertake the work in question, or contracting with an external organisation to perform the activity. The decision is often quite a difficult one, with the economic considerations becoming quite complex, and in turn overlaid by questions relating to corporate policy, and in some cases to government policy.

Contractual arrangements

When goods are to be bought, it is usually relatively easy to ascertain when a contract comes into existence, and when it has been completed, usually on payment for goods supplied according to the buyer's specification. In the supply of services the situation is often less clear cut. Suppose an architect is commissioned to design a suite of offices according to a specification laid down in terms of accommodation required, within budget figures determined by the client. The architect supplies proposals which meet the criteria, but are not to the client's aesthetic taste. The client requires an alternative design. Who pays? 'Not enough information' will be the correct response to this question, which nevertheless illustrates the type of difficulty which easily arises in arrangements for the supply of services.

Provision

Many services can only be acquired through the physical presence of the service provider of his or her employee. Gardening, or the servicing of a computer installation require the appropriate personnel to be 'on site'. However, banking or insurance services, for example, can be organised and provided remotely.

Complexity of acquisitions

While it is useful to look at the supply of services separately from the supply of goods, and to deal with such supplies in this chapter, it is the case that few contracts are purely for the supply of goods, and, equally, few are for services alone.

Figure 16.1 contains a list of nine different but typical organisational requirements, arranged in order with an item which is plainly 'goods' at the top, and a clear 'service' at the bottom. However, the supply of parts made to a customer's specification is not entirely a supply of goods. The parts will need to be shipped from supplier to customer, and there are other intangible considerations such as inspection and transfer of ownership (as opposed to possession) to take into account.

Fig. 16.1 List of typical organisational requirements

At the other end of the list, consultancy is, obviously, a service. Nevertheless it is difficult to envisage any kind of consultancy where no materials of any kind are involved. The consultant will usually hand over drawings, plans or other documents. Even when an oral presentation is to be made the physical resources for this to take place must be provided.

There are, of course, many supply arrangements which are clearly for both goods and services. A restaurant meal would provide a good example for the domestic purchaser, the contract hire of a fleet of motor vehicles would be an organisational example.

Resale

Unlike goods, services can not normally be resold. This means of course that the relationship between the service provider and the user of the service is a direct one. Intermediaries are not usually involved.

Variability

Services are, of course, provided by people, and people are individually unique. Standardisation, homogeneity and repeatability may be challenging requirements where goods are concerned; in the provision of services complete uniformity would be a goal verging on the impossible.

OUTSOURCING

Outsourcing is, essentially, the contracting out of non-core activities. That is not to say that the activities are unimportant, for example the Government has outsourced much of the computing activity required by various civil service departments and agencies. A difficulty is, of course, that a decision has to be made as to what really is core activity, and what is not. Mention was made earlier in the text of the concept of the anticipated virtual organisations, whose core activity will be managing and orchestrating contractors.

White and James (1993) define outsourcing as 'a contractual relationship between an external vendor and an enterprise in which the vendor assumes responsibility for one or more business functions of the enterprise'.

So, outsourcing is not a synonym for purchasing. It is concerned with the external provision of functional activity, and therefore outsourcing decisions are strategic in nature. They impact upon the nature and scope of the organisation. As such they are not taken at the operational level, but involve top management, and the consideration of a great variety of variables such as:

- Do we have candidate functions for outsourcing?
- How do we select?
- How do we assess ourselves?
- Who are the potential providers?
- How do we assess them?
- What sort of relationship will we form?
- How will we manage it?
- How do we ensure efficiency?

Outsourced functions normally lead to relationships where the vendor is providing services on a continuous basis. The determination of an appropriate relationship within which this continuous service is to be provided is likely to require a very great investment of time and effort at the planning stage. Additionally, of course, as with all relationships, there will be evolutionary change; change which will itself need to be managed.

SERVICE LEVEL AGREEMENTS

Service level agreements (SLAs) may be entered into between a client and supplier of services. They are defined by Hiles (1993) as 'an agreement between the service provider and its customers quantifying the minimum acceptable service to the customer'.

Most services are built up from a number of individual components, and a complete SLA will cover these in some detail. Examples are:

- Time of provision and of each type of service.
- Points of service delivery.
- Nominated service provider.
- Responsiveness.
- Documentation.
- Emergency arrangements.
- Hotline support.
- Dispute procedures.
- Training and staff development.

SLAs are also employed as 'proxy contracts' between Civil Service departments, divisions and branches. Because the Crown is indivisible so far as the law is concerned, contracts as such cannot be formed between the various elements of the Civil Service. SLAs in this context have no legal effect, but they are considered to be valuable as a means for setting out in a clear way the relationships, rights and obligations of the service provider and client.

Approaches to the provision of services

A basic distinction to be made when considering the provision of services is that between 'provider present' and 'provider not present' services. For many organisations, the provision of everyday services such as catering, cleaning and security involves the presence of the service provider's staff on the premises of the client concern. This of course adds another set of issues to be contemplated and determined connected with such matters as supervision, access, confidentiality, access and the 'host – guest' relationship. Some services, for example banking, insurance or credit rating will be undertaken at the provider's place of business, and some, such as transportation, will involve the presence of the provider for only some of the time during which the service is provided.

Occasionally there may be a choice as to whether the service provider will be present or not. For example, some companies, in entering into an arrangement with travel agents have agreed with the service provider that the agency maintains an office at the client's location.

Services may be provided on an occasional 'one-off' purchase, such as, for example the development and delivery of a training programme to meet a specific need. In other circumstances, call-off arrangements are sometimes entered into, where the service provider and client arrange a scale of charges, and in return for the commitment of the client not to buy outside the arrangement, preferential terms are offered. Contracts for repair services are commonly arranged on this basis. Such arrangements are most common in larger organisations with a range of locations at which the service might be required. Frequently, services are provided on a regular, planned and programmed basis, and some form of medium- to long-term agreement is entered into between provider and client. Routine cleaning services are generally provided in this way. Where this is the case it is desirable that some form of continuous assessment and improvement initiative is established and maintained, along the lines suggested by Figure 16.2.

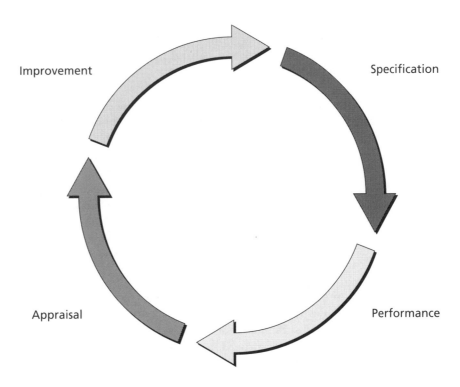

Fig. 16.2 The service cycle

EUROPEAN COMMUNITY PUBLIC CONTRACTS DIRECTIVE

The following notes are intended to highlight the main features of the directive; there are many matters of detail which are omitted, and the reader should not rely upon what follows as either a complete or an authoritative statement.

Council Directive 92/50/EEC relates to the co-ordination of procedures for the award of public service contracts. For the purposes of the directive, public service contracts means 'contracts for a pecuniary interest concluded in writing between a service provider and a contracting authority'. Provision is made, however, for a range of exclusions, including:

● Rent of land, existing buildings or other immovable property.
● Development of programme material by broadcasters.
● Contracts for broadcasting time.
● Contracts for certain telecommunications.
● Contracts for arbitration and conciliation services.

- Central bank services.
- Certain other financial services contracts.
- Employment contracts.
- Certain research and development service contracts.

Contracting authorities are State, regional or local authorities, associations formed by one or more authorities or bodies governed by public law. 'Service provider' means any natural or legal person, including a public body, that offers services.

The directive applies to public service contracts, the estimated value of which, net of VAT, is not less than ECU 200 000. Where services are subdivided into lots, the value of each lot must be taken into account, and for contracts which do not specify a total price, the basis for calculating the estimated value is either the total contract value for the duration, or if the duration exceeds 48 months, the monthly instalment multiplied by 48. In the case of contracts which are regular, or of contracts which are to be renewed within a given time, the contract value may be established on either the basic of the actual aggregate cost of similar contracts over the previous year, or the estimated aggregate cost during the 22 months following the first service performed.

A contracting authority in selecting a service provider may be required to do so under the following procedures:

- Open procedures under which any interested provider may submit a tender.
- Restrict procedures whereby only those providers who have been invited may submit a tender.
- Negotiated procedures where selected provider(s) are approached directly.
- Design contests where selection is based on a competition between providers, with the selection being undertaken by a jury.

Contracting authorities may elect to award the contract either on the basis of the lowest price, or the economically most advantageous tender, though in the latter case the criteria adopted must be made known to candidates or tenderers.

A requirement of the directive is that common advertising rules should apply. Contracting authorities are to make known their intended total procurement of certain categories of services, and also their intentions as to how they wish to award the contract. Moreover it is a requirement that the results of the award procedure should be notified to the Office of Official Publications of the European Communities, which they will then make public.

MANAGEMENT IN SERVICE PROVISION

As has been said, it is possible to express service requirements by means of a conformance specification or a performance one. Where conformance specifications are employed it is often the case that the specifications for even an apparently straightforward service are extremely long. Specifications for, for example, cleaning services, grounds maintenance or similar activities may run to very many pages and represent weeks of preparation time. The tasks and activities required to be performed must be explained in precise and unambiguous detail. To illustrate this point, the relatively small part of a grounds maintenance specification used by the Civil Service concerned with upkeep of soil borders includes a subsection on pruning and caring for roses which is in itself a fairly comprehensive guide to this branch of horticulture. The principal benefit arising from the use of performance specifications is, of course, that it can usually be readily seen whether the contractor has provided the service as agreed.

Frequently the situation is that the client is unable to produce a conformance specification, often because the reason that the service is being acquired from outside is that the client does not possess the time, knowledge or skill to do the work 'in-house'. When this is the case more attention will be paid to desired outcomes than to the manner in which the contract is performed. A contract for consultancy services will provide a good example of a situation in which this is likely to be the case. It may not be possible to prescribe exactly what it is that the consultant is expected to do, but it is reasonable to agree ground rules which govern aspects of the relationship. For example, questions such as working hours, observation of regulations, ownership of intellectual property arising from the work, terms of payment and so on can be formalised and agreed by the contracting parties.

Sometimes services are provided simply on the basis of an agreement between the parties based on a presumed joint understanding that a certain outcome is desired by the client and that the provider possesses the requisite competencies to undertake the work. Assumptions are frequently made, and these assumptions are often incorrect. The client expects work of sound quality, undertaken in a reasonable time and at a fair price. The problem is, of course, that few people will agree on the exact meaning of these expressions. There are many stories sold by clients of service providers treating them unfairly, and it is not unusual to hear service providers complaining about the unrealistic expectations of their customers.

While this text does not attempt to explain the legal aspects of purchasing and supply in general, it will be useful at this point to mention the 1982 Goods and Services Act and to highlight one or two features of that legislation. The first, obvious, point is that it does apply to services. Much of the legislation relating to trading is concerned solely with goods. The Act also applies to all situations where services are being provided. It is not a piece of 'consumer' legislation in that it protects all kinds of customers, including business or commercial organisations.

Some of the main provisions of the Act where it relates to services may be summarised as follows, though it should be remembered that this summary is not intended to convey anything other than an indication of the nature of the legislation: 'In a contract for the supply of service where the supplier is acting in the course of a business, there is an implied term that the supplier will carry out the service with reasonable care and skill.' Another implied term is: 'The supplier will carry out the service within a reasonable time.' Usually, though, the time will be agreed when the contract is made.

The Act limits the recipient's obligation to pay for services to 'a reasonable charge'. Of course, the above provisions do not, in themselves, indicate just what the word 'reasonable' should be taken to mean, and neither do they indicate what remedy is available to the recipient if the provider is deemed not to have been reasonable. We should probably need to turn to a member of the legal profession if, in practice, we felt that a service supplier was providing less than a 'reasonable' standard.

SUMMARY POINTS

- The purchase of services differs from goods in that the customer does not become the owner of a tangible good. Services cannot be stored and cannot normally be resold.
- Usually, results cannot be seen prior to the purchase of a service. Often, it is the actual service provider who is assessed. As services are provided by people and people are individuals, there can be no standardisation or 'repeat' purchase as for goods.
- Service Level Agreements quantify the minimum acceptable service to the customer and are agreed between the client and the service supplier. They are normally written into the contract.
- 'Provider present' services involve the provider's staff being on the client's premises. Access, supervision, confidentiality and safety matters must be addressed. 'Provider not present' services include banking and insurance where the service is provided remotely.
- The European Community Public Contracts Directive applies to public service contracts of over ECU 200 000. The contracting authority may select a service provider using open procedures; restricted procedures; negotiated procedures or a design contest. The results of the award are published by the Office of Official Publications of the European communities.

REFERENCES AND FURTHER READING

Allwright A (1986), *Contracting for Goods and Services*, Institute of Purchasing and Supply, Stamford.

Boyle E (1993), 'Managing organisational networks – defining the core', *Management Decision*, 31 (7).

Hiles A (1993) *Service Level Agreements*, Chapman and Hall, London.

Pagnoncelli D (1993), 'Managed outsourcing: a strategy for a competitive company in the 1990s', *Management Decision*, 31 (7).

Takal P F (1993), 'Outsourcing technology', *Management Decision*, 31 (7).

White R and James B (1996), *The Outsourcing Manual*, Gower Press, Aldershot.

CHAPTER 17

Buying for government and public services

Government expenditure on non-pay related areas is approximately £60 billion per annum. Main expenditures cover a vast range of goods; weapons systems, stationery and printed forms etc., furniture, uniforms, food, services and capital projects including consultancy services, banking services, information systems and services, the management of facilities, as well as medical services, road building and maintenance, and utilities.

OBJECTIVES OF THIS CHAPTER

- To appreciate the origins of European Law and the main principles which form the basis of procurement directives
- To introduce the three types of European Law and how they are administered
- To define public supply services and works contracts
- To outline the main provisions of the directives
- To examine the criteria relevant to supplier appraisal and bid evaluation under the EC procurement directives
- To evaluate the various contract pricing mechanisms.

Initiatives and policies such as market testing, contracting out, private finance initiative, competing for quality, NHS internal market, facilities management and partnering, all affect how goods and services are procured within central and local government. They help to shape both the approach to the market, the preparation of the specification and the evaluation of the most economically advantageous tender to meet the requirement.

There is a substantial difference between the approaches and methods adopted in relation to large and small procurement requirements. European legislation and particularly the procurement directives affect all public sector procurement because of the nature of Britain's relationship with the European Union. We must follow the 'teleological principles' adopted by the members of European Union. This means that the spirit of the directives flows through all levels of government procurement irrespective of value or size of individual expenditure on goods, services or works. There are few exemptions (though there are some). This spirit dictates open, fair and non-discriminatory policy in all our competitive tendering processes. European directives take primacy over national law irrespective of when the law was created.

With regard to lower value procurements, the directives have an effect upon the aspects of specification, evaluation of suppliers, service providers and contractors and on the evaluation criteria used for selecting the best value for money offer from amongst the competitive bidders. Higher value and larger scale procurements are additionally affected by the need to publicise many of the public sector requirements through the *Official Journal of the European Communities (OJEC)*. This has not only a strategic and procedural impact upon all the procurement, but places time implications upon the tendering procedure too.

This chapter will mostly deal with those larger procurements of goods and services which are subject to the full rigor of the European legislation. Works contracts will also be highlighted.

THE EU AND PROCUREMENT

All procurements made within the public sector should follow the EU's Good Procurement Practice guidance, which advises:

- A set of clear and concise objectives.
- A full understanding of the market and the law.
- A clear specification.
- Good sourcing and careful consideration when choosing suppliers, service providers and contractors.
- Well considered award criteria.
- Effective contract management.
- A sound supplier and contract performance review process.

PUBLIC ACCOUNTABILITY

Public sector purchasers are accountable to the public whose money is spent, including disappointed tenderers and potential suppliers. They must produce procedures and practices which will stand up to scrutiny during either government audits or to challenge through the courts of any purchasing decision that has been made. A primary purpose of public accountability is to prevent abuses of taxpayers money. A secondary purpose is to let it be seen that they have been prevented.

EU COMPETITION PROCUREMENT CYCLE FOR GOODS AND SERVICES

This public sector procurement contract cycle is based upon the cycle for procurement which includes the European Union competitive tendering procedures. The objective of the competitive tendering process is to ensure that a contractual relationship is formed with the most suitable supplier of goods or services in the market. The European dimension adds to that process additional steps to ensure wider market penetration is made, to encourage the

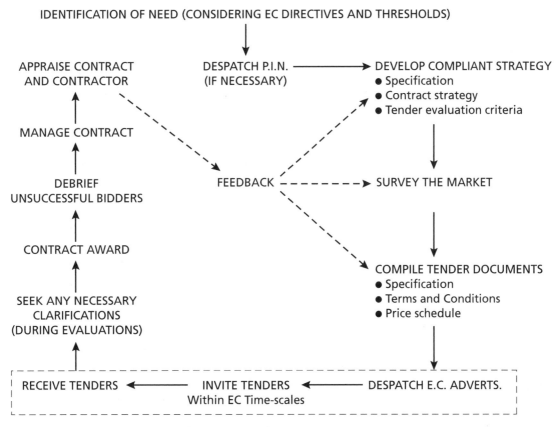

Fig. 17.1 The EU procurement cycle

achievement or at least the pursuit of a higher level of competition. This takes the form of time-scales to advertise the business in the market and for potential tenderers to respond.

EC PROCUREMENT DIRECTIVES

Origins of the European procurement law

The underlying legal basis for the EC procurement directives are contained in the Treaty of Rome, March 1957.

The main principles of this Treaty which carry through to the procurement directives aim to:

● **Increase the transparency of procurement procedures and practices throughout the community.**

This aim is to ensure that all member states follow the same procurement processes at the same time and by so doing that any member state will be able to 'see clearly' the particular stage that the procurement procedure has reached and have sufficient time and knowledge to join in if this is appropriate.

- **Aid the free movement of goods, services, capital and people between member states.**

The aim is to ensure that no discrimination will affect the business of the market and of its people. Qualifications, skills and experience of all its people should be recognised across the borders of the Union and so too the currency, goods and services of each member state.

- **Develop effective competition for public sector contracts.**

The European competition policy has been introduced for the public sector to facilitate the benefits that the use of forces of supply and demand in the market can offer. The private sector, while not working to the same ethos as the public sector, was deemed to be more efficient because of the market's pull and tug against quantity, price and quality etc. The public sector was deemed to have the largest levels of expenditure going through the common market and so was the sector which needed to be marshalled initially, to ensure that the common market and these competition policies worked.

The private sector is subject to laws of competition from the European Union, however, not these procurement directives.

- **Standardise specifications.**

This aim is to ensure that there is a common approach to the terminology and standards used within specifications across the member states. This aids non-discriminatory policies and ensures that a wider consideration of the market is taken.

- **Provide advance information of procurement needs to the marketplace.**

This aim ensures that any business for the European market is publicised early enough for the market to respond. The advance information mainly takes the form of publicity of intended procurement contracts in the *Official Journal of the European Communities,* although this also appears in product and service description coding systems which apply across the Union too.

There is a range of procurement directives covering procurement in areas of public works: the Consolidated Works Directive 93/37/EEC; Public Supplies, the EC Consolidated Supplies Directive, 93/36/EEC; the EC Services Directive, 92/50/EEC. Separate directives exist to cover the public procurement utilities.

The Compliance Directive, 89/665/EEC, places obligations upon the public sector to enforce the law contained within the procurement directives.

There are three types of European law: Primary law; Secondary Legislation which is what the procurement directives are known as in European law; and Case Law. The procurement directives are administered both by the European Commission, who is the watchdog body for the competition policy throughout the union and by the national courts of England, Wales, N. Ireland and Scotland. Britain operate their legal system using a 'dualist approach' to legislation. This has the effect of taking European law and ratifying it into national law through Parliament into 'Statutory Instrument'. Thus the

European directives become directly applicable to all member states from their date of implementation, but are translated to have the same meaning as the original law into national law as Public Sector Procurement Regulations. The European Commission set a time frame within which such ratification must occur. Due to this any public sector purchasing decisions which violate the Treaty may be challenged in the European Court of Justice by the EU Commission or our own or another member state, through the national court system.

The General Agreement on Tariffs and Trade (GATT) has had an impact upon the effects of this legislation on particular entities of the public sector. This agreement identified a series of entities which were included as those who must follow the full rigor of the EU procurement law. The provisions of the GATT Agreement were broadly similar to those found within only the former supplies directive. Since then other directives, as mentioned above now exist. The GATT Agreement was designed to establish an international framework of rights and obligations with respect to government procurement, and with a view to achieving liberalisation and expansion of world trade. (It thus had a lot in common with the procurement directives to follow.) This agreement has been superseded by the General Procurement Agreement derived from a more recently designated worldwide based organisation – the World Trade Organisation. Nevertheless, the original parameters set by the GATT Agreement in respect of identifying those entities who should follow the law still have effect. All government departments and their agencies, local authorities, and health trusts are mostly subject to this legislation. The designated level at which the contracting authority has been identified by GATT, reflects the boundaries around the various procurements within the government which must be aggregated together. The list of 'contracting authorities or entities' is recorded in the relevant statutory instrument.

- The public supplies contract regulations 1995, SI No 201.
- The public services contract regulations 1993, SI No 3228.
- The public works contract regulations 1991, SI No 2680.

A complete revision of the range of procurement directives is planned, which will no doubt reflect the development of various newer entities brought about through changes to the public sector's organisation and structure.

It is clear that the impact of the European Union's directives has been far reaching across the public sector. Heads of procurement organisations (contracting authorities) have been given the responsibility of ensuring compliance with the directives throughout the organisation (contracting authority), a task which has been particularly difficult in those departments where the purchase of goods and services has been fragmented.

In those areas where a planned and systematic approach to procurement does not yet exist, there is a danger that the directives are seen as a burden rather than a means of achieving better overall value for money. The procurement directives are having an effect on the organisational structure of purchasing and supply units across government departments as a whole; as they wrestle with the massive obligation to co-ordinate, aggregate, plan and forecast need over longer and longer periods of time. Government initiatives also coincide with these directives in so far as they also impact upon the way purchasing is done by government procurement officials. The EC directives tend to be operated best within a co-ordinated structure such as a centralised, commodity purchase group or satellite configuration. Decentralised procurement structures work less well since there is not the scope for the necessary co-ordination and management across departments and agencies. Life is often made more difficult as heads of procurement departments try to both manage and operate within devolved budget environments and a controlled legislative framework. As a result many changes in control and structure are appearing throughout the purchasing and supply function within the public sector.

ENFORCEMENT OF THE DIRECTIVES

By implementing the obligations of the compliance directive into UK law, aggrieved supplies and service providers can take action against non-compliant contracting authorities in the courts of the UK. They may take the form of, for example:

- Claims arising from a company's belief that they would have been awarded the contract had the purchasing process been properly conducted, i.e. the use of discriminatory specifications.
- Claims that the *OJEC* advertisement was improperly worded leading to failure of the company to respond.
- Claims that the company was improperly excluded from the purchasing process, i.e. during the use of unfair evaluation criteria.

Action in the UK concerning the possible breach of procurement regulations is brought in the High Court of England and Wales and N. Ireland and in the Court of Session in Scotland.

The first step to court in a case brought in the national courts (or European court), is the notification of the member state and the contracting authority of the alleged infringement, within three months of detection of the breach by the supplier, service provider or contractor, that they intend to go to court on the matter. By way of interim measures prior to final trial, these courts have the power to suspend the procedure leading to contract award, to ensure that natural justice can be satisfied prior to the award of any potentially defective contract. These courts can, too, suspend any decision that the contracting authority are about to make in the awarding procedure or make changes to any procurement documentation within the tendering procedure which amounts to a breach of the obligations placed upon them by the procurement law. This action stemming from the European procurement directives has had far reaching effect upon the premise that the British non-consumer law operates upon. Parties to a business contract were deemed, in original national contract law, to be sufficiently wise to contract virtually upon whatever basis they liked. This procurement law erodes that premise somewhat; the parties to business contracts now need to operate in a fair, open and just manner acting within the confines of the legislation. At the final trial, the courts may in addition to the other powers mentioned, award damages to the aggrieved supplier/service provider/contractor, if a contract has been entered into improperly.

The European Court of Justice can also repudiate a procurement contract which has been awarded improperly. The national courts, however, will not do this but may award damages to those who have suffered loss after the contract has been awarded.

DEFINITIONS OF PUBLIC SUPPLY, SERVICES, AND WORKS CONTRACTS

It is important to understand the various types of contract, and why they operate in relation to procurement practices and EC directives.

Public supply contracts

A public supply contract is for the purchase, lease or hire of goods and for siting or installation of those goods.

Public services contracts

A public services contract is when the purchaser engages a contractor (the service provider) to provide services. There are two categories of services: Part A, priority services (to which the services regulations apply in full); and Part B, residual services (where the tender is only subject to some of the requirements in the regulations, i.e. technical specifications, publishing of the contract post award, and making statistical reports to Treasury).

Design contests   Design contests are procedures for obtaining plans or designs, which involves a jury panel and offer prizes or payments or which may lead to the award of a services contract.

Public works contracts

A public works contract is where the contract is for civil engineering or building works or where the contracting authority engages a person to carry out for the purchaser, a work corresponding to specified requirements.

Works concessions contracts   Works concessions contracts are works contracts where the consideration given by the purchaser consists of or includes the right to exploit the work or works to be carried out under the contract.

Subsidised works contracts   Subsidised works contracts are works contracts which are awarded by a body other than a public authority for certain types of works where a public authority contributes more than half the cost.

The distinction between 'work' or 'works' used within the Public Works Regulations, has been explained as applying to contracts which involve building and civil engineering activities whether in the form of a specific service, for example, a work – painting; or in the form of a series of services leading to the completion of a work that has an economic or technical function, for example, works – the construction of a building.

THE MAIN PROVISIONS OF THE DIRECTIVES IN RELATION TO CONTRACTS

The provisions relating to contracts do vary from directive to directive in some aspects, and so these aspects will be dealt with separately. The following section outlines the main elements of the directives:

- Thresholds
- Aggregation rules
- Advertisements
- Procurement procedures
- Technical standards and specifications
- Evaluation criteria
  - Suppliers or service provider's appraisal
  - Supplier's or service provider's bid
- Contract award

Thresholds

The proposed tender will fall within the procurement directives if the estimated value is greater than the prescribed threshold. The threshold is calculated and revised bi-annually.

Table 17.1 Relevant thresholds for supply, works and services regulations

Regulation	European threshold	Sterling equivalent
Supply contract (GPA)	130 000 SDR	£ 104 435
Supply contract (non-GPA)	206 022 ECU	£ 160 670
Pre-information notice	750 000 ECU	£ 584 901
Services contracts (GPA)	130 000 SDR	£ 104 435
Services contracts (non-GPA)	206 022 ECU	£ 160 670
Pre-information notice	750 000 ECU	£ 584 901
Works contracts Pre-information notice	5 150 548 ECU	£4 016 744
Small lots services works	800 000 ECU	£ 62 389
	1 000 000 ECU	£ 779 867

All threshold figures are exclusive of VAT. The sterling figures are current at time of writing.

The directives provide guidance upon how to estimate the value of proposed tenders, these are referred to as aggregation rules and are dealt with below.

These rules and the above threshold figures interact, as once a contract value has been estimated using the rules, a contracting authority can determine whether the procurement will fall into the scope of the full procedures.

Aggregation rules

The method of calculating the value of the proposed services and supplies contracts depends upon the type of contract that is to be used. The rules generally offer four types of contractual procurement circumstance and, alongside each, a method of calculation relating to that circumstance is given.

- If the contract is for a one-off purchase, estimate the total value including all component parts, transportation costs, installation and commissioning etc.
- The value of a series of contracts, or repeat orders, for the same or similar 'products', should be estimated over a 12 month span (either historically or for the future). The requirement cannot be dis-aggregated to avoid the regulations.
- Fixed term contracts, should be estimated for the full duration of the contract. If a contract is to run for a three-year term, then it is the expenditure over the three years that represents the estimated amount. Similarly, if a contract is fixed for one year with two further year options to extend, then it is the three-year figure that should be taken as the estimate. This is so, as the period of consideration, in this case, is the three years.
- A series of contracts for an indefinite term or uncertain period, the total value should be calculated by multiplying the estimated monthly value by 48.
- Where there is a single requirement for services, and a number of services contracts have been, or are to be, entered into, then the total value of all the individual contracts must be calculated. A number of individual contracts may be removed from the total contract, if each contract is valued at less than 80 000 ECU (currently £62 389), and taken together they represent less than 20 per cent of the total overall valuation. The withdrawal of individual contracts from the total number is optional and is designed to encourage small companies to bid for government work and therefore expand (giving them the ability to grow in the future). The removed contracts would be subject to national competition tendering procedures. The remainder of the total contracts (after individual contracts have been removed) is subject to full European legislation irrespective of whether their value now places them below the relevant threshold value.

Aggregation rules which apply to public works contracts use similar principles. The estimated value applied for such contracts is to estimate the value of the whole works contract. Where the contract is part of a series necessary to carry out a project, it is the total value of the aggregated contracts which will determine if the contract falls within the scope of the regulations. Individual contracts, within a series of works contracts may also be removed from the total contract, if each contract is valued at less than 1 000 000 ECU and together they represent less than 20 per cent of the total overall valuation.

It is generally accepted that the valuation given to the estimates must be determined by calculating the highest possible value.

Advertisements

There is a requirement for the majority of EU procurements to be advertised in the *Official Journal of the European Communities* to comply with the aim to provide advance information. There are three kinds of advertisement that could be applied:

Pre-information notices

These have to be issued in respect of both supply and service works requirements. As the name suggests they are for information only and require no open form of response from the marketplace. Their purpose is to give advance warning to the marketplace of substantial business to come later (published later) in the financial year. This enables potential suppliers to plan ahead and to allow every opportunity for effective competition across the Community when the requirement is eventually advertised under one of the procurement procedures. It is required that:

- Notices are published at the commencement of the financial year or as soon as possible after forming the intention to procure.
- Only one notice be published for the specific 'product' per each contracting authority.
- Notices contain the total estimated contract value of the requirements for the coming twelve months.
- Notices must be issued where total estimated requirements equal or exceed a threshold, currently 750 000 ECU. (£584 901 services and supplies) (£4 016 744 works) These notices can be advertised voluntarily for goods or services below the relevant thresholds. When procuring services and works it is attractive for the contracting authority to do so as this provides a reduction in the relevant time-scale for publication of the later notices. Specific time scales will be discussed later.

In calculating the total value of the supplies or service requirements, to determine whether or not an indicative notice is required, only those anticipated contracts subject to one of the advertising procedures described later in this chapter, need be included. This excludes from the total those contracts that will *not* need to be advertised under one of the procurement procedures, either because they fall below the individual threshold, or because they are exempt in some other way.

Individual contract notices

If the estimated value of a contract requirement is equal to or exceeds the relevant threshold, then the anticipated contract in the majority of cases has to be advertised by the contracting authority using one of these notices. Some situations exist where contracting authorities are not required to despatch an advertisement of this kind, e.g. residual services, certain negotiated procedural aspects. To ensure impartiality, the potential contract requirement must not be advertised in the UK before the tender notice is sent for publication in the *Official Journal of the European Community* supplement for all to see. Furthermore, should a national advert be used at an appropriate time, it must not contain any information other than that published in the *OJEC*. A model notice is set out for use, for example, UK2100EN, used to place a pre-indicative notice for supplies requirements.

The Official Publications Office of the EU normally has 12 days in which to publish the notice in the *OJEC* supplement, starting from the date of despatch of the notice from the contracting authority.

As well as appearing in the *OJEC* supplement, tender notices are accessed by subscribers to the Tenders Electronic Daily (TED) database. Each individual contract notice unit is required to be no greater than about 650 words. A set of model notices are available, for example, for supplies contract requirements:

- UK2110EN – used to place an advertisement under the open procedure.
- UK2120EN – used to place an advertisement under the restricted procedure.
- UK2140EN – used to place an advertisement under the negotiated procedure.

This notice must contain enough relevant information that describes the circumstances under which the procurement procedure will operate. The name and address of the contracting authority, the description of the goods or services, the estimated value of the contract, amongst other important factors must be included to give the prospective bidders a window on the tender and potential contract.

The date of despatch of the tender notice by the contracting authority is a crucial reference point, because some of the minimum time limits allowed under the directives start from this date. The date of despatch means the date on which the tender notice is actually sent to the Official Publications Office, and not the date shown on the documents sent for publication, which could naturally be much earlier. To ensure that this rule is observed, the directives require procurement authorities to be able to provide evidence of the date of despatch.

Contract award notices

It is a requirement of the EC procurement directives that a contract award notice is published, no later than 48 days after the date of the contract. Furthermore, a contract award notice is required for any contract falling within the provisions of the directives even if it was not originally advertised in the *OJEC*. This applies whichever procurement procedure has been followed. The details to be published in the *OJEC* supplement include:

- The contract award criteria.
- The name and address of the selected supplier.
- The nature of the goods or services.
- The contract price or range of prices tendered.

The purpose of the notice is to tell the Commission and the marketplace how, when and why the business was settled. A model notice is also available (UK2180EN), and is used to notify the award of a supplies contract.

Procurement procedures

There are three main types of European procurement procedure that can be chosen by a contracting authority, the 'open' procedure; the 'restricted' procedure and the 'negotiated' procedure; and opportunity exists to *accelerate* two of the procedures in circumstances of extreme urgency outside the contracting authorities control. All of these procedures reflect the choice of approach that the contracting authority may decide to use to operate in the market when issuing tenders to potential suppliers, service providers or contractors. Each procedure has potential cost and resource implications which must be considered by the authority before any approach to the market is made. The variance between each of the procedures is in the degree of competition that will be sought in the event of the particular procurement campaign.

The open procedure

The open procedure is generally used where the contracting authority anticipates that competition is likely to be very limited because of the few, known, available suppliers or the specialist nature of the goods or service. The use of the open procedure increases the level of interest and competition to the maximum available, since all interested suppliers are invited to tender. However, the nature and value of the requirement needs to be such as to justify committing the large level of resources, which could well be needed, to manage a large volume of potential tenders effectively.

A prescribed minimum period of 52 days must be set aside from the date of despatch of the tender notice to allow the tenderers to return the completed tender documents. When the procurement is solely for service requirements then this time limit is reduced to 36 days if an indicative notice has been published. It is permissible to set a date, working backwards from the closing date for the procedures receipt of tenders, for a reasonable period, after which it would not be feasible for the contracting authority to despatch tender documents and the potential supplier return them completed.

The invitation to tender documents are sent to all suppliers who respond to the contract notice by the date specified. These documents must be sent within six working days of receiving the request to participate. When requested by the tenderers, additional information relating to the tender documents must be supplied by the purchasing organisation, not less than six calendar days before the deadline for receipt of the tenders. On some occasions, particularly in the case of the procurement of services, tenderers may require a site visit in order to complete their tender. When this is so, the period for receipt of tenders must be extended by a reasonable length.

The supplies and services directives do not set a specific time scale for the supplier appraisal phase of the procurement because, under the open procedure, the number of tenderers is unknown at the outset. Therefore the procurement organisation needs to plan sufficient resources, in terms of both time and effort, for this potentially time-consuming activity. However, if this procedure has been used to 'explore' the market potential, the number of responses could be very high, and the corresponding burden of supplier appraisal severe.

The open procedure has been drawn as a flow chart to give an outline of the process and the time scales required (*see* Fig. 17.2)

The restricted procedure

The restricted procedure has a two stage process and, as the name suggests, restricts the number of competitors that the contracting authority permits to enter the competition. This is the procedure most commonly used by UK government departments for their supplies and service requirements. The open

**Open procedure for the
procurement of supplies or services**

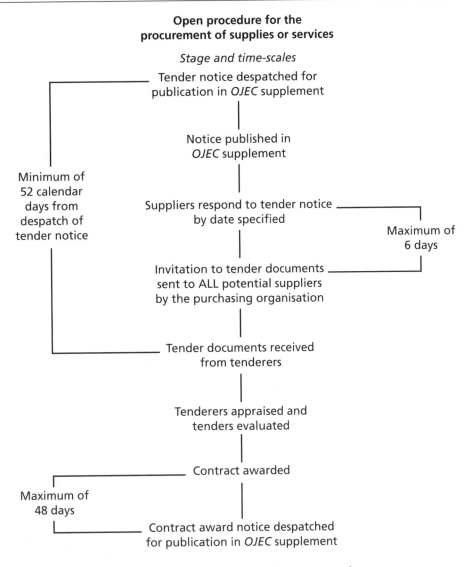

Fig. 17.2 Flow chart showing the process of the open procedure

and restricted procedures have been placed on the same footing as each other, so as to provide a free choice for contracting authorities to use either of these procedures. The open procedure has high resource and time implications, the restricted procedure aids the minimisation of such implications, through the ability to select those who it is felt most suit the criteria and legitimately rejecting the rest. Contracting authorities can make a selection of potential suppliers between a range of 5 and 20, where the number of competitors is specified. The choice of this procedure is often made when procurements are of the common variety which yield high numbers of potential bidders.

Under the restricted procedure, a tender notice advertising the requirement is despatched and published in the *OJEC* supplement. Interested suppliers will then notify the contracting authority of their interest. Under the open procedure *all* of these will be invited to tender. Under the restricted procedure the contracting authority will select, from among the interested parties, those who may submit tenders.

Under the normal restricted procedure, a prescribed minimum period of 37 days is set aside from the date of despatch of the tender notice to give interested suppliers sufficient time to respond. The information provided by the suppliers in response to the 'qualifications' section of the contract notice allows a supplier appraisal exercise to be conducted by the procurement organisation, so that only those suppliers who satisfy the purchaser's supplier appraisal criteria are subsequently invited to tender. No pre-set time span is designated within the directives for this supplier appraisal either, however, contracting authorities need to build in enough time to undertake this process. With this procedure it is important that the 'proper' criteria are used as the level of competition is reduced on the strength or weakness of them. No consideration of the specific goods or service to be offered can be assessed as there is no evidence available at this stage to consider on the matter. Time spent here will be well spent.

Under the normal restricted procedure, using the normal time-scales, tenderers are given a minimum of 40 calendar days from the date of despatch of the tender documents in which to complete and return their tender. This period may be reduced to 26 calendar days in service procurements where an indicative notice under the pre-information procedure has been used. When requested by the tenderers, additional information relating to the tender documents must be supplied by the purchasing organisation not less than 6 calendar days before the deadline for receipt of the tenders. On some occasions, particularly in the case of the procurement of services, tenderers may require a site visit in order to complete their tender. When this is so, the period for receipt of tenders must be extended by a reasonable length or ideally should be built into the original time-scale.

Accelerated restricted procedure

When using the restricted procedure, the normal time-scale may be shortened by adopting the accelerated procedure, but only when operational urgency makes impracticable any of the normal minimum time limits. It must not be used simply as a means of avoiding the normal time limits. The period from the date of despatch of the notice to the last date for receipt of requests to participate from suppliers, must be not less than 15 calendar days. In addition, the period for receipt of completed tenders must not be less than 10 calendar days from the date of despatch of the invitation to tender.

The justification for the use of the accelerated procedure must be stated by the purchasing organisation in the notice published in the *OJEC*.

The negotiated procedure

Under the EC procurement directives, it is permitted in certain circumstances to negotiate the terms of a contract with one or more suppliers. Depending on the circumstances, the use of this procedure may first need to be advertised in the *OJEC* with a negotiated procedures notice, or it may only need to be advertised after the award of the procurement contract.

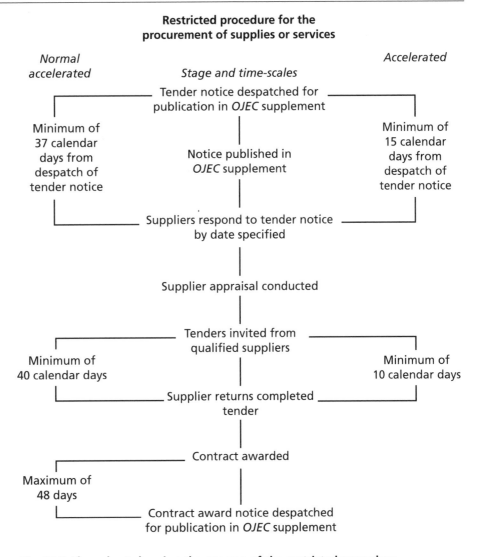

Restricted procedure for the procurement of supplies or services

Normal accelerated

Accelerated

Stage and time-scales

Tender notice despatched for publication in *OJEC* supplement

Minimum of 37 calendar days from despatch of tender notice

Minimum of 15 calendar days from despatch of tender notice

Notice published in *OJEC* supplement

Suppliers respond to tender notice by date specified

Supplier appraisal conducted

Tenders invited from qualified suppliers

Minimum of 40 calendar days

Minimum of 10 calendar days

Supplier returns completed tender

Contract awarded

Maximum of 48 days

Contract award notice despatched for publication in *OJEC* supplement

Fig. 17.3 Flow chart showing the process of the restricted procedure

Negotiated procedure *with* prior publication of a tender notice

The use of either the open or restricted procedures may, on occasions, produce irregular or unacceptable tenders. In these circumstances, if it is decided to pursue the requirement by negotiation, then the negotiated procedure may be used, as long as the original procurement procedure is substantially unchanged.

If the intention is *not* to include in the negotiations all of the suppliers who submitted tenders under the original procurement procedure, then it is necessary to publish a negotiated procedure notice in the *OJEC* prior to conducting the negotiation.

Under the services regulations the negotiated procedure may be used, with the need to prior publicise the negotiation intention, when the risks in the procurement make it difficult to price the requirement and when the nature of the services does not permit the drawing of a sufficiently precise specification.

The process requires a set period for the negotiated procedural advertisement to be placed, and permits a 37-day period for expression of interest to negotiate from the marketplace. Thereafter, the process can take as long as is necessary to complete satisfactorily. The requirement to advertise is deemed necessary because the competition has either been limited due to failure of a previous competition, or it is envisaged that this will be a difficult requirement to fulfil and therefore it is desirable to attract as much interest as possible.

When the negotiated procedure is employed as the method of procurement for either supplies or services, a written report is compiled by the procurement organisation to explain which of the permitted circumstances constituted the grounds for using that procedure.

Accelerated negotiated procedure

Under the EC procurement directives, it is permitted to use an accelerated negotiated procedure but only with prior publication of a tender notice. The period from the date of despatch of the accelerated negotiated procedure

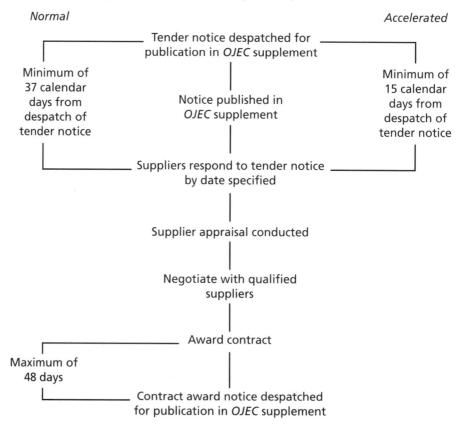

Negotiated procedure for the procurement of supplies or services with prior publication of a negotiated procedure notice

Normal   *Accelerated*

Tender notice despatched for publication in *OJEC* supplement

Minimum of 37 calendar days from despatch of tender notice

Notice published in *OJEC* supplement

Minimum of 15 calendar days from despatch of tender notice

Suppliers respond to tender notice by date specified

Supplier appraisal conducted

Negotiate with qualified suppliers

Award contract

Maximum of 48 days

Contract award notice despatched for publication in *OJEC* supplement

Fig. 17.4 Flow chart showing the negotiated procedure *with* prior publication of a procedure notice

notice to the deadline for receipt of requests to participate must not be less than 15 calendar days.

The justification for the use of the accelerated procedure must be stated by the purchasing organisation in the notice published in the *OJEC*.

Negotiated Procedure without prior publication of a tender notice

The negotiated procedure may be used without prior publication of a negotiated procedures notice in the following circumstances:

- When an open or restricted competition has failed due to irregularity and all of the previous participants in the tender exercise are to be invited to negotiate.
- When no tender has been received in response to a tender notice under the open or restricted procedures and the requirement is substantially unchanged.
- When the requirement is for research, experiment, study or development.
- When the goods or the service may only be provided by a particular supplier for technical, artistic or intellectual property right reasons.
- When additional requirement or replacement goods or services, for reasons of compatibility or disproportionate technical difficulties in operation and maintenance, needs to be met by the original supplier. (In the case of service procurement contracts, the limit on replacement or additional services may

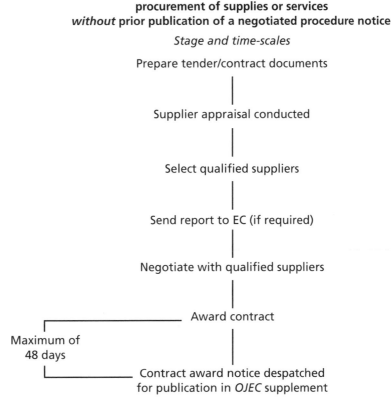

Negotiated procedure for the procurement of supplies or services *without* prior publication of a negotiated procedure notice

Stage and time-scales

Prepare tender/contract documents

Supplier appraisal conducted

Select qualified suppliers

Send report to EC (if required)

Negotiate with qualified suppliers

Award contract

Maximum of 48 days

Contract award notice despatched for publication in *OJEC* supplement

Fig. 17.5 Flow chart showing the negotiated procedure without prior publication of a procedure notice

only be bought to the value of no more than 50 per cent of the original contract, and applies for no longer than 3 years.)

● When the requirement is unforeseen and unforeseeable (urgent) by the contracting authority and the time limits prescribed under the open and restricted procedures cannot be met.

Technical standards and specifications

The EU procurement regulations require the contracting authority to use certain non-discriminatory terminology in pursuance of the aims of both the Treaty of Rome and the Procurement Directives. Specification detail needs to include such factors as the standards of quality, performance and safety required. In this respect, it is the responsibility of the purchasing organisation to ensure compliance with the requirements of the EC procurement directives upon the use of European Standards and common technical specifications. A common technical specification is a technical specification laid down in accordance with the procedure recognised by member states with a view to uniform application across the Community.

A European Standard is a standard approved by the European Committee for Standardisation (CEN) or by the European Committee for Electro-technical Standardisation (CENELEC). The supplies and service directives, Articles 7.2 and 14.2 respectively, require UK contracting authorities to use either a British Standard implementing a European Standard wherever such a standard exists, or common technical specifications.

If there is neither a British Standard implementing a European Standard, nor a common technical specification, or in the case where an exception applies, another standard may be used as long as it does not prejudice the principles of equivalence and mutual recognition of technical specifications.

There are, however, instances where it is permissible to derogate from the prescribed hierarchy of specifications. Again, like other exceptions, these are clearly defined. For example, where there exists a statutory duty in relation to, health or safety, technical reasons of conformance, or innovative reasons.

Evaluation criteria

Supplier's or service provider's appraisal

The supplier appraisal conducted when using one of the procedures prescribed under the EC procurement directives follows the same general methodology as that of any supplier appraisal. Typically, there are three main factors to consider:

1 Legality to operate as a supplier or service provider.
2 Minimum economic and financial standing.
3 Technical capacity to perform.

Financial information requested from potential suppliers would comprise:

● a copy of, or extracts from, the supplier's balance sheets, where publication of the balance sheet is required under company law in the country in which the supplier is established;

- appropriate statements from bankers; and
- a statement of the supplier's overall turnover, and its turnover in respect of the goods or services to which the requirement relates, for the previous 3 financial years.

Depending upon the nature, quantity and purpose of the goods to be supplied or service to be provided, the commercial and technical information requested as evidence of the supplier's capability might include:

- In the case of a service provider, the educational and professional qualifications of the supplier's managerial staff and those responsible for providing the service.
- A list of the principal deliveries effected or services provided in the past three years, with the amounts, dates and recipients, public or private, involved.
- A description of the supplier's technical facilities, their measures for ensuring quality and their study and research facilities.
- An indication of the technicians or technical bodies involved, whether or not belonging directly to the supplier, especially those responsible for quality control.
- Samples, descriptions and photographs of the product to be supplied.
- A statement of the service provider's average annual workforce and the number of managerial staff for the last three years.
- A statement of the tool, plant or technical equipment available to the service provider for carrying out the service.
- Certificates drawn up by official quality control institutes or agencies of recognised competence, attesting conformity to certain specifications or standards of goods, clearly identified by references to specifications or standards.
- An identification of the proportion of the contract which the service provider may intend to subcontract.

Suppliers responding to the notice who meet the minimum supplier appraisal standards are considered for business within the confines of the contract procedure chosen.

Evaluation criteria

Supplier's or service provider's bid

Within the EC procurement directives, a requirement exists to be open about the criteria to be used to select or reject a bid in the form of a tender from a potential supplier or service provider. The directives offer two choices upon which to base the choice:

- lowest price only, where the contracting authority may only select the lowest priced bid without consideration of any other factor; or
- the most economically advantageous tender, where the various sited value-for-money factors are weighed off against the price to allow recognition of quality, durability, delivery, after-sales service, etc. in the choice of the best offer to meet the requirement.

It is public sector practice to choose the value-for-money option when procuring goods, services and works contracts.

Contract award

There is now a requirement within the EC procurement directives to operate a debriefing policy for unsuccessful suppliers. The law states that if a request for a debrief from an unsuccessful tenderer is made to a public sector contracting authority then it must be met with a response within 15 days of that request.

STRATEGIC PROCESS

The entire European procedures necessitates a strategic plan to be adopted not only for each procurement but for each contracting authorities range of procurement responsibilities. The entire procurement will need to be co-ordinated annually and beyond to ensure compliance with these procurement procedures.

CONTRACT PRICING MECHANISMS

Once a contract is agreed, both parties are legally bound to fulfil their contractual obligations: in essence, the contractor completes the work in accordance with the specification with regard to quality and time; the contracting authority promptly pays the agreed price for all such work carried out. Why should this *ever* be the case? What is it about the price mechanism that might incentivise the contractor to perform?

It is a principle of government contracting that firm price contracts should be used wherever possible (firm prices are those prices not subject to any provision for variation). Firm price contracts are the most desirable type of contract for a purchaser because they give the contractor the strongest incentive for economy and efficiency: the less spent by the contractor in carrying out the work, the more they achieve by way of profit; the contractor 'keeps' every pound by which they 'beat' the price. The aim is to reward the contractor for legitimately keeping costs under control, while maintaining the contract quality requirements; in other words, efficiency is rewarded.

To obtain such a price from the market requires a clear, unambiguous specification and a relatively stable economy, so as to allow suppliers to cost and price the requirement with some certainty. For just as all cost 'savings' below the price will be *kept* by the contractor, all costs incurred above the price will be *met* by the contractor.

However, as soon as the risk of a loss is foreseen, possibly brought about by uncertainties within the requirement, the supply market may be less willing to contract on a firm price basis without the level of contingencies within the price quoted being pessimistically high.

In order to keep as much of the incentive of a firm price contract in those cases where uncertainty prevails, a target cost incentive contract arrangement is sometimes used. Here, it is not necessary to agree a *price* with the contractor, but only a *target cost*, a *target fee* and a *share ratio*. If the work is completed at the target cost, the contractor receives the target fee. However, if the contractor is more efficient and beats the target cost, then not only is the reward of the target fee achieved, but also the contractor's share of the cost saving. Conversely, if the contractor exceeds the target cost, the contractor receives the target fee but abated by the contractor's share of the cost overrun.

In a contract pricing mechanism where the contractor is incentivised to keep costs down, whether this be a firm price or target cost incentive arrangement, it is essential that the output required from the contract is specified in clear terms to ensure that the performance requirement is achieved; otherwise costs might be kept down at the expense of quality.

Quality or timing issues may be incentivised; if above average quality or quicker than average completion is required of a market, then a contractor might be rewarded in a similar way to a cost incentive. For example, for each day saved or for each batch of zero defects, the contractor might be awarded a share of the bonus sum. However, such multiple incentives need to be crafted with care; they need to be balanced to ensure that the quality of delivery bonuses available do not encourage wasteful expenditure.

SUMMARY POINTS

- European Directives take precedence over national law and dictate open, fair and non discriminatory policy. They ensure a wider market, and a higher level of competition is involved.
- Non compliant contracting authorities can be taken to court for several reasons including use of discriminatory specifications; misleading wording in the *OJEC* publication; unfair evaluation criteria. The court has power to award damages to the aggrieved supplier.
- The threshold value dictates whether or not a contract falls into the scope of the full procedures. Aggregation rules estimate the total value of connected contracts which may mean the directives apply. Advertising requirements of the directive are also covered in the chapter.
- European procurement has three types of procedure. With open, all those interested can tender. Restricted means only those invited are involved while negotiated procedures occur directly between the contracting organisation and supplier. Procedures can be accelerated in certain noted circumstances.
- European directives insist on non discriminatory terminology with clear unambiguous specifications. Potential suppliers are appraised legally, financially and technically in much the same way as any appraisal.
- Bid evaluation has 2 choices under EU directives: lowest price only or most economically advantageous tender. The latter tends to be the more popular. Unsuccessful tenderers may request, and are entitled to, a debrief.

REFERENCES AND FURTHER READING

Behan P (1994) *Purchasing in Government,* Longman in association with the Civil Service College, Ascot.

Central Unit on Procurement (1997) *Contracting for Strategic Services,* HM Treasury, London.

The Public Supplies Contract Regulations 1991, SI No. 2680.

The Public Supplies Contract Regulations 1993, SI No. 3228.

The Public Supplies Contract Regulations 1995, SI No. 201.

Trepte P-A (1993) *Public Procurement in the EC,* CCH Editions Ltd.

PART 4

Systems, controls and personnel

Chapter 18
PURCHASING SYSTEMS

Chapter 19
CONTROLLING PERFORMANCE,
EFFICIENCY & EFFECTIVENESS

Chapter 20
PEOPLE IN PURCHASING

Chapter 21
RESEARCH FOR PURCHASING
AND SUPPLY

INTRODUCTION TO PART FOUR

In this concluding part of the text we examine purchasing systems, control procedures and the most important asset of any organisation – people. There is a new chapter (21) in this section dealing with organisational buyer behaviour.

Chapter 18 explains the need for effective integrated systems in a complete and developed purchasing and supply function. We examine how different kinds of information systems are appropriate at different stages of development. The point is made that the development of truly integrated databases and electronic data interchange is seen as an important prerequisite for an effectively linked supply chain. Purchasing systems are described and basic purchasing documentation examined. Non-standard purchases are reviewed.

In Chapter 19 various methods are outlined for controlling purchasing performance, measuring both efficiency and effectiveness. In this chapter we suggest measurement and assessment methods and criteria appropriate for the stage of development reached.

Chapter 20 is concerned with people in purchasing. Well trained and motivated staff make a crucial contribution to the performance of the activity. Here we attempt to identify the skills and other attributes appropriate for purchasing staff in the 1990s, and sample training and development profiles are discussed. The education scheme of the Chartered Institute of Purchasing and Supply is described, and National Vocational Qualifications relating to purchasing and supply are explained. The question of ethics is also dealt with in this section.

The closing chapter, Chapter 21, looks at influential research conducted into organisational buyer behaviour and highlights its relevance to current purchasing practices and the evolving and developing perceptions of purchasing and supply held by suppliers and those concerned with marketing and related activities. This chapter gives indication as to how the area of purchasing research is developing, and provides some appreciation of the growing scope of this activity.

CHAPTER 18

Purchasing systems

INTRODUCTION

Purchasing is a function that has traditionally generated considerable quantities of paperwork. This paperwork was necessary to communicate information from one function to another in order to facilitate action, to indicate requirements to suppliers, and to obtain the necessary goods and services on time and to specification.

OBJECTIVES OF THIS CHAPTER

- **To identify the stages of purchasing development in relation to systems and procedures**
- **To appreciate the characteristics of an integrated system**
- **To outline the four types of data transmitted by means of Electronic data interface**
- **To assess how purchasing routines can be switched from a paper exercise to an 'on-line' communication**
- **To follow purchasing systems from origination, to selection and ordering through to completion**
- **To outline the differences between buying for high value contracts and for very low value orders.**

The advent of information technology (IT) and more integrated software systems has radically changed matters. Although the paperless office may still be in the future, and may never come about, simple transactions are today seldom paper based.

Table 18.1 illustrates how purchasing systems have developed in line with changes in IT, organisational structuring and new strategic concepts and shows the typical stages of systems evolution. Many organisations have passed through some of these phases as they strive towards totally integrated databases both upstream and downstream, that is, with suppliers and customers. This information, once generated, is, in theory, available to all those who require it, subject to security limits. Moreover the data should not have to be reformulated to fit other databases.

Strategically integrated databases are vital if the following concepts are to be fully developed:

- logistics;
- total quality management;
- flexible manufacturing;

Table 18.1 Development of purchasing systems

Stages of purchasing development	Standard of information system
Infant	Simple clerical system, not properly integrated. Few records kept.
Awakening	Recognition of accurate information important in purchasing area; manual system improved. Beginnings of computer system but not integrated with other company systems.
Developing	Beginnings of more integrated systems such as materials requirement planning (MRP). Linking computerised purchasing system with other function systems.
Mature	Fully integrated database throughout organisation, e.g. MRP II. All purchasing information generated by computer.
Advanced	The fully integrated database is now linked via EDI with major suppliers and customers – dramatic reduction in lead times and costs.

- automation;
- just-in-time; and
- reduced strategic acquisition costs.

In Figure 18.1 we can see a model of an integrated database. All the information of events is available as it happens, i.e. in real time. Every part of the organisation is linked. The effects of information changes in one function can be seen on other areas. Thus purchasing would have immediate information available on:

- orders placed/outstanding;
- turnover by supplier;
- stock position;
- accounts outstanding;
- production/customer requirements;
- vendor rating in terms of (a) delivery and (b) quality; and
- new developments/projects.

THE INTEGRATED COMPUTER SYSTEM

While even the most advanced systems will still generate considerable amounts of paperwork, this has been decreased considerably. Most computer hardware suppliers offer appropriate software packages that can be customised for the organisation involved. The secrets of a good integrated computer system are as follows.

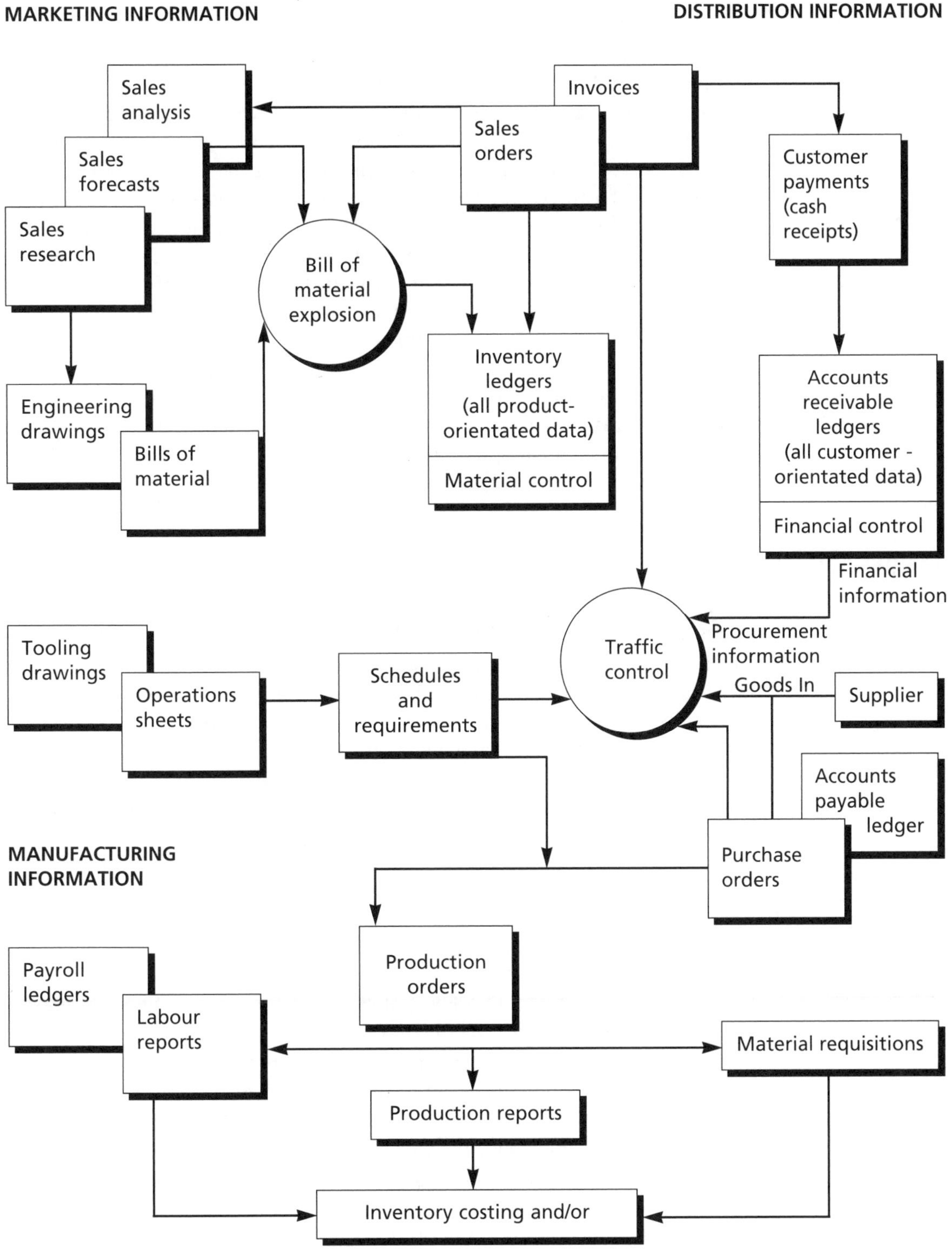

MARKETING INFORMATION

DISTRIBUTION INFORMATION

**MANUFACTURING
INFORMATION**

Sales
analysis

Sales
forecasts

Sales
research

Bill of
material
explosion

Engineering
drawings

Bills of
material

Inventory
ledgers
(all product-
orientated data)

Material control

Sales
orders

Invoices

Customer
payments
(cash
receipts)

Accounts
receivable
ledgers
(all customer -
orientated data)

Financial control

Financial
information

Procurement
information

Traffic
control

Goods In

Supplier

Tooling
drawings

Operations
sheets

Schedules
and
requirements

Accounts
payable
ledger

Purchase
orders

Payroll
ledgers

Labour
reports

Production
orders

Material requisitions

Production reports

Inventory costing and/or

Fig. 18.1 A model of an integrated database

Strategic planning

Select a system that suits your organisational requirements, not just for today, but one that can be developed as the organisation develops.

Many of the major computer organisations offer integrated packages which are built from discrete but compatible modules. Thus one can buy a system specially written to allow for total integration of the database at some time in the future. Without reasonable planning, organisations may buy computer software packages that suit particular functions (e.g. finance, production) but which cannot be integrated. There are indeed examples of large organisations that have grown in such a way that each function has not only developed its own software, but also has different hardware that does not allow integration of systems, or allows it at considerable cost.

Hewlett Packard, IBM and other major computer organisations, as well as many software houses, offer software packages consisting of the following modules that can be linked as and when required: materials management; production management; purchasing; sales order management; production cost management; general ledger; accounts payable and accounts receivable.

Adequate training

It is essential that highly developed systems are introduced only after staff have been properly trained to handle such systems effectively. There have been numerous examples of organisations introducing sophisticated software, only to find that operatives cannot handle the systems.

In many organisations we find that the input activities (i.e. stores, stock control and purchasing) have been neglected in terms of organisational development. Low salaries have sometimes been paid to stores staff and little training given. The introduction of new advanced systems, without attention to the human resources aspects, may lead to major problems in this area (e.g. computer input error, lost stocks, theft, damages). These problems can, if left unchecked, corrupt the total system and make it eventually useless. Those organisations that have successfully introduced integrated databases have spent considerable amounts of time and money in ensuring the right degree of expertise and commitment.

An example of a British Gas integrated logistics system is shown in Figure 18.2. This system integrates the general logistics of getting the workforce and materials on to gas drilling platforms located off shore.

The general developments in the systems area call for integration with other functions and the generation of all documentation by computer – thereby releasing the buyer to spend more of his or her time on other more effective purchasing activities such as negotiation, supplier development and cost reduction.

Eventually both customer and supplier databases will be linked with the buying organisation involved. Figure 18.3 illustrates the EDI linkage between buyer and supplier.

Having examined the general trend with information systems, we will now identify some of those activities in more detail, and shed further light on the transactions involved in the purchasing and supply areas.

TRANSACTION SEQUENCE

The normal sequence of activities involved in most purchase transactions begins when a need is perceived for some article or service and ends when the need has been met and payment made. Many purchases, however, are made to meet continuing needs, so that each transaction is part of a series. This affects the way suppliers are selected – often a long-term choice – and the way orders are placed – perhaps as delivery instructions against a long-term contract.

Forms and procedures used in purchase transactions vary considerably. Partly this reflects the differences between organisations and the operations they carry out. For instance retailing, offshore contracting, and mass production of consumer durables differ so much in what they do that they could be expected to use different documentation. Variations in procedure may also be due to individual preference and the custom and tradition of the company. Our research has also found many examples of forms and procedures which were capable of considerable improvement.

Purchasing systems can be considered under four main headings: originating, selecting, ordering, completing. Before examining these in detail, a note on electronic systems may be useful.

ELECTRONIC DATA INTERCHANGE (EDI)

Although face-to-face deals by word of mouth between buyer and seller have always been important in purchasing, and no doubt will continue to be so, most purchasing transactions between organisations have required a lot of paperwork. Increasingly routine communications such as orders, schedules and invoices go direct from computer to computer rather than by typed documents sent by post. Electronic data interchange is replacing paperwork interchange.

EDI is the transfer of data from one computer to another by electronic means, using agreed standards. Four main types of data transferred are:

1 *Trade data* This includes documents mentioned later in this chapter, such as request for quotation, purchase order, acknowledgement, delivery instructions, dispatch and receipt notes, invoice, credit note and statement.
2 *Technical data* This includes product specifications, machine tool settings, CAD/CAM data, performance data. In the manufacturing industry, design engineers in purchasing firms like to communicate from their workstations direct to their key suppliers' CAD systems. The result should be better designs produced in less time.

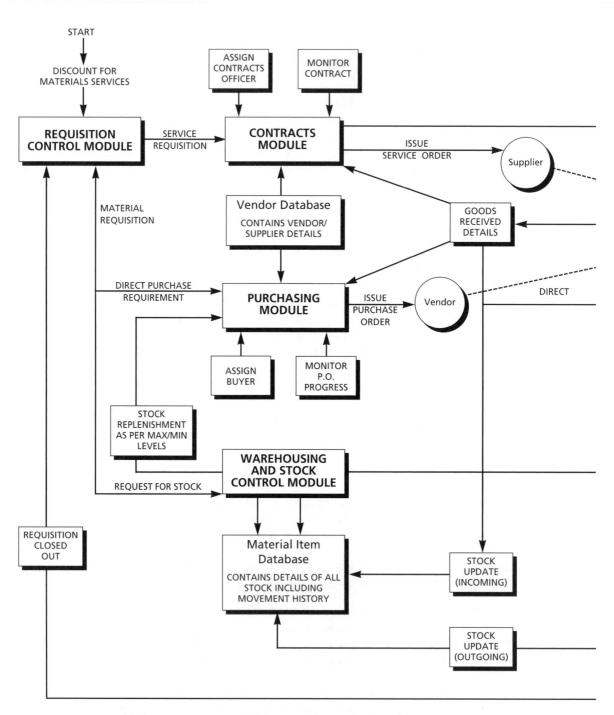

Fig. 18.2 An example of a logistical offshore management system (LOMS)

(*Courtesy:* British Gas Exploration and Production Ltd)

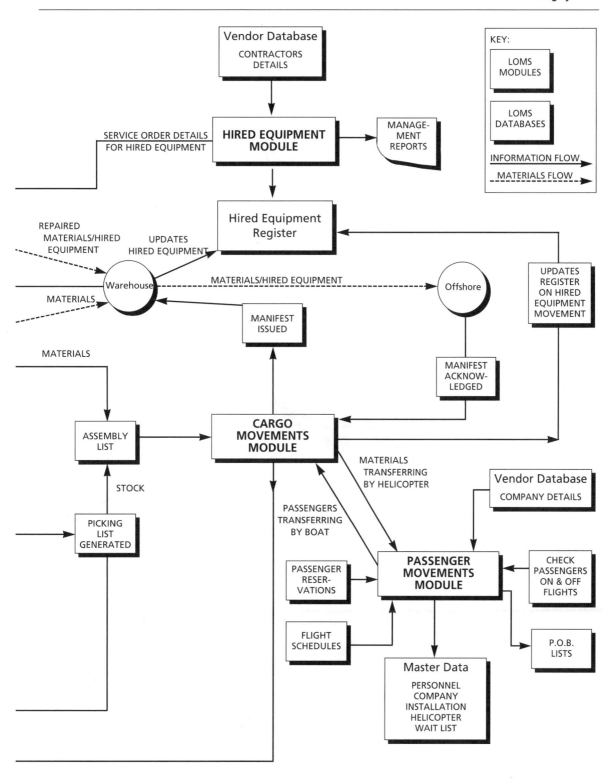

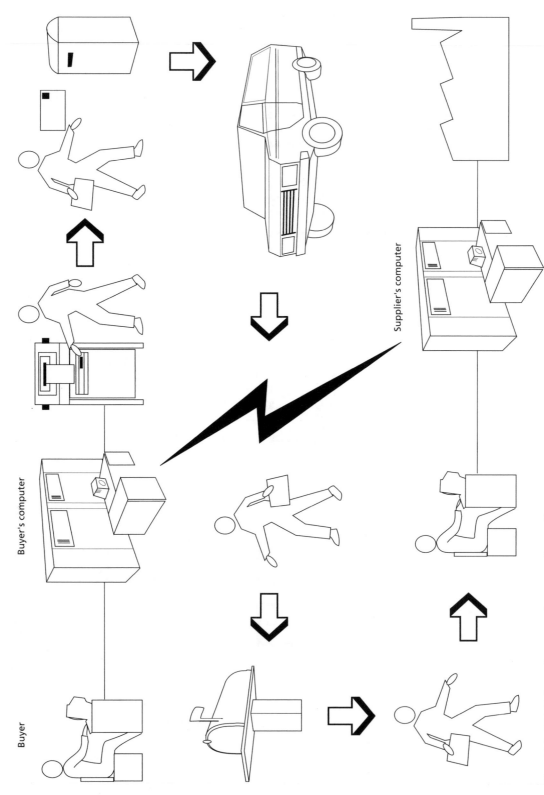

Fig. 18.3 EDI linkage between buyer and supplier
(*Courtesy:* IBM UK Ltd)

Supplier's computer

Buyer's computer

Buyer

3 *Query–response* An example of this is the airline system for querying prices and vacancies for passengers and cargo and making reservations after seeing the response. Similar systems enable a purchaser to check the progress of an order through a supplier's manufacturing and distribution sequence.

4 *Monetary data* Systems for electronic transfer of money computer-to-computer are now widely used, instead of making payment by delivering cheques or other paper documents by post or by hand. Examples include bank clearing systems, electronic payment of invoices, and Electronic Funds Transfer at Point of Sale (EFTPOS). With EFTPOS a retail customer may pay for goods by means of a credit card, which is checked by the POS reader at the till. The customer proves identity either by signature or by entering a Personal Identification Number (PIN). The till time-stamps and encrypts the data and calls the card-issuer's computer for authorisation. The transaction takes about half a minute. Funds are transferred from the purchaser's credit account to the retailer's account, either immediately or else overnight. The system operates on a network of minicomputers belonging to the banks. Another version introduced in 1989 under the name of SWITCH uses debit cards rather than credit cards to pay for goods and services at participating stores, restaurants, garages and retail outlets. Purchases are charged to the customer's current account in a day or two.

For EDI, data has to be set up in a way which can be interpreted by the receiving computers. Electronic links between sender and receiver, supplemented by temporary data storage facilities, are required in addition to the software which sets up or formats messages. These are normally provided by an independent network operator, such as International Network Services (INS) (Edict), and Istel (Tradanet). They are often called Value Added Networks (VAN).

EDIFACT (electronic data interchange for administration, commerce and transport) is being developed as a general standard. Specialised standards include EDICON (Electronic Data Interchange Construction), set up by the construction industry to devise and co-ordinate electronic trading methods from design, quotation and tendering through to invoicing; CEFIC for the chemical industry, EDIFICE for electronics, ODETTE for the auto industry, DISH and SHIPNET for international shipping, ANA for retail and distribution.

A considerable saving on postage, stationery and staff processing time is claimed for EDI. Further savings are due to shorter lead times, which lead to lower stocks. Against this fees have to be paid for access to the network, plus annual subscriptions and the cost of the hardware and software. Paperless trading of this kind is increasingly used by large retailers and manufacturers, and there can be little doubt that this is how large organisations will do business in future.

On-line materials databases

Materials information is increasingly available on-line from databases, which buyers can search for product description and specification, supplier names, prices and availability. Examples, amongst many, include:

- *World steel forecast* Annual time series and forecasts for the steel industry worldwide.
- *Magnesium forecast* Similar figures for magnesium.
- *Plastic chemicals* Time series, imports, exports, prices, sales and usage, etc.

Figure 18.4 gives a glossary of some widely used abbreviations.

Subcontract databases add a search facility to these registers of supplier information, so that buyers with one enquiry can obtain a tender list. Suppliers may also be able to obtain tender information on request.

AIM	Automatic Identification Manufacturers.
ANA	UK Article Numbering Association: sets TRADACOMS standards.
ANSI	American National Standards Institute: co-ordinates information on US national standards
CAD	Computer-aided-design: electronic drafting systems which convert rough sketches into finished drawings.
CAD/CAM	Computer-aided design/computer-aided manufacturing
DTP	Desk-top publishing: software which styles the printed output.
DICON	UK EAN: European Article Number.
EDI	Electronic data interchange.
EDICT	EDI for the construction industry.
EDIFACT	EDI for administration, commerce and transport.
EDIFACE	EDI for electronics.
EFT	Electronic funds transfer.
EFTPOS	Electronic funds transfer from point of sale.
TDI	Trading data interchange – US abbreviation for EDI.
TRADACOMS	Trading data communications standards; developed by ANA and used by TRADANET.
TRADANET	Value added network (VAN) operated in the UK by INS.
UPC	Universal product code; North American system for applying bar codes and article numbers to products.
VAN	Value added network; name for arrangements whereby computers can interchange data.

Fig. 18.4 Glossary of database abbreviations

PURCHASING SYSTEMS

Originating purchases

Purchases normally originate outside the purchase department, since the main function of the purchase department is to buy on behalf of the rest of the organisation. For instance when stock falls to order level, or new projects are launched, equipment needs to be replaced, or production programmes establish detailed requirements for parts and material, notification of some kind has to be made to the purchase department so that purchases can be made to meet these requirements.

Exceptionally, purchases may originate within the purchase department. Examples include a department store buyer who is also responsible for sales, a specialist raw material buyer in certain types of manufacturing and purchases made by the purchase department for its own use.

The purchase department may be notified of requirements by means of a purchase requisition, a document normally serving three purposes:

1 to request the purchase of the required goods or services;
2 to authorise the expenditure; and
3 to provide a record for audit and reference.

An example of a general purpose requisition is shown in Figure 18.5. When the department receives this, it is date-stamped and passed to a buyer. The buyer checks that the purchase request has been properly authorised, referring if necessary to an official list of authorised signatories with their cash limits. The description of goods on the requisition is also checked; after referring to records, correction may be needed before communicating with suppliers.

FRED SAUNDERS LIMITED	**PURCHASE REQUISITION**		Number	
Please order the following material:			Date	
Quantity or weight	Stock number	Description of goods		
Deliver to:			Time required	
Order no:	Supplier:		Dept.	Signed
Date:			Job no:	Authorised

Fig. 18.5 Example of a purchase requisition

Special purpose requisitions include travelling requisitions and buy lists. These save time and effort for repeat orders and regular purchases, eliminate copying errors and editing of descriptions, and provide an ongoing record of transactions. They are used for maintenance, repair and operating (MRO) items and they were in common use for stock replenishment and production requirements before computers took over. After ordering the goods and entering transaction details on the form, the travelling requisition travels back to its originator and is filed until next needed.

Buy-lists or blanket requisitions request the purchase of many items on one form. Stock control issues these schedules of requirements when using a periodic review system. Production planning systems such as materials requirements planning (MRP) or period batch control also produce buy-lists. These may not be printed out but retained in the computer system as planned orders until actioned by buyers.

Selecting

The next stage in the buying transaction is selecting. This may be a two-stage process, involving, first, selecting brand or make or specification, and second, selection of supplier. It may also have already been decided previously and may not need to be re-examined.

The simplest buying situation is the straight rebuy, when something has recently been purchased from a satisfactory supplier and the same thing is required again. A repeat order is normal and the possibility of change is not always considered. At reasonable intervals of time, however, it is good practice to contact other suppliers and see what the market has to offer even though the existing supplier seems satisfactory.

A modified rebuy occurs when some change has happened which makes it desirable to reconsider the situation. Perhaps the supplier wants to change the price, or delivery or quality performance has not been satisfactory, or the specification has been changed, or the quantity required has increased, or a new supplier has made an attractive offer.

The most interesting buying situation is when something is bought for the first time. The supplier's expertise may be used in drawing up the specification and many departments may be involved.

A normal part of the selection process is to send a request for quotation to a short list of qualified organisations. This gives full details of specification, quantity, contract conditions and date required, and asks the recipient to offer their price for the goods or work. In compiling this short list, buyers use their own trade knowledge and experience, departmental records, and the experience of colleagues in other departments. Trade directories and buyers' guides may be consulted. In addition to general guides such as British Telecom's *Yellow Pages* and *Business Pages*, there are many specialised directories. In printed form these are usually updated annually. Computer databases provide similar information about product description, suppliers and availability, and have the advantage that details can in principle be updated daily. A technical library which includes catalogues and other information useful in finding sources of supply is often kept. Often these information sources yield a long list of possible suppliers, without information about quality capability, financial status, performance record, and whether the firm is able to take on new work for completion within the period required. The usual procedure is to send to the firms on the long list a preliminary enquiry, known as a request for information (RFI), or prequalification questionnaire. This briefly outlines the requirement, and asks suppliers if they are able and willing to quote for the requirement to give the information needed to prepare a short list.

The request for quotation (RFQ) or enquiry form, which is sent to short-listed firms, is basically the purchaser's letterhead with a standard text preprinted to save typing and often it simply invites the addressee to bid for the goods or work specified. Sometimes, especially when large sums are involved, the RFQ may request prices for a number of alternative options: different total contract quantities, such as six months or twelve months requirements; different call-off options; variations in payment terms, supplier stockholding arrangements, and other aspects of the contract. These can provide the basis for subsequent negotiation.

RFQs may even ask suppliers to support their price quotation by a detailed cost analysis. There is no point in this when independent suppliers are competing for the contract, but some major purchasers buy on such a scale that potential suppliers are limited to one or two in any national economy and there may be other reasons why the purchaser is tied to a single source. If the market does not provide enough competition to ensure that the price is right, a mutually agreed cost basis has to be established.

In selecting suppliers for repeat purchases where several qualified suppliers are available, vendor rating provides a way to organise and present information about supplier track records. Useful as this information is, it must be remembered that past history does not provide a sure guide to future performance as managements change, new products are developed, new customers are found. Buyers need to keep in touch with future developments in their major suppliers, as well as taking account of their past performance.

Ordering

Having selected a supplier and agreed on the details, the next stage is to place an order. An order is an instruction to do something such as supply goods or carry out work. It is not in principle the same thing as a contract, which in this context is a business agreement for the supply of goods or services in return for a price. Contracts are subject to the law: contract law, the Sale of Goods Act and other statutes. They are also subject to any special terms and conditions agreed by the parties to the contract.

In many cases a single document, the purchase order form, incorporates both the order and the contract details. Normal practice is to make it a rule that all purchases, subject to a few specified exceptions, must be made by means of the official order form. This is for practical rather than legal reasons. The purpose of the rule is to establish clearly what the organisation is committed to accept and pay for, and to prevent sharp practice. Regular suppliers are made aware of the rule by printing it on the order form, or by stipulating that advice notes and invoices must quote the order number. Goods-receiving personnel are instructed not to accept goods which are delivered without an official order number.

Figure 18.6 is an example of a purchase order form. This is usually a multi-part form with copies for the supplier, the accounts department, the receiving department, the purchase department, and possibly additional copies for the progressing section and for the requisitioner. Some organisations send two copies to the supplier, the second copy being marked 'Acknowledgement'. The supplier signs and returns this acknowledgement copy to show that the order has been received and accepted at the price and under the terms and conditions stated. Some suppliers are unwilling to do this, and considerable pressure has to be applied to ensure compliance. Purchasing departments need to consider whether the effort required is justifiable in the case of every order. Certainly in the case of major contracts it is important to establish that the two parties are agreed on all major clauses, but in the case of minor orders this may not be so important.

The contract may cover more than one order. The contract may, for instance, cover the supply of aggregated requirements over a considerable period of time, or over a large geographical area as when headquarters staff sign contracts for common requirements at many divisions, plants or branches. Three solutions to the problem of which form to use have been observed:

1 The normal purchase order form is used for the contract. Special forms are used for the orders. These are called call-offs, contract releases, or delivery instructions.
2 A special form is used for the contract agreement, and goods are offered against it using the normal order form.
3 The same purchase order form is used for both orders and contracts. Some form of words is included such as: 'This is an order against contract number . . .' or 'This is a contract and goods should not be delivered until an order is placed'.

Period contracts are usually placed to cover one year's requirement and it is good practice to stagger renewal dates so that each month several contracts are reconsidered and renewed, rather than have all of them coming up for renewal in December, for instance.

Another version of the period contract is used when a manufacturing establishment knows that for the whole of the year it will require a certain component or material to make one of its products, but the quantity required is not exactly known because it depends on sales. A contract is then made for 50 per cent of the estimated annual requirement, and actual requirements as they arise are ordered against this contract. This arrangement is mutually advantageous. The advantage to the supplier is that they are assured of a substantial workload and can plan capacity and commitments accordingly. The advantage to the purchaser is first a lower price for a larger contract, and second better delivery times because of advance booking of capacity.

PURCHASE ORDER

Serial number

name, address,
telephone number, directors and similar information

date

Buyer's delivery address

Supplier's address

References (buyer's reference, supplier's reference, contract number, etc)

Delivery Date	Instructions for packaging and invoicing	Other details

Filing margin

Sizes

A4 210 × 297 mm (8¼ × 11¾ in)
A5 148 × 210 mm (5⅞ × 8¼ in)

acknowledgement of order
(if required)

reference to printed
conditions of purchase (if required)

Fig. 18.6 Purchase order format suggested by BSI

Blanket orders are another kind of period contract. The term literally means an order which covers a number of different items, but it has come to be used for a contract, usually with a local stockholder, for the supply of a large number of maintenance, repair and operating (MRO) items. A great variety of these is required by any large establishment, and individual requirements are usually for retail quantities. By consolidating the requirements into a single blanket agreement and arranging for a single monthly invoice for goods called off against the agreement, considerable savings in paperwork can be made.

Completing the transaction

The final or completion stage of a purchasing transaction occurs when work is completed or goods are delivered and accepted and payment is duly made. Just as the purchasing section does not normally initiate a purchase, so it does not normally carry the main responsibility for the completion stage, although it must be notified of receipts and inspection results and will normally deal with suppliers in connection with discrepancies in quantity or price, rejections and other problems.

The purchasing section also needs to evaluate supplier performance for future use in the case of straight rebuys and modified rebuys, as mentioned earlier. What is required is hard evidence rather than subjective impressions as to whether supplier performance has been satisfactory in respect of price, delivery, service and quality. This should be entered into the supplier record or the purchase record, where these are kept; otherwise it should be filed so as to be accessible the next time a purchase decision needs to be made.

The paperwork associated with the completion stage usually starts with an advice note received by post, which advises that goods have been dispatched (and consequently is sometimes called a dispatch note). This may be routed through the purchasing progress section, so that a note may be made on progress documents that goods are in transit, but must be delivered to the goods-receiving section the same morning. Each morning the goods-receiving section look through their collection of advice notes (and dispatch notes) to see if any are overdue, and immediately take appropriate action.

The document is sent separately by post if the consignment goes by road or rail, or with the goods if delivered by the supplier's own transport. Sometimes an additional copy of the advice note is included in the package marked 'contents note'.

Advice notes convey information about the dispatch of goods to both the parties to the transaction; the supplier bases their invoice on this document. Some companies include the advice note in their invoice set, the whole being prepared together, although the price is excluded from the advice note. Other companies produce both invoice and advice notes at the time they receive the buyer's purchase order, when they produce their own works order to manufacture.

When forming part of an invoice set, the advice note bears the same serial number. If it is separately prepared, it bears a number which is subsequently cross-referenced with the invoice. The form contains the purchase order number, date of dispatch, quantity and description of goods, how packed, number of packages, method of transport and other necessary information. It also enables the buyer to advise the sender and carrier of delay en route. In many cases it also includes instructions as to procedure should goods be received in a damaged condition.

Most organisations centralise goods-receiving in a section of their general stores. In some instances the transport may be directed to the point of use, to a sub-store or special storage bays (particularly for bulk raw materials), or to storage tanks for fuel oil and so on.

No matter where they are offloaded, the goods have to be checked for quantity, description and quality against the specification set out in the purchase order. This may necessitate weighing rail trucks or lorries on a weighbridge; measuring timber lengths and counting pieces; dipping a fuel tank before and after a delivery of fuel, and segregating and checking smaller items in a special section of the store.

The description of the goods and the checked amount received is then compared with the supplier's advice note and the relevant purchase order. Any discrepancies must be noted for purchasing to inform the supplier and carrier, if necessary. In some large companies the goods-receiving section contacts supplier and carrier direct without going through the buyer.

The goods-received record

Deliveries are checked for quantity and quality against the purchase order and the supplier's advice note. Many companies then produce a 'goods-received note' (GRN), though most modern systems are computerised and the information is keyed directly on to the screen at the receiving point. This form is usually prepared in duplicate or triplicate; it is serially numbered and written entries indicate the date, name of supplier, order number, description of goods, quantity received, how delivered, number of containers and the supplier's reference number. Any variations from the advice note, discrepancies or damage must be recorded. The goods checker signs the GR note to certify correct delivery.

Another method is to send a copy of the purchase order to the interested parties showing goods as being received. This obviates much writing and simplifies cross-referencing with the order in other departments.

A further method is to use the supplier's advice note. Then a GR note is only raised when goods are received without an advice note or when there is a multi-order delivery or a delivery involving a part-order.

Rejection of goods

When it is necessary to reject goods the supplier must be immediately informed of the quantity involved and the reason for rejection; at the same time, a request should be made for disposal instructions. Depending upon the type of goods and the reason for their rejection, negotiations between buyer and seller can lead to several methods of disposal. Goods may be returned for full credit, or for rectification at the supplier's works; they may be rectified at the buyer's works either by the supplier or by the buyer. In the latter case, the buyer should ensure that the supplier is prepared to accept a debit for the work done. Other possibilities include acceptance of the item at a reduced rate, having the item scrapped at the buyer's works and crediting the supplier with the scrap value and so on.

Goods rejected by the buyer are the property of the seller; therefore no work must be done on them or arrangements made to dispose of them without the seller's consent.

When goods are rejected, it is advisable to inform the supplier in writing and to request their confirmation of receipt of the advice and, if necessary, that they raise a credit note in the buyer's favour. In some systems, when the supplier has agreed to the goods being returned to them, a debit note follows the dispatch note to the supplier. Both methods have the desired effect of crediting the buyer's account for goods returned. The method used should fit the accounting procedures of the company concerned.

Deliveries in excess of the quantity ordered or advised, or of a superior quality, must also be notified to the supplier, the acceptance of goods being subject to agreement between the two parties.

Notification to carrier

When goods are delivered by public carrier and there is discrepancy or damage, the carrier as well as the supplier must be informed. This enables them to inspect and deal with any subsequent claim for compensation. Both supplier and carrier have to be informed of such discrepancies within the period allowed for this in the contract.

Containers

Many components and materials are delivered in returnable containers, and the charges made for many of these make it necessary to institute a system to control their return.

A simple method of achieving this is to prepare a daily list of returnable containers received, in duplicate. This shows the date received, name of supplier, identification marks or number, type and amount chargeable. One copy is sent to the dispatch department who complete the form showing the date the container was returned and the route. This is then sent to the invoice section via purchasing in order that it may be cross-referenced with the supplier's debit note for the containers and subsequently their credit note. Forms outstanding in both offices indicate the containers which have not been returned.

In some cases, the supplier hires the containers to the buyer at a daily or weekly rate: cable drums, gas cylinders and rail wagons are examples of these. Here, an efficient control system can reduce hire charges.

Invoices and payment

To ensure that goods paid for have actually been received and are authorised purchases, invoices are matched with goods received notes and purchase orders. If all three agree, the invoice is cleared for payment.

These checks are carried out either in the purchase department or in the accounts department. If they are done by the accounts department, copies of purchase orders, any subsequent amendments to them, goods received notes, damaged or shortage notification, etc., need to be sent to that department, which will refer any anomalies to the purchase department. Sampling methods are often used in invoice checking.

Some invoices cannot be checked against goods received documents, for instance pro forma invoices which are payable before goods are delivered, interim invoices, and bills for gas, water, electricity and insurance. Proper procedures for approving such invoices for payment need to be laid down.

Normally a period of credit (typically one month) is allowed for checks to be carried out and paperwork processed. Trade credit improves the purchaser's cash flow position, at the expense of the supplier. The purchaser can unfairly profit by delaying payment beyond the agreed period. This is bad business in the long run, since the supplier will allow for it in future pricing and buyers should honour their obligations. Many suppliers encourage early payment by offering settlement discounts, such as 3.75 per cent seven days, or 2.5 per cent monthly account.

NON-STANDARD PURCHASES

While standard purchase forms and procedures are suitable for most purchases, special systems may be adopted for a minority of transactions. Two types of purchase for which special systems are often used are very large contracts, at one extreme, and small orders, at the other end of the scale.

Purchasing for large projects

Large complex projects such as building offshore oil rigs, fully equipped hospitals and factories ready to go are carried out all over the world. Purchase departments on the client's side help in obtaining and analysing tenders, in comparing suppliers and in contract negotiation. Purchase departments on the contractor's side obtain information from subcontractors and suppliers which is needed in preparing the bid or tender. Once the contract is placed, the contractor needs to place a large number of orders and subcontracts, sometimes with the approval of the client or purchaser.

Often the expert knowledge and experience of contractors is used to convert the preliminary functional specification into a final build specification. Two-stage tendering is sometimes used. The World Bank suggests in *Guidelines for Procurement under World Bank Loans,* that the first stage could be to invite unpriced technical bids. Based on these, a technical specification would be prepared and used for the second stage, in which complete priced bids are invited.

It is admittedly difficult to reconcile the public accountability principle, that all tenderers have equality of information and are bidding for the same specification, with the common-sense purchasing principle that exceptional expertise on the part of a supplier should be used in preparing the specification. To expect a contractor with unique design and construction ability to tell the client the best way to do a job, without payment, and then in the second stage to lose the contract to a low bidder with less design capability, seems unlikely to work out. Such firms sometimes insist on negotiated contracts, or cost-plus contracts.

Negotiated or cost-plus contracts have the advantage that the chosen contractor is fully involved in the development of the specification from the beginning. The disadvantage to the purchaser is the lack of competition once the contractor has been selected.

Whatever procedure is adopted, it is unusual for the contract for a large complex project to result from a single offer which is accepted as made. Several meetings to discuss and negotiate terms and conditions, and aspects of the specification, may be required between purchaser and preferred tenderer (or tenderers). After all tenders have been received and appraised, one or two (or at most three) contenders will still be in the running, and final detailed negotiations are carried out to establish identity of views between the parties.

Delay in finalising contract terms or specification details leads to the use of letters of intent. These simply say 'we intend to place the contract with you' and in English law they are not binding on either party. Consequently they may not have the desired effect of enabling work to start unless the contractor is able to trust the purchaser.

An unconditional letter of acceptance on the other hand sets up a binding contract between the parties. Somewhere between the two is the instruction to proceed, which authorises the contractor to start work on specified parts of the contract and possibly states an upper limit to the expenditure which the contractor can make on the authority of the letter.

Purchasers usually follow up or accompany the letter of acceptance with an official order form, in order to get the contract into normal administrative and accounting procedures. Once the contract has been awarded, the main contractor will usually have to place subcontracts, and order equipment and materials. It is usual for the client to require that their approval be obtained for all major subcontracts. The procedure is shown in Figure 18.7.

Specifications are prepared, often after discussion with vendors, and incorporated in the enquiry documents. Further discussions with suppliers take place after the quotations are received (usually a month after the requests for quotation are issued, although it may be necessary to allow more time for very large subcontracts), and the contractor then prepares a bid analysis, which is discussed with the client. After appraisal and approval, orders are placed.

Bid analysis is further illustrated in Figure 18.8 which shows a typical form used for the purpose. It provides columns to list the various bids or quotations, compare them with the budget or control estimate, and make adjustments for freight and other extras. Space is also provided for a questionnaire on the selected vendor, to ensure that all the important aspects of supplier selection are considered.

Small orders

Most purchase departments have to process a large number of small orders. Administrative costs and paperwork can be disproportionate to the value of the transaction unless some simplified method is used for small orders.

Blanket orders, are a good example of a simpler method for small orders. Systems contracting is an American term which seems to denote a version of

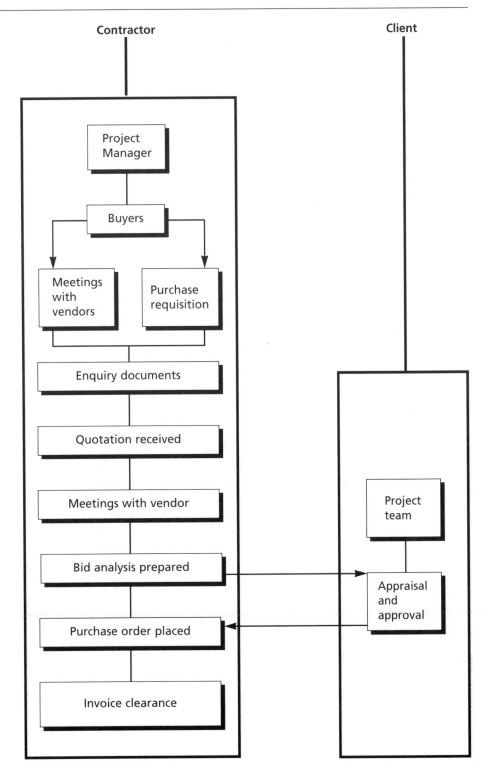

Fig. 18.7 Subcontracting procedure on a large contract
(*Source:* adapted from Stallworthy and Kharbanda, 1983)

Bid analysis for | Client | Job no | Requisition no

Vendors asked	(1)	(2)	(3)	(4)	(5)	(6)	Budget

Exchange rate used

Date

Escalation
Duties
Taxes
} Percentages included in above price calculations

Total percentage supplied to quoted prices

Freight, packing, handling etc amount

Total price delivered to be

Estimated entries

Above normal procurement cost

Total comparative cost for selection

Quoted delivery time | Schedule

Estimated delivery on site (including shipping time & shippage)

Questionnaire on selected vendor

- Is past record satisfactory?
- If no past record has shop been surveyed or investigated?
- Are shop facilities adequate?
- Is experience adequate?
- Is test equipment adequate?
- Are subcontractors or subvendors involved?
- If so is abnormal expediting/inspection effort required?
- Are extra exped/inspection costs expected due to shop location performance or subcontracting?
- Do prices represent a good deal under present market conditions?

All costs are tabulated in the currency indicated in the job procedure, namely

Selected vendor

Reasons

	Signature	Date
Compiled by		
Procurement recommendation		
Technical review & recommendation		
Project approval		
Construction approval		
Management approval		
Client approval		

Fig. 18.8 Bid analysis form
(*Source*: adapted from Stallworthy and Kharbanda, 1983)

the blanket order. Contracts are placed centrally; orders are placed locally using a simple release form like a stores requisition; suppliers deliver from guaranteed stocks direct to user locations, almost eliminating purchaser-held stocks; a simple bulk invoice in tally sheet format is submitted monthly. Stockless purchasing is the aim, with big reductions in paperwork and administrative delays.

Blank-cheque-with-order systems were invented by Kaiser Aluminum, originally to simplify invoice processing and payment of bills. What happens is that the company's order form includes a blank cheque which the supplier is required to complete. On receipt of the order they make up the requirement and arrange for it to be dispatched, at the same time completing the cheque portion with the relevant net invoice total and depositing it in their bank. Each cheque is limited to a maximum (say $1500). The supplier is expected to deliver the ordered amount at the agreed time, together with an advice document which the buyer uses for audit purposes in addition to its more usual use. The supplier is not allowed to deliver on more than one occasion against any order. If they cannot deliver in full they can only receive payment for that which is delivered and the order is considered complete by the buying company.

Companies using this system claim considerable administrative savings in the accounts payable area. Most indicate that they have considerably reduced the part-order problem. All have negotiated discounts in return for the method of payment and many state that suppliers give their orders priority over other customers who do not operate such schemes.

Another way to reduce administrative costs involves the supplier depositing goods in the buyer's stores, which the latter pays for on an 'as used' basis. Generally speaking, the supplier arranges for periodic visits to be made to the store area to check the number of items in the various categories involved which have been used. They then replenish the stock to the agreed level and invoice, usually on a monthly basis, for those used. A single contract covers the agreed period. This indicates the price of each item against a code and description. The monthly invoices are paid against this contract with the buyer auditing the levels and usages on a periodic basis. Items stocked are the property of the supplier until used.

Apart from a reduction in paperwork, other advantages include: reduction in 'stock-outs'; no obsolescence and reduced stockholding costs for the buyer. The supplier is said to benefit in having a 'captive' market; regular liaison with the users in the buying company; and reduced paperwork.

SUMMARY POINTS

- In order to achieve world class concepts, it is necessary to implement a fully integrated database that links all aspects with up to date 'real time' information.
- The system adopted must suit the organisational requirements. There must be sufficient training given to those using the system which is often the weak link. Once up and running, the system will free up the buyer to pursue more effective activities.

- The chapter outlines how different types of requisitions are dealt with. Selection of brand and supplier depends on whether it is a 'first time' buy, modified rebuy, or a straight repeat. There are many means of sourcing goods and services. If a new company is to be approached it may be requested to complete a pre-qualification form.
- Purchase orders are copied to various functions. An acknowledgement copy may be forwarded to the supplier to be returned, signifying acceptance of terms and conditions.
- Any defect in the delivery and the purchaser informs the supplier and carrier (in case of a claim on insurance). Goods can be returned for full credit or rectification. They may be accepted but at a reduced cost. If they are rejected, they remain the property of the supplier.
- Larger projects are complex to manage and often use a two stage tendering process where the technical specification is firstly prepared on unpriced technical bids. Based on this, priced bids are invited. Low value systems need to be simplified so that the cost of processing is less than the value of the order. Blanket orders, blank cheque with order and consignment stock agreements all reduce the purchasing department's involvement and pass the responsibility on to the user.

REFERENCES AND FURTHER READING

Anon (1990), *Practice of Purchasing: A Supervisory Study Guide*, Chartered Institute of Purchasing and Supply.

Armstrong V and Jackson D (1992), *EDI for the Purchasing and Supply Manager*, Chartered Institute of Purchasing and Supply, Stamford.

Baily P (1991), *Purchasing Systems and Records*, 3rd edn, Gower, Aldershot.

Brazier I (1993), 'The office of the 90s', *Purchasing and Supply Management*, May.

Emmelhainz M A (1986), 'Electronic data interchange in purchasing', *Guide to Purchasing*, 1 (17), National Association of Purchasing Management (USA).

Heinritz S, Farrell P, Giunipero L and Kolchin M (1993), *Purchasing, Principles and Applications*, 8th edn, Prentice Hall, New Jersey.

Kennedy P D (1994), 'The purchaser and the pendulum', *Purchasing and Supply Management*, January.

Marshall I (1993), 'Keeping Jimmy operating', *Purchasing and Supply Management*, March.

Monks J G (1988), *Operations Management*, McGraw-Hill.

Scheuing E E (1989), *Purchasing Management*, Prentice Hall.

Stallworthy E A and Kharbanda O P (1983), *Total Project Management*, Gower, Aldershot.

CHAPTER 19

Controlling performance, efficiency and effectiveness

In purchasing the calculation of the number of requisitions dealt with by a buyer in any one day may tell us something about his or her efficiency at passing paper. The number of items received on time and the number of items which fail to meet the specification will, also, be of benefit in that regard. However, his or her effectiveness may be more concerned with establishing vendors who have the potential to supply for many years to come – competitively. Also with, for example, reducing the number of these suppliers so that co-makership and just-in-time approaches may be managed to the best effect. These ideas are developed in this chapter.

OBJECTIVES OF THIS CHAPTER

- To examine efficiency in purchasing in relation to its stage of evolution
- To identify Van Wheel's 5 stages of purchasing development
- To consider the benefits of measuring performance
- To analyse the basic questions in 'best practice' benchmarking
- To evaluate reporting systems and the information that should be included
- To consider the role of budgets.

In much of the literature relating to purchasing, the measures of performance which are discussed primarily relate to operational activities. Yet effective purchasing must involve activities, objectives and measurement relating to both tactical and strategic issues. As Herb Simon argued, we should ask 'Are we doing the right things?' before we ask 'Are we doing them right?'

Nevertheless, we still need to be concerned with the measurement of operational action. Indeed, in that respect measurement can be one of the major influences for improvement. It is our intention in this chapter to discuss approaches to performance control and measurement from the point of view upon which this book is based. That is that purchasing is a management function which has strategic, tactical and operational aspects. The effectiveness of purchasing professionals in meeting the criteria involved will, in part, be a function of the effectiveness of the approaches used to measure their performance in each of these fields of activity.

A second point needs to be made at the outset. Just as organisations differ so does the role played by the purchasing professional, which means that there is not one single generally applicable approach which may be used to measure purchasing performance. It follows that the peculiarities of each organisation need to be studied carefully so as to ensure that the measurement approaches which are used are appropriate.

Finally it is important to recognise that while most effective measurement systems are quantitative, there are qualitative factors which are important. In addition there are those managers who eschew formal measurement systems and rely upon intuition. While we cannot recommend such an approach for most managers, there are successful people whose brains seem to be attuned to picking up masses of data from a variety or sources and interpreting it into management action.

There is little doubt that intuitive perceptions are important in all systems involving people, and there may be no substitute for intuition. Nevertheless, few people are willing or have the necessary skills to operate exclusively on this basis. Most need to supplement whatever skills of this kind they have with systematic collection and analysis of data, even though this entails staff time and costs.

One problem in measuring purchasing performance is that it is difficult to isolate responsibility: quality failure may be due to poor tooling provided by the buying company as much as to poor source selection; delivery failure may result from production control changing schedules frequently, or from late requisitioning; poor supplier performance might stem from the buying company being slow payers. The point is that many functions are involved in one way or another with the purchasing process. They may influence supplier performance in a variety of ways by their actions, yet the complex interrelationships make it difficult to segregate the effect of that influence. This is one of the arguments for management by objectives where corporate objectives are supported by a network of interconnected sub-objectives. It is also a basic thrust behind the growing interest in what might be termed 'collective' approaches – materials management, logistics management, physical distribution management, and materials administration. These all aim to group authority and responsibilities in ways which allow control and measurement. A department which indents for materials, stores them, purchases those materials and schedules supplies to production can be held responsible for total material performance. Such approaches may be conceptually and administratively attractive, but it is still desirable for management to gauge how well the function is performing.

MEASURING PURCHASING PERFORMANCE

One can examine efficiency in purchasing in relation to its stage of evolution. At very early stages of development, purchasing invariably has a low status and is reactive in operation. Its effectiveness or otherwise is seen in terms of its ability to handle transactions. While it is important that transactions are handled efficiently, achieving strategic purchasing objectives can often assist in simplifying or reducing them.

Measurement that centres on the generation of transactional activities in itself often perpetuates the view that purchasing is essentially a reactive clerical function. One might find, for example, that purchasing in an organisation is subordinate to the finance director. This person's view of purchasing may be that the function should:

- encourage competition by placing numerous enquiries;
- change suppliers regularly;
- pay the lowest price; and
- delay paying suppliers for as long as possible.

These objectives could in turn lead to the following results:

- Too many suppliers offering materials at the lowest price, with no incentive to look at longer-term aspects that could lead to strategic savings.
- An enormous amount of expediting time could be spent by the buyer because suppliers are not paid on time.
- Too many short-duration orders again increasing administrative effort rather than longer-term arrangements that could perhaps cover a number of years.
- Buyers wastefully involved in routine ordering rather than the computer scheduling supplies when required.

More advanced purchasing organisations such as those in Ford, IBM, Rover, Nissan or Marks & Spencer would argue that the buyers' time is much better spent on such tasks as negotiation, supplier development, cost reduction, and internal interface development than on routine administrative activity.

Measurement criteria

Figure 19.1 shows the likely measurement criteria as the purchasing and supply function develops. The figure illustrates how, as the focus of the purchasing activity changes, so the methods used to evaluate performance also change. Initially measurement is clerically orientated and superficial; as the function develops, measurement criteria become more tactically and strategically based, and the range of measurement criteria increases.

This framework of criteria is based on work undertaken by Van Wheel (1985) and allows for five stages of development:

1 Where purchasing is essentially reactive and fragmented, performance criteria are few or even non-existent. The main objective for the activity is to convert requisitions into orders and get the supplies in.

2 As the function develops, it is likely to be given the responsibility for handling the paperwork involved in the purchasing system. At this point, in judging the function's contribution, clerical efficiency is probably the main criterion.

3 In the third stage of development, the role is being viewed more in respect of its commercial usefulness to the organisation. At this stage a chief buyer or a purchasing manager might be appointed. While clerical and systems

Position of purchasing	Status	Purchasing performance measurement	Focus on
Fragmented purchasing carried out mainly by functional areas; small clerical purchasing function	Low	Very few; staying within agreed budgets	Getting the goods in
Purchasing function established; mainly clerical; functional area still involved in buying	Low but improving; reporting via other function to top management	Mainly measuring clerical efficiency of the function, i.e. orders and requisitions outstanding	Clerical efficiency
Purchasing function commercial	Recognised function with purchasing manager reporting to functional head, e.g. Finance Director; all purchasing carried out by purchasing dept	Clerical buying efficiency; i.e. savings, cost reduction, negotiating efficiency	Clerical buying efficiency
Purchasing function commercial, but elements of strategic involvement	Reporting directly to MD; purchasing manager	As above, plus supplier development and intra-organisational interface development	As above, plus beginning to measure overall effectiveness on a longer-term basis
Purchasing is a strategic business function	Reporting to MD/Board; purchasing director heads function	As above, but concerned with strategic development JIT, etc.; measurement of 'total costs of supply'	Strategic effectiveness

Fig. 19.1 Measurement criteria for the purchasing and supply function

efficiency are being measured, the function would also be expected to begin to show savings against budgets or costs. At this stage savings or cost reductions are likely to be measured.

4 At the next important stage of development, purchasing is seen as being of more strategic importance. At this point, concern and hence measurement criteria are established to assess key supplier developments through vendor-rating schemes. As the profile of purchasing becomes higher, its interface with other functions becomes more significant and this may also be

measured. At this stage the purchasing manager is reporting to the chief executive of the organisation. Almost certainly concern will be shown for total acquisition costs and there will be less emphasis on lowest price.

5 Finally, at the fifth stage purchasing is recognised as being of strategic importance, with the head of the function probably at director level. Here measurement is centred around strategic effectiveness. Purchasing's ability to make world class concepts work would be measured, and thus there would be considerable interest in, for example, the following matters:

(a) moves towards co-makership and strategic supplier alliances;
(b) education of the supply base;
(c) improving the strategic profile of suppliers;
(d) improvements in the supply chain; and
(e) each supplier's adoption of EDI, JIT, TQM and zero defects philosophies.

Measurement criteria are dynamic and must develop as the organisation develops. Clerical efficiency gives way to cost effectiveness and eventually strategic effectiveness. Figure 19.2 illustrates how measurement criteria change as the function develops.

As one might imagine, the move from one level of development into another is probably accompanied by a range of other changes. Often the transition is far from smooth.

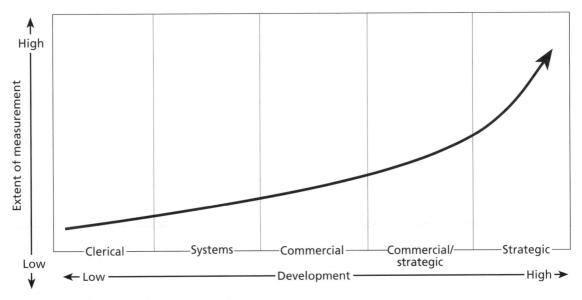

Fig. 19.2 Purchasing performance development

Why measure performance?

Five main benefits are commonly considered to result from performance measurement:

1 Almost 75 per cent of the respondents to a survey believed that inability to measure purchasing performance had hindered management recognition of the function. If a general manager has no means of measuring the effect of a function on his or her overall performance, he or she is unlikely to regard it as of great importance. If he or she has only crude ways to measure performance, these are what will be used, in the absence of more sophisticated means. Crude performance measures of purchasing performance tend to be negative, indicators of failure rather than success (e.g. when production supplies fail to arrive or fail to pass inspection).

2 Improved performance ought to be encouraged by reports of actual performance measured against some kind of standard. An Olympic sprinter who knows that the Olympic record for the 100 metres is x seconds has something to aim for in training. In the Olympics he or she will have two aims, one, to beat the record and, two, to win the race. If there were no records kept, no times taken and each athlete ran on his or her own, it is doubtful whether the speeds common today would ever have been achieved.

3 A third benefit is the establishment of ground rules against which people can be measured. Thinking through a task in this way should enable the manager to develop profiles for recruitment, training, pay and promotion. Many formal staff-reporting schemes are built around this basic concept, that there must be something to measure and some means of measuring.

4 Such data should be invaluable in the organisation of the function and relationships with the wider organisation. In the event of a reorganisation, the data on the various jobs involved will be available.

5 Finally, if staff believe that their efforts will be recognised, they are likely to be better motivated with consequent benefits to morale.

Measurement areas

What is measured in companies where some form of evaluation is practised? Common areas for the measurement of purchasing information are:

- operational purchasing;
- co-ordination with other functions;
- purchasing organisation and system;
- budget performance;
- creative performance;
- policy development; and
- planning and forecasting.

Typical measures which are used in relation to the first of the areas listed above are included in Figure 19.3

Co-ordination with other functions is difficult to measure, important as it is in the overall performance of the purchasing function. Measures which have been used include: the number of complaints from other department managers regarding purchase performance; the number of complaints to other managers by the head of purchasing; and the number of panic purchases. All these are, to say the least, difficult to come to terms with as meaningful measures. One

Area	Measure
Quality	Percentage of rejects in goods received Percentage of parts rejected in production Percentage of raw materials rejected in production
Quantity	Percentage of stock which has not moved over a specified period Number of production stockouts Number of small-value orders Number of emergency orders Comparison of stock with target stock
Timing	Supplier's actual delivery performance against promised Time taken to process requisitions Time taken up with remedial action
Price	Prices paid against standard Prices paid for key items compared with market indexes Prices paid against budget Price at the time of use against price at the time of purchase
Operational costs	Cost of processing an order Progressing costs as a percentage of total Operational costs (including telephones, telex, etc.)

Fig. 19.3 Some commonly used measures of operational purchasing performance

firm uses (i) periodic attitude survey across departments, and (ii) a sampling method relating to key operational meetings and the content of the minutes.

The system and procedures involved in purchasing might reveal lack of control within the department or between departments; they could highlight either staff or system inefficiency and may be indicative of poor management as well as poor liaison.

The aptness of the organisation to its environment and the suitability of the staff who work within it are also important.

Creative performance is difficult to appraise. However, questions which might be asked include: What has been achieved through value analysis? What has been developed in supplier price/cost analysis? Has the department been successful in locating alternative economic sources, particularly where there was previously a monopoly supplier? Has the department, in conjunction with its suppliers, contributed to productivity and efficiency on the company's production line? What additional services are available to user departments, as a result of purchasing initiative, which will contribute to their efficiency?

Policy development is another important area which does not lend itself to quantitative measurement; surprisingly few organisations have thought through their policies. Examples of purchasing policy areas which might repay study are:

- make or buy;
- the degree of centralisation;
- reciprocity;
- intercompany trading (in groups);
- single or multiple sourcing;
- working with suppliers towards JIT; and
- co-makership arrangements.

Criteria which might be used in judging the quality of the department's efforts include: Is there a clear statement of policy? Is that policy understood and applied by the relevant personnel? Have policies been updated as conditions change?

Planning and forecasting is an increasingly important aspect of purchasing work. The basic question is: Is the function involved with long-term and short-term planning within the company at all? If it is, to what extent, what is the quality of the input, and what is the time horizon? How good are the forecasts which underpin the planning input? Perfection in forecasting is not to be expected, but a reasonable improvement both in forecast accuracy and in the quality of the accompanying comment should be achieved over the years. Forecasts may be concerned with: the industrial relations environment; supply and demand; prices; technological development; legal and social changes which may affect supply markets.

To conclude this section, we include a short summary of the findings of an extensive US survey (Monczka, Carter and Hoagland, 1979). This survey examined the methods used to measure purchasing performance in leading US organisations. It would be interesting for the reader to compare these findings with those of Stevens (1978), who worked with a UK population.

The category rated most highly by the survey population was *price effectiveness*. It appeared that actual-to-plan price effectiveness measures were seen to be most effective:

1 When purchasing and non-purchasing (e.g. industrial engineering, cost accounting) personnel participated in developing the plan (or performance measures).
2 When the plan was established about three months prior to implementation.
3 When revision was allowed based on significant changes in the purchasing environment up to one month before the starting date.
4 When plans were based on *forecast* prices in addition to price change requests from suppliers.

Furthermore, such evaluation was considered more effective when the aggregate material budget was broken down into (i) purchase family groups, (ii) purchased line items, and (iii) product selling categories.

Other measures used by respondents included:

- *Cost savings* Both cost reduction and cost avoidance, with the caveat that they were best rated when they were precisely defined.
- *Workload* Measures here included workload in, workload current, and workload completed.

- *Administration and control* The administrative budget was rated most highly in this group.
- *Efficiency* These included various lead-time and labour-efficiency measures. However, they were rated low because the public sector in which they were most widely used thought little of them.
- *Material flow control* Time phased material flow reports showing requirements and promised shipments over an extended period. Users had greater confidence about the accuracy and validity of this.

Other measurement factors

Supplier performance/ characteristics

Supplier quality and delivery performance measures were used. Measures included business dollar volumes and their supplier characteristics. The factors which appear to improve the effectiveness of supplier quality and delivery measurement systems include the ability to classify performance by:

- supplier;
- purchased item; and
- buyer;

all encompassed within a timely reporting system. In addition, precise definitions were necessary to define 'lateness', 'poor quality' and 'significance of the problem'.

Procurement planning and research

These measures were considered effective in directing purchasing effort towards planning.

Competition

Measures used to stimulate competition were found on a selective basis. Those organisations which used them rated these measures highly.

Inventory

The measures most commonly used here were: value of inventory, inventory turnover rates, consigned inventory value and projected inventory value levels.

BENCHMARKING IN PURCHASING AND SUPPLY

As we have seen, there are numerous approaches to the assessment of both the performance of the purchasing and supply function of an organisation, and the performance of the concern's suppliers. Some have argued that the evaluation of supplier or vendor performance is also an appraisal of purchasing performance, in that it is appropriate that the reputation of purchasing should be dependent upon the quality and suitability of the suppliers recruited.

Various monitoring and measurement approaches are employed in the activity of purchasing. It is sometimes found useful to calculate key ratios, and to watch for changes in the ratios. Examples include: purchase expenditure;

sales, number of orders placed; expenditure, salary costs; number of transactions, and so on. It is widely argued that if you cannot measure a variable and you cannot control it, then the data which are collected on purchasing activity are usually valuable as instruments of control as well as performance indicators.

Benchmarking is more than another name for the kinds of monitoring, assessment and measurement so far mentioned. The idea behind benchmarking is not simply to seek statistics or other evidence as an indication as to whether a new or existing supplier, or the purchasing function itself, is meeting specifications or requirements. The idea is to discover 'best practice' wherever it might be found, and to attempt to identify and isolate the variables that accompany or are part of this best practice. The thinking is that once this has been done, the variables can be transported as leading indicators (benchmarks) back to the researching organisation, with a view to focusing attention on how the performance might be matched (or bettered). Note that benchmarking is not concerned with copying the methods and systems of other organisations; the attention is given mainly to the factors which are identifiable as demonstrating that an organisation is successful. The term 'best practice benchmarking' occasionally confuses; it is the benchmark which is seen as most readily transferable, and hence most valuable, not the practice.

Given then that benchmarking is not simply attempting to replicate other successful organisations, it should also be clear that it is nothing to do with industrial espionage. The primary concern is with measurement and assessment, not for its own sake, but to keep in touch with current best-practice achievements, with a view to matching or exceeding that performance in your own organisation.

There are five basic steps in benchmarking, as follows:

1 *What are we going to benchmark?* Almost anything that can be measured in purchasing might be benchmarked. Outstanding deliveries, rejection rates, production interruptions or price-paid indices are some examples.

2 *Who are we going to benchmark against?* We first need to identify best practice. An obvious way to do this is to seek advice from our suppliers as to whom they regard as good trading partners. We might also look at organisations which are successful by the accepted measures of market share or profitability, and consider their purchasing operations. Industry observers or professional bodies might give us the right kinds of leads.

3 *How will we get the information?* Much useful information is in the public domain. Much is published in the management journals and trade press, and many successful managers and organisations are very happy to share information. Your personal contacts can help, and of course if a competitor is interested in benchmarking, and the leading ones are likely to be, there is mutual benefit in exchanging information.

4 *How will we analyse the information?* Benchmarking is not concerned with information for the sake of information. Collect only the data you need, and attempt, as far as is possible, to compare like with like. Statistics, ratios and other 'hard' information is usually more valuable than opinion or anecdote.

5 *How will we use the information?* Basically, if you discover that somebody is doing better than you are in a particular area of activity, set out to catch or overtake them. Set new standards for your own performance, and devise an appropriate methodology for meeting those standards. This of course means that adequate resources need to be deployed, which in turn requires that top management is enthusiastic about benchmarking. We cannot, unfortunately, simply adopt benchmarking as another valuable purchasing management technique. It is unlikely to achieve its potential unless undertaken as a matter of organisational policy.

OTHER INDICATORS OF PERFORMANCE

Since, as we have argued elsewhere in this text, we believe that purchasing is a primary business function, one general measure might be involvement in the business, and the quality of that involvement will be a key factor in measuring effectiveness. For example, is the function involved in (new) product development from the conceptual stage through to production? What is the extent of the function's market knowledge? In a strategic sense this might involve keeping abreast of developments in markets other than those which are being used at present, for example, in another part of the world. Yet another measure which is being used increasingly these days is competitive benchmarking. The idea here is that the company concerned provides data to a neutral third party as do, say, twenty other companies. The neutral organisation then provides a set of league tables which rank performances without listing the names of the companies concerned. This approach has been widely used in the electronics industry.

Product knowledge is yet another measure of involvement in the business, and this includes awareness of competing products and the components or materials from which they are made. Stemming from consideration of competing products is the need for purchasing to be fully involved in the strategies which are developed to ensure business survival. For example, where life cycles are shortening it is vital that the company which is competing in those markets increases the pace of innovation. Few organisations can do that in isolation, the majority need to involve, motivate and manage key suppliers to work with them (e.g. co-makership). A key aspect of measuring purchasing performance is to consider such issues and the same might be said of productivity improvement and quality programmes.

Then in an age when EDI is fundamental, measures regarding the development and implementation of information systems may well be important. For example, one UK retailer targeted its purchasing staff to have their top twenty suppliers EDI-connected within twenty months.

Finally, it is worth registering the point that one measure of the effectiveness of a purchasing function can be its own measurement systems. For example, does it measure the performance of key suppliers? Is this information used for control and management purposes? Does the data obtained from this process influence source decision making?

REPORTING TO MANAGEMENT

Whatever system is used in the evaluation of procurement effort, some kind of report indicating the scope of activity of the department, its objectives and its performance in meeting the requirements of the organisation needs to be produced. It will include by exception reports on current and projected market conditions and other pertinent information for top management, for example: data on new products; new materials and processes; information on the development of supply sources; and market intelligence on key raw materials, together with pertinent recommendations for related company policy and strategy. More than one chief executive has told the authors that they regarded such procurement reports as key indicators of the level of performance of the function.

It is not only the quality of the information which is important, but also the manner in which it is presented: only a report which is professionally presented is likely to be given attention by busy top management. What to include in the report? How often should such reports be made? and How should it be presented? are questions which can only be answered in specific cases. However, a useful rule of thumb is 'report when necessary'. Some managers will be required by their company to present a report at given intervals but, even so, pertinent reporting at other times may be called for. Reports should be presented when relevant; for example, where market conditions are unsettled, or the material content of a product is particularly high, weekly market reports may be required, plus quarterly and/or annual reports which carry details of important activities of the department during that period.

All reports should be concise, generally including an executive summary of the data as the first page; back-up data can be presented in graph, chart or diagram form. Statistics in the body of the text should be limited to summary information but, if necessary, these may be backed by fuller statistics included as an appendix. When a conclusion or recommendation is called for, it is usually included at the end, although some reports begin with this. It is useful to have a frontispiece indicating the title of the report and the key contents by page.

In all reporting, useful advice is 'If in doubt – leave out'. Report as a member of a management team. Ask yourself: What is my objective in presenting this information? What does the recipient want in the way of information? When does he or she want it? Just because he or she wanted it last year/month/ week, it does not necessarily mean that he or she still does.

In undertaking an assignment, one of the tasks of a consultant is to ascertain how effective is the purchasing function. In effect he or she will be making a judgement about the performance of the function having regard to a variety of factors. Each consultancy project will differ depending upon, for example, the type of organisation being reviewed, the market it serves and the markets from which the organisation buys. However, there are basic areas which would be included in most instances. Some of these are listed below so that the reader might undertake a survey of his or her own organisation for, in itself, this process will be a useful measure of performance. It should be noted that the list which follows should be augmented as necessary by ideas discussed earlier in this chapter.

Organisation

To whom does the most senior purchasing person report? Are there effective links with key decision makers in the field of product development? At what level of seniority is the top purchasing person? (Generally speaking, we have found that the more layers above him or her in the organisation the less effective he or she is.) What view do members of the most senior management team have of purchasing's importance.

Information

Does purchasing have access to key data early enough? Does purchasing contribute key data on a proactive basis? Does purchasing have up-to-date key data available to it on an as-needed basis (e.g. point-of-sale data in retailing; immediate inventory position in manufacturing)? Has purchasing promoted the use of EDI with its key suppliers? Are purchasing systems up-to-date? Is it regarded as the source of key data on supply matters?

Strategic management

Is purchasing fully involved in the organisation's strategic planning process? Does a strategic plan for purchasing exist? Is that plan reflected in the overall business plan? Were those business plans (where they exist) influenced by purchasing input? What benefits ensued? What strategic actions are currently being undertaken by purchasing? What new supply options are being developed? What market monitoring is undertaken? What key threats have been identified by purchasing? What key opportunities have they identified?

Suppliers

What supplier relationship policies are in being? What programmes are in place to improve supplier performance? What supplier visit programme is in place? Which functions accompany purchasing in these visits? Are longer term considerations taken into account in measuring suppliers/potential suppliers? Are co-makership programmes in place?

Staffing

How do purchasing staff compare in quality terms with other key functions? (Sometimes company grading systems can be helpful in this regard.) Is the function adequately staffed in numerical terms? What staff development programmes are in place? Are purchasing staff *au fait* with existing (and planned) information technology? Is the level of supply market knowledge good enough? Are they creative? How is their negotiation effectiveness measured? How sound are their interdepartmental relationships?

BUDGETS

Budgets are one of the traditional controls of business and are used in organisations of all types. The basic concept of the budget, as Mr Micawber pointed out, is to balance expenditure with income. The budget should help ensure that expenditure is not exceeding income on an *ongoing basis*; it is not a once-a-year exercise.

A budget is derived from the plans which have been formulated and should allow for subsequent comparison, evaluation and control of the efforts made to meet the objectives set out in the plan. In the company setting, each departmental head usually prepares a budget. The purchase budget is developed in conjunction, for example, with the sales, production and labour budgets. All these sub-budgets are prepared in relation to the relevant financial projections and overall company estimates with regard to, for example, return on investment (ROI), turnover and growth. Whether this is done formally in a large concern or informally on the back of an envelope by the owner of a small business, it is an attempt to co-ordinate and control the major parts of the business. In each case, these parts are expressed in monetary terms and by this means an overall budget may be constructed which is made up of interlocking individual budgets. Figure 19.4 represents a typical budgetary system.

The budgetary control system will depend upon the requirements and resources of the particular organisation, but it usually starts with an estimate of

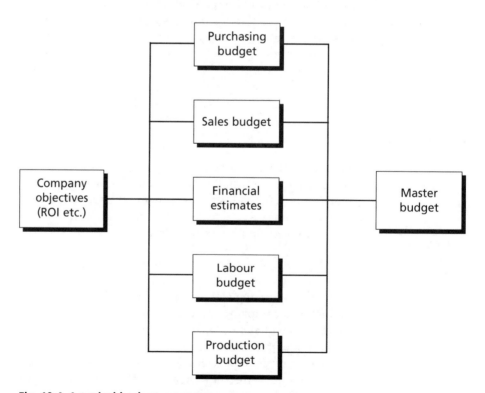

Fig. 19.4 A typical budgetary system

income for the period. Once this has been done, and objectives in, for example, return on investment (ROI) terms have been stated, top management will require their senior managers to submit their plans for achieving the desired results. Usually these managers will have contributed the data upon which the estimates were based. The process is iterative: it results in due course in a master budget made up of elements which support each other and the whole.

Sometimes budget planning is undertaken in conjunction with the corporate planning timetable. Thus it is usual for an annual budget to be prepared which, in turn, is divided into period budgets within the twelve months in question. Some organisations do this on a calendar-month basis whereas others use thirteen periods each of four weeks; certain companies operate on a weekly basis and have fifty-two budget periods during the year.

It is sometimes thought that the sales budget must be the starting point, in that the amount of material purchased and the machinery and labour utilised will depend upon the volume of goods sold. Although this is true in the majority of cases, it is not necessarily so; for example, the owner of a small business may not be in a position financially to meet his or her estimated demand. Consequently, at least in the short term, he or she may be obliged to budget against a financial constraint. When labour is in short supply this may be a constraint, and in times of materials shortage, the amount available will govern the volume of goods produced and sold.

Where the sales budget is the starting point, the marketing department will estimate the sales which can be achieved during the relevant period. This may be broken down by product or product groups and include an addendum indicating market potential. This latter information may be used in longer-term budgeting, as a basis for, for example, expansion plans and changes in the product range or mix. In certain circumstances, it could also indicate the desirability of withdrawing from certain markets or rationalising and/or contracting the product range.

Following the sales budget, production will review plant and manufacturing resources in the light of this budget. The production budget will estimate raw material, component costs, wages and overheads in relation to the desired production level. Accurate information from procurement in formulating both these budgets is important.

A budget system, if it is to be used for control, should include objective estimates. Because of the many variables in business, sales forecasts can rarely be completely accurate and inaccuracy reacts upon production and procurement. Because of this, some companies have introduced alternatives into their budgets to provide planned flexibility. This necessitates managers making objective estimates of probabilities and stating the assumptions upon which those estimates are based. There can be little effective control if, for example, the sales manager deliberately understates sales or the purchasing manager overstates prices, presumably believing that they will receive recognition when actual performance is compared with budget and they have been able to beat their estimates.

A budget can be a performance measure, although its major purpose is to control. However, clearly there can be little real control if each contributor to the budget pads his or her estimate; for example, if the procurement manager puts forward an inflated estimate of the prices he or she expects to pay, this will be built into both production and sales budgets and will affect the prices which marketing set for the coming period and, as a key variable in the marketing mix, could have an adverse effect on market share. If marketing underestimates sales volume, planned production schedules could be disrupted and procurement opportunities (e.g. bigger volumes) could be lost. Despite the difficulties of forecasting, all concerned in budgeting should strive for accuracy. It is poor management to allow padding of budget estimates: padded standards do not allow the measurement of performance or motivate improvement in performance; they also fail to control.

The purchase budget

The purchase budget is based upon the sales and production budgets. In theory, the supplies function extrapolates materials requirements from the production budget, projects prices and orders materials, phasing deliveries in accordance with production schedules. However, actual sales may differ from estimates, not only in total but by product or product range, and this could disrupt material call-off. The longer the budget period the more difficult this becomes. It will be seen that controlled flexibility is necessary in successful budgeting.

For central control, the purchase budget should be presented in a manner which allows fast consideration of the effects of change. It is for this reason that some companies present their materials budgets as unit prices x volume. Changes in either variable may then be accommodated quickly, particularly where the system is tied to a computer. Timing of purchases is vital in respect of cash management, which needs to control the amount of cash required during each period. Deviations from budget, to take advantage of an unusual supply opportunity, should be discussed with financial management, as should changes which reduce expected expenditure (e.g. arrangements for consignment stocking which reduce inventory holding). It is important that the 'budget to performance' comparison is made promptly to allow management to act quickly. Computers can present comparative data on an ongoing basis with benefits in control terms.

When the preliminary programme of purchases is constructed, the procurement manager has to take into consideration:

- current material/component stocks;
- outstanding orders for relevant production materials;
- agreed stock levels and current lead times;
- the production schedule for the period in question;
- price trends of key materials and components in the long term; and
- unit prices in the short term.

The task of estimating prices and price trends requires the consideration of many things including:

- political or economic factors, world or domestic, which may affect prices;
- labour relations and availability of labour to major suppliers;
- comparative currency changes and levels of inflation in pertinent countries;
- possible changes in import duties, transit and insurance charges, dock charges, etc., as they affect goods from overseas;
- indirect effects on component prices due to fluctuations in prices of raw materials to suppliers;
- the position of long-term contracts as regards fixed prices or escalation clauses;
- the supply position of materials and components in relation to overall demand; and
- lead times and the potential effects of having to purchase from more expensive alternative sources in the event of a failure.

The supplies manager may not be able to forecast exact requirements at the beginning of the budget period nor may his or her price forecasts be absolutely accurate. However, a continuing survey of the supply markets in which he or she deals can prove helpful; and performance improves through practice. This can contribute to efficient purchasing and lower costs.

The departmental operating budget

The direct cost to an organisation of a procurement department is controlled by a departmental operating budget. Along with other departmental heads, the procurement manager makes an estimate of the costs which will be incurred during the budget period. This estimate is usually produced annually and will include:

- total departmental salary bill;
- total expenses for the period;
- total cost of departmental supplies; and
- capital expenditure.

More detailed budgets break down the second and third points into items such as heat and light, area occupied (rent), postage, telex and fax, telephone, travel and entertainment costs and rental of machinery. The major part of the operating expenses of a procurement department will be salaries.

Both budget systems have the same basic advantage: the manager is forced to forecast future changes, to plan to reach stated objectives, and to monitor progress. Clearly, the budget can only be as good as the estimates upon which it is based and, since business involves so many variables, forecasts can be wrong. However, a good budget system will be flexible enough to allow for this. Apart from changes in external environments, the budget can signal deficiencies within the organisation. Variations from budget, both inside and outside the organisation, will only be *signalled* by the budget system. The responsibility for adapting and correcting still lies firmly with the manager.

DISPOSING OF REDUNDANT STOCK, SCRAP OR WASTE

Despite the considerable efforts which have been made to improve the management of materials in many organisations some redundant material has to be disposed of. The same thing can be said of scrap or waste and, frequently, the task of disposal is vested in the purchasing department. The following short section is designed to suggest something of the role which an effective purchasing department might play in the process.

One important point is to consider why the redundant or scrap materials have arisen. Some waste is inevitable, but careful consideration of the reasons behind the surplus can have a profound effect on the economies of an operation. One simple example which illustrates the potential concerned a metal fabricator. In this case the weekly volume of scrap from the company's flame-cutting facility was investigated by a trainee. He noted that the metal left between the blanks which had been cut out appeared to be excessive. As a result, using a new, computer controlled machine in the process, scrap was reduced by some 20 per cent.

In another case the machining time involved in finishing a complex casting was considerably reduced as a result of an investigation which started with an examination of alloy steel swarf arisings. Both examples suggest that, periodically, those who have to dispose of waste/scrap materials may find that economic advantage is best obtained by avoiding the 'production' of the waste in the first place.

The type of scrap involved here is, of course, only one of the many which may arise. Others can come about as a result of poor storage, damage while in stock, the materials/components being faulty on arrival, the product becoming obsolescent or production methods being changed. Again in many cases of these and other types, prevention is always better than disposal.

One company which sought to obviate as much of this kind of waste as possible started their investigation by analysing ten different cases which originated during the previous five years. Their most dramatic success involved two cases where they were able to improve liaison between sales, production and purchasing so as to co-ordinate the introduction of new products (and the demise of older products) more effectively. In one case, the purchasing department, not being aware of the new product launch plans, had ordered what became obsolete material relating to the previous design two weeks before the planned date of the new product introduction.

Managing disposal

Space does not permit full treatment of this subject for the variety of types of material which need to be disposed of is extremely wide. However, there are some useful points which apply in many cases and which should be noted.

When considering how to dispose of scrap materials, questions to be considered might be:

- Can we dispose of material within the business (or group)?
- Can the item be cannibalised for useful parts prior to scrapping?

- Can we sell the items in the marketplace rather than scrap? (e.g. back to supplier if redundant stock.)
- If we are to sell material as scrap, can we get a better price if we segregate by type or size or by bailing into cube form or cutting to smaller sizes?
- Can we come to an agreement with a merchant whereby they provide skips/containers for housing the scrap prior to collection?

Clearly the costs associated with disposing of materials need to be kept in mind when examining the issues involved. It makes no sense to install some sophisticated scrap system if the cost of doing so is greater than the money received. Usually effective negotiation with a bona fide scrap dealer can provide the buyer with useful guidelines within which to operate.

It is extremely important to ensure that the control systems associated with scrap disposal are clear and watertight. As a principle it is far better not to become involved in ready cash transactions. While converting the scrap into cash in the business as quickly as possible is a sensible requirement, scrap disposal services are not always offered by bona fide businesses. Where cash payment is an acceptable alternative for some reason it is important that the system ensures that checks on what passes to the merchant and what cash is paid in return are properly documented. Where valuable scrap (e.g. gold, silver, platinum) is involved, security arrangements have to be made to a higher degree than would be the case with other materials.

Finally, it is essential that buyers who are concerned with the disposal of significant amounts of scrap or waste material should keep in touch with market trends. Scrap prices fluctuate as do the prices of materials from which the waste arises.

SUMMARY POINTS

- The chapter discusses the relative ease of measuring operational activities which are quantitative as against tactical and strategic activities which are qualitative.
- At the lowest level of development, purchasing is often a clerical function, using an adversarial approach to sourcing. Price is the major decision factor between competitors, which are changed regularly. At the highest level, purchasing is recognised as a strategic business function, playing a vital part in the adoption of world class concepts.
- The higher the degree of purchasing development, the greater the extent of measuring performance. Measurement leads to recognition of the function; sets targets and establishes ground rules from which policies can be formed.
- Benchmarking aims to discover 'best practice' wherever it might be found. The idea is to identify key characteristics of best practice and adopt them.
- Budgets are derived from objectives such as required Return on Investment. A figure is given which is the estimated expenditure required to meet the desired ROI. This budget figure is then used as a control comparing actual expenditure with projected. If necessary, corrective action can be taken.

- Redundant stock, scrap or waste is a cost to an organisation. The most effective way to reduce it is to avoid the production of waste. Waste occurs through obsolescence, theft, poor storage conditions, damage in transit. With careful management, it can be disposed of profitably!

REFERENCES AND FURTHER READING

Davies O (1985), 'Measuring purchasing performance', in *Purchasing Management Handbook,* Gower Press, Aldershot.

Department of Trade and Industry (1993), *Benchmarking,* DTI, London.

Leenders M R *et al.* (1989), *Purchasing and Materials Management,* 9th edn, Irwin, Homewood, Ill.

Monczka R M (1974), 'Buyer performance evaluation; major considerations', *Journal of Purchasing and Materials Management,* November.

Monczka R M, Carter P L and Hoagland J H (1979), *Purchasing Performance: Measurement and Control,* MSU (USA).

Paperman J B and Shell R L (1977), 'The accounting approach to performance measurement', *Journal of Purchasing and Materials Management,* Summer.

Power S (1993), 'Thoughts on performance appraisal', *Purchasing and Supply Management,* September and October.

Van Eck A, Van Weele A J and de Weerd H (1982), 'Price–performance evaluation', *Journal of Purchasing and Materials Management,* Summer.

Van Wheele A J (1985), 'New concepts in measuring purchasing performances', *Journal of Purchasing and Materials Management.*

Wells P E and Rawlinson M (1993), 'Playing the system', *Purchasing and Supply Management,* April.

Wieters C D (1976), 'The design and use of supplier performance rating systems in selected industries', unpublished dissertation, Arizona State University.

Zenz G J (1975), 'Evaluating materials management', *Journal of Purchasing and Materials Management,* Autumn.

CHAPTER 20

People in purchasing

In this text we have indicated that the scope of purchasing and supply has become broader, and the emphasis more strategic. New concepts, systems and procedures are continually being developed. It will not be possible for organisations to benefit from the competitive advantage that a developed purchasing function can bring unless they have staff with the appropriate knowledge, skills and competencies to put ideas into practice. This chapter concerns itself with the ways in which human resources in purchasing and supply are matched with organisational needs.

OBJECTIVES OF THIS CHAPTER

- To observe that successful organisations match human resources to organisational needs
- To appreciate the importance of motivation and just reward to attract and retain high calibre staff
- To consider individual needs when planning a training programme
- To look at the routes available to attaining professional purchasing qualifications. To understand the NVQ/SVQ levels of competence in purchasing and how they are measured
- To appreciate the principles and standards of purchasing practice and ethical conduct.

STAFFING DEVELOPMENT

Staff profiles need to be linked in some way with strategic needs. We indicated in Chapter 4 that the role of the buyer and support staff is very much affected by the stage of development reached by the organisation. If we examine the developing role of a buyer, a progression can be seen. This progression will be developed in this chapter, which deals with the ways in which human resources in purchasing and supply are matched with organisational needs.

Figure 20.1 illustrates the general 'buyer profile' likely to be required by organisations at different stages of purchasing development. At stage 1 the function is seen as essentially clerical and reactive, but by stage 5 it has become proactive, with little involvement in routine buying activities – ordering, scheduling, and expediting are now clerical or automated tasks with minimal buyer involvement.

Stage of development	General characteristics and responsibilities of incumbent
Infant	No special qualifications; order clerk approach; over 80 per cent clerical.
Awakening	No special qualifications; some basic buying, i.e. routine ordering; 60–79 per cent clerical.
Developing	Formal school-leaving qualifications demanded; involvement in negotiations; sourcing and routine buying purchasing function recognised; 40–59 per cent of job content clerical.
Mature	Business qualification required; specialist commodity buyers potential integration with other functional areas; involved with all aspects of new product development; major part of job is negotiation, and supplier development/cost reduction; 20–30 per cent of job content clerical.
Advanced	Professional or postgraduate qualification needed; buyer involved with more strategic elements of the job; more concern with total acquisition, cost, managing the supplier base, etc.; less than 20 per cent of work is clerical.

Fig. 20.1 Buyer profile

A problem facing some organisations is their lack of awareness that salaries must reflect the contribution required from a buyer. We have seen numerous advertisements calling for a buyer but offering the salary of an order clerk. At the higher stages of purchasing development the skills and knowledge required are of a high order, and need to be appropriately rewarded.

MOTIVATION

Many factors influence the way in which people behave. The morale of a group of people will be a key factor in their success or failure as will the ethics or culture of a business. For example, where an organisation is structured so as to discourage entrepreneurial drive, buyers will tend to avoid risk, and the necessary skills and competencies of people in such an environment will be different from those who operate in freer concerns.

In other organisations there will be buyers who contribute fully to strategic planning discussions or who are involved in new product development. Again, these people will tend to be different and behave differently from those who are concerned with what we might call operational/supply purchasing and their perceptions of their roles, and their colleagues perceptions of them, will be quite different.

The way in which people are managed, directed, rewarded and punished will affect the way in which they behave. Effective communication, the development of trust and confidence, opportunities and training will all impact upon the success of any organisation. Without well-motivated people who are able and well trained, even the most brilliantly conceived plans and strategies can fail. Some would argue that it is far better to have a less than perfect system which people understand and want to make work than a highly sophisticated one without their understanding and commitment. As many sporting contests illustrate, a highly motivated team whose members work for and with each other can beat a team of less motivated people even if they have greater talent.

Motivating people to work well is a topic that has exercised the minds of many people. Theories abound, but there would seem to be one common ingredient – job interest. If the manager can demonstrate and recognise the contribution of his or her staff to corporate well-being, this is favourable to individual and group motivation.

It is important for the manager to recognise that creating the climate in which people can be motivated to use their talents is a key part of his or her job. This is not easy to do, particularly where staff attitudes are not what they should be. Oxenfeldt (1966) illustrates this in a case where a policy-orientated executive had replaced another who had had a narrower view of his task. He illustrates the differences between the two men by using three categories, as in Figure 20.2.

Of course, the right attitudes need to be developed throughout an organisation. The procurement function needs to project an image of efficiency and professionalism, as well as a propensity to collaborate with colleagues in other departments. Stuart Lauer (1967) describes changes made in the procurement activity of a Westinghouse plant:

> Eventually we submitted a report to the management of plant X. The opening paragraph was headed: 'Management Philosophy', and pointed out all criticism of the purchasing operation came back to the question of management philosophy; what can and should a purchasing department do? The buyers were very efficient in expediting and in routine clerical work. Very little creative buying work was being done. But very little had been expected. Management emphasis on the routine side of procurement had resulted in minimising the efforts to reduce operating costs and an overall lack of planning and organisation in the department.
>
> If the division wants this department to be primarily a routine clerical operation, then people of this calibre should be employed and paid accordingly. If, however, there is a need and an apparent opportunity for the purchasing department to influence product cost, this should be reflected more adequately in the organisation, manning and objectives set forth and met by the department. For the last five or six years the management of plant X have had a very low expectation of the purchasing organisation in areas other than getting material into the plant on time. *This, in our opinion, should change drastically and the level of performance of all the people in the purchasing organisation should be raised and measured on much broader criteria.* [emphasis added]

Lauer's final words emphasise individual direction, motivation and measurement. When a group of people and/or an organisation structure or

Area	The traditional buyer	The new man
ATTITUDES (opinions and beliefs)	His job commenced with requisition: he was a service department to production	He saw the function as having profit-earning potential: believed that he should contribute to long-range plans as an equal partner
COGNITIONS (knowledge and assumptions)	No financial, statistical or analytical knowledge. Assumed all books were for academics. Assumed that his job was largely concerned with 'trouble shooting' for production	An MBA; considerable financial/quantitative bias; assumed purchasing to be a vital element in corporate well-being thus necessitating creative input to corporate plans and policies
VALUES (goals, fears, aspirations)	Concerned with status. Present job being ceiling of his ambitions but with a progressive salary. Goals to make savings, resist price increases and make sure that production never ran short	Aspirations to reach the board; anxious to eliminate weaknesses in personal management knowledge in order to be able to do a better job. Goals to achieve overt objectives through better planning management, creativity and close collaboration with other company executives

Fig. 20.2 Oxenfeldt's dispositional difference

system are being analysed with a view to improving performance, it is essential to understand the roles which are to be performed, the standards which have to be achieved and how performance will be evaluated. Where there is clear understanding of these issues between manager and managed, the chances of developing effective functional team performance are greatly enhanced.

THE RIGHT PEOPLE

Since it is difficult to make silk purses out of sows' ears, it makes great sense to attempt to recruit good people in the first place. So, what kind of people should a purchasing manager be looking for? A particular business environment may suggest specific requirements. However, there are useful guidelines which can be of general application. A piece of research by Reck (1978) suggests some of these.

Reck considered the question 'What differentiates more effective from less effective purchasers?' He concentrated on personality and socio-economic factors. Among other things, the study concluded that effective purchasers 'tend to have a more positive self image'. This finding, of course, might well be applied to any field of management. However, given the role which the purchasing person has to fill, it is reasonable to argue that this requirement is more significant in his or her profession than in most. For example, he or she has to interface with senior people in his or her own organisation as well as in others. The person may need to relate to a wide spectrum of industries and technologies, and will need to ensure that a balanced view is taken of the technical/commercial mix. Also to do his or her job efficiently and effectively, he or she will need to be able to conceive of the business he or she is in as a complete entity. It is unlikely that any 'shrinking violet' will be able to perform effectively in demanding circumstances.

A second finding was that the purchaser tends to have a 'superior ability to communicate with others'. This finding is as pertinent as that already discussed. Indeed, it might be argued that it is self-evident. Whether this is so or not, our traditional methods of selecting purchasers have not always taken this into account, or so it would seem, if we judge from the comments of purchasing managers, on staff which they have inherited.

A third finding was that the effective purchaser tends 'to have a superior ability to use interpersonal skills'. Among the areas cited in this respect were departmental co-ordination, negotiation and inter-firm co-ordination.

Finally, Reck found that 'more effective purchasers tended to be more interested in developing themselves professionally . . . They also tended to have achieved a higher level of formal education than their less effective counterparts.' Our own evidence in observing the purchasing scene over the past thirty years confirms this. We find, for example, greater evidence of a desire to be more professional (and be seen to be so) among this group, and during this period we have seen many more graduates recruited into the function. Several top jobs have been filled by young, ambitious individuals whom we remember as new entrants to the profession within the last decade or so.

In closing this short section we would not wish to leave the reader with the impression that buyers should all conform to this list of characteristics. As a famous soccer manager told a group of managers recently, 'When you build a team you don't want all lead violinists – or it will never work. You want some workmen or roadsweepers as well. The secret is in the blend.' Perhaps the problem faced by some purchasing organisations is that they are populated entirely by the latter.

Who are the right people? The answer depends upon the tasks to be performed, the environment within which the work is to be done, and the conceptions of the manager as to his role. Chapter 3 on building an organisation with input to corporate plans in view, develops this discussion. However, one useful technique which might be employed by all kinds of organisations is that of developing job and person descriptions, but a basic principle here is to ensure that neither becomes a straitjacket.

THE JOB DESCRIPTION

Any job description relates to a particular task which is required to be performed in the specific business environment concerned and an example of such a document is included here. The job described is undertaken in an engineering environment which is organised on a project basis. In the company concerned, a purchasing manager is assigned to each major project.

Job description: project purchasing manager

This manager:

1 Reports directly to the senior project manager and liaises with the other project managers.
2 Provides a full purchasing service to the senior project manager, which includes subcontracting, ordering equipment and material, expediting, inspection and shipping.
3 Represents the senior project manager in meetings with the clients for whom he or she is responsible on all purchasing matters.
4 Prepares purchasing procedures for the project, agrees them with the senior project manager, corporate purchasing management and the client and ensures that they are adhered to.
5 Directly supervises the chief subcontracts buyer, chief buyer, senior project expeditor and senior project inspector.
6 Reviews and agrees regularly with senior project manager and with corporate purchasing management the workforce requirements for the project.
7 Maintains close liaison concerning all purchasing activities with corporate purchasing management.
8 Supervises the preparation of: conditions of contract and subcontract; list of suppliers and subcontractors; detailed inspection procedures; shipping documentation; and all other documentation relating to purchasing for the project.
9 Agrees with the client the names of firms to be invited to tender and attends the opening of tenders meetings when sealed tender procedure is applicable.
10 Continually monitors and reviews progress of purchasing work, prepares monthly purchasing status reports, attends and reports to monthly meetings at which the whole situation as regards purchase orders and subcontracts is considered in relation to the time-scale for the contract.
11 Signs bid summaries before submission to client, corporate purchasing management and senior project manager, after ensuring that laid down procedure has been complied with.
12 Supervises the placement of all purchasing commitments by letter of intent, purchase order, contract form or in any other manner.
13 Ensures that copies of purchase orders, correspondence and any other relevant documents are passed to senior project manager, client and any other person as required by laid-down procedure.

14 Obtains from suppliers and subcontractors schedules of work compatible with the project programme.

15 Makes sure that any negotiations about orders or subcontracts are properly conducted and takes personal responsibility if they are of a critical nature.

16 Ensures that invoice queries from the invoice checking section are promptly dealt with by the procurement staff.

'Organisational' job description

A well-used question among consultants and management teachers asks the directors of a business: 'What business are you in ?' The question stems from an *Harvard Business Review* paper of long ago entitled 'Marketing myopia'. In this the author argued, among other things, that the US Railroad Companies would still be predominant businesses today if they had realised that they were in transportation rather than railroads. Then, says the author, they would have been open to the opportunities which evolved in, for example, air transport. Whatever the merits of this argument, it is useful to ask what job the organisation has to do through the same question. In its turn the answers to this question will suggest the various tasks which individuals will need to perform. The following example was developed with respect to a group purchasing activity.

Group purchasing – key roles

Group purchasing – key roles

The key roles of the group purchasing organisation fall into three categories: direct purchasing, staff, and other.

1 *Direct purchasing*   The group purchasing organisation is responsible for: all common UK contracts; key major materials purchased for more than one site; major capital purchases; and co-ordination with other group companies in other countries with regard to purchasing matters.

2 *Staff*   In this area, the responsibilities of purchasing cover: purchasing management audits; advice on recruitment and selection (in all cases); recruitment and selection in specified cases; staff training and development; staffing requirement advice; and purchasing consultancy advice.

3 *Other*   The group purchasing organisation is also responsible for: the market research library; economic forecasting; currency management; legal advice; purchasing policies; development of group purchasing information systems; and socio-political forecasting.

TRAINING AND DEVELOPMENT

Having selected the right people, and established a helpful environment, systems and organisation, it is important to ensure that purchasing staff are well trained. Such development should be concerned with the particular needs which individuals in the organisation have. Those needs may be concerned with their present job, or with one which they will do in the future, and that future job may result as often from technological developments as from promotions. Obviously it is necessary to establish clearly these needs before organising programmes of training, yet it is not unknown for that important step to be omitted.

One company used a matrix approach to determining needs. Their form is shown as Figure 20.3. The simple idea is that the broad skills listed at the left-hand side of the matrix are considered in respect of each of the other skills which are shown across the top. An X is then placed in the column where the other skill is appropriate for the general skill. By representing this for each general skill, a profile of the skills necessary to perform the task in question will be developed. Training programmes may then be tailored to satisfy the various aspects of the skill in question. The knowledge requirements at the right-hand side may be dealt with in a similar way.

KNOWLEDGE, SKILLS, ATTITUDE

The matrix in Figure 20.3 indicates two of the three elements which a management development programme might aim to satisfy. The third is attitude. Knowledge comprises the things people need to know to carry out particular tasks; skills are the abilities they need to have to perform the function; and attitude involves the manner and spirit with which they approach the job. These are simplified descriptions, but suffice for present purposes.

Knowledge includes both general and specific education as well as job knowledge. In development terms, the analysis of particular needs starts at recruitment; for example, applicants for given posts rarely measure up exactly to the specification and may need some remedial development immediately.

New employees should have the right knowledge when they are recruited. So a reasonable general question might be, what should the level be, say, for people new to business? For example, consider the problem as it relates to a graduate. What should his or her discipline be? Does it matter if it is ancient Greek, or Welsh literature? Or should it be relevant to the job in some way, like economics or finance?

Some companies are indifferent to the type of degree. They argue that what they need is a trained mind, whatever the specialism of the graduate. The specific knowledge training programme which they used on recruitment will be assimilated quickly and the new employee will quickly fit into the company environment. Others argue that a relevant degree makes assimilation easier and, as one manager put it, 'despite the impracticalities of economic theory, they are aware of the business process'.

There is a small but increasing number of British first degree programmes with purchasing as a major theme. They seem to have in common the fact that they provide a broad integrative foundation in general business, with specialisation developing as the course progresses. Figure 20.4 is a schematic representation of the UK's first named degree in purchasing and supply chain management which is offered at the University of Glamorgan.

		Broad skills	Calculation	Data analysis	Decision making	Design liaison	Leadership	Labour management	Negotiation	Problem solving	Planning	Strategic management	Supplier selection	User liaison
Knowledge	Product knowledge													
	Technical knowledge													
	Supply market business knowledge													
	End market business knowledge													
	Company business knowledge													
Other skills	Computer compatible													
	Cost analysis													
	Financial analysis													
	Meeting management													
	Team working													
	Conceptual thinking													
	Creative thinking													
	Logical thinking													
	Modelling													
	Forecasting													
	Researching													
	Evaluating													
	Motivating													
	Delegation													
	Questioning													
	Listening													
	Preparation													
	Work planning													
	Report writing													
	Selection													
	Interviewing													
	Human relationships													

Fig. 20.3 Needs analysis matrix

SEMESTER ONE	SEMESTER TWO
Economy and environment Business law Business financial statements Information technology 1 Business skills Business seminar (non-assessed)	Fundamentals of marketing Organisations and people Financial planning and control Quantitative methods Information technology 2 Business seminar (non-assessed)
SEMESTER THREE	SEMESTER FOUR
Business environment (company analysis) Financial analysis and interpretation Information and research Management and organisational behaviour Risk and uncertainty Project placement seminar (non-assessed)	Purchasing and supply Design and innovation Political economy of European integration Business planning and enterprise Operations management Project placement seminar (non-assessed)
SEMESTER FIVE	SEMESTER SIX
Placement	Placement
SEMESTER SEVEN	SEMESTER EIGHT
Dissertation Corporate strategy Buyer/seller relationships Materials management Option	Dissertation Corporate strategy Law of trade Transportation systems Option

Options: Entrepreneurship, Global marketing, Ethics, Business forecasting, Distribution, Marketing analysis and forecasting.

Fig. 20.4 Schematic representation of a BA (Hons) degree in purchasing and supply chain management   (*Courtesy:* University of Glamorgan)

From the UK viewpoint, an influential approach to qualification is that promoted by the Chartered Institute of Purchasing and Supply in its professional diploma; this course of study is based upon a general management programme. Purchasing is seen as a broadly based function which has to interact with most other functions within the organisation, while operating in an outside environment.

Certainly, recruits to the function need not have the same educational background. The findings of the survey discussed earlier may not be applicable to a company, say, in the pharmaceutical industry: a science-based graduate might meet their particular need, while a company involved in constructing petrochemical plant may need a trained chemical engineer. The selection process will relate not only to the education of the applicant, but also to his or her other attributes as a potential businessperson. Many organisations in the UK and elsewhere, when recruiting graduates who have not specialised, require them to take the IPS diploma examinations. Figure 20.5 gives the framework of the current CIPS education scheme. There are requirements with regard to entry qualifications for the foundation stage.

JOB-RELATED KNOWLEDGE

Once the new employee has joined the organisation, his or her knowledge training will follow several routes. The educational aspects will either have been dealt with prior to him or her joining, or they will be undertaken in parallel with on-the-job training. This latter training will be designed to meet several needs; for example, it will be necessary for the person concerned to become familiar with the organisation structure, with people and procedures, and with terminology. A variety of approaches have been used to meet these needs, including arrangement for the person to work in several departments in the organisation in turn as an introduction to the company. Some companies have comprehensive induction, while others believe that 'on-the-job' training supervised by experienced people affords the best introduction if it is coupled with a good operating manual and sensible job rotation. Other methods include company meetings, departmental meetings where the newcomer is given a specific role (e.g. observer or secretary), and assisting and/or observing experienced people on projects, assignments or negotiations. Once again, the suitability of these or other approaches in particular cases will depend upon the needs of the person in question. However, a well thought-through programme of induction and on-the-job training, coupled with other inputs as relevant (e.g. short courses, programmed learning), is preferable to some *ad hoc* approach.

Skills

It is difficult to conceive of skills training which does not add to knowledge in some degree. In most cases, the person concerned will be developing a particular skill while gaining further knowledge about, for example, when, where and how to use those skills. None the less, the emphasis of development in areas such as negotiating, participating in meetings, and interpreting data, will be on improving the ability of the man or woman in that aspect of their task.

Skills may be developed in a variety of ways. On-the-job training is widely used although, for best results, some basic instruction and guided reading relative to the skill is advisable. Books can introduce the employee to the basic concepts to avoid pitfalls; coaching by the immediate supervisor should complement the reading. To use a sporting analogy, the young player is told that in order to catch the ball successfully he or she 'should keep his/her eye on it' as it approaches. In practice, the player will learn the wisdom of this

SCHEME OF STUDY

The syllabuses of the CIPS are designed to provide a comprehensive framework for study and examination of the role and management practices of a broad-based purchasing and supply profession, the scope of which has greatly expanded in recent years. It now extends far beyond the frontiers traditionally delineated by such terms as 'buying' and 'stores management'. Its functions embrace all the activities within the supply chain, that is to say:

(a) specification of requirements;

(b) sourcing and acquisition of materials and services;

(c) negotiation and management of contracts and projects;

(d) control and movement of materials into and through production and other operational processes;

(e) inspection, quality assurance, handling, storage and distribution to the point of need;

(f) control and disposal of waste and redundant materials.

This wide range of responsibilities illustrates the vital, strategic role which the profession plays in corporate management. The need to co-ordinate the management of all the activities within the supply chain from sourcing and acquisition, through production where appropriate, and distribution to the customer, has become increasingly recognised in recent years. The syllabus requires students to study the ways in which such co-ordination can best be achieved, depending upon the nature of the business concerned, to create competitive advantage through simultaneous achievement of high customer service levels, optimum investment and value for money. The terms 'logistics', 'supply chain management', 'materials management' and 'total procurement' are amongst those used to describe this co-ordination but, whichever term is used, the aim remains to optimise the profession's contribution to the corporate goal.

The Foundation and Graduate Diploma Schemes

THE FOUNDATION STAGE
- Management Princples and Practice
- Introduction to Purchasing and Supply Chain
- Management
- Economics
- Quantitative Studies
- Business Accounting

Entrance requirements

One of the following is a minimum:

(1) Five/four GCSE (at grade 3 or higher) or GCE passes (including English Language and a quantitative subject) of which at least two/three must be at Advanced Level. Note that 2AS Level passes may be substituted for 1 Advanced Level pass (likewise 4 for 2)

(2) BTEC or SCOTVEC National Award, OND/ONC (any discipline) or BEC/SCOTBEC/SCOTVEC equivalent.

(3) Five/four passes in the Scottish Certificate of Education (including English Language and a quantitative subject), of which at least three/four must be at Higher Grade.

(4) First and Second Certificate in Purchasing and Stores.

(5) Suitable employment experience, support of present employer and an age not less than 23.

Fig. 20.5 Framework of the current CIPS education scheme

GRADUATE DIPLOMA

The new CIPS scheme is designed to be flexible and to enable you to choose subjects that are of interest and relevant to your job. In addition to the four compulsory Core subjects, students must pass at least one Specialist Option subject and three other subjects chosen from the *Specialist Option* and/or *Elective* list.

Core Subjects
- Purchasing and Supply Chain Management I: Strategy
- Purchasing and Supply Chain Management II: Tactics and Operations
- Purchasing and Supply Chain Management III: Legal Aspects
- Purchasing and Supply Chain Management IV: Case Study

Specialist Options
- Purchasing
- Stores and Inventory Management
- Distribution (C66)
- Commercial Relationships

Elective Subjects
- Project
- Operations Management
- Marketing
- Project and Contract Management
- International Purchasing
- Retail Merchandise Management

Fig. 20.5 Continued

advice but it will be necessary for his or her coach to reinforce that learning as the player progresses.

People have different aptitudes and speeds of learning and, indeed, the ability to learn differs from person to person.

Other approaches to skills development are through company-based assignments, in-company and external training programmes, and various permutations of these with on-the-job training. In all skills training, the old adage 'practice makes perfect' applies. As has been stated before, the starting point for skills training is a careful analysis of needs.

NATIONAL VOCATIONAL QUALIFICATIONS

During the 1980s there were a number of government policy initiatives connected with education and training. A major intention was to increase the vocational relevance of qualifications. A problem was posed by the fact that there were few identifiable standards of occupational competence. Following considerable debate the National Council for Vocational Qualifications and the Scottish Vocational Education and Training Council were established to facilitate the identification of industry/occupational standards which could be accommodated in national qualifications.

National Vocational Qualifications (NVQs) are the qualifications which emerged from this initiative. They are based on standards set by industry and are designed to be flexible. Each NVQ is composed of a number of units that set out the standards which should be reached. Each unit is, in a sense, a small qualification in its own right. The unit sets out exactly what the candidate must be able to do and the standard which must be attained. People select which units they do, and are awarded certificates to show the unit credits they have achieved.

The benefits of NVQs have been identified in detail. For example, *employers* are able to:

- Identify people's training needs.
- Recognise staff achievement.
- Provide a structured training programme for their staff.
- Chart employees' promotion prospects.
- Demonstrate a commitment to quality and investment in people.
- Select the right staff and retain a committed workforce.
- Provide a better service to clients.
- Improve the company's performance and profitability.

Employees are able to:

- Gain recognition of their abilities.
- Obtain a nationally recognised qualification.
- Progress through a clearly defined qualifications system.
- Achieve enhanced career prospects.
- Improve their knowledge about all aspects of their job.

The Purchasing and Supply Lead Body has published national standards of competence in purchasing, which is essentially the set of *units of competence* from which a prescribed range must be selected and attained for the appropriate NVQ to be earned and awarded. Three levels are involved in the purchasing qualifications, which have been defined as follows.

Level 2

Competence in a significant range of varied work activities, performed in a variety of contexts. Some of the activities are complex or non-routine, and there is some individual responsibility or autonomy. Collaboration with others, perhaps through membership of a work group or team, may often be a requirement.

Level 3

Competence in a broad range of varied work activities performed in a wide variety of contexts and most of which are complex and non-routine. There is considerable responsibility and autonomy, and control or guidance of others is often required.

Level 4

Competence in a broad range of complex, technical or professional work activities performed in a wide variety of contexts and with a substantial degree of personal responsibility and autonomy. Responsibility for the work of others and the allocation of resources is often present.

The Chartered Institute of Purchasing and Supply, as a centre approved by City and Guilds to offer NVQs in purchasing, has supplied information on assessment and certification, and an overview of the set of units of competence (*see* Figures 20.6, 20.7 and 20.8).

ASSESSMENT

Assessment primarily takes place in the candidate's normal working environment and is carried out by appropriate managers or supervisors or, where necessary, by an external assessor. Principally, it comprises observation of the candidate's activities and products (e.g. reports and records) and oral questioning to test underpinning knowledge. The assessment is subject to overall scrutiny by external verifiers who ensure that national standards in assessment are maintained.

Each candidate will:

● undertake an initial self-assessment which is discussed with the assessor to identify his or her needs in terms of training and experience

● produce evidence of prior learning for accreditation by their assessor to ensure that they do not have to retrain in areas in which they are already competent

● devise, with the help of their assessor, a personal action plan

● gather evidence against the Standards

● undergo assessment by their accredited assessor

CERTIFICATION

To gain an NVQ at Level 2, 3 or 4, candidates are required to successfully complete a number of units:

● **Level 2** – 7 units

● **Level 3** – 9 units

● **Level 4** – 10 units

Certificates are issued to candidates once they have achieved all the relevant units of competence required for each level. Candidates who prove their competence in one or more units will receive a Certificate of Unit Credit.

Fig. 20.6 NVQ assessment
(*Courtesy:* Purchasing and Supply Lead Body)

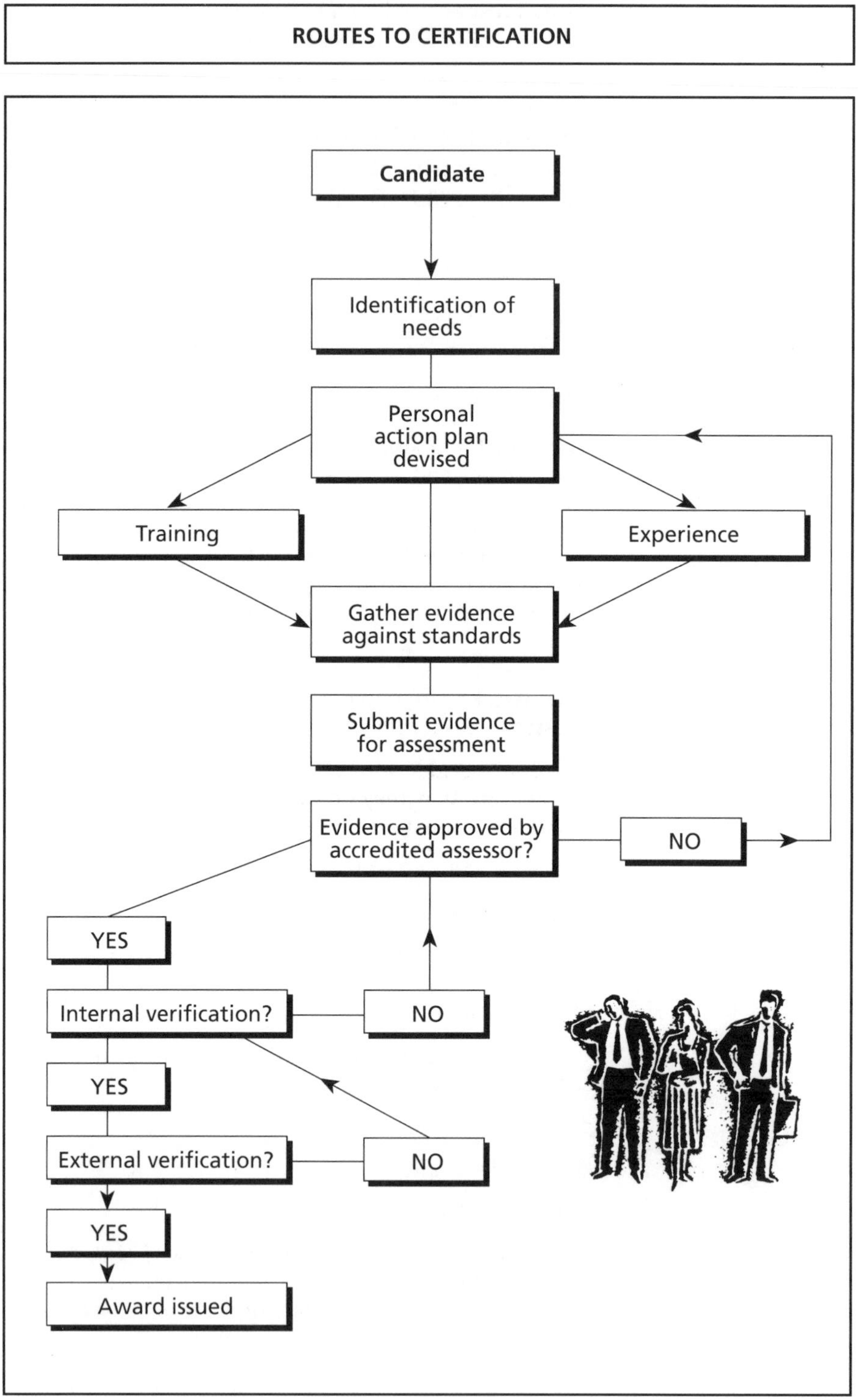

ROUTES TO CERTIFICATION

Fig. 20.7 Routes to certification
(*Courtesy:* Purchasing and Supply Lead Body)

NVQ and SVQ Qualifications Frameworks

National Vocational Qualifications
Scottish Vocational Qualifications

What is contained in this document

This document shows the frameworks for the NVQs and SVQs in Procurement at Levels 2, 3 and 4. They are based on the new Procurement standards valid from November 1996 to March 2000. Key points:

- Each framework contains the titles of the units and elements of competence at the relevant level.
- Each framework contains a mix of mandatory and optional units to provide flexibility to the qualification design.
- Each framework contains at least two of the following categories:
  - *Mandatory Units* These apply to all procurement professionals and are mandatory within the framework
  - *Specific Optional Units* These units have been selected to represent specialisms within which different procurement professionals operate. At levels 3 and 4 there are two groupings of Specific Optional Units (two groups of six at level 3 and two groups of four at level 4)
  - *Non-Specific Optional Units* These units have been selected to provide greater depth and variety to the qualification and apply to some, but not all, procurement professionals.

Each candidate will be required to complete a set number of units to obtain the SVQ or NVQ. For candidates this means:

	Level 2	Level 3	Level 4
Mandatory Units	5	4	4
Specific Optional Units	–	3	3
Non Specific Optional Units	2	*	*
Total	7	9	10

*No set number but further units must be selected from the Optional Units or the Specific Optional Units to reach the total required.

Fig. 20.8 Units of competence
(*Courtesy:* Purchasing and Supply Lead Body)

Procurement – Level 2 Qualification Structure

7 Completed Units for a Level 2 SVQ or NVQ comprising:

5 Core Units (Section 1) + 2 Optional Units (Section 2)

Section 1   CORE UNITS *(all units to be completed)*

001 Contribute to the health and safety and security of the working environment	**004 Store, retrieve and supply information****
1.1 Contribute to the maintenance of the health and safety of self, other workers and members of the public	4.1 Maintain an established storage system
	4.2 Supply information for a specific purpose
1.2 Contribute to the maintenance of security and confidentiality	**007 Progress the delivery of goods and services**
	7.1 Maintain agreed delivery position of goods and services
002 Maintain effective professional relationships with other people	7.2 Resolve variations in supply
2.1 Maintain effective professional relationships with external contacts	**008 Improve service reliability for customers***
	8.1 Respond promptly to the service needs of customers
2.2 Maintain effective professional relationships with colleagues	8.2 Use customer feedback to improve service reliability
	8.3 Work with others to improve service reliability

Section 2 OPTIONAL UNITS *(two units to be completed)*

003 Contribute to the installation and improvement of procurement systems	6.4 Recommend supplier after evaluation of quotations
3.1 Contribute to the installation and testing of procurement systems	6.5 Place orders for the supply of goods and services
3.2 Contribute to the improvement and integration of procurement systems	**029 Contribute to the establishment of inventory and materials requirements**
	29.1 Provide data for schedules, demand forecasts and materials requirements
005 Contribute to improvements in supplier performance	29.2 Monitor loadings, delivery requirements and materials supply
5.1 Contribute to resolving user complaints	29.3 Contribute to the review and improvement of forecasting
5.2 Provide feedback and support to supplier	
006 Acquire specified goods and services	**030 Contribute to the optimisation of inventory and stock levels**
6.1 Provide information on goods and services to users	30.1 Monitor the applicability of inventory levels
6.2 Select potential suppliers for the supply of goods and services	30.2 Implement specified changes in inventory levels
6.3 Obtain quotations for the supply of goods and services	30.3 Reconcile stock levels against requirements

*Standards developed by Customer Service Lead Body
**Standards developed by Administration Lead Body

Fig. 20.8 *(continued)*

Procurement Level 3 Qualification Structure

9 Completed Units for a Level 3 SVQ or NVQ comprising:

4 Core Units (Section 1) + 3 Specific Optional Units (Section 2A or 2B) + 2 further Options (selected from Section 3 Non Specific Options and/or remaining units from Section 2)

Section 1 CORE UNITS *(all units from this section to be completed)*

009 Contribute to the development of policies and plans 9.1 Obtain information to assist the evaluation of policies and plans 9.2 Present information for the development of policies and plans **010 Maintain the effectiveness of procurement operations** 10.1 Contribute to the identification of objectives for procurement operations 10.2 Contribute to the improvement of operational effectiveness	**011 Create and maintain effective professional relationships with other people** 11.1 Create and maintain effective professional relationships with suppliers and other external parties 11.2 Create and maintain effective professional relationships with other members of staff **043 Provide information and advice for action towards meeting organisational objectives*** 43.1 Obtain, evaluate, record and store information 43.2 Provide information and advice

Section 2 SPECIFIC OPTIONAL UNITS *(three units from this section from either 2A or 2B)*

2A Supply and Contract Management

014 Monitor and evaluate supplier performance and continuity of supply 14.1 Assess supplier's capacity to supply 14.2 Monitor supplier performance and vendor rating of supplier **015 Contribute to the establishment and evaluation of current and future requirements for supply** 15.1 Provide information on goods and services to users 15.2 Agree purchasing and technical specification with users 15.3 Contribute to the establishment of type and duration of supply agreement **016 Negotiate improvements in supplier performance** 16.1 Resolve user complaints with supplier 16.2 Provide feedback, assistance and advice to supplier 16.3 Co-ordinate improvements in supplier performance	**023 Contribute to the development of a contract strategy and plan** 23.1 Provide information for contract objectives and strategy 23.2 Develop a contract implementation plan **024 Let contracts for the supply of goods and services** 24.1 Identify and evaluate potential contractors 24.2 Produce contractual documentation 24.3 Establish an agreement 24.4 Award a contract **025 Monitor and review the contract delivery** 25.1 Monitor contract costs against budget 25.2 Monitor contract progress 25.3 Close standard contracts 25.4 Undertake post-contract review

Fig. 20.8 *(continued)*

2B Materials Management

031 Contribute to the planning of inventory and materials requirements
31.1 Determine the planning timescale
31.2 Identify inventory and materials requirements
31.3 Identify available capacity
31.4 Contribute to capacity control

032 Identify and establish scheduling requirements
32.1 Calculate capacities and loadings
32.2 Calculate delivery requirements
32.3 Create and maintain production schedules

033 Contribute to the optimisation of inventory levels
33.1 Contribute to the setting of inventory levels
33.2 Monitor and adjust inventory levels

034 Contribute to the implementation of changes in inventory
34.1 Contribute to the identification of possible changes to inventory
34.2 Implement changes to inventory

035 Contribute to controlling the stock take system
35.1 Maintain records of stock
35.2 Identify and reconcile stock discrepancies

036 Progress delivery and monitor the quality of supplies
36.1 Maintain agreed delivery schedule for supplies
36.2 Monitor the quality of supplies
36.3 Investigate complaints and resolve variations in supply

Section 3 NON SPECIFIC OPTIONAL UNITS (available as options)

012 Contribute to the establishment and improvement of procurement systems
12.1 Contribute to the specification and design of procurement systems
12.2 Contribute to the installation and testing of procurement systems
12.3 Contribute to the improvement and integration of procurement systems

044 Contribute to the provision of personnel*
44.1 Contribute to the identification of personnel requirements
44.2 Contribute to the selection of personnel

045 Contribute to the planning, monitoring and control of resources*
45.1 Plan for the use of resources
45.2 Monitor and control the use of resources

046 Contribute to the training and development of teams, individuals and self to enhance performance*
46.1 Contribute to planning the training and development of teams and individuals
46.2 Contribute to training and development activities for teams and individuals
46.3 Contribute to the assessment of teams and individuals against training and development objectives
46.4 Develop oneself within the job

047 Contribute to planning, organisation and evaluation of work*
47.1 Contribute to planning work activities and methods to achieve objectives
47.2 Organise work and assist in the evaluation of work
47.3 Provide feedback on work performance to teams and individuals

Fig. 20.8 (continued)

Procurement Level 4 Qualification Structure

10 Completed Units for a Level 4 SVQ or NVQ comprising:

4 Core Units (Section 1) + 3 Specific Optional Units (Section 2A or 2B) + 3 further Options (selected from Section 3 Non Specific Options and/or remaining units from Section 2)

Section 1 CORE UNITS *(all units from this section to be completed)*

017 Provide commercial input to decision making	**018 Develop the effectiveness of procurement operations**
17.1 Identify and evaluate commercial issues impacting on organisational planning	18.1 Establish objectives of procurement operations
17.2 Evaluate supply market issues	18.2 Review and improve the effectiveness of procurement operations
17.3 Evaluate alternative commercial strategy options	
	049 Indicate and implement change and improvement in services, products and systems*
048 Exchange information to solve problems and make decisions*	49.1 Identify opportunities for improvement in services, products and systems
48.1 Lead meetings and group discussions to solve problems and make decisions	49.2 Evaluate proposed changes for benefits and disadvantages
48.2 Contribute to discussions to solve problems and make decisions	49.3 Negotiate and agree the introduction of change
48.3 Advise and inform others	49.4 Implement and evaluate changes to services, products and systems
	4.95 Introduce, develop and evaluate quality assurance systems

Section 2 SPECIFIC OPTIONAL UNITS *(three units from this section from either 2A or 2B)*

2A Supply and Contract Management

019 Determine conditions in the market for supplies	22.3 Negotiate improvements in supplier performance
19.1 Establish own organisation's position in the marketplace	**024 Let contracts for the supply of goods and services**
19.2 Identify market changes likely to affect supplies	24.1 Identify and evaluate potential contractors
19.3 Determine competitiveness of supplies from the market	24.2 Produce contractual documentation
19.4 Identify beneficial developments relating to supplies and sources	24.3 Establish an agreement
	24.4 Award a contract
020 Establish and maintain strategic sourcing arrangements	**026 Establish contract strategy and plan**
20.1 Evaluate the case for strategic sourcing	26.1 Identify objectives to determine a contract strategy
20.2 Establish strategic sourcing arrangements	26.2 Develop and monitor a contract implementation plan
20.3 Maintain and improve operations and arrangements for strategic sourcing	
	027 Administer the contract
021 Establish and evaluate current and future requirements for supply	27.1 Monitor and maintain costs against contract budget
21.1 Prepare purchasing and technical specification	27.2 Maintain contract compliance
21.2 Establish the type and duration of supply agreement	27.3 Monitor and control contract progress
	27.4 Deal with contractual claims from contractors
	27.5 Close the contract
022 Establish supplier status and secure improvements in supplier performance	**028 Improve contract performance**
22.1 Determine viability and status of potential supplier	28.1 Identify and implement improvements in contract performance
22.2 Monitor supplier performance and continuity of supply	28.2 Undertake post-contract review
	28.3 Identify and implement improvements in contracting

Fig. 20.8 *(continued)*

2B Materials Management

037 Plan and reconcile inventory and materials requirements and capacity
37.1 Evaluate the business impact of the planning timescale
37.2 Establish requirements and available capacity for materials and inventory
37.3 Control capacity against requirements

038 Define and establish production schedules
38.1 Define production capabilities
38.2 Evaluate loadings
38.3 Establish delivery requirements
38.4 Generate and maintain production schedules

039 Capture and forecast demand
39.1 Monitor and control methods for capturing demand
39.2 Review and improve forecasting methods

040 Manage materials requirements
40.1 Establish materials requirements
40.2 Specify materials supply requirements
40.3 Control materials supply

041 Optimise inventory levels
41.1 Set inventory levels in relation to organisational policy
41.2 Control and maintain inventory levels

042 Determine inventory service levels
42.1 Evaluate the impact of inventory service levels
42.2 Specify changes to inventory profile

Section 3 NON SPECIFIC OPTIONAL UNITS *(available as options)*

013 Establish and improve procurement systems
13.1 Specify and design procurement systems
13.2 Install and test procurement systems
13.3 Improve and integrate procurement systems

050 Secure effective resource allocation for activities and projects*
50.1 Justify proposals for expenditure on projects
50.2 Negotiate and agree budgets

051 Develop teams, individuals and self to enhance performance*
51.1 Develop and improve teams through planning and activities
51.2 Identify, review and improve development activities for individuals
51.3 Develop oneself within the job role
51.4 Evaluate and improve the development processes used

052 Plan, allocate and evaluate work carried out by teams, individuals and self*

52.1 Set and update work objectives for teams and individuals
52.2 Plan activities and determine work methods to achieve objectives
52.3 Allocate work and evaluate teams, individuals and self against objectives
52.4 Provide feedback to teams and individuals on their performance

053 Recommend, monitor and control the use of resources*
53.1 Make recommendations for expenditure
53.2 Monitor and control the use of resources

054 Contribute to the recruitment and selection of personnel*
54.1 Define future personnel requirements
54.2 Contribute to the assessment and selection of candidates against team and organisational requirements

*Standards developed by MCI (Management Charter Initiative)

Fig. 20.8 *(continued)*

INTERRELATIONSHIPS

Earlier in this chapter we mentioned the importance of buyers being effective in interfacing with people in other functions. In our view the skills associated with this aspect of the purchasing task rank highly amongst those necessary for effective purchasing, and this is particularly true when life cycles are shortening or when market demands fluctuate frequently. Sound liaison with colleagues enables buyers and others to perform effectively.

For example, in the development of a (new) product, effective liaison between designers, production, marketing and purchasing staff is essential if the product is to be delivered on time and be of the correct quality. As far as the purchasing staff are concerned they can only be effective if they have the associated people-skills to win the respect of their colleagues. It follows that managers should consider such traits and abilities when selecting staff and be prepared to enhance them through training.

In a 1987 study, Anklesaria and Burt found that in order to be effective in such liaisons, purchasing personnel needed five characteristics:

1 An educational background in engineering and/or an MBA type qualification.
2 Experience in dealing with engineers.
3 Ability to read blueprints.
4 Analytical and conceptual design capabilities.
5 Convergent learning style capabilities.

They argued that understanding these requirements should assist purchasing managers in selecting suitable people and in mapping out their development programmes.

While we would be prepared to argue with some of the detail in these findings, what we can say is that they illustrate the importance of being able to use the language of other professionals. While it is not necessary to be an engineer to interface with one, at the least it is essential to be able to discuss their requirements with confidence. That ability should extend into being able to liaise with engineers in other organisations as well as in the buying company.

It is a sobering thought that purchasing staff interface with more functions than the majority of other specialists. It follows that the skills and knowledge required to undertake the purchasing task properly are greater than most. Further, the behavioural skills which need to be brought to bear are at least as important as those which have been mentioned. The challenge of the task, therefore, is one which requires all-round 'business people' to perform it. In our view, where the challenge is taken and individuals seek to make themselves broadly proficient, the purchasing job is an excellent route through which future general managers or managing directors might move. At its worst the function is a mere administrative buying service for production. At its best it is a proactive, business-related function which offers challenges which will test the more highly motivated people in any organisation.

Those who manage the function have a task which is no less challenging and that task is to select, develop, motivate, and lead individuals who elect to become purchasing professionals.

ETHICS

We feel that it is appropriate in this chapter about human resources to make mention of ethics and professional practice. There are a number of published 'codes'; below we reproduce the principles and standards of purchasing practice published by the National Association of Purchasing Practice in the United States, and the CIPS ethical code.

PRINCIPLES AND STANDARDS OF PURCHASING PRACTICE

The following principles and standards of purchasing practice are published in the United States by the National Association of Purchasing Management:

1 To consider, first, the interests of his or her company in all transactions and to carry out and believe in its established policies.
2 To be receptive to competent counsel from his or her colleagues and to be guided by such counsel without impairing the dignity and responsibility of his or her office.
3 To buy, without prejudice, seeking to obtain the maximum ultimate value for each dollar of expenditure.
4 To strive consistently for knowledge of the materials and processes of manufacture and to establish practical methods for the conduct of his or her office.
5 To subscribe to and work for honesty and truth in buying and selling and to denounce all forms of manifestations of commercial bribery.
6 To accord a prompt and courteous reception, so far as conditions will permit, to all who call on a legitimate business mission.
7 To respect his or her other obligations and to require that obligations to him or her and to his or her concern be respected, consistent with good business practice.
8 To avoid sharp practice.
9 To counsel and assist fellow purchasing agents in the performance of their duties whenever occasion permits.
10 To co-operate with all organisations and individuals engaged in activities designed to enhance the development and standing of purchasing.

THE ETHICAL CODE

This code is published in the UK by the Chartered Institute of Purchasing and Supply.

Introduction

1 In applying to join the Institute, members undertake to abide by 'the Constitution, Memorandum and Articles of Association, Rules and By-Laws of the Institute'. The Code set out below was approved by the Institute's Council on 26 February 1977 and is binding on members.

2 The cases of members reported to have breached the Code shall be investigated by a Disciplinary Committee appointed by the Council; where a case is proven, a member may, depending on the circumstances and the gravity of the charge, be admonished, reprimanded, suspended from membership or removed from the list of members. Details of cases in which members are found in breach of the Code will be notified in the publications of the Institute.

Precepts

3 Members shall never use their authority or office for personal gain and shall seek to uphold and enhance the standing of the Purchasing and Supply profession and the Institute by:
   (a) maintaining an unimpeachable standard of integrity in all their business relationships both inside and outside the organisations in which they are employed;
   (b) fostering the highest possible standards of professional competence amongst those for whom they are responsible;
   (c) optimising the use of resources for which they are responsible to provide the maximum benefit to their employing organisation;
   (d) complying both with the letter and the spirit of:
      (i)   the law of the country in which they practice;
      (ii)   such guidance on professional practice as may be issued by the Institute from time to time;
      (iii) contractual obligations;
   (e) rejecting any business practice which might reasonably be deemed improper.

Guidance

4 In applying these precepts, members should follow the guidance set out below:
   (a) *Declaration of interest* Any personal interest which may impinge or might reasonably be deemed by others to impinge on a member's impartiality in any matter relevant to his or her duties should be declared.
   (b) *Confidentiality and accuracy of information* The confidentiality of information received in the course of duty should be respected and should never be used for personal gain; information given in the course of duty should be true and fair and never designed to mislead.

(c) *Competition* While bearing in mind the advantages to the member's employing organisation of maintaining a continuing relationship with a supplier, any arrangement which might, in the long term, prevent the effective operation of fair competition should be avoided.

(d) *Business gifts* Business gifts, other than items of very small intrinsic value such as business diaries or calendars should not be accepted.

(e) *Hospitality* Modest hospitality is an accepted courtesy of a business relationship. However, the recipient should not allow him or herself to reach a position whereby he or she might be or might be deemed by others to have been influenced in making a business decision as a consequence of accepting such hospitality; the frequency and scale of hospitality accepted should not be significantly greater than the recipient's employer would be likely to provide in return;

(f) when it is not easy to decide between what is and is not acceptable in terms of gifts or hospitality, the offer should be declined or advice sought from the member's superior.

5 Advice on any aspect of the precepts and guidance set out above may be obtained on written request to the Institute.

SUMMARY POINTS

- The level of an organisation's development defines the buyer profile. At infancy, the organisation requires an order clerk, efficient at performing routine, repetitive tasks. At the advanced level, an organisation will employ professional, possibly post graduate staff who are fully capable of dealing with the strategic elements of the business.

- The chapter outlines the characteristics a purchasing manager should look for during recruitment. Effective purchasers tend to have a positive self image with the confidence and ability to communicate at all levels both within and out with the organisation. They tend to have a higher level of education (which they are keen to continue) and a proactive attitude – reflected in the manner and spirit with which they approach their work. Above all, they are team players.

- Organisations provide training by induction courses, on the job experience, external courses or a mix of all three. This can be enhanced and formalised by the pursuance of a professional purchasing qualification, the most recognised being membership of the Chartered Institute of Purchasing and Supply. This can be studied through a college course or can be achieved through assessment in the work place using the National Vocational Qualification route. Both routes are explained in the chapter.

- The author concludes the chapter with guidelines on the principles and standards of purchasing practice (published in the USA) and the CIPS ethical code. Most organisations adopt these practices alongside their own purchasing procedures.

REFERENCES AND FURTHER READING

Altier W J (1986), 'Task forces – an effective management tool', *Sloan Management Review*, Spring.

Anklesaria J and Burt D N (1987), 'Personal factors in the purchasing/engineering interface', *Journal of Purchasing and Materials Management*, Winter.

Armstrong M (1988), *A Handbook of Human Resource Management*, Kogan Page, London.

Barnes J G and McTavish R (1983), 'Segmenting industrial markets by buyer sophistication', *European Journal of Marketing* 17 (6).

Carter J R, Monczka R M, Clauson K S and Zelinski T P (1987), 'Education and training for successful EDI implementation', *Journal of Purchasing and Materials Management*, Summer.

Chartered Institute of Purchasing and Supply (1995), Education Scheme.

Day R L, Michaels R E and Perdue B C (1988), 'How buyers handle conflicts', *Industrial Marketing Management*, May.

Howeler S (1980), 'Curriculum proposal for a purchasing degree', *Journal of Purchasing and Materials Management*, Spring.

Lauer S (1967), 'Westinghouse Plant X', in Baily and Farmer (eds), *Purchasing Problems*, Purchasing Officers' Association, London.

Leich D N (1975), 'Organisation development and procurement', in Farmer and Taylor (eds), *Corporate Planning and Procurement*, Heinemann, London.

Oxenfeldt A R (1966), *Executive Action in Marketing*, Wadsworth, London.

Parasuraman A (1981), 'Role clarity and job satisfaction in purchasing', *Journal of Purchasing and Materials Management*, Autumn.

Pedler M, Burgoyne J and Boydell T (1986), *A Manager's Guide To Self Development*, 2nd edn, McGraw-Hill, Maidenhead.

Purchasing and Supply Lead Body (1997), NVQ and SVQ Qualifications Framework, Stamford.

Reck R R (1978), 'Purchasing effectiveness', *Journal of Physical Distribution and Materials Management*, Winter.

Smith D (1992), 'Purchasing's contribution to company environmental performance', *Purchasing and Supply Management*, July.

CHAPTER 21

Research into purchasing and supply

The study of organisational buyer behaviour (OBB) has been of considerable interest to those involved in the marketing activity. Interest in buyer behaviour has centred around who makes the purchasing activity and how it can be influenced. A better understanding of the organisational buying process can be the difference between success and failure in marketing products and services.

OBJECTIVES OF THIS CHAPTER

- To identify the principal sectors of purchasing research
- To gain an insight into organisational buyer behaviour and how it can be influenced
- To explain models of organisational buyer behaviour
- To look at the growing contribution to research by purchasing specialists
- To redefine performance measurement in line with the development of the purchasing function
- To introduce the UK Purchasing Research body IPSERA.

Until comparatively recently the bulk of the research in this area has tended to come from researchers with marketing backgrounds – either university academics or marketing practitioners investigating such areas as:

- How long does the buying process take?
- Who are the key influencers?
- What is the composition of the decision-making unit (DMU) or buying centre?
- How advanced is the purchasing function?
- How do purchasing view their relationship with sellers?
- What is the nature and relationship of bondings with major suppliers?
- How does the buying process change between production/non-production items or high risk/low risk?

The list could, of course, cover many pages. This work is naturally of interest to buyers themselves, hence this chapter.

It is not surprising that these and many other such questions concerning the buying decision are of interest. If the selling organisation influences the main decision makers and puts together the right deal it might win a multi-million pound contract

Organisational buyer behaviour research is taught on many university Master's programmes and in a more limited number of first degrees in business and marketing. It is interesting to note that there is a relatively small number of universities teaching purchasing as part of a first degree, and even fewer have a specialist Master's degree in that subject. Research conducted by *purchasing* specialists is therefore more limited but now growing rapidly.

In this chapter we will identify the principal sectors of research and discuss the implications for the purchasing practitioner. We will give a much more intensive bibliography at the end of this chapter containing what we believe to be major pieces of research in the purchasing area. Throughout this edition we have, of course, acknowledged important pieces of research where we have felt this to be appropriate.

In the final section of this chapter we will highlight some of the major new contributions now coming from purchasing specialists. This area of research is now growing rapidly and should be of interest to all purchasing practitioners.

RESEARCH REVIEW

Buying centre/decision-making unit

One of the earliest pieces of research into the buying decision was undertaken by Buckner (1967) in a study called *How British Industry Buys*. This important pioneering research indicated that organisational buying decisions were affected by a number of specialists, such as designers, engineers, buyers, and others that comprised the 'buying centre' or decision-making unit (DMU). In some instances purchasing was not even involved, or had little impact in the decision to buy.

Further research revealed that the composition of the DMU varied considerably, depending on how important the item was, its value, and its degree of essentiality. Research by Wind (1978) indicated that involvement in the buying centre was a function of the amount of risk and the levels of expenditure involved. Studies indicate many factors dictating the composition of the DMU, and the more recent of these, such as that by Jones (1994), indicate that the more developed the purchasing function is, so the greater is the involvement of the purchasing specialist in the unit.

Organisations where the purchasing function is well developed now see purchasing as a major, if not *the* major decider in the DMU. Yet if one looks back at the development of the purchasing function in many organisations, in the past it was usually not even consulted over large items of expenditure.

Buying process

Research into the various stages of the buying process is now well advanced. The initial research in this area was conducted by Robinson and Faris in the early 1960s. They divided the buying process into eight activity stages: Wind (1978) extended this into twelve stages (*see* Figure 21.1).

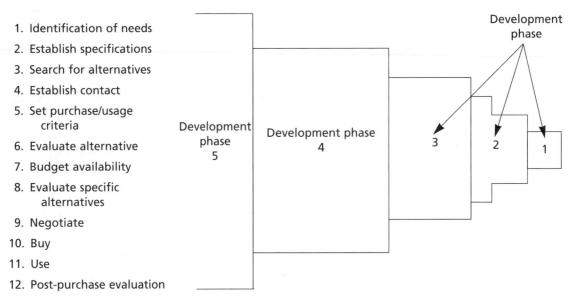

1. Identification of needs
2. Establish specifications
3. Search for alternatives
4. Establish contact
5. Set purchase/usage criteria
6. Evaluate alternative
7. Budget availability
8. Evaluate specific alternatives
9. Negotiate
10. Buy
11. Use
12. Post-purchase evaluation

Fig. 21.1 Twelve-stage classification of OBB buying process
(Source: Wind, 1978)

Marketing executives are eager to find out who are the key decision makers at each of these stages. In those organisations where the purchasing activity is seen as clerical and reactive, their involvement tends to be limited to a small number of the stages. Where purchasing is seen as being of strategic importance, however, they could be involved in all the stages.

Product/purchase/classification

The involvement of the buying function in sourcing and other decisions has been shown to depend on the type of product or service involved. Over the years, many different types of classification have been identified and commented on. One of the most quoted models is that by Robinson and Faris who identified three major buying classification stages: new buy, modified re-buy, and straight re-buy. These categories are now standards for buying classifications.

New task or buy This is a requirement to buy a product not purchased before. Such a buy is likely to involve many different departments within a company: purchasing, designers, accounts, production and so on.

Modified re-buy In this case a product that has been sourced previously has experienced a variation which will necessitate changes to normal supply procedures. These changes will have to be approved by various 'influencers' in the DMU.

Straight re-buy Here a supplier has been selected and there is a continuing relationship based on agreed and understood procedures. Purchasing tends to be the major influencer in the straight re-buy situation, and will remain so, provided other variables do not change.

In those organisations where the function is seen as strategic, purchasing has had to become more involved in all types of buys.

Buying characteristics and development

It is not surprising to find a large volume of literature in this area. Earlier finds tended to characterise the buyer as superficial with fixed ideas, but further research by, *inter alia*, Hankinson and Woatz revealed a very complex personality.

Browning and Zabriskie (1980) examined literature covering nearly two decades and provided valuable evidence of the growing interest in professionalising the purchasing function. In 1975, *Business Week* reported that the purchasing executive was receiving increased recognition, status and compensation. His or her duties had become less clerical in nature and more tactical and strategic. Bird and Mazze (1976) further reinforce this idea.

Barath and Hugstead (1977) reported that: 'increased professional status restricted rather than extended the role of purchasing agents, and led to their use of rule-evading tactics in resolving conflicts with engineering and production'. This could be due to concentration at the time on the more essential roles within purchasing, or a general recognition that they could not be a 'Jack of all trades' as they began to specialise. One would, however, still expect the purchasing function to be more involved with strategic interfaces when requested. The conflict recorded by Barath and Hugstead is also noted by Lambert, Broughton and Banville (1986). This role conflict is likely to increase as purchasing evolves.

Buyer–seller relationships

Sellers naturally have a considerable interest in the characteristics of the buyers they are likely to conduct business with. Successfully profiling the buyer enables the seller to select appropriate responses and deals.

Research has revealed a considerable amount of buying inertia in terms of re-sourcing supplies. Buyers tend to stay with the same suppliers over many years. There are many sound as well as dubious reasons for doing this; Figure 21.2 summarises some of these reasons. Increasingly it is being argued that a long-term relationship with key suppliers, if properly managed, will yield more benefits than problems.

Positive	Negative
● High costs involved in re-sourcing.	● Too complicated to resource.
● Relationship is long-term and 'mutual'.	● Buyer is not looking for alternatives.
● Lower cost of supply is possible with present source.	● Lack of knowledge of alternatives.

Fig. 21.2 Reasons for buying inertia in the re-sourcing of supplies

Traditional approach – dyadic and systems models

Traditional research into industrial buyer behaviour has tended to study buying behaviour and selling behaviour independently from each other. However, the way in which a buyer acts or reacts depends not upon any one variable studied separately, but upon many. Therefore, we should look at the totality of any activity.

1 The dyadic approach argues that buying is an interactive process which cannot be studied in isolation from selling and that the buyer–seller dyad should be the basic unit of analysis.
2 The systems view goes further. It takes the dyad as a sub-element and asserts that buying behaviour can only be understood as a total process influenced by all inputs/outputs affecting the whole organisation.

Traditionally, buyer behaviour has been examined with the aid of stimulus-response models. Another assumption sees buying behaviour in terms of interactive constructs, for example, in terms of independence.

A significant criticism of the traditional literature is that it tends to take a short-term view of any relationships and assumes in nearly all models that a buyer acts rationally. What is rational in the short term may not be so when looked at through the historical perspective.

In the price negotiation situation, a buyer may be loath to force suppliers to reduce prices, knowing that this could lead to the supplier going out of business, or perhaps failing to make the necessary investments later on. The buyer may even fear future repercussions from the seller when market conditions change. The outcome of price negotiations is the result of the interaction of many variables, both past, present and for the future. The renegotiation of prices therefore will depend on those interactive forces rather than on an individual response.

The interaction approach

This approach acknowledges buyer–seller interdependence and recognises the overall interaction between the buyer and seller as they attempt to influence each other. Many of the studies concerning the industrial buying process have been separated from studies of industrial marketing activity. Buyer–seller situations such as the price renegotiating process, concern independence. This interdependence may be due to such factors as customised products and investment, different problems associated with industrial markets and the effects of the actions of buyer and seller on each other.

At the very heart of this approach is the nature of the relationship between buyer and seller. The approach sees the relationship as being made up of individual episodes, which comprise the detailed pattern of contact between the two sides. Price renegotiations are made up of just such episodes and cognisance must be taken of previous episodes when a new episode is about to start. Neither party is likely to be able to make changes without consideration of the reaction of the other. Thus in a price renegotiation situation, the seller would normally inform the buyer he is seeking a price increase and negotiations between the two would normally follow.

Literature in the field of buyer behaviour has tended towards analysis of discrete purchasing decisions with little allowance for the dynamic and continuing complex relationships. Interaction is often taking place between companies at different stages of development within a changing environment. The interaction approach firmly challenges the view that the buyer is passive or can be treated in a general way. One must examine each individual buyer–seller situation to understand the nature of any relationships.

The interaction approach challenges the view of an atomised structure in industrial markets where it is assumed that buyers and sellers can be changed easily. The interaction approach instead lays great emphasis on stability in buyer–seller relationships. Of course, not all relationships between buyer and seller are close. Much will depend on the products in question in relation to such factors as market structures, availability of alternatives, value of business involved and so on. Thus the purchase of stationery, where competition between sellers may be high, would not lead to the same type of relationship as where, for example, one buyer was purchasing a product supplied by a monopolist. Considerable sums of money may be invested by both sides in a relationship: that is, in systems, human resources and physical resources that are only applicable in a specific buyer–seller relationship.

The complexity of such a relationship requires a study of each individual episode in the context of the overall relationship. Thus a supplier requesting a price increase which is thought excessive and one which the buyer is not able to reduce, would not necessarily lead to the buyer looking for a lower-priced product elsewhere. It would be necessary to view this episode in terms of the overall relationship. A failure to reduce a price increase may be an episode that could worsen the relationship; a number of such episodes could lead to the total breakdown of the relationship.

MODELS OF ORGANISATIONAL BUYER BEHAVIOUR

There have also been attempts at describing organisational buying behaviour using various conceptual models. These models are useful, particularly for marketeers attempting to predict and understand purchasing decision making. In one early model (see Figure 21.3) developed by Webster and Wind, organisational buying behaviour is seen as a complex process involving many people and goals, and with potentially conflicting decision criteria. It often takes place over an extended period of time, requires information from many sources and encompasses many interorganisational relationships. This model demonstrates the importance of the buying centre and the roles involved (i.e. user, influencer, decider, buyer and gatekeeper). Environmental influences are seen as being subtle and persuasive as well as difficult to identify and measure; included here are such influences as physical (e.g. geographic climate, ecology, technology), economic, political, legal and cultural factors.

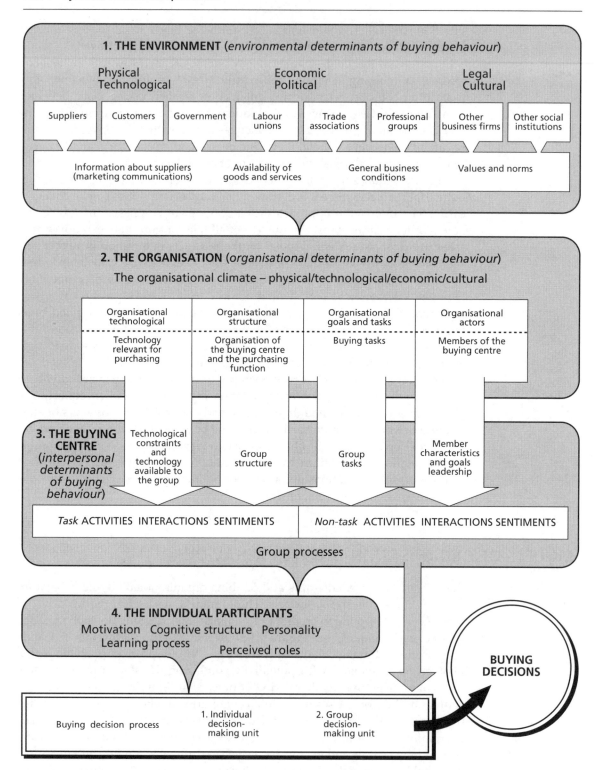

Fig. 21.3 A general model for understanding organisational buying behaviour
(*Source:* Webster and Wind, 1972)

Webster and Wind argue that environmental impacts have four distinct impacts:

1 They define general availability of goods and services.
2 They define general business conditions.
3 They determine the values and norms guiding interorganisational and interpersonal relationships between buyers and sellers. These values and norms may be codified into laws, or they may be implicit in cultural, social, legal or political forces that are seen as being the dominant source of values and norms.
4 They influence the information flow into the buying organisation, affecting behaviour.

Organisational factors cause individual decision makers to act in a different mode to the one they would follow if they were functioning alone or in another organisation. Organisational buying behaviour is seen as being motivated and directed by the organisation's goals and is contained by its financial, technological and human resources. This class of variables according to the model are primarily task-related. In order to understand the influences of the formal organisation, Levitt' classification of variables is used, in which organisations are seen as being multivariate systems composed of four sets of interacting variables: task, structure, technology systems and people. Together these four interacting sets of factors define the information, expectations, goals, attitudes and assumptions used by each person in their decision making.

Buying tasks are seen as a subset of organisational tasks and goals that evolve from the definition of a buying situation. The model goes on to define five stages in the buying process. The organisational structure's subsystems of communication, authority, status, rewards and work flow are all contained in the model. Finally, the model looks at the buying centre and individuals involved in buying behaviour.

Hill and Hillier in their analysis of the model comment that: 'although the model is a valuable contribution to a theory of organisational buyer behaviour, in that it indicates a whole range of factors which can directly or indirectly influence the evaluation of buying decisions, it still tends to provide a static representation of a dynamic situation'. The model does, however, move us nearer to an understanding of the organisational buying process, but it lacks operational clarity.

Sheth model

Following on from the Webster and Wind model, we have the Sheth (1978) model (*see* Figure 21.4). This model looks at information flows rather than environmental factors and is more dynamic than previous models. It acknowledges the existence of a buying centre consisting of buyers, engineers, users and others. Moreover it reasons that the actions and expectations of individuals are influenced by previous experience and that information received is often subject to perceptual distortion.

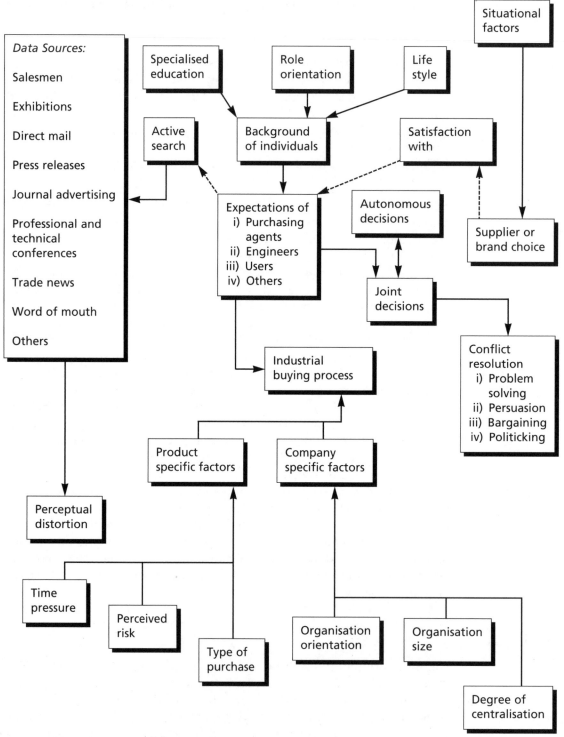

Fig. 21.4 Sheth integrative model of industrial buyer behaviour
(*Source:* Adapted from model devised by Jagdish N. Sheth)

RESEARCH UNDERTAKEN BY PURCHASING SPECIALISTS

As was mentioned earlier in this chapter, since the beginning of the 1990s there has been a tremendous growth in research activity into the purchasing areas from purchasing specialists. There are a number of reasons for this development:

- The recognition that the purchasing and supply activity if properly developed can give organisations a strategic advantage.
- The recognition that good supply chain management can reduce costs of incoming goods and materials.
- Purchasing and supply can make a major contribution by studying value streams i.e. where is value added and where can costs be reduced.
- The Chartered Institute of Purchasing and Supply's initiative in establishing several Chairs of Purchasing and getting purchasing recognised as a major function in its own right.
- The recognition of the strategic role of the activity, through the work of Porter (mid-1980s), Lamming (1993), Cox, (1995) and Womack and Jones (1997).

PURCHASING OVERVIEW

The following few pages attempt to give a very general overview of the contributions from the purchasing specialists who are now having a major influence on practitioners in this area.

The purchasing and supply function has historically been regarded as a relatively unimportant activity in many organisations. Its status and influence have been relatively low, particularly when compared with other functional areas such as finance and production. The purchasing activity has, however, seen considerable changes in its status over the last twenty years as a result of both internal and external factors affecting its development. Reasons for the growth and the changing status of the function are contained in the literature about purchasing (Reck and Long, 1988). Essentially, the reasons for its development revolve around such factors as a recognition of the strategic importance of the activity and its importance in reducing organisational costs, particularly through supply chain integration. The ability of purchasing to fulfil a strategic proactive role within the organisation is affected by its existing stage of development. Therefore, it is highly unlikely that a reactive clerical purchasing activity could take on board concepts such as supply chain management (MacBeth and Fergusson, 1990), lean supply (Lamming, 1993), or understand concern over strategies, acquisition cost and total cost of acquisition (Schilleweart, 1996).

Development of the purchasing function – overview

The purchasing function as Shealy (1985) reminds us, is found in all types of business. He remarks, however, that there is a distinction between 'the function and the purchasing department', and that many of the functions of purchasing may well be fragmented within an organisation. It can be demonstrated that the degree of involvement by purchasing in decision making is an important indicator as to the stage of purchasing evolution reached within an organisation.

As we have stated in earlier chapters, the more developed the purchasing activity the greater its role tends to be. Thus a buyer in an organisation involved in such areas as:

● world class concepts;
● lean supply;
● strategic acquisition costs;
● cost of ownership; and
● managing the supply chain

would need totally different skills to his or her counterpart of twenty years ago or a buyer still involved in typical clerical and transactional duties.

Purchasing development is likely to be irregular because of the different demands placed on it by different organisations. A major problem faced by purchasing occurs when the organisation demands a proactive strategic function but in reality has a transactional clerical activity. Purchasing effectiveness can be defined as the 'ability of the purchasing activity to achieve those organisational objectives expected of it'.

Purchasing activity and functions

The purchasing activity need not necessarily be contained within the purchasing department. It is likely that as the activity develops and gains recognition within an organisation, a separate purchasing function will develop. It is also likely that the purchasing department itself, in order to evolve will at some stage in its development, devolve more routine purchasing back to user departments (Lamming and Cox, 1995).

Furthermore, the functions of the purchasing department are also likely to vary considerably from organisation to organisation, depending on their stage of development (Jones, 1997).

Evolution of purchasing – strategic implications

The Purchasing and Supply Lead Body see the activity as being involved in purchasing and supply chain management (1997) that is, 'Helping to provide the interface between customer and supplier in order to plan, obtain, store and distribute as necessary, supplies of materials, goods and services to enable the organisation to satisfy its external and internal customers'.

One might expect, for example, that purchasing in its early stages of evolution may become involved in a wide range of activities. As corporate awareness develops regarding the purchasing activity, more detailed and specific functions may be identified. For example, price negotiations and cost reduction are seen as being a particularly important part of the purchasing function. Savings achieved in this area could be considerable. If purchasing's efforts are directed into too many areas, then its ability to make such savings and offer positive contributions is reduced, i.e. the opportunity cost argument.

The literature reveals that as purchasing develops, a more significant proportion of a buyer's time is spent on the more 'strategic aspects' of purchasing and less on the operational activities. This is shown in the work of Freeman and Cavatino (1990), Gracia (1993) and Fletcher (1993). And it is particularly true when purchasing becomes more involved in strategic management of the supply chain, as discussed by Sysons (1992) and (1993), Stannack and Batchelor (1994), Cox, Hughes and Ralf (1995). After identifying the likely range of purchasing activities we can examine the factors affecting its scope.

During the 1990s, with the accelerated growth of world class concepts, there has been a heightened awareness of 'input activities' within an organisation. Bolnijn and Kumpte (1990), Farmer and Ploos (1991) and Andersen Consulting (1993) draw attention to the need for a more developed purchasing and supply activity to assist in the development of such strategies. More recently Hamer and Champy (1993), Hines (1993) and Lamming (1993) identified the possible requirements of the purchasing function into the next century and the need for accelerating development in a number of areas.

This recognition that a strategically developed purchasing activity can add value in the supply chain is particularly well documented by Stevens (1994), Lamming (1995), Hines (1995), Sysons (1995).

JIT – an example of 'total corporate involvement'

While historically many developments within organisations have not necessarily required major commitments from purchasing, the newer developments, many vital to corporate survival, can only be developed with 'total corporate involvement'. One can select, for example, JIT, one of several world class strategies, to illustrate why it is essential to develop the purchasing function both operationally and strategically. The basic objective of JIT is to produce the required item at the required time, in the right quantity. The introduction of such a concept is said to lead to:

- significant reductions in inventory work in progress, and finished stock;
- decreased lead times;
- improvements in quality and productivity;
- increased adaptability and flexibility to change;
- lower costs of production; and
- elimination of the production of unnecessary items.

In order for the philosophy to work effectively, a high degree of co-operation is required both from functions within the organisation and from outside suppliers. Considerable effort is required from the purchasing department to really make the philosophy work. If purchasing is seen as a clerical activity, then there is little chance of the philosophy ever working. JIT requires a high degree of sophistication and skill from those in the purchasing department or function, Bertoto (1991) and Andersen Consulting (1993).

Successful application of JIT depends to a very great extent, on the buying firm's suppliers. As Manoochehri (1994) observes, 'suppliers must be able to provide the buyer with frequent deliveries of small lots of high quality parts with delivery geared precisely to the buying firm's production schedule', he continues, 'to achieve such harmony it is essential for the buyer to work closely with suppliers'.

Hohn, Pinto and Bragg (1983) stress the need for purchasing to provide the organisation with quality materials in a reliable manner, at the lowest practical long-term cost.

> In the past, to achieve this objective, purchasing managers have emphasised things such as negotiation skills, competitive buying, cost reduction techniques, multiple sourcing, and policy and procedure development. Consequently, evaluation of suppliers generally is based on the quality, delivery and pricing aspects of their performances. An overriding principle has been that through free competition in the market place, major purchasing objectives can be achieved most effectively.

> They continue 'Utilisation of a JIT purchasing system does not alter the fundamental objective of the purchasing function. However, the basic approach used in achieving the objective is different. The JIT purchasing concept assumes that most long-term material cost reductions are possible only through a significant reduction in a supplier's cost. Therefore purchasing staff must work with suppliers in achieving this long-term cost reduction.

The above has important repercussions for both the organisations and purchasing departments concerned. It means:

- longer-term contracts;
- fewer suppliers (too many suppliers, as Manoochehri (1984) observes, 'leads to problems of co-ordination, supplier development costs, and higher long-term costs');
- sharing information with suppliers concerning costs and future business;
- helping suppliers by giving them assistance where necessary;
- generally moving away from the old adversarial relationship; and
- identifying strategic relationships more in terms of win–win deals.

It has been generally accepted that effective implementation of the JIT concept has been a major factor contributing to Japanese industrial success in recent years. American and European organisations have also recorded considerable success with the introduction of JIT, as has been noted by Barratt (1984), Olsbero (1985), Hill and Vollman (1986).

The concept, however, is heavily dependent on a well-developed purchasing function and certainly pressure to introduce this concept or philosophy organisationally will reveal any purchasing deficiencies. As Rajan and Treville (1986) remark, 'getting from Just in Case to Just in Time is highly dependent on a developed purchasing culture'. This in turn will require the development of good relationships with key suppliers, as described by Hosford (1994) and Madombi and Schrunder (1995). The improvement in relationships and the quality of the bondings are also likely to be indicators of development.

Strategic development

Systems are generally becoming more corporate in scope requiring rapid accurate responses from all function areas. This means that because such systems are strategic in their impact on the organisation, all functions must contribute effectively to them. Again, developments in MRP and MRP II have had and are having important repercussions on purchasing development.

Other world class strategies

The developments of MRP II, logistical management and JIT are strategic in nature, and all rely heavily on good functional development. In order for such concepts to work effectively, purchasing must be represented at a corporate level. Such new developments also require the function to be reasonably well developed. Indeed one could see major problems arising within organisations where purchasing is essentially undeveloped and clerical in its operations. Therefore, it is extremely difficult to visualise any of the above concepts working effectively in organisations where purchasing is not well developed. However, cases are reported from time to time, about organisations where MRP II or JIT is proving impossible to develop effectively. While many reasons are given for such failures, it is interesting to note that in nearly every case, the purchasing function was found to be essentially clerically reactive.

The measurement of purchasing performance

As the activity has developed so measurement of its performance has required redefinition.

A number of points emerge from the surveys undertaken:

- The purchasing function is being more extensively measured as its role becomes more strategic, Evans and McKenzie (1988), Polastri (1985), Brady and Willets (1985), Bilborough and Dale (1985), Leonard (1986), and Van Weele (1985).
- Different variables become the focus of attention depending on whether the activity is seen as being clerical or strategic, Van Weele (1985), Kraljic (1983), Lancaster (1984), Ramsey (1986) and Hoppenbrouners (1994).
- The types of variables used to measure purchasing performance and the scope and depth of such control systems are indicative of the stage of development reached within the function, Richards (1975), Reck and Long (1987), Hill (1972), Oliver (1987).
- Newer developments such as JIT, logistical management and total quality control are requiring far more breadth and depth in measurement criteria, Farmer and Ploos (1991), Adams and Niebuhr (1985), Leonard (1986), Gracia (1993), Wagner (1987).
- A developing concern with 'lean thinking' (Womack and Jones 1996), and that one must look at ways of measuring how waste can be reduced throughout the supply chain in order to reduce costs.

The current position of purchasing

Rich *et al.* (1996) believe that purchasing has now reached a watershed; it has undergone a process of 'gentrification' from academics, the CIPS and practitioners, who may have overstated the role of purchasing development overall, particularly in terms of its place in a fully integrated corporate structure. But it must not be forgotten, however, that the development of world class concepts, lean supply, value chains etc. require a strategic, proactive function.

An article by Stanwick and Jones (1996) explores shifts in the conceptualisation of the purchasing function. They consider the effects of these changes suggesting that they are so fundamental that they call for a redefinition of the profession. In turn they identify a four-stage purchasing evaluation structure based on:

1 product-centred purchasing
2 process-centred purchasing
3 relation purchasing
4 performance-centred purchasing.

This four-stage approach is also recorded by Stannack and Scheuing (1996) and similar purchasing development ideas are noted in this research.

Outsourcing and purchasing

With the growth of outsourcing particularly from the 1990s onwards there has been a wealth of articles considering the outsourcing of the purchasing activity, including Evan (1996) and Cobbett (1994), Benmeridja and Benmeridja (1996).

Outsourcing of the purchasing function may indeed make sense if the purchasing function is poorly developed and incapable, because of its stage of development, of making the contribution to strategic goals that are expected of it. In the public sector outsourcing of the purchasing function may also be likely because such factors as outmoded ideas in the areas of regulations, sourcing policy and tendering procedures are affecting good purchasing practices (Anderson, 1996).

As purchasing activity develops one is also likely to see purchasing organisations devolving the authority to buy and manage low value items and transactional business, either internally or externally, so that they can evolve to take on board more strategic aspects of supply chain management i.e. in order to evolve it must devolve.

Whether the purchasing activity is provided in-house or outsourced we still need to know objectively what its current stage of development is and how it needs to be developed to meet future corporate needs.

CONCLUSION

We are now witnessing purchasing's coming of age in the academic area. Purchasing specialists from various universities and organisations are now making their own contributions to advancements of the activity. It is interesting to note that real advancement in the marketing area occurred when the subject/discipline was adopted and developed by the universities as a subject in its own right. Purchasing is not as advanced but we are beginning to see rigour injected into its development.

In the early 1990s, we also saw the development of IPSERA. This is the major UK research arm of purchasing. Further development of the activity hinges on its ability to sell itself as a useful activity both to academics and practitioners. This in turn will affect how others view the activity and will help to shape its growth and development in the future.

SUMMARY POINTS

- Until fairly recently, most research in purchasing behaviour has been carried out by academics/researchers with marketing backgrounds. This stems from the theory that a better understanding of the organisational buying process will enable more effective marketing.
- The author differentiates between dyadic and systems research. Dyadic argues that buying and selling are interdependent processes – a decision reached by one party will have considered the reaction of the other. The systems approach looks at buying behaviour as a result of inputs/outputs affecting the whole organisation.
- The chapter outlines models of organisational buyer behaviour and indicates the factors and influences which can directly or indirectly affect the evaluation of buying decisions.
- As discussed in an earlier chapter, the more developed the purchasing function, the greater its role and involvement tends to be in the attainment of world class concepts. The functions of the purchasing department will vary according to their stage of development – the further the development the more time spent on strategic issues and the less on operational tasks.
- Strategically developed purchasing will be represented at corporate level, adding value in the supply chain, enabling the adoption of JIT philosophies and utilising MRP II systems.
- Many articles exist stating the need to measure purchasing's contribution to the organisation taking into account variables that impinge on its performance. Stanwick and Jones (1996) take this a stage further calling for a redefinition of the profession, identifying a four stage evaluation structure – product centred purchasing; process centred purchasing; relation purchasing and performance centred purchasing

REFERENCES AND FURTHER READING

Aljian G W and Others (1994), *Purchasing Handbook*, New York, McGraw-Hill, Latest edition.

Ammer, Dean S (1974), 'Is your purchasing department a good buy', *Harvard Business Review*, March/April, pp 29–34.

Andersen Consulting (1993), *The Lean Enterprise, Benchmarking Project Report*, London.

Banting P, Ford D, Gross A and Holmes G (1985), 'Similarities in industrial procurement across four marketing countries', *Industrial Marketing Management*, May.

Barath R and Hugstead P (1977), 'Professionalism and the behaviour of procurement managers', *Industrial Marketing Management*, June.

Barath R M and Hugstead P S (1979) 'The effects of professionalism on purchasing managers', *Journal of Purchasing & Materials Management*, pp 25–32.

Bevan J (1988), Comakership, *Management Decisions*, pp 20–25.

Bilborough C and Dale B (1985), 'The role and influence of factory level purchasing within a corporate structure', *International Journal of Physical Distribution and Materials Management*, vol 15, (1), pp 39–45.

Bird M M and Mazze E M (1976), 'Measuring efficiency of the industrial purchasing departments', *Industrial Marketing Management*, March.

Bird M M and Mazze E M (1976), 'Measuring efficiency of industrial purchasing departments', *Industrial Marketing Management*, June.

Brady J L and Willetts B P (1985), 'Student attitudes towards the purchasing managers job', *Journal of Purchasing and Materials Management*, Spring.

Bolwijn P T and Kumpte T (1990), 'Manufacturing in the 1990s, productivity, flexibility and innovation', *Long Range Planning*, 23 (4), pp 44–59.

Bonfield H and Speh T (1977), 'Dimension of the purchasing role in industry', *Journal of Purchasing and Materials Management*, June.

Brand G T (1972), *Industrial Buying Decisions*, Cassell, London.

Browning J M and Zabriskie N B (1980), 'Professionalism in purchasing: a status report', *Journal of Purchasing and Materials Management*, March.

Browning J M and Zabriskie N B (1980), 'Professionalism in purchasing: a status report', *Journal of Purchasing and Materials Management*, August, pp 46–52.

Buckner H (1967), *How British Industry Buys*, Hutchinson, London.

Campbell N C G (1985), 'An interaction approach to OBB', *Journal of Business Research*, vol 13, February.

Cannon S (1994), 'The purchasing and supply function – redefined', *Purchasing and Supply Management*, September 1994.

Cox A, Hughes J and Ralf M (1995), 'Facilitating strategic change – The key role for purchasing leadership', *Purchasing and Supply Management*, November.

Cunningham M T and Howse E (1982), 'An interaction approach to marketing strategy' in Hakansson (ed) *International Marketing and Purchase of Industrial Goods*, IMP Group.

Chaddick J R and Dale B G (1987), 'The determination of purchasing objectives and strategies', *Journal of Materials Management*, August.

Drucker P (1973), *Managing For Results*, Pan, New York.

Evans E and McKenzie N (1988), 'How much is your purchasing department costing you?', *Management Accounting*, April.

Farmer D H (1978), 'Developing purchasing strategies', *Journal of Purchasing and Materials Management*, 14 (3), Fall.

Farmer D H (1981), 'Input management', *Journal of General Management*, Summer, pp 65–77.

Farrington B (1978), *Industrial Purchase Price Management*, Unpublished PhD Thesis, University of Brunel.

Farrington B and Woodmansey M (1980), *The Purchasing Function Management Survey*, Report No. 50, BIM Foundation.

Foxall G R (1980), 'Marketing models of buyer behaviour: a critical review', *European Research*, September.

Freeman V and Cavatino J (1990), 'Fitting purchasing to strategic firm frameworks, processes and value', *Journal of Purchasing and Materials Management*, June, pp 86–98.

Godiwalla J M, Warde W and Meinhart W A (1979), *Corporate Strategy and Functional Management*, Praeger, New York.

Gracia B (1993), 'Upstreaming purchasing – from department to function', *2nd Pserg Conference*, University of Bath, April.

Hakansson H and Wootz B (1975), 'Risk reduction and the industrial purchaser', *European Journal of Marketing*, vol 9.

Hamer M and Champy J (1993), *Re-Engineering the Corporation: A Manifesto for Business Revolution*, Nicholas Brealey Publishing, London.

Hill R and Hillier J T (1989), *Organisational Buyer Behaviour*, Macmillan, London.

Hill A V and Vollman T E (1986), 'Reducing vendor delivery uncertainties in a JIT environment', *Journal of Operations Management*, vol 6 (4), August.

Hines P (1993), 'Integrated materials management; a post Porterian paradigm', *Proceedings of the 2nd Pserg Conference*, University of Bath.

Hines P (1994), *Creating World Class Suppliers; Unlocking Mutual Competitive Advantage*, Pitman, London.

Hosford N (1994), 'Partnerships – what's really going on?' *Purchasing and Supply Management*, August.

Jones D M (1983), 'Price negotiations', MSc thesis, Lancaster University.

Jones D M (1997), 'Purchasing development', unpublished PhD thesis, Strathclyde University.

Kellog C D (1970), 'The human element in industrial technical purchasing', *Industrial Marketing Research Association Journal*, May.

Kennedy A M (1981), 'Comments on marketing models of buyer behaviour', *European Research*, April.

Kraljic P (1983), 'Purchasing must become supply management', *Harvard Business Review*, September–October, pp 86–94.

Lambert D and Allen B (1976), 'The buyer as marketing practitioner', *Journal of Purchasing and Materials Management*, vol 12 (2), Fall pp 19–23.

Lamming R (1993), *Beyond Partnership Strategies for Innovation and Lean Supply*, Prentice Hall International UK Ltd, Stamford.

Lamming R and Cox A (1995), 'Strategic procurement management in the 1990s – concepts and cases', *Chartered Institute of Purchasing and Supply*.

Lancaster G (1984), 'A new role for purchasing people', *Purchasing and Supply Management*, January, pp 27–35.

Leigh T W and Rethan A J (1985), 'User participation and influence in industrial buying', *Journal of Purchasing and Materials Management*, Summer.

Leonard R (1986), 'Measuring individual areas of performance', *Purchasing and Supply Management*, February, March and April.

Lister P (1967), 'Identifying and evaluating the purchasing influence', *I.M.R.A. Journal*, August.

Lyles M A (1981), 'Formulating strategic problems: empirical analysis and model development', *Strategic Management Journal*, vol 2, pp 61–75.

MacBeth D K and Ferguson N (1991), 'Strategic aspects of supply chain management', *Integrated Manufacturing Systems*, 2:1 pp 9–12.

MacBeth D K and Ferguson N (1994), *Partnership Sourcing: An Integrated Supply Chain Approach*, FT/Pitman, London.

Miles R E and Snow C C (1978), *Organisational Strategy, Structure and Process*, McGraw-Hill, London.

Mintzberg H (1979), *The Structuring of Organisations*, Prentice-Hall.

Olsbero G (1985), 'Japanese industrial structure – a challenge to the world', *I.F.P.M.M. Journal*, pp 56–62.

Paterson R L (1985), 'Procurement belongs in management', *Journal of Marketing Education*, Fall.

Polastri P R (1985), 'Estimating the effects of inflation on prices; a practical approach', *Journal of Purchasing and Materials Management*, Spring, vol 21, pp 9–16.

Porter M E (1990), *The Competitive Advantage of Nations*, Macmillan, London.

Quinn B (1972), 'Aha! here's a man who's really thinking of the business we're in. He's not just a buyer', *Modern Purchasing*, January, pp 15–18.

Ramsey J (1985), 'We have no one to blame but ourselves,' *Purchasing and Supply Management*, December, pp 25–29.

Reck R R and Long B (1988), 'Purchasing, a competitive weapon', *Journal of Purchasing and Materials Management*, Fall, pp 2–8.

Robinson P and Faris and Wind T (1967), 'Generalised simulation of the industrial buying process', *Marketing Science Papers*, June.

Robles F (1984), 'Buying in a matrix organisation', *Industrial Marketing Management*, August.

Saunders (1994), *Strategic Purchasing and Supply Chain Management*, Pitman Publishing, London.

Schilleweart N (1996), 'Total cost of acquisition as an instrument for supplier evaluation', 'Paper for IPSERA Conference', April, Eindhoven.

Shealy R (1985), 'The purchasing job in different types of business', *Journal of Purchasing and Materials Management*, Winter, pp 17–20.

Sheth J N (19730, 'A model of industrial buyer behaviour', *Journal of Marketing*, October.

Shields D (1982), 'Changing purchasing's philosophy', *Purchasing*, April.

Stannack P M and Batchelor J (1994), 'Partnership sourcing as a teaching/learning process', '3rd International Conference of International Purchasing & Supply Education', University of Glamorgan, March.

Stevens J (1995), 'Global purchasing in the supply chain', *Purchasing and Supply Management*, January, pp 31–34.

Sysons R (1989), 'The revolution in purchasing', *Purchasing & Supply Management*, September, pp 16–21.

Sysons R (1992), *Improving Purchasing Performance*, Pitman, London.

Sysons R (1995), 'The road to purchasing excellence', *Purchasing and Supply*, August, pp 19–23.

Van Eck A and Vanweele (1982), 'Price performance evaluation – a conceptual approach', *Journal of Purchasing and Materials Management*, Summer, pp 2–9.

Webster F and Wind T (1965), 'Modelling the industrial buying process', *Journal of Marketing Research*, May.

Webster F and Wind T (1972), *Organizational Buying Behaviour*, Prentice Hall, New York.

Williams A J (1987), 'Causes of purchasing myopia', *Industrial Marketing & Purchasing*, vol 2 (1), pp 19–24.

Womack J P, Jones D T and Roose D (1990), *The Machine that Changed the World*, Ranson, New York.

Womack J P and Jones D T (1996), *Lean Thinking*, Simon and Schuster, New York.

INDEX